Cultural Influences on Global Marketing

Cultural Influences on Global Marketing

First
Edition

Constantine G. Polychroniou

University of Cincinnati

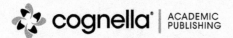

cognella® | ACADEMIC PUBLISHING

Bassim Hamadeh, CEO and Publisher
Jennifer Codner, Senior Field Acquisitions Editor
Michelle Piehl, Senior Project Editor
Christian Berk, Associate Production Editor
Jess Estrella, Senior Graphic Designer
Stephanie Kohl, Licensing Coordinator
Natalie Piccotti, Director of Marketing
Kassie Graves, Vice President of Editorial
Jamie Giganti, Director of Academic Publishing

Printed in the United States of America.

ISBN: 978-1-5165-3632-0 (pbk) / 978-1-5165-3633-7 (br)

I dedicate this edition to my wife Carole-Christina and my children Georgia, Helena, Jioanna, and also my granddaughter Alexandra for their incessant encouragement and unflinching support throughout my career!

CONTENTS

PREFACE

This book has come into existence following many years of teaching and relevant research in the field of internationalization and globalization of markets. Textbooks that I had used in the past did not engage the concept of culture in a way that emphasized its importance to the success of foreign marketing operations. The impact of international marketing, amidst the frenzy of a globalizing environment, has demanded a repositioning of the traditional international marketing course. The difference between domestic and international marketing is not on methodology but rather on *systems* and *environments* that are different because foreign markets function differently. The reason for the difference is *culture*. Culture, which is what I call the last frontier to achieving market homogenization, prescribes the idiosyncrasy of the political economy of the market. That is, culture affects the political, economic, and regulatory systems of the market. As economies face an increasingly competitive environment due to increased trade and less protectionism, companies that operate in foreign markets find imperative the need to be more cost-efficient in their effort to deliver comparatively greater value to their market and safeguard profitability. The feasibility of cost efficiencies depends on company marketing strategy and cross-border market convergence. The greater the similarity of cross-border markets, the greater the potential homogeneity. The level of homogeneity, in turn, affects the degree of cost efficiencies a marketer may enjoy.

Cross-border relative homogeneity allows the marketer to employ *standardization* in their marketing mix (program), which enhances cost efficiencies. The trend in our current cross-border market environment is for companies to seek cost efficiencies, which calls for standardization and the use of a global marketing strategy. As mentioned earlier, cross-border relative market homogeneity requires intercultural similarity. This is the case because cultural values, customs, habits, rules, and relevant cultural attributes affect the formation of attitudes, perceptions, and expectations, which dictate behavioral patterns and behavior.

It is pivotal, therefore, that the international marketer should focus on how the foreign market's culture affects marketing behavior; i.e., purchasing, consumption, and decision making. Cultural awareness, sensitivity, and empathy become key to marketing success in foreign markets. They allow the marketer to develop effective communications and successfully manage their foreign presence.

As an author, I have painstakingly gleaned the most critical and vital concepts of forward-thinking cross-border cultural marketing from a plethora of relevant published materials. The selected topics in this book offer an opportunity to the student to develop a solid understanding of the interworkings of contemporary globalized marketing and a functional appreciation of the broad effect of culture on the marketer's success in a way that no other book has offered before. Therefore, the book's emphasis on the influence of *culture* on the success of cross-border marketing is undoubtedly the *core value* of this book.

INTRODUCTION

This book offers the reader the opportunity to engage in topics, which, in a globalized environment, are critical to the success of the contemporary international marketer. These topics encompass all activities that an international marketer must focus on in order to ensure success in cross-border marketing. Furthermore, both the selection and ordering of those topics guarantees concept continuity, essential to better understanding the intricacies of the marketing process in foreign markets. Finally, select cases offer marketing experiences that international marketers have encountered in their cross-border marketing ventures. Following is a description of the topics discussed in this book.

Introduction

This section unfolds in thirteen chapters. These chapters address the fundamental issues concerning the contemporary international marketer, operating in an increasingly dynamic globalizing environment.

The new realities of a global marketplace have changed the traditional approach to addressing the needs of the foreign market and pose distinct challenges to the international marketer as the impact of cross-cultural awareness has become critical in the formulation of the marketing program and the designing of marketing strategies.

Topics focus on the impact of the foreign cultural environment on international marketing operations, the impact of culturally influenced consumer behavior, and the formulation of the marketing mix. The choice of strategy—be it *global* or *multi-domestic*—is discussed, leading to foreign market *entry* methods, *trade* agreements (that is, *multilateralization versus regional trade agreements*), the *political* and *regulatory* environment, marketing *communications*, cross-cultural *negotiations*, economic *integration*, and global *value* creation.

These critical topics attempt to offer a practical paradigm of the "everyday" issues that an international marketer encounters in today's globalizing environment.

With the above in mind, the chapters have been structured so that they will help the marketer assume strategic positioning, focusing not only on the marketing mix and conventional marketing methodology, but critically on how marketing success may be impacted by cross-cultural exchange and how to manage such reality. The approach undertaken in this book is innovative because the new dynamic that characterizes the evolution of trade and the development of international markets is the increasing cross-cultural exchange. Such exchange is becoming preeminently pivotal for marketing success in global markets.

Each chapter begins with a brief yet complete description of its contents, preparing the reader to better focus on the issues.

1

Chapter 1 begins with cultural influences, cultural traits, and cultural components, such as values, customs, habits, cues, norms, mores, artifacts, and more. The topics of cultural knowledge and cultural attitudes and behaviors are discussed. The chapter addresses the concepts of *individualism* and *collectivism,* defining and exploring their impact on cultural behavior. It becomes evident how cultural attitudes and behaviors are fashioned under different sets of values that individualism and collectivism embrace. Furthermore, the concept of *diversity* and its importance in a thriving global environment, as is evident, assumes a critical role in the interchange of individualism and collectivism, producing a viable symbiotic relationship between the two.

1.1 Overview of Components of Culture

Geoffrey Paul Lantos

OBJECTIVES

- To enable you to recognize and categorize the different elements that constitute culture.

- To help you understand how marketers infuse their marketing communications with cultural components to appeal to members of society and allow you to experience how they appeal to consumers.

- To have you witness how advertising reflects changes in cultural components over time and differences in these elements across cultures.

Background

This exercise broadly categorizes various **cultural components** (**cultural cues**), the basic elements constituting a society's culture. These components are illustrated with marketing examples and advertisements that incorporate them. The four broad categories of cultural cues are summarized in Exhibit 1: symbols, material artifacts, cognitive components (knowledge and attitudes), and behaviors.

Symbols: Making The Intangible Tangible

Symbols are objects, characters, and other concrete, tangible representations of abstract, intangible ideas. Cultural communication uses symbols to convey information quickly and easily, something advertisers strive to do. Symbols come in several forms:

- Tangible items are physical representations of cultural ideas. The terrorists who attacked the World Trade Center and Pentagon on 9/11 chose those buildings because they symbolized U.S. financial and military power.
- Words are used to verbally communicate cultural ideas. Marketers are interested in the meanings and images conveyed by the words they select to communicate with customers.
- Pictorial images, colors, shapes, numbers, animals, and music can all be symbolic, and their meanings can differ across cultures. While

EXHIBIT 1.1 Components of Culture (Cultural Cues)

Symbols: Tangibles, words, images, pictures, colors, shapes, numbers, animals, music, product semiotics, trade characters, advertising icons.

Material components/cultural artifacts: Visible, tangible items, including commercial products.

Cognitive components/abstract elements:

 Cultural knowledge:

  Cultural values/social values/core values

  Cultural beliefs: Cultural truisms/folk wisdom, superstitions, common knowledge, myths, legends

  Language

  Religion

  Politics

  Cultural attitudes

 Cultural behavior and activities:

  Cultural norms:

   Customs

   Conventions

   Etiquette

   Rituals

   Mores: Legal codes, moral (ethical) norms

  Cultural activities

the number 7 is lucky in the United States and Morocco, it is unlucky in Ghana and Kenya. A dove represents serenity and peace in the United States but death in some Asian cultures.

Marketers have been embarrassed by cross-cultural symbolic gaffes. Merrill Lynch used a bull to represent strength, but some foreign customers viewed it instead as a source of meat. An advertiser in England and Ireland displayed the "V" peace sign, which in those nations is equivalent to an American giving someone the finger. Samsonite offered suitcases in purple and black in the Mexican market where, unfortunately, these colors are associated with death and mourning.

As is true of all aspects of culture, symbols change over time. The letter "X" used to stand for pornography ("X-rated"), but it now means extreme, edgy, and youthful (as in Generation X, ESPN's X Games, and Nissan Xterra).

Semiotics (**semiotic studies, semiology**) is the study of signs (i.e., something that has meaning, such as words, images, body language, etc.) and symbols. **Product semiotics** investigates unique symbolic qualities of products and brands. Porcelain china and paper plates both hold food, but one is more appropriate for serving guests a fine meal and the other is better for burgers at a picnic. The cigar has always been looked upon as a symbol of success, achievement, and celebration. The Harley-Davidson motorcycle represents rugged individualism, freedom, and rebellion.

Many brands use **trade characters** (**advertising icons, product mascots**), people or animals that symbolize a brand. Betty Crocker stands for the motherly care the company puts into preparing their baked products. The Energizer Bunny represents longevity, perseverance, and determination. Ronald McDonald personifies fun and family values.

Cultural Artifacts: The Material Components Of Culture

Cultural artifacts (**material components**) are physical aspects of society. They include tangible items such as homes, cars, books, appliances, tools—in fact, all commercial products.

Certain cultures are associated with specific products. The United States is the land of hamburgers, hot dogs, blue jeans, and Coca-Cola. The Netherlands is associated with tulips, wooden clogs, and Gouda cheese. Britain is known for tea, rain boots (Mackintosh), and Shetland sweaters.

Some products are associated with specific eras. The 1900–1909 period ushered in the Ford car, Crayola crayons, and the Teddy Bear; 1910–1919 gave birth to the telephone, crossword puzzles, and construction toys such as Erector sets and Tinkertoys; the 1940s launched Tide detergent and Timex watches; the 1950s introduced TV dinners and muscle cars with huge tailfins; the 1960s birthed Handi-Wrap plastic wrap and Ziploc bags; and the 1970s introduced VCRs, disco music, and the smiley face, whose 1990s descendant was the happy face emoticon typed on computer keyboards ☺.

Some of these products have not changed at all (crossword puzzles and the Teddy Bear). Others evolved slowly (new colors of Crayola crayons and new formulas of Tide detergent), while others have changed radically (you would not still drive an early Ford auto for everyday transportation) and some no longer exist (button shoes and girdles).

Cognitive Components: The Way We Think

The **cognitive components** of society's "collective consciousness" are thoughts, values, ideas, and other intangibles that influence and help define a society. Cultural knowledge and cultural attitudes are two categories of cognitive components.

CULTURAL KNOWLEDGE
Cultural knowledge is a general awareness shared by a society's citizens. It includes cultural values, cultural beliefs, language, and summary constructs such as religion and politics. **Cultural values** (**core values, social values**) are abstract ideals about general goals and desirable means for achieving those goals that are widely shared in a society. They are a culture's beliefs about what is and is not desirable regarding goals or ends (terminal values) and the means to achieve those goals (instrumental values). Examples of American cultural values focused on goals are accomplishment, activity, comfort, efficiency and practicality, and social recognition. Cultural values focusing on means for attaining goals include ambition, cheerfulness, cleanliness, courage, and self-control.

Marketing efforts should appeal to society's dominant core values whenever possible. G.I. Joe, an American cultural icon, represents the American values of heroism, patriotism, and courage.

Some ideals are **ethical values**, standards for acting morally and doing the right and proper thing. Ethical values are either good and helpful (e.g., freedom, equality, and nondiscrimination) or bad and harmful (e.g., deception, violation of rights, and injustice).

One of the most important ingredients in ethical decision making is the central role of ethical values. It is especially important to be aware of these values when traveling abroad since standards of right and wrong may be different, such as the acceptability of bribery and of treating women as second-class citizens. Although *culture relativists* say, "When in Rome, do as the Romans do," *cultural absolutists* say that moral truths exist regardless of society—certain actions are just plain right or wrong, that is, a society may be endorsing unethical values, as when the United States permitted slavery.

Cultural beliefs, a second general type of cultural knowledge, are a society's ideas about reality that may or may not be true. The following are common cultural beliefs:

- **Cultural truisms** (**folk wisdom**). These pithy sayings express commonly held beliefs such as "Time is money" and "You can't teach an old dog new tricks." As is true of all cultural elements, cultural beliefs change over time. During the 1920s, many people believed that education was wasted on a girl and a woman's place was in the home. Many cultural truisms are not universally accepted. Some say, "Absence makes the heart grow fonder," while others insist "Out of sight, out of mind." Many believe that "Knowledge is power," but others insist "Ignorance is bliss" and "What you don't know won't hurt you."

A provocative example of a marketing cultural belief is that green M&Ms are an aphrodisiac. This is an example of an **urban legend**—a cultural belief passed along from person to person that is not true. The M&Ms legend reportedly started circulating among randy college guys during the 1970s. After decades of skirting the legend, M&M/Mars finally cashed in with TV commercials and print ads featuring the seductive female M&M character, Green, sporting bedroom eyes and luscious lips.

- **Superstitions** are ideas that result from ignorance, fear of the unknown, or trust in magic or chance. Examples include the beliefs that astrology can help foretell the future, one should play his or her "lucky number" in a lottery, and 13 is an unlucky number. Marketers were in seventh heaven about a calendar quirk on July 7, 2007, and its link to the lucky number 777. Hotels, casinos, and retailers held 7-centric promotions and events, such as Wal-Mart's "Lucky in Love Wedding Search," in which seven couples won a July 7 wedding ceremony and reception.
- **Common knowledge** is a set of educated beliefs shared by most members of society, such as computer literacy and common courtesy.
- **Myths** are stories containing symbolic elements expressing a society's key values, ideals, emotions, and dreams. These often feature a clash between good and evil and serve as a moral guide. Superman, Dr. Jekyll and Mr. Hyde, E.T., and Santa Claus, whose modern image was developed in the 1930s through a series of Coca-Cola ads, are all mythical.
- **Legends** are stories about revered people who are a combination of myth and history. Legendary figures include Elvis Presley, Babe Ruth, Davy Crockett, Paul Bunyan, Princess Diana, John Lennon, and Michael Jordan.

Language, a third type of cultural knowledge, permits effective communication within a society. Marketers must be careful with literal translations from one language to another, as idioms and figures of speech do not smoothly translate. You might run into difficulty if you tell a Frenchman he is "out to lunch" and he orders pate or, explain to a Spanish woman that you are "tackling some problems" and she assumes you fight bulls.

A fourth kind of cultural knowledge suggests that certain topics shouldn't be discussed among polite company—religion and politics. Consequently, marketers should exercise caution when incorporating religion and politics into their marketing communications so as not to offend people. **Religion** is a belief in and reverence for a supernatural power(s) recognized as the creator(s) and governor(s) of the universe. Religious beliefs influence what people regard as truth on big-picture issues such as the nature of reality, the meaning of life, the existence and nature of the afterlife, and the makeup of morality. Religious beliefs affecting CB include "It is wrong to eat meat," "Don't smoke tobacco," and "Don't go shopping on Sunday."

Politics concerns the activities and affairs of government and politicians. Marketers are ever vigilant to monitor and lobby for or against laws passed by legislatures and interpreted by the judiciary on issues such as product safety, fair pricing and distribution, and deceptive advertising. But many marketers are loath to get involved. When asked to endorse an opponent of conservative Jesse Helms in a North Carolina U.S. Senate race, Michael Jordan observed, "Republicans buy shoes, too."

CULTURAL ATTITUDES

Cultural attitudes are very general positive or negative evaluations in society regarding issues and practices, such as the proper roles of men and women in society, whether smoking in public is acceptable, and whether ironing clothes is necessary. For instance, Europeans are less inhibited about their bodies than Americans are, so there is little social stigma in men unzipping and peeing in public if nature calls. This illustrates that cultural attitudes give rise to cultural behavior.

Cross-cultural attitudes are reflected in advertising. Slapstick violence in humorous advertising is accepted in the United States but not in Europe. However, the U.S. ad market is more squeamish about sexual images and nudity compared with Europe and many other parts of the world.

Behavioral Components: The Way We Act

Cultures vary with regard to how people behave in certain situations. The two categories of behavioral components are cultural norms and cultural activities.

CULTURAL NORMS

Cultural norms are informal societal rules or standards for appropriate or inappropriate behavior. Such behavioral standards determine what is "normal," i.e., the way things ought to be. Cultural norms permeating society include customs, conventions, etiquette, and rituals.

Customs are norms handed down over generations that define culturally acceptable behaviors in specific situations, often special occasions. For example, it is customary to hold ceremonies for such milestone events as weddings and graduations, and it is expected that ham will be served at Easter dinner and turkey at Thanksgiving dinner.

Conventions are norms regarding the conduct of everyday life. They concern the proper way to do things such as entertain guests, landscape a yard, and dress for work. Conventions, like most aspects of culture, evolve slowly. Recall that during the 1990s, dress in the American workplace became more casual, with employees switching from gray flannel suits to gray flannel shirts. Children once carried books to school either in their arms or in a briefcase, but they now lug them in backpacks. During the 1970s, a 10 percent tip in a restaurant was fine; in the 1990s it had risen to 15 percent; and now it is approaching 20 percent. However, in most countries tips are still only 10 percent and in some countries there is no tipping at all or it only exists in certain cities.

Conventions related to CB can change. During the energy shortage of 2001, some hotels began charging "energy fees" in addition to their posted and advertised rates, thereby breaking the convention that customers should not have to pay such surprising add-on charges.

Etiquette (decorum) is the set of rules that govern socially acceptable behavior. If you violate rules of etiquette, you are rightly considered ill-mannered, or even uncivilized, but not immoral.

Standards of etiquette vary among cultures. For example, territoriality is a person's defense of their territory, or personal space. In the United States, people stay about three to four feet away from others, whereas in some European countries people stand almost nose to nose.

A **ritual** (**ritual behavior**) is a series of expressive, symbolic behaviors that occur in a fixed sequence and are frequently repeated over time. Rituals can be mundane, everyday, and private activities. They include grooming rituals such as shampooing and shaving daily or brushing one's teeth after every meal. Rituals can also be important and public, such as **rites of passage**. These ceremonies recognize people's change in social status, life situation, or other significant events. Examples include birthday parties, retirement dinners, graduation ceremonies, and bar mitzvahs.

Rituals frequently are associated with **ritual artifacts**, items used in conjunction with rituals, such as a retirement gold watch, a communion cup, or a white wedding gown. Associated with Christmas are Christmas trees, mistletoe, wreaths, and colored lights. Birthdays bring to mind candles, cake, and wrapping paper. Gift giving is a public ritual that involves purchasing, exchanging, and evaluating gifts at these rites of passage.

Social and entertainment events are often ritualistic and goods-laden, such as dinner and the theater, baseball games and hot dogs, and Super Bowl viewing parties. Holidays are also often rich in ritual, presenting marketers opportunities to sell ritual artifacts. Thanksgiving, Christmas, Easter, and the Fourth of July all include ritualistic consumption such as feasting and gift giving.

MORES

Mores are norms with a strong moral overtone. They usually prohibit forbidden behavior, such as incest, cannibalism, and the exhibition of skin by women in fundamentalist Muslim countries. Violating a more constitutes a moral breach and usually results in some sort of social sanction, such as peer disapproval, ostracism, or even imprisonment. The two important types of mores are legal codes and moral norms.

Legal codes are a code of laws adopted by a town, state, or nation enforcing mores via government sanctions for wrongdoing. There are laws that marketers are obliged to obey concerning matters such as selling cigarettes and alcohol to minors, gambling, consumer protection, price discrimination, and truth in advertising.

Moral norms (ethical norms) are standards of behavior that require, prohibit, or allow certain specific actions to avoid causing harm to others (e.g., prohibitions against stealing, lying, and injuring) or to help people (e.g., encouragement of donating money and time to charities). For example, most people in the United States feel it is wrong for youngsters to consume alcoholic beverages.

CULTURAL ACTIVITIES

Cultural activities involve how people in a society spend time and money. We can be occupied with leisure or work, be alone or with others, or pursue sports or the arts.

Acceptable activities change over time. For example, ballroom dancing was thought to spark sexual passions in the early 1900s, as was jitterbug dancing during the 1940s and the Twist in the 1960s. In the early 2000s "freak dancing" or "dirty dancing," in which boys thrust their pelvises into girls' behinds, caused consternation among parents, and songs such as Sisqo's "Thong Song" and "Bootylicious" by Destiny's Child encouraged this practice. What do you suppose dancing will be like in the 2020s?

Review Questions

1. Describe the four major categories of cultural cues and examples of specific types of elements included in each category. Explain the marketing relevance of each of these categories.
2. What are the major types of symbols? Which ones are marketers most likely to use?
3. How do cognitive components of culture differ from material artifacts? What are the major types of cognitive components marketers can tap into?
4. Cite examples of cultural behavior and activities and how they present marketing opportunities.

In-Class Applications

1. Identify and explain which cultural components are found in the following scenarios. Classify each broadly (i.e., symbols, material artifacts, cognitive components, cultural attitudes, and cultural behavior) and narrowly (e.g., words, superstitions, and customs).

   o *Scenario A. Bob Courts Candy.* Bob has an important first date tomorrow with the captain of the cheerleading team, Candy. He wants to do it right, so he purchases a pair of Calvin Klein slacks and a bottle of CK cologne.
   o *Scenario B. Dick Does Digital.* Dick is shopping for a digital TV. He wishes to be on the leading edge with his home entertainment center. Dick knows it will be expensive, but wants to impress his friends with his technological savvy as well as entertain them in style.
   o *Scenario C. Lynn Goes Online for Goodies.* Lynn has been invited to her friend's home for dinner. She offers to bring a dessert. Pressed for time because she has a demanding full-time job, she orders a dessert and bottle of wine from the Peapod online home shopping service. They promise to deliver to her door within three hours.
   o *Scenario D. Professor Looks Very Professionally Professorial.* Arthur Vary is trying to cultivate an intellectual image for himself as a newly minted assistant professor of marketing, so he decided to buy a pair of eyeglasses even though his vision is 20/20. Professor Vary also took up pipe smoking to look contemplative, although he knows it is unhealthy. Further, Arthur invested in a classical music collection to craft the academic image and lined his office bookshelf with all of the complimentary review copies of textbooks received from publishers to make it appear that he is well read. Professor Vary also invested in a cap and gown for the many academic convocations

and graduations he knows he will be attending during his career.

- ○ *Scenario E. Herr Krauss Goes Native.* Heimlich Krauss, a German citizen, recently moved to New York City to head up the marketing function within a U.S. subsidiary of his corporation. He wanted to adjust to the United States as quickly as possible. In order to do so, Mr. Krauss took to drinking Coca-Cola, bought a Chevrolet, frequented McDonald's, and shopped at Sears. He also bought a German-English dictionary and some English language CDs to improve his command of the language. Heimlich then began regularly attending New York Yankees games, where he patriotically stood for the national anthem, splurged on hot dogs and Budweiser beer, took a seventh-inning stretch, and rooted for the Bronx Bombers.

2. Identify an example of each of the four broad categories of cultural characteristics that has influenced your CB or the behavior of college students in general. Note any significant differences between American and international students in the class.

3. One way to generate new product ideas is to use trend extrapolation, which means to identify a broad current change in society (demographically, technologically, socially, politically, etc.) and assume it will continue into the future. Analysts then ask what new needs or wants this trend creates and what new products could be developed to satisfy the emerging needs and wants.

   What new product ideas are suggested by each of the following cultural trends?

   a. Sit-down meals are giving way to grazing as time-strapped consumers eat on the run throughout the day.
   b. People are down-aging, acting younger and younger (e.g., 80-year-old marathon runners).
   c. Weddings are becoming more formal, individualistic, and expensive.

   d. People want to simplify their lives—"less is more."

4. Identify as many cultural cues as you can in each of the ads from U.S. media in Exhibits 5.2 through 5.6. Which of these elements might not work well in some other foreign cultures? Why not?

Written Applications

1. Answer Question 3 in the In-Class Applications. For one of your new product ideas, suggest several other cultural trends with which it would be consistent. Then, check your assumption by surveying about six target market members (be sure to clearly describe that market) to see whether they find it an attractive new product idea and why or why not. Do any of them mention any of the trends?

2. Answer Question 4 in the In-Class Applications. Identify and describe specific societies in which one or more of these ads might not be acceptable.

3. Visit one or more of the following Web sites, which contain archives of advertisements:

   - ○ Adflip.com: The world's largest archive of classic print ads.
   - ○ Ad*Access at http://library.duke.edu/digitalcollections/adaccess/: Over 7,000 advertisements printed in U.S. and Canadian newspapers and magazines between 1911 and 1955.
   - ○ adclassix.com/rareads.htm: A specialist in original vintage ads.
   - ○ AdForum.com (AdForum allows you to search by country as well as by time period): http://adland.tv/: Carries 40,000 TV and radio spots in Quicktime format. The site is strong in both U.S. and international ads.

   On these sites, find two ads from different time periods (e.g., the 1940s and the 1980s) and two ads from different countries (e.g., the United States and France). Discuss differences reflected in cultural characteristics found in each ad.

REFERENCES

Berger, Arthur Asia. (1984). *Signs in Contemporary Culture: An Introduction to Semiotics.* New York: Longman.

Demirjian, Turan Senduger, and Tian, Robert. (2007). *Perspectives in Consumer Behavior: An Anthropological Approach.* Fort Worth, TX: Fellows Press of America.

de Mooij, Marieke. (2004). *Consumer Behavior and Culture: Consequences for Global Marketing and Advertising.* Thousand Oaks, CA: Sage Publications.

Hawkins, Del I., and Mothersbaugh, David L. (2004). *Consumer Behavior: Building Marketing Strategy,* 9th ed. Boston: McGraw-Hill Irwin.

Hofstede, Geert. (1980). *Culture's Consequences.* Beverly Hills, CA: Sage Publications.

Holbrook, Morris. (1987). "Mirror, Mirror, on the Wall, What's Unfair in the Reflections on Advertising." *Journal of Marketing,* 51, 3, 95–103.

Hoyer, Wayne D., and MacInnis, Deborah J. (2007). *Consumer Behavior,* 4th ed. Boston: Houghton Mifflin.

Kramer, Thomas, and Block, Lauren. (2007). "Conscious and Nonconscious Components of Superstitious Beliefs in Judgment and Decision Making." *Journal of Consumer Research,* 34, 4, 783–793.

Laermer, Richard. (2008). *2011—Trendspotting for the Next Decade.* New York: McGraw-Hill.

Lantos, Geoffrey P. (1987). "Advertising: Looking Glass or Molder of the Masses?" *Journal of Public Policy and Marketing,* 6, 104–128.

Letscher, Martin G. (1994). "How to Tell Fads from Trends." *American Demographics,* December, 38–41.

McCracken, Grant. (1986). "Culture and Consumption: A Theoretical Account of the Structure and Meaning of Consumer Goods." *Journal of Consumer Research,* 13, 1, 71–84.

Mick, David. (1986). "Consumer Research and Semiotics: Exploring the Mythology of Signs, Symbols, and Significance." *Journal of Consumer Research,* 13, 2, 196–213.

Milner, Laura M., Fodness, Dale, and Speece, Mark. (1993). "Hofsted's Research on Cross-Cultural Work-Related Values: Implications for Consumer Behavior." In W. Fred Van Raaij and Gary J. Bamossy (eds.), *European Advances in Consumer Research.* Amsterdam: Association for Consumer Research, 70–76.

Pollay, Richard W. (1986). "The Distorted Mirror: Reflections on the Unintended Consequences of Advertising." *Journal of Marketing,* 50, 2, 18–36.

Rokeach, Milton. (1973). *The Nature of Human Values.* New York: The Free Press.

———. (1979). *Understanding Human Values.* New York: The Free Press.

Rook, Dennis W. (1985). "The Ritual Dimensions of Consumer Behavior." *Journal of Consumer Research,* 12, 3, 251–264.

Samuel, Lawrence R. (2002). *Brought to You By—Postwar Television Advertising and the American Dream.* Austin, TX: University of Texas Press.

Schwartz, Shalom H., and Bilsky, Wolfgang. (1987). "Toward a Universal Psychological Structure of Human Values." *Journal of Personality and Social Psychology,* 53, 3, 550–562.

Sproles, George P. (1981). "Analyzing Fashion Life Cycles—Principles and Perspectives." *Journal of Marketing,* 45, 4, 116–124.

Sunderand, Patricia L., and Denny, Rita M. (2007). *Doing Anthropology in Consumer Research.* Walnut Creek, CA: Left Coast Press.

Vinson, Donald E., Scott, Jerome E., and Lamont, Lawrence R. (1977). "The Role of Personal Values in Marketing and Consumer Behavior." *Journal of Marketing,* 41, 2, 44–50.

Zakia, Richard D., and Nadin, Mihai. (1987). "Semiotics, Advertising and Marketing." *Journal of Consumer Marketing,* 4, 2, 5–12.

1.2 *I* to *We*—From Individualism to Collective Identity

Juana Bordas

I was born into a *We* culture in which seven people lived in a tiny house with one bath room. There was no concept of private space—a person never went to his or her room; the whole house was common ground. A *We* culture meant my mother, Maria, dressed us up on Sundays and marched us to church, where we took up the whole pew. She watched over us like an eagle circling the morning sky. She only had to give us that look to scare us into perfect piety. **We** *cultures have a strong sense of belonging and sticking together.*

A *We* culture meant my mother hurried home from church, took off her black mantilla, and then cooked the Sunday chicken, which was carefully divided so that every other Sunday I got a leg. **We** *cultures share everything.* A *We* culture meant that on Saturday mornings everyone scrubbed doors, walls, and windows, shook rugs, took out the mattresses for a good airing, and washed down the sidewalks. **We** *cultures work together so everyone benefits.*

The preparation for a *We* orientation starts early in life. Latino babies are never left at home with a babysitter. At Sunday gatherings or *fiestas*, babies are passed around like precious treasures. People anxiously wait their turn to sing to the baby, pinch its cheeks, and make it laugh. Babies are called *preciosa* and told over and over how *linda* (pretty) they are! At parties, they are bounced from lap to lap. When the music starts, they are sashayed onto the dance floor and rocked to a ranchero or salsa beat. Latino babies get accustomed to people at an early age; that is how they become *We*. **We** *cultures center on people.*

One time when I had a bad tooth, my mother took me to the dentist, and then we went to see the movie *The African Queen*. It is a vivid memory, because it is the only time I remember one-on-one time with my mother. *We* meant I was never alone or just with another person. **We** *cultures are collective and relish togetherness.*

No one gets left out of a *We* culture. Uncle Huey showed up on a sweltering August day to the warm embrace of my father. He would spit brown tobacco off the front porch and aggravatingly clear his throat ten times a minute. His trousers hung off him like the laundry on my mother's clothesline. We pleaded with our Papí, "He is embarrassing, *pleeeze s*end him back home." This was to no avail. No matter how obnoxious he was, he was part of the *We*—he was my uncle. **We** *cultures are impeccably inclusive.*

For Latino Catholics, first Holy Communion is a solemn and festive day, one's first encounter with the heavenly host—a baby step into spiritual maturity. As the big day approached, I was worried. We didn't have any money and all the young girls would be kneeling before the holy altar in fancy white dresses. My mother took the precious cotton brought from Nicaragua out of the old trunk, she had been saving for herself. She measured me here and poked me there. She sewed late into the night after working all day, cooking the family dinner, and putting her children, us, to bed. A week later, she proudly held up a simple white dress with lace stitched around the collar, where she pinned a cotton flower bought at Woolworth. The other girls had store-bought dresses with lace and taffeta, but my dress was the most beautiful because no one else's Mom had sacrificed so much. **We** *cultures put benefiting the whole before the individual.*

I still can't imagine how my mother with her broken English figured all this out! Where did she find the money to do these things? It was her total dedication to the *We*, that unbroken promise that her family and children came first. *We* was all she knew. She passed on that sense of a family and culture of togetherness to me. *We* was embedded deep in my soul. I didn't understand it then, but it sustained me when I left my family to go to college and live in the strange land of the *I*'s. *In* **We** *cultures the I exists only in relationship to others, not as a separate entity.*

I and Individualism or *We* and Collectivism

Anthropologists who study and categorize cultures make broad distinctions between collectivist or *We* cultures and those that are more individualistically or *I* oriented. American Indians, Latinos, and African Americans are considered collectivist cultures, whereas North Americans and western Europeans are considered individualistic. In *Managing Diversity: People Skills for a Multicultural Workplace,* Norma Carr-Ruffino comments that most of the world's cultures, as well as women in all societies, are collectivist.[1] This is understandable, as individualism is a historically new phenomenon that grew out of the Protestant ethic and European intellectualism. We should not look at collectivist or individualistic cultures as distinct categories, but rather recognize that in today's rapidly changing and interdependent world, cultures are blending aspects of both. For instance, to function successfully in dominant culture organizations, people of color have learned the individualistic orientation.

The previous principle, *Sankofa*, reviewed the roots of individualism; we will now take a closer look at collectivist or *We* cultures. Our goal is to understand the nuances of both orientations and to consider how these have influenced leadership. In this way, we can integrate the best of each viewpoint into a multicultural leadership model.

It is important to clarify that the term *collectivist* does not refer to today's political concept of socialism,

> We should not look at collectivist or individualistic cultures as distinct categories, but rather recognize that in today's rapidly changing and interdependent world, cultures are blending aspects of both."

but rather to an ancient, tried-and-true form of social organization. Collectivist *We* cultures have been on the earth for a very long time; their traditions and histories go back many generations. These cultures, therefore, are stable, with highly defined and specific rules, and they change more slowly than individualistic cultures. Collectivist cultures are usually portrayed as tightly woven and integrated. As noted previously, these cultures cherish group welfare, unity, and harmony. To maintain these, people behave politely, act in a socially desirable manner, and respect others. The family, community, or tribe takes precedence over the individual, whose identity flows from the collective. People work for group success before personal credit or gain.

Individualistic cultures, on the other hand, appeared relatively recently in history, and they are more loosely integrated. Change and risk taking are embraced. Individuals are *highly differentiated* from others. Self-identity and self-interest are keystones. To grow up means to become independent, autonomous, and responsible for one's own life. Individual freedom and choice are highly valued. In these cultures, individual needs supersede collective ones. This is not considered selfish. The individual serves society by living up to her or his potential. Achievement and getting things done take priority.

Whether a culture is individualistic or collective depends on the degree to which individuals' beliefs and actions are independent of those of the group. *We* cultures emphasize group opinions and actions, and they stress psychological closeness. Individual goals are integrated with those of the collective. Individualistic cultures, on the other hand, emphasize personal opinions. Being able to think for yourself signifies intelligence and competency. Competition with others is considered healthy, motivating, and beneficial. Calling attention to oneself or standing out from the group is a way to advance.

The extent of one's individualist or collectivist orientation determines how much control one assumes in life. The independent focus says, "To a very great extent, I control my life, determine my reality, choose my experiences, and shape my destiny. I am the captain of my own ship." Collectivist cultures are more in tune with natural cycles and believe in a life power that is external to them. These forces influence their lives. They also take into account what other people think, want, and need. These lessen individual freedom of choice.

People from collectivist cultures, therefore, have a greater belief that things happen to them. The Spanish language contains a passive tense in which innate objects or others assume responsibility: "The glass fell"; "The taxi left me"; "It didn't call my attention." Similar verbal constructs can be found in the Zulu and Xhosa languages as well as those of other African tribes.[2] This signifies an external source of control, which simply means there are many more factors than just what *I* want that must be consulted and considered.

Culture, the lens through which a group of individuals defines reality, has been described as *collective programming*. Cultural determinism proposes that a person's values, beliefs, and worldview are riveted on this early conditioning. Today's diverse society and global marketplace require leaders to free themselves of this type of conditioning in order to attain a broader cultural perspective and repertoire. The next section reviews early *We* cultures that have existed since prehistoric times. Considering these antecedents provides insights for understanding how leadership in Anglo society is different from leadership in communities of color.

Our First Culture Was a We Culture

Before there was an *I* culture, *We* ensured our continued existence. Those who adhere to man's evolutionary heritage coming from anthropoids—the great

> "Culture, the lens through which a group of individuals defines reality, has been described as collective programming. Cultural determinism proposes that a person's values, beliefs, and worldview are riveted on this early conditioning."

apes—can witness even today their cooperation, strong sense of family, and mutual care. Genomics has confirmed that fully 99.4 percent of our DNA is similar to that of the anthropoids. Our genetic footprints follow their path. Much early human behavior was patterned on the great apes and their communal behavior.[3] Obviously, no "lone wolf" survived and evolved alone. In fact, the idea of the lone wolf is a misnomer because wolves are in fact wedded to their pack. Our immense journey has been a journey of *We*—a collective one. The long, dependent childhood we live through before we can live on our own means that someone fed us, cleaned us, and made sure we were safe, warm, and dry. ***We** is the reason we are alive.*

Primitive times were brutal and treacherous, with wild terrains, hunger, predatory animals, and tempestuous weather. Early humans had to be constantly alert—ready to defend themselves or to take rapid flight and flee the threat. Alone, a person would die from the elements and a multitude of dangers. The tribe was the warm bear robe essential for protection. Whether for hunting, taking care of domesticated animals, raising children, planting or harvesting, or preparing medicinal and herbal remedies, the tribe brought people together for preservation, safety, comfort, ritual, and celebration.

Through tribal living, human beings developed complex and mutually beneficial ways of working together, including the differentiation of roles based on one's abilities or lineage—today, this is still the basis of organizational development. The herbalist, the potter, the fire keeper, the weaver, the warrior, the chief, the ruling council, and the hunting party, all first came into form when humans lived in tribes. Just as important, the tribe uncovered and explained the meaning of the universe and man's place in it. In times when the mysteries of life were stupefying, humans looked to the medicine man, the chief, or the wise woman to explain events in the natural world and provide guidance.

Tribes were the vehicles for a collective human identity or the sense of *We* to evolve. Even today, many tribes dress in identical clothes, wear their hair the same, adorn themselves similarly, and follow the daily rituals that give meaning to their lives. Contemporary American teenagers who long to belong cling to this tribal tendency by looking and acting *like, you know*, the same.

Individualistic cultures would have us believe that survival of the fittest was an everyman-for-himself instinct in a dog-eat-dog, competitive environment. In actuality, the collective lifted man to the top of the evolutionary pyramid. In her notable book *Calling the Circle,* visionary author Christina Baldwin uses the term *first culture* to refer to the time when humans lived in tribes or small communities in which everyone was needed and included and everyone belonged. Baldwin points out that human beings survived and thrived because of their ability to care for each other, work together, and help one another. *We* was our "competitive evolutionary edge" over other species. Survival of the fittest was a cooperative and reciprocal experience.[4]

Riane Eisler's landmark work *The Chalice and the Blade* documents early societies across Europe, Asia, and the Americas in which people worked in partnership, living in harmony with nature. She notes that human survival was largely due to the cultivation of highly sophisticated ways of working together that included collaborative decision-making structures. Eisler describes many Neolithic cultures as ones in which "social relations are primarily based on the principle of linking rather than ranking, [and] may best be described as a partnership model where both men and women worked together for the common good." First cultures by necessity were tight as a drum, and their foundation was *mutual assistance* and *loyalty.*[5]

> **Human beings survived and thrived because of their ability to care for each other, work together, and help one another. We was our competitive evolutionary edge over other species. Survival of the fittest was a cooperative and reciprocal experience."**

To understand the deep groove that "the tribe" or collective existence has made in our memory banks, consider that humans have first appeared about

195,000 years ago.[6] For over 80 percent of this time span, humans lived in caves, surrounded by a tribe that provided protection, love, warmth, food, family, and a sense of identity.[7] Human beings are social animals; *We* have always lived in groups. Through our long evolutionary journey, our reliance on each other was linked directly with the need for survival—the strongest instinct we have. First cultures, therefore, are humanity's home base.

We Is the Tribe, Community, and *Familia*

The mutuality of early cultures has survived in its most vibrant forms among indigenous people and in Indian, Latino, and African American communities, in which sticking together has been a survival tactic. This is evident today in their collectivist orientation, which centers on the common good rather than on individual gain. As in early cultures, an individual is defined by one's group and relationships.

American Indian leadership, for instance, is based on a great deal of introspection and work on identity—both individually and collectively, for the two are intertwined. Individuals are like strands of straw making up a woven basket that is decorated with traditional designs and colors. The basket is the tribe, holding individuals in place and giving them a sense of unity, identity, and sustenance.

LaDonna Harris, president of Americans for Indian Opportunity, observes how this works: "In Native cultures, *strong personal identity and collective identity stand side by side*. A good tribal person must have self-worth, positive qualities and skills, and be as healthy as possible so they can contribute to the community. The collective is only as strong as the individuals who give it life." Benny Shendo Jr.

> "The reality is you can be collective and still be an individual. You can be totally yourself, a real character, but you are yourself within this spectrum of community and tribe first."
>
> —Benny Shendo Jr.,
> Jemez Pueblo

concurs: "The tribe and community are central, then the extended family, the clan, and then perhaps the individual. Yet, people are secure in their personal identity. In the Anglo culture, individualism is stressed. The reality is you can be collective *and* still be an individual. You can be totally yourself, a real character, but you are yourself within this spectrum of community and tribe first."

Shendo reflects on the collective identity: "For Native Americans, who you are depends on what tribe you belong to. Your rights, like the right to live on our lands, for example, come from your tribal membership. It's not about the individual. In all Indian cultures, the tribe is paramount because it's that community, that group of people who create the collective identity, the songs, traditions, and culture ... When I meet Indian people, the first thing they say is 'what tribe are you?' That's how we establish our initial relationship, and it is a collective identity."

The first premise of the American Indians Ambassador Program reflects this point of view: "The strength of the Indian peoples, both collectively and individually, is the tribe. It is our culture, family, community, and tribe that define our role in society and our self-identity." Collective identity is in sharp contrast to individualism, which touts personal achievement and competition. There is no concept within any American Indian tribe of winning at the expense of others.[8]

Similarly, a core belief in the Hispanic culture is that other people come first. This drives a humanistic set of values that are other-centered rather than self-centered or individualistic. The Latino tendency toward collectivism is evident in the treasured value of *la familia*, which broadly refers to groups with a special affinity who provide assistance and support. Latinos cherish belonging, group benefit, mutuality, and reciprocity. Interdependency, cooperation, and mutual assistance are the norm. Unlike the Anglo emphasis on the nuclear family, the Latino *familia* is elastic and grows to include *padrinos* or *madrinas*—godparents for baptisms, weddings or confirmations, and *"tías"* or *"tíos"*—honorary aunts or uncles.

Then again, in Latino culture, while simply walking down the street with a close friend, a person may be suddenly introduced as a *compadre* or *comadre*, indicating that he or she is now considered family. Even sponsors for *quinceaneras* (a religious ceremony in which a young woman is presented to the community), wedding anniversaries, or baptisms become part of the family. Latinos have an open-door policy when it comes to *We*. The value of *bienvenido*—welcome and hospitality—implies an inclusiveness that makes for a dynamic and expanding family much like a tribe.

This tradition has roots in both the indigenous and the Spanish cultures that are the ancestry of Latinos. The large extended families in Spain ensured that a relative or close friend was contacted when a need arose. The Aztec culture was organized in multiple family groups who governed themselves and worked as a unit. The growing of crops, building of homes, trading, and caring for children were all based on a *We* orientation. This reflected the Aztec belief that human beings are related to one another and that what one does to another affects oneself. Today these tendencies can be found in the Latino values of helping one another and being of service.

African American ancestors came from tribal cultures that mirror a similar sense of connectedness, interdependence, and reciprocity. Dr. Jim Joseph, in his insightful book *Remaking America,* termed this the *cosmology of connectedness.* "The idea that a person cannot be fully understood apart from the community which determines his or her personhood was fundamental to the African view of moral duty and social obligation."[9]

African Americans carry on this collectivist tradition. Because the plight of slavery was a communal one, everyone suffered under the same yoke. Black people faced discrimination and racism by "sticking together." The *We* in the song "We Shall Overcome" indicates an understanding that solidarity is their source of strength and salvation. Indeed, since the practice of slavery tore families apart, African Americans don't know if someone is a blood relative or not, so they refer to each other as brother, sister, or cuz (cousin). When walking into a room, although Black people may not know each other, they recognize they are related through a common history, faith, and culture.

Dr. Joseph believes the large family patterns that Black people develop, which include stepparents, peer group members, community leaders, meeting brethren, teachers, and special friends, is also a legacy inherited from the African world. He surmises, "While the bonds of the extended family were severed by the massive transcontinental displacements that brought Africans to American shores, the spirit of community not only survived but took on new forms and meaning."[10]

African Americans continue to have an immutable group identity. In 2005, Kanye West, the controversial rap singer, was chosen by news columnist Barbara Walters as one of the most fascinating people of the year. When asked to describe himself, his first word was *Black!*[11] Likewise, when I am working with African American youth, when I give them a sheet with the question "Who are you?" repeated ten times, for almost every teenager "Black" is the first choice. The White culture does not have that kind of centralized identity with people of their race or color.

The highly developed sense of We—*community, extended family and tribe—has kept communities of color intact for the past five hundred years. That strong sense of* We *was their survival, hope for tomorrow, and anchor of mutual protection, support, and celebration.*

> Black people faced discrimination and racism by "sticking together." The We in the song "We Shall Overcome" indicates an understanding that solidarity is their source of strength and salvation.

I Is Contained in *We*

I and we are not a dichotomy. The *I* is intrinsic to the *We* orientation—individuals must be strong for the collective to thrive. *We* do not have to choose one or the other. This concept of *both and* rather than *either or* is a thread that runs through collectivist cultures. Because they are more tightly woven, there is a sense of wholeness in which many things, including differences, can exist at once. Just as the corn stalk grows tall on its own but only fully matures when many are planted and cross-fertilization occurs, the *I* is nourished in the rich soil that has been cultivated by the collective not just today, but for many previous generations.

The challenge is to balance communal good with individual gain—to reach the higher ground of interdependence. This implies a social imperative whereby personal gain cannot be shouldered at the expense of the common good. Today, the widening gap between the haves and have-nots and the stark social inequities that go with it indicate that the pendulum has swung too far in the *I* direction. Balancing individualism with collectivism may sound easy; however, it proposes a new *cultural equilibrium* that runs contrary to social conditioning and the historical antecedents of the dominant culture.

As previously noted, individualistic cultures are competitive and acquisitive. When these cultures clashed with collective ones, the *We* has always been relegated to the underdog position. Even today, individuals from collective cultures may feel exploited or ripped off when they sacrifice for the group or organization and are not recognized for their hard work or are passed up for promotion. The question is, how do we balance the *I* with the *We*? If we can accept that human beings have an innate drive for connectedness and taking care of one another, then returning to a *We* perspective and a mutual sense of responsibility is a natural homecoming. Einstein once remarked that our sense of separateness was "a kind of optical illusion." To live in a mutually caring world, he continued, we must undertake a deliberate change in perspective. "Our task must be to free ourselves ... by widening our circle of compassion to embrace all creatures and the whole of nature ..."[12] Einstein's unified field theory runs contrary to our individualistic and autonomy-focused culture; it resonates instead with the holistic worldview of indigenous communities.

Shifting from an *I* to a *We* orientation implies an alteration in values whereby social responsibility and looking after the common good is embraced. Almost unanimously, across collective cultures, it is understood that the excessive accumulation of wealth or power by a few hinders the well-being of the society as a whole. For this reason, deep sharing is a cultural touchstone and wealth is defined as being able to give to others. Principle 3, *Mi Casa Su Casa*, explores how people in communities of color have passed this trait

from one generation to another and are expected to treat each other with a generosity of spirit.

NEXT STEPS

I to *We*—From Individualism to Collective Identity

Understanding our group or collective heritage lays the foundation for appreciating our diversity

Participants bring the oldest picture they have of their grandparents or *antepasados* and something that represents their culture. Each person shares the story reflected in the picture. (In the oral tradition of communities of color, people embellish, use flowery language, and use their imagination!) Their cultural gifts are also shared. These are placed on a table that has been draped with a nice cloth and decorated with flowers and even candles. People comment on what they have learned about each other's history and unique backgrounds. This exercise creates a cultural collage of people's backgrounds and family histories.

Create a collective history for your community or organization

Traditionally, people grew up in the same place, knew each other's families, and had a common history and values. Today we are a mobile society in which people from many origins and places live and work together. Building trust is a key leadership challenge when people are diverse and do not know each other, and when newcomers must be integrated into the organization. Creating a community or organizational timeline acknowledges individual experiences, discovers mutual history, and nurtures a common ground.

STEP ONE: PREPARING A COMMUNITY OR ORGANIZATIONAL TIMELINE

A long piece of paper with the words "Our History and Significant Milestones" is placed on the wall. The years are posted on top, starting with the organization's founding or the initial time period that has affected the group. Increments of five to ten years are posted, ending with the present year.

STEP TWO: EXPLORING OUR CONNECTIONS

People reflect on significant global or societal events that impacted their lives; important life decisions, achievements, or events; milestones or changes in the organization or community. What is each person's history with the organization? When did he or she become a member? If the history is not known, people who can remember this can be invited to share their memories, which provides an opportunity to thank and learn from early contributors or founders.

These are recorded individually and then similarities, differences, and unique perspectives are discussed in small groups. The groups then pare down their experiences to three to five significant ones that they would like to share with the large group or their community. (Record these on sticky notes so they can be posted on the timeline.)

STEP THREE: INTEGRATING OUR EXPERIENCES AND ACKNOWLEDGING OUR HISTORY

People reflect on the trends and patterns they see on the timeline. The whole group discusses what they have learned about each other, the societal influences that have affected them, and the organizational or community changes. Understanding a company's beginnings and founding vision can inspire a sense of purpose and belonging.

Recommended readings and resources

- For more information on completing a timeline, see *Future Search: An Action Guide to Finding Common Ground in Organizations and Communities* by Marvin Weisbord and Sandra Janoff (Berrett-Koehler, 1995).
- *From Me to We: Turning Self-Help on Its Head* by Craig Kielburger and Marc Kielburger (Wiley, 2004)

NOTES

1. Norma Carr-Ruffino, *Managing Diversity: People Skills for a Multicultural Workplace* (Andover, UK: International Thomson Publishing, 1996).
2. Michael Boon, *The African Way: The Power of Interactive Leadership* (Cape Town, South Africa: Zebra Press, 1996), 18.
3. Kate Prendergast, "Updating Our Origins; Biology, Genetics and Evolution: An Interview with Steve Jones," *Science and Spirit* 10, no. 5 (2000): 24.
4. Christina Baldwin, *Calling the Circle* (Newberg, OR: Swan Raven, 1994).
5. Riane Eisler, *The Chalice and the Blade* (San Francisco: Harper and Row, 1987).
6. "Modern Forms of *Homo sapiens* First Appear about 195,000 Years Ago," http://www.talkorigins.org/faqs/homs/species.html (accessed December 1, 2006).
7. HRDQ, "Mastering the Change Curve," http://www.hrdq.com/home.htm.
8. For more information on the American Indian Ambassadors program, see Americans for Indian Opportunity, http://www.aio.org/programs.html (accessed August 1, 2006).
9. James A. Joseph, *Remaking America: How the Benevolent Traditions of Many Cultures Are Transforming Our National Life* (San Francisco: Jossey-Bass, 1995), 74.
10. Ibid.
11. Barbara Walters, "The 10 Most Fascinating People of 2005," *ABC News Special*, November 29, 2005.
12. For Albert Einstein quotes, see http://www.heartquotes.net/Einstein.html (accessed August 24, 2006).

DISCUSSION QUESTIONS

1. What is cultural knowledge, and how can it help the international marketer succeed in the foreign market?

2. What are the cognitive components of a culture? What are cultural attitudes, and how might those affect a market's success in a foreign market?

3. What is the difference between individualism and collectivism?

2

C **hapter 2** introduces the reader to culture's importance to the orderly functioning of a politico-economic environment. For instance, the chapter discusses the impact of culture on business strategy, its implementation, and its impact on the design of organizational frameworks. It introduces the reader to critical cultural differences, and it offers practical guidelines for conducting business in different cultural environments. The chapter discusses the Hofstede model, which demonstrates how culture may affect export marketing and how cultural understanding affects business exchange. It defines and explains the difference between *agenda-oriented* and *relationship-oriented* cultures. It also discusses how values in such cultures affect business or market behavior and how different cultural values affect agreements. Finally, the chapter offers strategies and tactics with which to effectively navigate through cultural differences.

2.1 Understanding Foreign Cultures

Shaoming Zhou, Daekwan Kim, and
S. Tamer Cavusgil

This chapter will help you

- develop an appreciation for differences in cultures and societies across the globe;

- identify the impact of culture on business strategy and its implementation;

- introduce research-based frameworks that classify global cultural dimensions;

- become familiar with some of the dimensions of cultural differences;

- develop and recommend some practical guidelines for doing business in a foreign cultural setting;

- learn about resources that can provide information on various national cultures.

C ulture is one of the least understood aspects of doing business abroad. Culture manifests itself in many forms and is present in all interactions within a society (Calantone, Kim, Schmidt, & Cavusgil, 2006; Kim & Cavusgil, 2006; Nakata & Sivakumar, 1996, 2001; Steenkamp, ter Hof-stede, & Wedel, 1999). Three elements can be used to define culture:

- **A culture is learned by people.**
- **A culture is shared by all members of a society.**
- **One element of a culture affects other elements of the culture.**

The first element, that a culture is learned by people, means that culture is not a hereditary trait, such as hair color. Rather, culture is a framework through which people evaluate their environment and make decisions. The second element, that culture is shared by all members of society, is what makes the framework into a culture rather than a personal preference or personality. It should be noted, however, that the society in question must be strictly defined when discussing culture. For example, in the United States, there is a general national culture that can be described as individualistic, but there are subcultures, such as African American, that can be described as collectivist. In other words, a national culture has its own subcultures at different levels, such as regional or organizational subcultures. The third element, that one element of a culture affects other elements of the culture, relates each element of a culture to the other elements.

For example, a person's social status within a culture will affect the vocabulary that person uses.

At the broadest level, a country has a national culture that reflects nationally consistent attitudes, behaviors, and norms. Within this, different classes of professionals have their own professional culture that is based on the training and the requirements of their profession; for example, lawyers, doctors, and engineers might have certain attitudes that are more reflective of their professional training rather than broad-based national cultural considerations. A third dimension of culture is organizational culture. Organizational culture reflects the work ethic and the patterns of inter- and intraorganizational interaction between employees. Such work ethics and interaction patterns vary significantly from one organization to another.

Business executives who hope to profit from their travel have to learn about the history, culture, and customs of the countries they visit. Business manners and methods, religious customs, dietary practices, humor, and acceptable dress vary widely from country to country. Understanding and heeding cultural norms is critical to success in international business. A lack of familiarity with the business practices, social customs, and etiquette of a country could weaken a company's position in the market, prevent it from accomplishing its objectives, and ultimately lead to failure (Calantone et al., 2006).

Therefore, before entering a new market, it is important to understand how culture can potentially affect you and your business. For instance, in Muslim countries, social norms require that people not drink alcoholic beverages. However, in actuality, alcoholic beverages are popular in some areas.

Raju (1995) created a model that illustrates several levels at which culture can affect business transactions. Three of these levels are discussed below.

- Buying behavior: This has to do with the perceptions people of a culture hold regarding imported products, the value of brand equity in a society, the existence and strength of brand loyalty, and the impact of social norms on buying behavior.
- Consumption characteristics: Issues in consumption include the product versus service consumption in the culture, social class and reference group influences, and urban versus rural consumption patterns. An example of this would be food consumption in Brazil. In urban areas, Brazilians are beginning to eat on the run, favoring snacks and quick meals. In rural areas, however, the traditional large, sit-down meal is still predominant.
- Disposal: Resale, recycling, and remanufacturing considerations constitute the disposal level. In addition, some cultures are strongly influenced by social responsibility and the environmental implications of product disposal.

How well prepared are you to conduct business in cultures other than your own? Are you familiar with the cultural factors that play a fundamental role in international business transactions? You need to appreciate that different cultures require different behavior patterns by exporters. Products, strategies, and technologies that are appropriate in one culture might be dismal failures in another.

One of the primary challenges of international business is the ability to operate effectively in foreign cultural settings. The challenge for business managers is to remove the blinders imposed by home cultures, a somewhat difficult but essential task if operations in foreign cultures are to succeed. It is important to understand that cultural differences will have an effect on the way you do business overseas. The greater the involvement of your firm abroad, the greater will be your reliance on an understanding of foreign cultures for your firm's growth and survival.

Roles of Culture in Export Marketing

Operating in a foreign culture impacts your export marketing activities in two key areas: demand side impact and management impact. On the demand side, you are now dealing with customers who have different behavioral patterns than those you are accustomed to. Customers vary in many dimensions, including purchase behavior, communication aspects, and product preferences. Understanding such differences is critical in creating values for customers across countries. In addition, in a foreign culture the management of your business operations becomes quite different from what it is at home. Negotiating skills, levels of initial trust, and the control of middlemen become harder to determine when you operate in a different environment, and the implementation aspects of business strategy become substantially different.

Furthermore, personal interactions pose the most risk in terms of cultural influences on business success. For example, in Japan, a manager's smile accompanied by the words "I don't think so" carries the same meaning as an American manager's "Absolutely not!" That's because in a collective society, people try to avoid saying "No" to prevent other people from losing face. In Egypt, a training exercise that required the managers to stand on a blanket and turn the blanket around without stepping off had to be canceled. The reason? One of the managers was a woman, and the men in Egypt were forbidden to touch her. Because each culture is different, it is best to research each individual culture as part of your market research effort.

An understanding of interactions in different cultures is often a fundamental prerequisite to marketing products or services abroad. There are two aspects that managers need to address:

1. Gain a more than superficial understanding of people and their behavior.
2. Make sure that your message is getting across.

Every culture has its own subtle relationships between words and actions. Getting people to understand what one means and wants is one of the primary tasks of management. Such communication is not only necessary but also an important means of furthering incentive-based plans and productivity. Moreover, sensitivity to daily habits, such as the importance of 4-hour lunch breaks in some societies, or the physical distance between people engaged in conversation, can be among the most vital aspects of the business relationship in export marketing.

Understanding Cultures

Many psychologists and cultural anthropologists have defined factors that provide dimensions for comparing cultures. Some of the commonly used approaches are the six questions approach, the four dimensions approach, and the Hofstede model.

The Six Questions Approach

Florence Kluckholn and Fred Strodtbeck (1961) developed a set of six questions that compare cultures across six dimensions:

1. What do members of a society assume about other people? That is, are other people good, bad, or a combination?
2. What do members of a society assume about the relationship between a person and nature? In other words, do they believe in establishing a harmonious relationship with nature or are they willing to turn nature to their advantage?
3. How do people act in a society? Are they individualistic or do they perform tasks in groups?
4. How are plans formulated and accomplished in a society? Is the status quo accepted or is it challenged? Are plans formed and implemented according to preestablished schedules?
5. What is the conception of space in a society? How close do people stand to each other when communicating? What are the differences in terms of public and private space?
6. What is the dominant temporal orientation of a society? Is it past, present, or future?

The Four Dimensions Approach

Another classification scheme was developed by Edward T. Hall (1990). His work emphasizes four dimensions along which cultures can be compared:

1. The amount of information that needs to be transferred if a message is to be stated
2. The concept of space
3. The importance assigned to time and schedules

4. The speed of information flow between individuals and organizations

The Hofstede Model

The third major conceptual approach to viewing cultures was developed by Geert Hofstede (1980), an IBM employee, who surveyed IBM employees across 40 countries to define cultural dimensions. He developed and presented a framework that had four main factors:

1. Power distance: This denotes the degree to which individuals in a society automatically accept hierarchical or power differences among individuals.
2. Uncertainty avoidance: This attribute measures the degree to which individuals in a society are comfortable in working within uncertain circumstances. It also examines their relative degree of comfort in working with long-term acquaintances rather than strangers.
3. Individualism versus collectivism: Individualistic cultures stress individual performance and achievement, whereas collectivist cultures tend to view work, performance, and achievement as group processes and outcomes. This aspect especially impacts organizational culture.
4. Masculinity versus femininity: Masculine cultures tend to be aggressive and favor the acquisition of material wealth. On the other hand, feminine cultures are comparatively subdued.

Applications of Cultural Understanding in Business

Culture can be viewed using different conceptual aspects. However, there are some practical, readily usable ways that will help you understand foreign cultures. Some important attributes that differ across cultures include the following:

- Deal focused versus relationship focused
- Rigid time and scheduling (monochronic) versus fluid time (polychronic)
- Informal business culture versus formal business culture
- Low context versus high context
- Expressive/verbal communication versus reserved/nonverbal communication

Deal Focused Versus Relationship Focused

Deal-focused cultures tend to be very task oriented. There is an urgency to get to business without too many preliminaries. Small talk is usually not necessary before a business conversation. Agreements in such a culture tend to be very specific and legal. Contracts are a standard form of business agreement. In case of disputes there is an impersonal, legalistic, and contract-based approach to dispute settlement. Typically disputes are resolved through litigation.

In relationship-focused cultures, personal trust and relationships are very important. There needs to be personal rapport and understanding before business conversations can begin. In some cases, managers make international trips only to cultivate the relationship, and avoid discussing business at all. The real business is often taken care of over the phone after the trip.

Rigid Time Versus Fluid Time

Depending on how people in a society use time, the culture in the society is considered either monochronic or polychronic. In monochronic cultures, punctuality is very important. The clock is worshipped and schedules are set accordingly. Agendas for business meetings are usually preestablished and meetings are rarely interrupted. In fluid time (polychronic) cultures, there is less of an emphasis on punctuality. Scheduling is loose, and in some cultures to keep someone waiting signals authority and superiority and may be deliberate.

Informal Business Culture Versus Formal Business Culture

Some cultures stress an informal mode of interaction between people. These cultures are more egalitarian compared to other more hierarchy-oriented cultures.

In formal cultures, people are addressed using suffixes and a strong code of etiquette is followed. For instance, in Japan, a very formal society, employees commonly wear dark suites and workplace uniforms are very common. Using suffixes or addressing others by their titles in front of the last name is routinely expected in Japan. Western managers, even after years in a business relationship, often do not remember the first names of Japanese managers, as they rarely use them.

Low Context Versus High Context

Introduced by Edward Hall, the contexts of cultures are used heavily to understand the communication orientation of foreign partners. In low-context cultures, people tend to emphasize direct, explicit, and frank communication. The meaning of words is clear and straightforward. The context of the communication is rarely interpreted as a meaningful element of communication.

However, in high-context cultures, "saving face" is crucial. Communication tends to be indirect, polite, and vague. Much of the meaning of what is said is implicit. Meaning is found more in the context surrounding the words, rather than the words themselves. This mode of communication stems from the desire to maintain smooth and harmonious relationships.

East Asians mask negative emotions by remaining expressionless or by putting a smile on their face. Showing impatience, frustration, irritation, or anger disrupts harmony and is considered rude, offensive, and therefore unacceptable. High-context cultures can be found in some Latin American countries (Mexico and Venezuela) and in some newly industrializing countries (Korea and Thailand). Low-context cultures are found in North America and the Scandinavian countries.

Expressive Communication Versus Reserved Communication

In cultures that place importance on expressive communication, primarily words and the meanings of words convey the message. People tend to be loud in their communication, and facial expressions are also used to convey meaning. On the other hand, reserved communication stresses body language, listening, and pauses. People tend to be soft-spoken and maintain a certain distance when communicating. Sometimes touch behavior like shoulder patting, elbow grabbing, back slapping, or holding hands is used to convey a important message.

Common Cultural Differences

There are numerous cultural elements, and some show more apparent difference than others. The following dimensions represent areas of major differences across cultures:

- Linguistic differences
- Concept of space
- The meanings associated with different aspects of body language
- The value and significance attached to material possessions
- The importance assigned to trust in relationships
- The form of agreements

Linguistic Differences

In exporting it is quite possible to do well without learning or understanding a foreign language. Most international business people speak some English and therefore have a common language to facilitate transactions. However, words and expressions sometimes convey different meanings across countries. Even if they convey correct meanings, the communications can be slow enough to make some impact on the transactions. Therefore it is important for exporters to understand that it is possible that a similar language may be spoken in two countries, but the interpretation of certain words or expressions is very culture specific.

The Concept of Space

The physical distance that people prefer to keep from each other is also a very interesting dimension of culture, as it varies quite significantly across cultures.

In the Middle East and Latin America, you may feel crowded, people stand very close to each other and may lay their hands on you. If you back away from someone who stands too close, you may be perceived as cold, unfriendly, or distrustful. In Scandinavian countries and West Germany, on the other hand, the conversation distance between people is greater, thus giving the impression that they are a little cold and distant. In Asian countries like Korea, Japan, and China, it is not uncommon to observe someone whispering in the ear of another person.

Body Language

Body gestures and eye contact signal different behavior patterns and feelings that are often unique to certain cultures. For example, the habit of people of the same sex holding hands is shunned in the U.S. or Canada, although it is a very common practice in Africa, Asia, and the Middle East, especially among females.

Hand gestures such as the OK sign (thumb and forefinger), which is also the symbol for "Made in America," may have a vulgar, indecent connotation in Latin America or the Middle East. (Interestingly, such a sign can mean money and change from a payment in Korea.) Instead, one should beckon to a person be extending the arm and hand, holding the hand out palm down, and closing it repeatedly. Also, diet conscious Americans may feel complimented if you tell them that they are slim. In other countries, however, heaviness is a sign of health, wealth, and status. Such a statement would not be a compliment.

Not all cultures regard eye contact as acceptable behavior. Eye avoidance is accepted as normal in some oriental countries such as Japan and Korea, and in many instances it is used to indicate superiority. In some African countries, prolonged eye contact may be regarded as disrespectful.

The Significance of Material Possessions

Americans are often characterized as being materialistic and gadget crazy. Lacking a fixed class system and having a very mobile population, Americans have become highly sensitive to how others make use of material possessions. We use everything from clothes to houses as a complex means of ascertaining each other's status.

In the Middle East, on the other hand, status is determined through other indicators such as family, connections, friendship, and education. The desire for technology and modernization is not shared by all. Modern gadgets may not always be sought after; in certain cultures, social graces are more important than material things. However, in some countries, such as Japan, Korea, and Turkey, high-technology items are in great demand. The Japanese often take great pride in expensive items and tasteful arrangements in their homes that are used to produce the proper environment.

The Importance of Trust in Relationships

Some societies encourage the formation of loose friendships. Friends come and go in a highly mobile society. Lifetime friendship is extremely rare. There are few well-defined rules governing our obligations to friends, consequently we move to a very personal level very quickly when we engage in conversation. We use first names and prefer informality. We feel comfortable about teasing and criticizing each other in public, with little regard for the target person's face. However, such behaviors are frowned on in many other countries. Particularly in collective societies, saving "face" is very important. Latin Americans and Arabs are slow to make friends, but are very loyal to the people they do consider friends. The Chinese prefer to do business with people they know. Such a business network among Chinese businessmen in Asia is called *Guanxi*.

Approaches to Agreements

As mentioned above, in Southeast Asia and China, "face saving" is very important and seems to play a quite crucial role in business relationships. It is wise to avoid embarrassing or confrontational behavior in these societies. In one case where a Swedish firm was negotiating for a project in Thailand, the chief negotiator from the Thai side insisted on better terms of payment, although his arguments were based on incorrect information. The Swedish negotiator, knowing this, promised to look into the matter. Later, when they were alone, the Swedish negotiator told him that his information was incorrect; the Swedish negotiator did not say this earlier to avoid embarrassment. The Thai negotiator appreciated this gesture and became very helpful in future negotiations.

Not only saving face, but also different timelines in negotiations with business partners from different parts of the world play a role. Many exporters have found that their Asian counterparts often take a much longer timeline in finalizing an agreement. It is important to be patient with the pace of negotiations to avoid any misinterpretation of intentions.

There are few different types of rules for negotiating agreements:

- Rules that are spelled out as regulations or laws
- Mutually agreed upon moral practices, taught to the young as principles
- Informal customs to which everyone conforms without being able to state the exact rules

All societies favor one of these or another. In the North American culture, businesspeople tend to rely on written contracts or agreements. To Americans, signing a contract means negotiations have been completed. In the Arab world, a manager's word is just as binding as a written contract. In fact, a written contract may violate a Muslim's sensitivities and reflect on his honor. Therefore understanding which types of rules the society emphasizes helps in interpreting the true meanings and implications of an agreement with a foreign partner.

Self-Referencing

The typical reaction of a person to a foreign culture is called self-referencing. This is a process in which we form judgments about other people by evaluating them against our own past experiences and cultural programming. We tend to see others through our own colored lenses. This behavior can lead to serious misperceptions and a lack of understanding, potentially resulting in export failure. Successful negotiators have the ability to process information from three different perspectives during negotiations:

- Monitoring your own words and actions
- Understanding the meanings the other side gives to those words
- Monitoring and understanding the words and actions of the other side

Culture has a strong bearing on how business negotiations are conducted and concluded. It is important to ascertain the following:

- Determine the background, status, and expected negotiating approach of your foreign partners
- Make sure that whatever is said is communicated clearly and is understood as such
- Understand issues of timing associated with talking
- Say whatever is appropriate at the right time

It is also important to understand the organizational culture and the risk-taking tendencies of individuals, as these have a strong bearing on the outcomes associated with negotiations. There are major differences in negotiating styles between Americans and most other cultures, especially East Asian countries. Therefore it is important to develop an appreciation for the negotiating approaches of these people before attempting to conclude a deal.

Navigating the Cultural Differences

Your international business counterpart will realize that you are a foreigner, make some allowances for your behavior and lack of knowledge, and will forgive any inadvertent cultural faux pas. Of course, he will be more impressed by the knowledge you have acquired prior to entering his country. Always remember that your personal image will be linked to the company.

If you consider something morally objectionable, culturally insensitive, or socially outrageous in a foreign country, it may be a good idea to try and understand why a foreign culture acts as it does before passing judgment. The golden rule of business etiquette is to be open-minded, nonjudgmental, patient, and flexible.

Try to be more formal and polite with foreigners. Being conservative in formality and politeness will always help. Show respect for your hosts by making formal introductions with full names and titles. Never call an individual by his first name until invited to do so. Also, remember that in some countries, to call a business partner by his first name is unacceptable. And it will never hurt to try to learn the correct pronunciation of their names.

There are different ways of shaking hands and acknowledging the other person. Bowing your head slightly or a nod might be customary in many countries (e.g., in Japan and Korea). The French prefer a quick handshake, the Chinese pump the hand, and the Arabs offer a limp hand. There are numerous others you may want to be familiar with before going on a business trip to a foreign country. Here are several more suggestions.

Socializing

If you are invited to a social affair, accept the invitation as a sign of respect for your hosts. In some countries it is considered rude not to accept an offer of hospitality. Many cultures use social occasions as a means to get to know you, your company, and your country. Business is usually not discussed during these social events, but you never know. For instance, Korean businessmen may discuss and decide some business matters at such informal social events.

Business Cards

You should have business cards with your information printed in the local language on the reverse side; this is very common practice among export managers, even in the United States. In some countries business cards are treated quite reverently, as indicators of status. Do not bend, write on, or put away the business card while in the company of the presenter. Try to glance at the information on the business card as you receive it and talk about it briefly. This will be appreciated by the presenter.

Gifts

Presenting business gifts may be unusual in the United States, but in many countries gifts are not only accepted but are expected. Flowers are a must when visiting a French home for dinner. Chrysanthemums, which represent mourning, should be avoided. Do not buy perfume for a woman in Europe unless she or her husband requested that you purchase a certain type for her.

Brand name gift items are appreciated, particularly in Japan and Korea. Always bring a gift when visiting a home in Japan. Bringing several extra gifts is a great idea if you are going to Japan. Wrap nonlogo gifts and avoid bold colors, dark grey, and black-and-white combinations. The black-and-white gift wrapping combination is reserved for funerals in many parts of Asia. The color red is appreciated, as it is associated with healing and good health.

In the Arab world it is good idea to give something with intellectual value, such as a book. This complements the Arab's concept of an educated self.

Adapting the Container and Package Size

An exporter who is aware of foreign cultural sensitivities, tradition, and heritage increases its chances for success abroad. Such knowledge is especially beneficial when designing containers and packaging for export. In Japan, product packages are generally smaller than those in Western countries. For instance, consider the package size for detergent. In Japan, the best-selling package size of detergent is less than one-quarter of what is popular in the United States. Also, you will have a really hard time finding mouthwash in the typical size found in the United States. The typical size of mouthwash packages in Japan is about one-third the size of those in the United States. So is the package size for fruit juices. Why are they small in Japan? It is probably because most Japanese people either hand carry the items or use a bicycle and thus cannot carry products in a large package size.

The typical family size would be another fact to consider in determining the size of the package. In the United States, families have an average of less than four members. However, it goes up substantially in numerous emerging markets. This means a family pack of product should have more units in those countries than in the United States.

In India, inexpensive, reusable containers must be used. In fact, many countries stipulate that a products packaging or container must be reusable. In the Ivory Coast, for instance, cylinders are used as measuring cans, and packages with plastic lids become salt and pepper shakers.

The Significance of Numbers and Colors

Certain numbers, colors, shapes, or phrases can be important when marketing in another country. In many cultures, different numbers can have either positive or negative connotations; for example, the number 7. The number 13 is associated with bad luck throughout Western societies. Different numbers have different meanings for different cultures, and to disregard or ignore their meaning could hurt your sales prospects in those markets. A leading U.S. golf ball manufacturer targeted Japan as an important new market by virtue of the expanding popularity of golf in that country. Special packaging in sets of four was developed for export. The company's sales were well below their anticipated volume. Research eventually targeted packaging in fours as a primary factor for lagging sales; four is the number of death not only in Japan but also in some other Asian countries, including Korea.

Cultural preferences should also be considered with regard to color. Some cultures prefer bold colors, some more subtle ones. For instance, most African countries prefer bold coloring, and they especially favor the colors of their flag. In Korea, red is strictly avoided in writing a person's name, as they relate the color to bloodshed and thus is seen as life threatening, although it is generally well accepted for other purposes. West Germans dislike red because of its association with Communism, while the Danes and Czechs like red. An exporter who is aware of these cultural preferences can color his packaging appropriately.

Shapes That Matter

The shape and size of a package is also susceptible to cultural overtones. In Colombia and Romania, triangular and circular packages attract customers. Circular and square shapes are preferred in Taiwan, because they represent completeness and correctness, while a triangle represents complications. Although most shapes are quite neutral to U.S. exporters, it is important to understand that shape can affect how well your product sells in other countries.

Consumer Purchasing Behavior

In the United States, men buy diamond rings for their fiancées, however, in Germany, for example, young women tend to buy diamond rings for themselves. Advertising campaigns must consider such cultural traits. In many countries, including Western ones, wives are involved in the purchasing decisions of major items. However, the role of wives in purchasing decisions is much less significant in Arab countries.

Cultural Attitudes That Work

As a businessperson interacting with other cultures, you cannot afford to be insensitive to the existence of cultural differences. Differences do exist, and to ignore this fact is to invite embarrassment, if not disaster. The following points should help you cope more effectively with cultural differences.

Avoid Cultural Bias

We tend to view other cultures through the lens of our own culture. We accept our own culture as the norm and view everything else as strange. Our acceptance of our own culture tends to condition how we react to different behavior, values, and systems. Consequently we must be conscious about such "built-in" bias.

Develop Empathy and Sensitivity for Foreign Cultures

We need to develop empathy for other points of view. We must avoid ethnocentrism and appreciate the differences in cultural patterns and traits. Try to understand where the other person is coming from and why such different cultures prevail in their countries. Remember, you can only criticize those who eat dog meat in Asia when you are ready to be criticized by Hindus for eating beef.

The Importance of Experiential Knowledge

The key to successfully doing business in a foreign culture is using common sense derived from experience. It is advisable to begin exporting to relatively similar markets and then move into culturally dissimilar markets over time. Employees can be briefed beforehand on the norms of a foreign culture, but still it is important to realize that direct experience will be very important as well. Sometimes anthropological models can provide help in dealing with cross-cultural business situations. However, acquiring factual and interpretive knowledge about other people and cultures will certainly help.

Watch Out for Overgeneralizations

Sometimes, given your understanding of the cultural dimensions of various cultures, you might tend to stereotype a certain group or individual that might be different from the larger cultural grouping as a whole. Such overgeneralizations can stem from misidentifying social and ethnic groups within societies. Be wary of such generalization.

Learning Local Language

All in all, cultures are closely intertwined with language. Therefore learning the local language is the most effective way to begin navigating a foreign culture. This will expedite the cultural learning process, reducing the time required to understand a foreign culture.

If you are interested in obtaining some hands-on information on the culture in a country, you should visit the following Web sites:

- http://www.buyusa.gov/home/export.html
- http://www.fita.org
- http://www.executiveplanet.com

A good collection of country-specific books is offered at http://www.worldbiz.com.

Successful export marketing is a learning process. Learning about people's attitudes, preferences, ways of living, and ways of doing business can help exporters to navigate foreign cultures. In doing so, just remember that learning a foreign culture involves a significant level of individual adaptation, tolerance, flexibility, curiosity, and knowledge. When such cultural maturity is translated into a product adapted to locally prevailing requirements, an exporter can move on to the next level of business.

REFERENCES

Calantone, R., Kim, D., Schmidt, J., & Cavusgil, S. T. (2006). The influence of internal and external firm factors on international product adaptation strategy and export performance: A three-country comparison. *Journal of Business Research, 59*(2), 176–185.

Hall, E. T. (1990). *Beyond culture.* New York: Anchor Books.

Hofstede, G. (1980). *Culture's consequences: International differences in work related values.* Beverly Hills, CA: Sage.

Kim, D., & Cavusgil, S. T. (2006). Does online information disclosure matter to etailers? A cross-cultural study. *International Journal of Internet Marketing and Advertising, 3*(1), 89–104.

Kluckholn, F., & Strodtbeck, F. (1961). *Variations in value orientations.* San Fran-cisco: Row Peterson.

Nakata, C., & Sivakumar, K. (1996). National culture and new product development: An integrative review. *Journal of Marketing, 60* (January), 61–72.

Nakata, C., & Sivakumar, K. (2001). Instituting the marketing concept in a multinational setting: The role of national culture. *Journal of the Academy of Marketing Science, 29*(3), 255–275.

Raju, P. S. (1995). Consumer behavior in global markets: The A-B-C-D paradigm and its applications to Eastern Europe and the Third World. *Journal of Consumer Marketing, 12*(5), 37–56.

Steenkamp, J.-B., ter Hofstede, F., & Wedel, M. (1999). A cross-national investigation into the individual and national cultural antecedents of consumer innovativeness. *Journal of Marketing, 63*(2), 55–69.

DISCUSSION QUESTIONS

1. Describe the four dimensions of the Hofstede model.

2. In terms of managing the foreign culture, what should an international marketer do in order to increase their likelihood of success in a foreign market?

3. What is the difference between high-context and low-context cultures?

4. How do deal-focused cultures differ from relationship-focused ones?

5. What cultural elements represent areas of major differences across cultures?

6. Why is knowing the foreign culture important to an international marketer?

7. What is ethnocentrism?

3

Chapter 3 focuses on defining the concept of *cultural competence*. It describes the importance of cultural competence in an environment of increased diversity in which cultural differences may stymie intercultural symbiosis. The chapter compares dimensions of individualism and collectivism, and it shows how such dimensions may affect attitude formation and behavior. It also discusses concepts such as *monochromic time*, *polychromic time*, *low-context*, *high-context*, and what cultural environments such concepts represent. Finally, the chapter engages the discussion on how a business could increase its cultural competence; that is, how it could increase its cultural understanding. Cultural competence, being as critical as it is, becomes the focal point of cross-border marketing strategy. The chapter outlines elements or dynamics that may either encourage or impede cultural competence.

3.1 Cultural Competence

Geraldine Hynes

P art One lays two "cornerstones" or basic concepts that are the foundation on which the framework of this book is built. The first cornerstone is *diversity appreciation*. [...] We discussed the increasing diversity of the workforce and considered four competitive advantages that diversity offers. We also examined communication strategies that you, as a manager, can adopt to capitalize on the advantages of workforce diversity.

This chapter describes our second cornerstone, *cultural competence* (Figure 3.1). Diversity brings with it different cultural norms, leadership styles, and communication patterns, so you can see the critical link between cultural competence and your success as a manager. If you know how to navigate among cultural differences, you will be equipped to develop positive relationships with your employees, leading to productivity, profits, and organizational success.

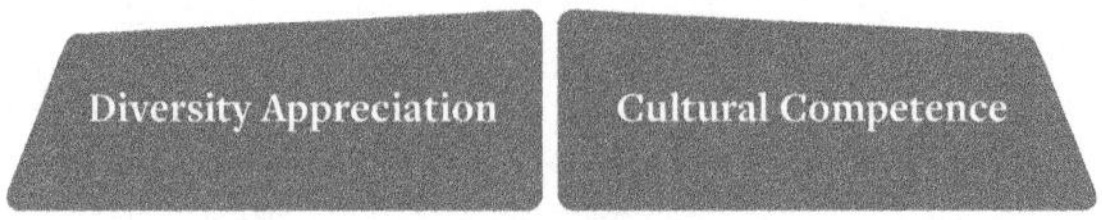

> Diversity Appreciation   Cultural Competence

FIGURE 3.1 Cornerstones of the Sequence for Success

What Is Cultural Competence?

Corporate response to the increasing diversity of the workforce varies widely, but cultural competence is generally valued. Cultural competence is defined as being "comfortable working with colleagues and customers from diverse cultural backgrounds."[1] Cultural competence is known as the "third wave" of diversity thinking—after affirmative action and inclusion. Indeed, today's employers consider intercultural skills as a top consideration when hiring. In a recent survey of 318 executives from both private sector and nonprofit organizations, 96 percent agreed that it's mandatory for their new hires to be culturally competent.

Reactions to diversity in business:
1. Affirmative action
2. Inclusion
3. Cultural competence

Briefly, a culturally competent manager understands that culture profoundly affects workplace behavior and attitudes. Furthermore, a culturally competent manager knows how to navigate relevant cultural differences in order to maximize workers' loyalty, satisfaction, productivity, and ultimately the bottom line. The Economist Intelligence Unit recently surveyed 572 executives in multinational organizations around the globe. The business leaders overwhelmingly agreed that cultural competence improves revenues (89 percent), profits (89 percent), and market share (85 percent). The executives widely agreed that managerial communication skills are essential for workforce productivity.[2]

Why Culture Matters

Let's take a closer look at the notion of culture so we can see why it's such an important factor in managerial success. Culture is what we grow up in. Beginning in childhood, we learn acceptable behaviors, customs, and habits. We also adopt the beliefs, values, and moral attitudes of the society in which we mature. A body of common understanding develops. We know what to expect, and we know what is expected of us.[3]

Culture is what we grow up in.

Defined in such a way, culture includes the religious system to which we are exposed, the educational system, the economic system, the political system, the legal system, morals, recreational outlets, mores governing dress and grooming, standards of etiquette, food and how it is prepared and served, gift-giving customs, quality and quantity of communication among the people, greeting practices, rituals, modes of travel available, as well as the many other aspects of our lives.

There is some evidence that culture can even affect our personalities. For instance, a series of studies of people who spoke both Spanish and English showed that switching languages significantly affected personality variables such as extraversion (or assertiveness), agreeableness (superficial friendliness), and conscientiousness (achievement).[4] Bilingualism is becoming more common in the United States, especially among the younger generation. According to the U.S. Census Bureau, Millennials are the most diverse generation in history, with one in four speaking a non-English language at home.

Furthermore, culture can influence the way we see the world. If you show pictures of a monkey, a panda, and a banana to someone from Japan and ask which two go together, chances are that the Japanese will pick the monkey and the banana, because the former eats the latter. Show the same pictures to someone from Great Britain and she or he will select the panda and the monkey, because they are both mammals. Westerners typically see classifications where Asians see relationships.

There is strong evidence that these differences in worldviews begin in childhood. In another study, Japanese and American children were asked to look at a tank of large fish, small fish, and some aquarium plants and rocks. When they were asked what they saw, the Japanese kids described the groups of fish and the environmental elements. The Americans talked about the big fish.[5] The researchers concluded that the

FIGURE 3.2 What do you see in this picture?

collectivist Japanese culture encourages youngsters to focus on groups, while the individualist U.S. kids learn early on to focus on standouts (Figure 3.2).

Malcolm Gladwell explored the importance of culture in his best-seller, *Outliers: The Story of Success*. He concluded, "cultural legacies are powerful forces. They have deep roots and long lives. They persist, generation after generation, virtually intact ... and we cannot make sense of our world without them."[6]

A Closer Look at Cultural Differences

What are the "deep roots" of cultural differences that Gladwell was referring to? One of the most extensive studies of cultural differences was conducted at IBM Corporation by a Dutch management thinker, Geert Hofstede. He surveyed more than 116,000 IBM employees in 40 countries. A massive statistical analysis of his findings revealed six dimensions of national culture as shown in Figure 3.3: power distance, uncertainty avoidance, individualism/collectivism, masculinity/femininity, high and low context, and monochronic/polychronic time.[7] Examining Hofstede's framework can help you anticipate and then solve possible problems caused by misunderstandings between employees from different cultures.

Power distance indicates the extent to which a society accepts the fact that power is distributed unequally. It is reflected in the values of both the more powerful and less powerful members of the society. The Philippines, Venezuela, and Mexico are countries with high power distances; and Denmark, New Zealand, the United States, and Israel are a few of the countries with low power distances.

> High/low power distance: The extent to which society accepts the unequal distribution of power.

A manager in a culture with high power distance is seen as having dramatically more power than a subordinate would have. This manager, who usually is addressed respectfully by title and surname, might favor a controlling strategy and behave like an autocrat. For instance, within the British Houses of Parliament,

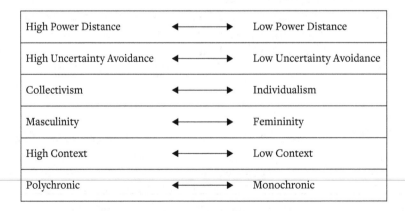

High Power Distance	⟷	Low Power Distance
High Uncertainty Avoidance	⟷	Low Uncertainty Avoidance
Collectivism	⟷	Individualism
Masculinity	⟷	Femininity
High Context	⟷	Low Context
Polychronic	⟷	Monochronic

FIGURE 3.3 Hofstede's Dimensions of Cultural Differences

lawmakers can move to the head of the line at restaurants, restrooms, and elevators, while clerks, aides, and secretaries who work in Parliament must stand and wait. In a culture with a lower power distance, however, a manager is seen as having little more power than a subordinate, is often addressed by first name, takes her place in line, and manages by using an equalitarian communication strategy.

Uncertainty avoidance relates to the degree to which a society feels threatened by uncertainty and by ambiguous situations. People within such a society try to avoid these uncertainties and ambiguous situations by providing greater career stability, establishing and following formal rules, not allowing odd ideas and behaviors, and believing in absolute truths and the attainment of expertise. Greece, Germany, England, and Japan have strong uncertainty avoidance, while Hong Kong, Denmark, the United States, and Sweden have weak uncertainty avoidance.

> High/low uncertainty avoidance: The extent to which society feels threatened by ambiguity.

If you are managing subordinates whose culture values uncertainty avoidance, you will have difficulty getting them to embrace change. Most likely, they will prefer the status quo. To reduce resistance, try to get your people involved in the new strategy and highlight the benefits of change.

On the *individualism/collectivism* dimension, *individualism* suggests a loosely knit social framework in which people are expected to take care of themselves and their immediate families only. *Collectivism*, on the other hand, is a tight social framework in which people distinguish between in-groups and out-groups. They expect their in-group (relatives, clan, organization) to take care of them; and because of that, they believe they owe absolute loyalty to their in-group. The United States, Australia, and Great Britain are the most highly individualistic countries on Hofstede's scale, while Pakistan, Colombia, Nigeria, and Venezuela are more collectivist countries.

> Individualism/collectivism: The extent to which society prefers loyalty to the group over loyalty to the individual.

If you are a manager from an individualistic culture and you are participating in negotiations with business professionals from a collectivist culture, you will be frustrated when they resist making decisions. They must first collaborate to reach consensus. You may ask to talk to a "decision maker," but there won't be one. Try to be patient while the other group spends so much time in conference.

Masculinity/femininity is the fourth Hofstede dimension. Masculinity includes assertiveness, the acquisition of money and things, and not caring about the quality of life. These values are labeled masculine because, within nearly all societies, men scored higher in these values than women. Japan, Austria, and Mexico were among the most masculine societies. Feminine cultures, by contrast, value family, children, and quality of life. Denmark, Sweden, and Norway are considered feminine cultures.

> Masculinity/femininity: The extent to which society values quality of life.

Consider the following example. In the United States, people are judged at least partly on their ability to make a good salary. Frequently, this judgment precludes traditional U.S. feminine values of caring for children. Despite the passage of the Family Leave Act in 1993, the majority of U.S. working men and women do not take the full time they are eligible for when dealing with family and medical problems.

The fifth cultural difference in Hofstede's model is *context*. In a *high-context* culture, much information is gathered from the physical context or environment or the person's behavior. People look for meaning in what is not said—in the nonverbal communication or body language; in the silences, the facial expressions, and the gestures. Japan and Saudi Arabia are high-context countries, as are Chinese- and Spanish-speaking countries.

> High/low context: The extent to which society gathers information from the environment.

In a *low-context* culture, the most information comes from the language. In such a culture, communicators emphasize sending and receiving accurate messages directly, usually by being highly articulate. Canada and the United States are low-context cultures. As you might suspect, negotiations between low-context and high-context cultures can be tricky. The value of contracts and documents used in business-to-business transactions will vary by culture. In high-context countries, agreements are sealed with handshakes between those with strong personal relationships.

The sixth dimension of cultural differences, according to Hofstede, is *monochronic versus polychronic time*. In a monochronic culture, such as Germany, the United States, and most westernized nations, we talk about saving time, wasting time, making time, and spending time. We measure time by the clock, often in nanoseconds. In hyper-punctual countries such as Japan, pedestrians walk fast and bank clocks are accurate. In Western businesses we read quarterly returns and define "long-term" projections as those going out 3 to 5 years into the future. Time is linear.

> Monochronic/polychronic: The way a society perceives time.

In polychronic cultures, such as Spain, Latin America, and most Asian countries, time just *is*. These cultures trace their roots back thousands of years. Time is measured by events, not the clock. Thus, promptness diminishes in value, and being "late" is a sign of status. In Ecuador, for instance, politicians, military officers, and business people are less punctual than blue-collar workers are.

People in polychronic cultures are more patient, less interested in time management or measurement, and more willing to wait for their rewards than those in monochronic cultures. And the fact that polychronic cultures typically are less economically successful than monochronic cultures is not a compelling reason for change.

Developing Cultural Competence

All of us can benefit from increasing our understanding of cultural differences. Now that we have explored the deep roots of some of these differences, as described in Hofstede's model, you can see that culture has a profound effect on each of us. As a culturally competent manager, you will recognize that culture determines why your employees

- Prefer authoritarian or democratic leadership
- Need more or less personal space and privacy
- Perceive punctuality as important or not
- Are future-oriented or look to the past
- Are factual or intuitive in decision making
- Value individual achievement or loyalty to the group
- Focus only on the words or on everything except the words

When observing employee conflicts, other managers may not notice that the underlying issue could be cultural. They might think, "What's wrong with you? You shouldn't be so upset." But culturally competent managers will recognize that cultural background strongly influences the way employees respond to any situation.

Once you recognize how pervasive a person's culture is and how different it may be from yours, you can then begin to appreciate the complexity of good management. If you want to succeed in our highly competitive global marketplace, you will need to see and accept things as others see and accept them.

Cultural differences can affect work relationships in domestic as well as multinational corporations. Subcultures in the United States, primarily labeled by geographic region, may affect workers' behavior, communication style, and values just as much as national cultures do. My personal story as a Yankee who works in Texas provides an example of domestic cultural differences, as I described in the Preface of this book.

Understanding your workforce includes recognizing and respecting the cultural roots of their attributes, whether international or domestic, and trying to adapt to their culturally based values and behaviors. As a culturally competent manager, you will take better advantage of this type of diversity and see it as an asset to be valued, not a liability to be dealt with.

Barriers to Cultural Competence

The biggest roadblock to cultural competence is our own cultural values. From an early age, we are taught that our way of doing things is the right way, and everyone who is different is wrong. This bias against difference is natural and normal, not pathological, and mostly subconscious. But every day our biases determine what we see and how we judge those around us. We have biases about almost every dimension of human identity.

> Bias is a normal psychological reaction to difference.

We are attracted to and tend to like people who are similar to us, not different from us. The perceived similarities may or may not be real. When people think they're similar, they expect to have positive future interactions. Therefore, the discovery of similarities and differences is crucial in developing relationships. Here's how it works:

Think about a time you had to interview a job candidate. When the candidate walked in and greeted you, you immediately noticed her gender, race, dress, appearance, speech patterns, handshake, and even body size. And you immediately formed judgments based on those outward factors. If you perceived those factors to be similar to yours, you probably formed a positive impression of the candidate. If you perceived those factors to be different from yours, you probably formed a negative impression. As the interview went along and you gained more information about her background, experiences, and skills, you probably paid most attention to the information that confirmed your first impressions and disregarded the information that conflicted with them. That normal mental process can lead to bias and discrimination. It can also lead to costly hiring mistakes.

Overcoming the Barriers

How can you avoid scenarios like the one above? Howard Ross, the founder of Cook Ross, an international diversity consulting company and author of *Everyday Bias* and *Reinventing Diversity*, suggests four strategies for developing cultural competence:

1. *Recognize and accept that you have biases.* Bias is a normal psychological phenomenon. Rather than feel guilty about your biases, take responsibility for them. Once you accept them, you can begin to limit their impact.
2. *Practice "constructive uncertainty."* Slow down decision making, especially when it affects other people.
3. *Try to interact regularly with and learn about people you feel biased against.* Exposing yourself to positive role models will reduce the risk of discrimination.
4. *Look at how you make decisions.* Consider the impact of environmental factors, time of day, and your physical and emotional state in order to identify barriers to perception.[8]

Strategies for developing cultural competence:
1. Recognize and accept that you have biases.
2. Practice constructive uncertainty.
3. Learn about people that you feel biased against.
4. Look at how you make decisions.

Let's apply Ross's four strategies to the job interview scenario described earlier. If your first impression of the candidate is negative because you perceived her outward characteristics (age, appearance, race, gender, voice, handshake) to be different from yours, what should you do? The first step is to recognize your bias and the possibility of premature judgment. Next, deliberately decide that you won't jump to conclusions. Ask questions and listen closely to her responses. Try to penetrate well below the surface so you can exchange information more accurately. Bring in another interviewer whose opinions you respect and then compare impressions afterward.

It's true that similarities make it easier to build relationships at work. It's also true that most work groups develop their own subculture over time; members adapt their values, behaviors, attitudes, and even appearance so they fit into the workgroup and gain a sense of belonging. However, different traits and outlooks will give your team balance, opportunities for growth, and possibilities for learning new ways of thinking. Becoming aware of your mental processes will help you to become culturally competent so you can make better decisions, whether it's about hiring or anything else. [...]

Three Cases of Corporate Cultural Competence

After examining the roots of cultural differences and what's involved in becoming culturally competent, let's look more closely at how three very high-profile corporations respond to their multicultural environments.

Our first case is Walmart, the largest retailer in the United States, Canada, and Mexico, and the second largest in Britain. Worldwide, more than seven billion people shop at a Walmart each year. But Walmart stores failed in Germany. Why? For one thing, many Germans found the idea of a smiling greeter at the entrance to be off-putting. In fact, many male shoppers interpreted it as flirting. For another thing, German labor unions objected to Walmart's non-union hiring practices.

Walmart also has been insensitive to cultural values in Brazil and Mexico, where the company's stores focused sales campaigns on items the people in those countries don't use—golf clubs and ice skates. Cultural competence was in short supply in Korea, too, where Walmart built stores with shelves so tall that customers had to use ladders to reach the products.[9] These examples of failed management and sales tactics at Walmart demonstrate what can go wrong when decision makers lack cultural competence.

Our second case is Honda Motor Company, one of the most successful multinational companies in the world, employing 140,000 people globally. Astonishingly, Honda has been profitable every year since its inception in 1949. The Honda business model, known

as lean manufacturing, is built on Eastern principles that emphasize

- Simplicity over complexity
- Minimalism over waste
- A flat organization over a complex hierarchy
- Perpetual change

Staying true to this cultural framework is the secret of the company's excellent performance. Just how does Honda do it? Jeffrey Rothfeder spent 5 years researching the company and describes in his book, *Driving Honda*, how the organization's processes align with their bedrock principles. Take one of these principles, for example—"respect individualism." Given the Japanese culture's emphasis on teamwork, this principle is surprising. Most companies encourage workers to team up toward a common goal. But Honda views collaboration from the vantage point of the individual, not the team. Honda sees the individual's capabilities, decision making, knowledge, and creativity as the source of the group's performance. In short, Honda practices cultural competence.

This quote from the founder, Soichiro Honda, captures the profound respect for individualism:

This emphasis on individualism and creativity translates into physical aspects of the workplace. Honda factories are flat environments. The offices are open bullpens with desks; there are no private dining rooms—just a cafeteria, and no reserved parking spaces. Employees have no job descriptions. The result, according to Rothfeder, is enthusiastic, efficient, productive workplaces with high morale and frequent communication.

Our third case study of cultural competence is Zappos, the largest online retailer of shoes, clothing, and accessories. Amazon bought the company for $1.2 billion in 2011. Similar to the Honda work environment, Zappos's corporate headquarters in Las Vegas has no offices, although there's a nap room. CEO Tony Hsieh eliminated job titles, instead creating a flat organizational chart.

Zappos requires its managers to spend significant time listening to employees. In his best-seller, *Delivering Happiness*, Hsieh wrote that he required his managers to spend 20 percent of their time away from their desks.

> In the ocean you see a bunch of fish and they're going every which way. And something happens, a stimulus happens where one lines up, then another, and another, until they all line up and they go together in the same direction, perfectly. Later, they separate again to find their own way and nourishment. That's also how successful teams and businesses work."[10]

The upshot is more opportunities for people to enjoy their work and to be self-reliant and responsible. Hsieh estimates that because of Zappos's flat and lenient culture, workers are 20 to 100 percent more productive.[11]

Hsieh recognizes that a workforce with different likes and dislikes, personalities, and ways of interpreting the world is the best source of improvements. As in Honda's culture, with its emphasis on respect for the individual, Zappos capitalizes on employees' cultural differences. The principle of individualism is tied to salaries and all other business activities. It's not just window dressing.

These three cases, Walmart, Honda, and Zappos, demonstrate what can go right when a company aligns and recalibrates its strategic goals with the company's basic principles, and what can go wrong when it doesn't. The takeaway is that maintaining a consistent corporate culture and being sensitive to the cultural environment are fundamental aspects of doing business.

Culture and Communication Style

At this point you may be thinking, "All this sounds true enough; it goes along with what I've seen in my own career. But the concept of cultural competence is pretty abstract. My job description doesn't cover establishing and maintaining the company's culture. What are some concrete actions I can take to enhance my cultural competence and help the company to succeed?"

The answer is that cultural competence is reflected in your communication style. Every day, when you interact with coworkers, subordinates, customers, suppliers, and other stakeholders, everyone's culture acts as a lens through which your messages are filtered. Similarly, their messages to you are filtered through your own cultural lens. Being sensitive to unintended distortions of the messages' meanings equals cultural competency.

> Cultural competence is reflected in communication style.

Cultural Sources of Misunderstanding

Various cultures view feedback differently. For example, managers in the United States and Europe typically prefer direct communication; they deliver feedback that is explicit, honest, and authentic. In Asian cultures, communication is expected to be more vague and indirect, and managerial feedback is more likely to be nuanced because bluntness might injure the employees' self-esteem. Furthermore, Asian cultures value silence. Silence, like talk, communicates.[12]

> Cultural sources of misunderstanding in conversations:
> - Degree of directness
> - Silence
> - Loudness and pitch
> - Appropriate topics
> - Touch
> - Eye contact

Here is an example of communication style differences that are culturally based. It is part of a conversation between a Chinese police officer in Hong Kong and his supervisor:

Chinese police officer:	My mother is not well, sir.
English supervisor:	So?
Chinese police officer:	She has to go into hospital.
English supervisor:	Well?
Chinese police officer:	On Thursday, sir.

The meaning of this exchange is clouded by cultural differences in communication style. The Chinese officer is hoping that his boss will realize what he wants and offer this before he has to ask for it. In British English, however, it is more typical to start with the request and then give reasons if required. So, the English version of this conversation would be something like this:

Chinese police officer:	Could I take a day off please?
English supervisor:	Why?
Chinese police officer:	My mother is not well and must go to the hospital.[13]

Typical British English speech patterns are similar to U.S. patterns in their degree of directness. When people from Asian cultures are more indirect, Westerners may view them as evasive. A Westerner lacking cultural competence might impatiently prod the speaker to "get to the point." On the other hand, a culturally competent Westerner would understand that the Asian roundabout pattern is used to avoid the risk of hurt feelings and is therefore often a more relationship-sensitive communication style.

Naoki Kameda, a prominent Japanese business communication researcher, explains that the indirect communication style represents important values, based on the "3Hs":

- Humanity—warm consideration for others
- Harmony—efforts not to hurt the feelings of others
- Humility—modesty[14]

By comparison, a direct style seems pretty self-centered, doesn't it?

Communication Style and Empathy

It's easier to communicate with others when you understand and agree with the cultural values behind their communication style preferences. Furthermore, if you can empathize with the other person, share his feelings, and relate to his intentions, then you might even adopt his communication style during the interaction. All you have to do is ask yourself, "If I were on the receiving end, how would I react to this message?" Then adjust your communication style so the receiver's understanding is closer to what you intended. [... E]ffective business communication leads to stronger relationships and feelings of empathy and trust. These emotional conditions, in turn, lead to improved performance, productivity, and organizational success.

 Successful business communication is about 10 percent business and 90 percent human relations."
—A. Wilson, 1975

Summary

Along with diversity appreciation, cultural competence is a cornerstone for getting along, getting it done, and getting ahead at work. Culturally competent managers understand that culture profoundly affects workplace behavior and attitudes, and they know how to navigate relevant cultural differences in order to maximize workers' loyalty, satisfaction, productivity, and the bottom line.

While bias against difference is natural and normal, it can restrict thinking and prevent the development of workplace relationships, empathy, and trust. Culturally competent managers recognize that culture is a lens that filters messages. They develop flexible communication styles to overcome barriers and increase shared meaning.

ENDNOTES

1. Hart Research Associates (2013). *It Takes More than a Major: Employer Priorities for College Learning and Student Success* (Washington, DC: Association of American Colleges and Universities).

2. D. Bolchover (2012). "Competing Across Borders: How Cultural and Communication Barriers Affect Business" (The Economist Intelligence Unit Ltd. Report), p. 11.

3. N. Sigband, A. Bell (1986). *Communicating for Management and Business*, 4th ed. (Glenview, IL: Scott Foresman), pp. 69–70.

4. N. Ramirez-Esparza, S.D. Gosling, V. Benet-Martinez, J.P. Potter, J.W. Pennebaker (2006). "Do Bilinguals have Two Personalities? A Special Case of Cultural Frame Switching," *Journal of Research in Personality* 40, pp. 99–120.

5. R. Nisbett (2004). *The Geography of Thought: How Asians and Westerners Think Differently...and Why* (New York, NY: Free Press).

6. M. Gladwell (2008). *Outliers: The Story of Success* (New York, NY: Little, Brown and Company), p. 175.

7. G. Hofstede (1980). "Motivation, Leadership and Organization: Do American Theories Apply Abroad?" *Organizational Dynamics* Summer, pp. 42–63.

8. H.J. Ross (2014, August 3). "An Appeal to Our Inner Judge," *New York Times*, p. D3.

9. J.W. Neuliep (2012). *Intercultural Communication: A contextual Approach*, 5th ed. (Thousand Oaks, CA: Sage Publications), pp. 374–5.

10. J. Rothfelder (2014). *Driving Honda: Inside the World's Most Innovative Car Company* (New York: Portfolio/Penguin), p. 134.

11. T. Hsieh (2013). *Delivering Happiness: A Path to Profits, Passion, and Purpose* (New York, NY: Grand Central Publishing).

12. W.B. Gudykunst (1998). *Bridging Differences: Effective Intergroup Communication*, 3rd ed. (Thousand Oaks, CA: Sage Publications).

13. This example is from A. Kirkpatrick (2009). *World Englishes: Implications for International Communication and English Language Teaching* (Cambridge, England: Cambridge University Press) as reported in N. Kameda (2014). "Japanese Business Discourse of Oneness: A Personal Perspective," *International Journal of Business Communication* 51, no. 1, pp. 93–113.

14. N. Kameda (2014). "Japanese Business Discourse of Oneness: A Personal Perspective," *International Journal of Business Communication* 51, no. 1, p. 102.

DISCUSSION QUESTIONS

1. Describe cultural competence and explain why it is considered pivotal to a marketer's success in a foreign market.

2. How can an international marketer develop cultural competence and overcome cultural barriers?

3. How do cultural awareness, cultural knowledge, and cultural competence differ from each other? What is their individual impact?

4. What are the barriers to developing cultural competence?

5. What are some cultural sources of misunderstanding in cross-cultural communications?

4

Chapter 4 addresses the dynamics of subcultural influences and their impact on subcultural segmentation. It also discusses the bases used for subcultural segmentation and helps the reader to understand its importance. Subcultural segmentation allows the marketer to increase their understanding of the market segment, effecting a more successful targeting. Subcultures are used as bases for effective segmentation. For instance, ethnic background, religion, gender, age, geographic attributes, etc., are viable subcultures. Furthermore, the chapter discusses the conditions for using sub-subcultural segmentation as marketers attempt to penetrate the market using unique consumer behavioral patterns. A discussion on strategies for marketing to subcultures sheds light on the importance of subcultural characteristics to the marketer's success.

Culture and Buyer Behavior

Donald L. Brady

Donald L. Brady

McDonald's Corporation, a U.S. firm, is the world's largest food service provider, with more than 30,000 restaurants in more than 100 countries, serving around 52 million customers each day. McDonald's and Coca-Cola are the two most well-known brands in the world. Regardless of the market, the management of McDonald's pursues founder Ray Kroc's goal of providing quality, service, cleanliness, and value to offer customers 100 percent total satisfaction. To accomplish this goal, management must be culturally sensitive, and India and the countries of the Gulf Cooperation Council (GCC) are two excellent examples.

Over 80 percent of India's 850 million people are Hindu. Approximately another 12 percent are Muslim. Together, these two religions, comprising about 92 percent of the population, have dietary uniqueness that affects their way of life. This fact presented a real problem for McDonald's, whose primary product is a beef hamburger. Since the cow is taboo for Hindus (the cow is "aghanya," which means it may not be slaughtered), beef is not eaten. For the Muslims, beef may be eaten only if it is "halal," which means lawful or permitted. Meat must meet certain conditions established by Islamic law from the Quran before it can be eaten. These requirements include: No pork content or meat from a reptile or meat-eating animal; it must be slaughtered only by a Muslim in the prescribed Islamic manner; it must contain no blood or blood by-products and no alcohol. For the people of India, chicken and lamb are the meats of choice, and many people forgo meat completely and are vegetarians. Obviously, for Arabs in the GCC, any

Chapter Objectives

After reading this chapter, you should

- know what being sensitive to a culture means and involves;
- understand the role of culture in developing international marketing strategy;
- be able to define and explain the kinds of cultural knowledge the international marketer needs to know and appreciate;
- know what the self-reference criterion is and how to avoid it;
- understand the different cultural strategies management may employ;

- be able to decide and plan which cultural strategy is appropriate for various international marketing situations; and
- appreciate the impact of cultural change for international marketing strategy.

beef meat served must be halal.

To conform to local customs and culture in these countries, McDonald's management has tried to be as sensitive to Indian and Arab lifestyles as possible. In India, McDonald's has formed fifty-fifty joint ventures with Amit Jatia, who owns and operates all the restaurants in western and southern India, and Connaugh Plaza Restaurants, PL, which owns and operates all the restaurants in northern India. In the GCC countries, the restaurants are owned by local Arabs. For example, the twenty-five restaurants in the United Arab Emirates are owned by Emirates Fast Food Corporation with Emirati Rafic Fakic as the managing director. Menus have been modified to conform to religious practices and to accommodate the local palate and preferences. In India, nonbeef and vegetarian offerings such as the McVeggie Burger, McAloo Tikki Burger, McCurry Pan, and the Chicken Maharaja Mac are provided. Restaurant operations have been reengineered to assure vegetable products are 100 percent vegetarian. Vegetable products are prepared using separate equipment and utensils, pure vegetable oil for cooking, and cheese and sauces completely vegetarian and eggless. Separation of vegetarian and nonvegetarian foods is maintained throughout procurement, cooking, and serving.

In the GCC, only 100 percent pure beef with no additives, fillers, or flavor enhancers is served. The beef is halal, from only prime cuts of flank and forequarters, and grilled in a double-sided hot plate. No oil or shortening is used during food preparation. Products that appeal to local tastes such as McArabia Chicken and McArabia Kofta have been added to the menu. Additionally, local sourcing is employed for all food and supplies used in the restaurants.

In India, health and safety is assured by utilizing "Hazard Analysis Critical Control Points" throughout the supply chain to monitor health and hygiene. Perishable products are maintained in a "Cold Chain" from supplier to restaurant. Community involvement is an important component of marketing strategy. McDonald's management supported the Nalanda Foundation's "girl-child" initiative because of the cultural inclination that many Indians have to favor the boy child more than the girl child. The purpose of the foundation's initiative is to assure educational benefits and other privileges young girls deserve but are frequently denied. Support was also provided for Pulse Polio, which was an initiative intended to make India polio free by 2005. In the GCC, refreshments were provided to volunteers and McDonald's restaurant employees who helped clean up beaches. A series of workshops was sponsored to help raise awareness of environmental issues such as environmental management, recycling, environmental law, corporate social responsibility, and ecotourism in the Middle East.

In March 2005, McDelivery, a home delivery service to neighborhoods that are no more than seven minutes away from a McDonald's restaurant by road, was begun in India. Although McDonald's is a fast-food business, management has positioned it as a family restaurant in India. To provide convenience to the family, particularly those who find traveling to the restaurant difficult, home delivery is an attractive service. Remaining culturally sensitive has been a business necessity at McDonald's.

Sources: Based in part on information from McDonald's USA at http://www.mcdonalds.com/; McDonald's India at http://www.mcdonaldsindia.com/; and McDonald's, "Welcome to McDonald's UAE," at http://www.mcdonalds.com/content/countries/uae.html.

Culture

One of the most important considerations for success in international marketing is appreciating and understanding cultural differences between the foreign country and the domestic country. Culture has been suggested to be the root cause of most international marketing blunders.[1] Most assuredly, an optimum international marketing strategy cannot be developed without taking the foreign culture into account.

Culture Defined

What exactly is a nation's culture? The term *culture* can have multiple meanings. From a business perspective, we can consider **culture** to refer to a distinct way of life for an aggregate of people. Thus, within a single country, various segments of society can have some common and some different cultural components. The citizens from all segments may share certain characteristics that identify the entire nation, or each group may be unique. Think of culture as a society's way of living—the entirety of learned behavior that influences conduct and lifestyle. Culture is influenced by everything that affects a society's way of life. Culture determines what is acceptable and what is not. Culture includes, but is not limited to, concerns regarding beliefs, habits, customs, morals, laws, religion, education, family, cuisine, work, and art. Cultural beliefs and values are learned by living in a society and are passed on from generation to generation.

Since it is learned, culture is dynamic and evolves over time. Each new generation is influenced by the cultural value of the previous generation. And because the world is becoming smaller due to advances in technology and communications, cultures can influence each other. The desired aspects of other cultures are attractive and can be absorbed into any culture through contact. Therefore, every culture can have an influence on another culture because of the exposure caused by travel, TV, and other interactions.

Importance of Culture

Why should the international marketer be concerned with culture? Culture is basic to any society and influences how people live. Part of people's way of living is their buying behavior. Therefore, culture influences how, when, where, and why products and services are bought. Managers must be knowledgeable about culture because aspects of culture can have an impact on consumers' wants and needs and how those wants

Exhibit 4.1 Malchev Supermarket

The sign on this small neighborhood grocery store reads "Supermarket."

and needs are satisfied. The more thoroughly a culture is understood the greater is the likelihood that an ideal marketing strategy can be developed. The uniqueness of the culture that can influence strategy development can be taken more fully into account. With an understanding and appreciation of the culture, the likelihood of making inadvertent mistakes in decisions is minimized and international marketing errors can be reduced. Culture, then, is pervasive in all international marketing efforts and requires a high priority in management's decision making.

Cultural Knowledge

What kinds of cultural knowledge does the international marketing manager need to succeed internationally? Two kinds are important to the manager:

- factual knowledge
- cognitive knowledge

Factual Knowledge

Factual knowledge is knowledge about a culture that can be learned. The manager can obtain the knowledge by reading a book, talking to people from the foreign country, or experiencing the culture directly by living in the foreign country. Factual knowledge is absolutely required to be successful. Without factual knowledge, the manager will make cultural blunders. Before entering any country, sufficient effort must be devoted to acquiring the factual knowledge that will influence consumer acceptance of the firm's products or services. The international marketer must understand the following major components of culture that constitute factual knowledge:[2]

- education
- language
- politics
- religion
- social relationships
- technology
- values

EDUCATION

Education is concerned with learning a culture's appropriate behavior. As people mature, they are taught appropriate ways to act as functioning members of society. Therefore, the education process is unique to each culture.

Education can be formal or informal. Informal education occurs through observation and involvement with others at home and in a variety of social settings. A child learns to take turns by observing the order in which peers are served. Older children learn what kind of respect is given to adults by interacting with them. This kind of education is acquired by living it. Daily, people assimilate information without really being cognizant of doing so. Much of a person's socialization process is realized through informal education. For example, by interacting with others in Turkey, people learn that speaking with your hands in your pockets or crossing your arms on your chest is considered rude and should be avoided.

Formal education is learning in a structured environment such as a school. A culture's approach to formal education influences its citizens' occupations and ultimately the class structure of society. Some cultures place a greater importance on formal education than others. Differences exist in terms of the emphasis on literacy, availability of education based on gender, and availability of secondary and higher education. For example, formally educating women is not considered important in India. And, the Wahabi branch of Sunni Islam, Saudi Arabia's official religion, preaches that education for girls is counterproductive.

Attitudes and availability of formal education affect workers' understanding and appreciation of technology. Therefore, care and maintenance of machines may not be considered important where formal education is not stressed. Appropriate training will not be available from local sources and must be provided within the firm. If management doesn't provide its own training, equipment will be neglected, resulting in maintenance problems, production stoppages, and expensive repairs. Education level will influence the type of people that can be hired to perform particular kinds of jobs. That in turn can affect the firm's productivity and efficiency. As a result, management may have to centralize operations to ensure that workers understand manufacturing processes and adhere to required service and maintenance schedules.

LANGUAGE

Language is the primary means by which cultural awareness is communicated, and therefore it defines social life. However, language is meaningful to each culture in its own unique way. How a society understands its surroundings is determined by its use of its language. Approximately 6,900 different living languages are spoken in the approximately 230 nations of the world.[3] Each of these unique languages can constitute a unique culture. Obviously, some countries have more than one language and therefore more than one culture. An example is Belgium, which is divided into two culturally autonomous sections, with Flemish speakers in the north and French-speaking Walloons in the south. Of the world's living languages, only 347 (about 5 percent) have one million or more speakers; these few are spoken by 94 percent of the world's population.[4] Since only 6 percent of the world's people speak the remaining 95 percent of the languages, these languages tend to be of less concern to the international marketer.

Language is important to the international marketer because of the potential to misunderstand the meaning and enunciation of words, that is, what is implied by what is said and how people express themselves. In some cultures, for example in Saudi Arabia, people will say "yes" when they really mean "maybe" or "no." They agree simply to be polite. People are expected to know these courtesies are always extended so feelings are not hurt. In some cultures, such as Syria's, not being embarrassed is extremely important. Syrians often find admitting they were wrong is difficult. Thus, during business negotiations, care must be given to choosing words so that the person who forgoes the most has a comfortable way out, permitting prestige and reputation to be retained. If you do not understand the culture, you can easily unintentionally insult a foreigner by what you say. Word emphasis and voice inflection can also influence the meaning of what was said. Thus, how you state your communication is important, as well as what the actual communication is, so that the understanding is clear.

Communication can be complicated when workers speak different languages or when they speak different dialects of a language. A dialect is a variation of a language that is unique to a region or a group of people, such as American and British English, or the English spoken in Boston and that spoken in the southern United States.

Exhibit 2 lists a few countries and the number of languages spoken in each. When different dialects or different languages are spoken in a factory, management must hire translators, have signs printed in multiple languages, and find creative ways to coordinate understanding. In cultures lacking in technology, words may not exist to adequately explain the complexities of high-technology machines or products. Management must learn the uniqueness of a culture's language to understand and appreciate acceptable communicating behavior.

Nonverbal language is also important. How people behave and project themselves can communicate more distinctly than what is spoken. Thus, body language, gestures, and movements can project meaning. For example, the thumbs-up gesture that signifies everything is alright in the United States means "screw you" in Australia. During business meetings in Japan, displaying an open mouth is considered rude. In Germany, smiling and laughing are considered inappropriate during business meetings. A person is considered to be thinking deeply when arms are folded across the chest in Japan. Hand gestures such as the thumb and first finger forming a circle means alright in some cultures but signifies homosexuality in Turkey and "screw you" in others.[5] Syrians are known to utilize a high level of nonverbal communication during business meetings. Hand gestures are prevalent, and close association, including touching, is common. Bulgarians shake their head from side to side to indicate yes and up and down to signify no. Therefore, the manager should be aware that nonverbal language, just as verbal language, can have a different meaning from culture to culture, and what you do can communicate just as compellingly as what you say.

Exhibit 4.2 Number of Languages Spoken in Selected Countries

Country	Number of Languages
China	235
Germany	27
Ghana	79
India	415
Italy	33
Japan	15
Kenya	61
Mexico	298
Nigeria	510
Russia	105

Source: Raymond G. Gordon Jr., *Ethnologue: Languages of the World,* 15th ed. (Dallas TX: SIL International, 2005). Online version at http://www.ethnologue.com/.
Note: One language may be spoken in more than one country. For example, Mandarin Chinese is spoken in China and Indonesia.

POLITICS

Politics are associated with the political system in a country and affect what is permissible for people. Politics ultimately influence economic conditions and the ability of people to achieve economic independence. Thus, the bureaucratic incentives or disincentives that surround people's lives influence behavior. [...]

RELIGION

Religion is people's beliefs about organizing and interpreting conditions over which they have no control or which they do not fully comprehend or understand. Religion helps people explain and confront social problems such as inequalities in status, income, and well-being. Religion also explains injustices and suffering and provides an incentive for doing what is socially correct instead of what is selfishly desired. Religion is not supportable with scientific or logical arguments and is based on faith. What is appropriate has been spiritually commanded and is therefore irrefutable and accepted by faith.

Formal religions such as Islam, Christianity, and Hinduism include various beliefs that regulate behavior and affect a person's underlying demeanor. Religious events, holidays, and activities influence lifestyle in ways that can affect business culture and marketing efforts. For example, Hindus do not eat beef, Muslim Ramadan limits activity, and Irish Catholics and Protestants do not interact. Formal religion can affect work schedules, which must be interrupted for prayer and religious holidays. Formal religion can also affect social behavior which, for example, may make doing business with women difficult in some countries. In Saudi Arabia, society is male dominated and women, except relatives, do not have the right to interact with men.

Informal religions also exist in many countries. Superstition, ancestor worship, spirit worship, and magic are examples. Informal religious practice, as well as formal religious activity, can disrupt business. For example, if an undesirable unexplained event, such as an accident, occurs at work, it may be considered to have been caused by some other unhappy occurrence

Exhibit 4.3 The Blue Mosque

The Blue Mosque in Istanbul, Turkey, is a place of worship for people of the Muslim faith.

Exhibit 4.4 Backgammon Game

Two men playing backgammon are obscuring part of the window display of a business establishment.

such as the passing of a loved one or the howling of a wild animal. A shaman or spiritual leader may be consulted for guidance and performance of a ritual to remove the evil spirit. Some cultures claim to be nonreligious or atheist.

SOCIAL RELATIONSHIPS

Social relationships are widely varied. What is socially acceptable in a given culture depends on norms and codes of conduct developed within organizations such as the family, business, and religion. For example, the use of promotional pieces that include unmarried men and women clasping hands in public and talking about personal hygiene might be unacceptable in some cultures because such a social relationship is considered inappropriate.

Societies determine the appropriate distance between communicants. In some cultures, such as in the United States, invading another person's space is unacceptable; while in others, like Syria, people will talk face-to-face and touch each other when emphasis is required. Displaying the sole of your shoe will be considered an insult in Iran and Turkey. A youngster drinking beer in Germany or drinking wine in France is socially acceptable. Colors can have special meanings. For example, green is the traditional color of Islam, is associated with nature in the United States, and is a symbol of sickness in some Asian cultures. Men in Austria are taught to rise when a woman enters the room. The use of titles is important to Germans. Germans also shake hands at the beginning of a business meeting and again at the conclusion. Saudis do not shake hands but rather clasp hands firmly and briefly. Indians also do not shake hands, but instead hold the palms together at chin level as if praying and nod or bow slightly. In China, business cards should be presented with both hands and a slight bow. Immediately upon receipt, the card should be examined intensely for a few minutes before being placed away.

Social considerations influence whether a culture is individualistic or collectivistic.[6] **Individualistic cultures** tend to emphasize the importance of the individual over that of the group. Individuals are flexible in social settings and give precedence to their own self-interest. **Collectivistic cultures** tend to emphasize the group over the individual. Individuals are loyal to the group regardless of personal sacrifices that have to be made. As a general rule, Western countries tend to be more individualistic, and Eastern countries tend to be more collectivistic.

Social norms help determine apropos behavior. Class status, occupation, and wealth can influence a person's position in society and determine what behavior is socially appropriate. For example, in Germany, age tends to take precedence over youth. The oldest person will enter first unless a younger person holds a higher position in the firm. A positional hierarchy is important in Italian firms with little fraternization between work-position levels. Rank and status are also important for business relationships in China and Syria. The international marketer needs to learn what is considered socially acceptable behavior to avoid costly and embarrassing mistakes.

TECHNOLOGY

Technology refers to the infrastructure system that satisfies a society's needs for what constitutes a comfortable way of life. Included is the importance of possessing the variety of machines that may be considered necessary to provide a comfortable and happy life. Technology concerns a society's acceptance of research and development and attitude toward newness and change.

The appropriate style of life and values of a society influence the kinds of technology that are acceptable. The level of technology with which people are comfortable and that they consider important influences the kinds of products they are willing to buy, and therefore, reflects the mechanical complexity of the business environment in which people can work. New and complicated technologies may not be embraced when introduced, or considerable training will be required to acclimatize employees. Problems can be encountered during training because the native language may not have words for all of the new technology. Therefore, a literal translation is not possible, and the technical word will have to be retained from the originating language or new words created to express a comparable meaning.

A culture's level of technology will also influence the ability to introduce innovations. An electric hair curler may not be appreciated or acceptable in a culture where it is traditional to braid hair or style it with beads. Likewise, an electric frying pan may not sell well where preparing a meal requires cooking the food in direct contact with the flames. The fact that such a product can save time is not valued by the culture because personal attention and love are required during food preparation to produce an acceptable meal. The manager must learn what technology is acceptable to a culture and use that information in decision making.

VALUES

Values are filters used to determine priorities among alternative actions a person can take. Values determine which of several behaviors are most appropriate for a certain situation. What one culture values another may eschew. For example, punctuality is a virtue and expected by most Germans, while tardiness is of little concern to the Syrians. In countries such as the United Kingdom and Bulgaria, arriving late for engagements is socially appropriate and expected. Values usually relate behavior to underlying assumptions about power, rank, and often religion.[7]

Values can pertain to anything that influences a person's acceptable behavior. Values may include issues such as a culture's position and attitudes toward time, achievement, work ethics, adroitness, wealth, and change. Some cultures, such as the German, have a lineal view of time while others, such as most Middle Eastern and Latin nations, have a circular view of time. The lineal view holds that lost time cannot be recaptured, and a missed opportunity may be gone forever; it promotes a sense of urgency. In the circular view, time is seen as moving in a circle. What is not done now can be done later; thus a missed opportunity will return at a later time. There is not the same sense of urgency about time as in the lineal view. The international manager can learn that because of differences in values, arriving early for an appointment is impolite in Brazil, children should not look at their parents while talking to them in Tanzania, and business is not discussed before a period of socializing in Japan, Syria, Mexico, and Saudi Arabia.

Cognitive Knowledge

Cognitive knowledge is the ability to think and feel comfortable in a foreign culture so that the factual knowledge can be understood and appreciated. Involved is the ability to use reason, perception, and intuition to assimilate the cultural conditions. Knowing what is acceptable in the culture is not the same as knowing why that behavior is appropriate. Appreciating the culture (making it part of one's being) permits a deeper comprehension of the differences and fine points of life. A manager with cognitive knowledge can think and function more comfortably in the culture, akin to the way the local people do.

Even with cognitive knowledge, some customs should not be embraced by the international marketer. **Cultural exclusives** are behaviors from which foreigners are excluded. Cultural exclusives are only appropriate for participation by a member of that culture. People from other cultures should avoid involvement, and trying to participate, regardless of one's cultural appreciation, is considered in poor taste or offensive. For example, a Christian should not worship in a Muslim mosque.

Appropriate actions are expected and must be embraced if the international marketer is to be accepted. **Cultural imperatives** are behaviors that foreigners must observe to be successful. For example, in countries such as Syria, Saudi Arabia, and Spain, developing friendship and trust may be necessary before business can be conducted. Failure to build the personal relationships precludes the possibility of negotiating any business association.

The international marketer may selectively embrace most other cultural practices. **Cultural electives** are behaviors that foreigners may observe but are not required or expected to respect by members of the culture. Practicing elective behavior is neither harmful nor helpful. These are cultural practices that should be understood and appreciated, and embraced if the international marketer feels comfortable with them. One will not be viewed less highly or more highly for participation. For example, in some cultures, men customarily greet each other with a kiss on the cheek. The international marketer may use this form of greeting or refrain from it. A local businessperson will not feel slighted if a kiss is not offered, because they recognize that you are not one of them. The international marketer needs to realize whether an exclusive, an imperative, or an elective is involved, and be able to respond appropriately.

Self-Reference Criterion

Why is increasing one's cultural IQ so important? Managers need to be as intimate with the foreign culture as possible to help them develop cultural empathy. **Cultural empathy** means putting yourself in the foreigners' position so you can understand and appreciate their perspective. This permits you to share the foreigners' emotions and feelings and to clearly understand them. Obtaining cognitive knowledge helps make this possible, but simply possessing cognitive knowledge does not guarantee that cultural empathy will exist. Cultural empathy requires sensitivity to perspectives different from your own so the foreign market can be objectively evaluated. Cultural empathy precludes cultural apathy and ignorance. Failure to practice cultural empathy is the cause of many international marketing mistakes.

Failure to adequately appreciate the foreign culture is known as the **self-reference criterion** (**SRC**).[8] The SRC is a tendency to consciously or subconsciously view the foreign culture in terms of your own cultural experiences. Imposing your cultural values, or failing to have cultural empathy, typify the SRC. No matter how well you learn and appreciate the foreign culture, you know and understand your culture better. Therefore, you need to be constantly aware of putting your thinking in the foreign culture and discounting your own culture. Not recognizing the SRC is a common mistake made by international marketers; causing indiscretions to be easily committed unintentionally. For example, the SRC is active in the manager who, while developing marketing strategy, thinks back to familiar experiences with consumers in the home country and assumes those behaviors will be similar in the foreign country. This manager unknowingly lets familiar values override the values of the foreign culture and thereby becomes a casualty of the SRC.

Making decisions without an adequate knowledge of the foreign culture, whether intentional or not, is likely to result in SRC mistakes. The SRC may provide one good argument for minimizing the involvement of expatriate managers in foreign markets.

A four-step process should be followed to help minimize the chances of committing the self-reference criterion:[9]

1. Identify the factors such as traits, values, needs, habits, and economics that contribute to the success of the marketing program in the domestic market.
2. Identify the factors such as traits, values, needs, habits, and economics in the foreign culture that may influence the success of the marketing program.
3. Compare the two lists of factors for differences. Any differences constitute potential SRC problems.
4. Pay attention to significant differences, which serve as a warning signal that the marketing program must be modified to accommodate more thoroughly those factors that are different in the foreign culture.

The idea is to isolate and identify differences between your own values and those in the foreign culture. Attention can then be centered on the recognized differences so appropriate adjustments can be made. In this way, your own cultural prejudices can be ascertained, thus reducing the likelihood of allowing them to inhibit your thinking and decision making.

Cultural Strategy

Obviously, the firm's marketing strategy must be developed with consideration for the culture in which it will operate. However, how important is it to conform to the local cultural norms and values? To what extent must management coordinate with accepted business practices? How much freedom does management have to be creative with marketing strategy? When developing marketing strategy, the manager can react with one of three responses to the foreign market's cultural environment. The manager's approach may be

- culturally congruent,
- culturally distinct, or
- culturally disparate.

Culturally Congruent Strategy

To employ a **culturally congruent strategy,** management follows a marketing program that is similar to those of the local competition. The product line will need to include: Models already on the market, distribution in acceptable outlets, standardized promotion, and a competitive price. The objective is to minimize channel and consumer resistance by not upsetting the status quo. Consumers' buying habits are not disrupted, and they do not have to learn new purchase behaviors. The philosophy followed is that of "When in Rome, do as the Romans do." Although this approach appears to offer the advantages of cultural empathy, it also provides little differentiation for the firm and for the ability of the product to better solve the customers' problem or satisfy their needs. Trying to be "Roman" may not be a good idea because Rome is already full of Romans (competitors) appealing to the customer in similar ways. Therefore, Rome may not appreciate nor need another Roman (identical competitor). Also, trying to be Roman may be difficult. The Romans are good at being Romans (successful competitors) and may outperform a foreigner in their own market. Therefore, being different, or at least distinctive in some way, may be more desirable for the outsider.

Culturally Distinct Strategy

With a **culturally distinct strategy** management remains culturally similar in most of the marketing program but introduces one or a few changes that possess cultural dissimilarities. Although these differences may be contrary to acceptable cultural norms, if accepted, they offer some benefits not available from the competition. The dissimilarities allow management to differentiate the firm and its product in some manner from the local competition. No efforts are made to encourage consumers to accept the cultural differences. Management expects the benefits customers will realize from the cultural dissimilarity will be recognized and ultimately accepted. Thus, disruptions will be minimized and society will not feel pressured to change. Since management makes no concerted effort to convince consumers of the advantage of the cultural dissimilarity, the acceptance process may be slow and people may not realize or appreciate the benefits offered. If rejected by the society, an otherwise good marketing program may be unable to achieve its potential or become completely unsuccessful.

Culturally Disparate Strategy

A **culturally disparate strategy** is used when management deliberately ignores the prevailing cultural norms. The cultural dissimilarities are extensive, and management undertakes intentional efforts to change the culture by convincing people that the new method is more advantageous. The intent is to accelerate the rate of acceptance by altering those aspects of the culture that are most likely to offer resistance. A considerable investment in advertising and communications with potential customers is required. No guarantee exists that the efforts to change the culture will succeed. Attempts to change parts of a culture can have negative effects on consumers' attitudes and cause them to boycott the firm and its products. However, if successful, management stands to gain considerable market share at the expense of local competition.

Strategy Implementation

Management must assess the cultural climate and decide which of the three cultural approaches is most desirable. Suppose consumers in the foreign market are accustomed to buying unsliced bread from a bakery. Would the international marketer be more successful by introducing bread that is shaped differently, sliced, and sold in a grocery store or by opening a lot of bakeries and selling the traditionally shaped, unsliced bread? Researching the market can help answer these questions. Ultimately, management must implement the strategy approach that is believed to have the greatest chance of success.

Cultural Change

As the world grows smaller because of improvements in communication, transportation, and technology, the opportunity for cultures to touch each other increases. As a result, cultural exchange occurs and desirable aspects of other cultures are espoused and embraced. Therefore, by operating in a foreign country, management acts as a change agent influencing the dynamic nature of the culture. Your presence in the foreign culture introduces characteristics of your own culture. To the extent that the foreigners accept differences in marketing strategy, management has been responsible for changing the foreign culture. The rate of cultural change depends on the propensity of society to accept the change. As a result of cultural change, many foreign cultures are becoming Americanized as they embrace U.S. ways and values. In some instances, foreigners welcome these changes while in others, Americanization of the culture is feared and shunned. For example, in Iran the Shah was overthrown in 1979 because the American conduct he embraced clashed with religious beliefs.

One of the reasons for protectionist trade policies (tariff and nontariff barriers) is the fear of foreign intervention in the society. Fear that foreign investors will gain too much control of the economy and that their business practices will be contrary to national goals contributes to government regulation of international marketers. Therefore, the international marketer must remain flexible and be a good corporate citizen of the foreign country. Management should adapt to the foreign culture and practice cultural empathy. Appreciation of and respect for the culture should be built into the marketing strategy.

CHAPTER SUMMARY

Culture is an extremely important consideration for the international marketer. Culture influences how a group of people lives. Therefore, culture permeates people's decision-making and buying behavior. How they shop, what they buy, where they buy, and how they buy are influenced. The international marketer must learn and understand the foreign culture if the most successful marketing strategy is to be developed.

The two kinds of cultural knowledge management needs are factual knowledge and cognitive knowledge. Factual knowledge is the minimum required knowledge and can be learned. Information about a culture's language, education, religion, values, technology, social relationships, and politics comprise the factual knowledge managers must know. Cognitive knowledge takes factual knowledge one step further by permitting the manager to value and feel a part of the culture. Cognitive knowledge provides an appreciation of cultural exclusives, imperatives, and electives.

The international marketer must stay alert to avoid the self-reference criterion. The self-reference criterion is viewing the foreign culture in terms of your own cultural experiences. The self-reference criterion is responsible for many mistakes made in international marketing. To avoid this, managers need to identify factors in the foreign culture that are different than in the domestic culture and would adversely affect marketing strategy. Managers must practice cultural empathy.

When developing an international marketing strategy, management may utilize one of three cultural approaches. A culturally congruent approach is as similar to the foreign culture's accepted values as possible. A culturally distinct approach introduces strategy changes that include minor cultural differences and allows the culture to discover the benefits of the changes. A culturally disparate approach introduces strategy changes that include major cultural differences and attempts to persuade consumers to accept the changes.

The international marketer is a cultural change agent. The firm's presence introduces aspects of the domestic culture to the foreign culture. Management must be sensitive to the foreign culture's propensity to accept change and must act in a way that shows respect for the foreign culture.

KEY TERMS

Cognitive knowledge

Collectivistic cultures

Cultural electives

Cultural empathy

Cultural exclusives

Cultural imperatives

Culturally congruent
strategy

Culturally disparate
strategy

Culturally distinct strategy

Culture

Education

Factual knowledge

Individualistic cultures

Language

Politics

Religion

Self-reference criterion
(SRC)

Social relationships

Technology

Values

REVIEW QUESTIONS

1. What is culture?

2. Why is a foreign culture important for the international marketer to understand?

3. Describe cultural empathy.

4. Is it really possible for you to perceive and understand situations from a foreigner's point of view? Why or why not?

5. Talk to a foreign student and identify three differences between that student's culture and your own.

6. Explain the difference between factual knowledge and cognitive knowledge.

7. Give an example of how the international marketer can make mistakes by communicating improperly in a foreign advertisement.

8. Explain how the international marketer can avoid becoming a victim of the self-reference criterion.

9. Select a product and country of your choice. Which of the three cultural marketing strategies is most appropriate for marketing this product in that country? Why? Provide arguments supporting your strategy decision.

10. What risks does management face when following a culturally disparate strategy?

NOTES

1. James A. Lee, "Cultural Analysis in Overseas Operations," *Harvard Business Review* 44 (March–April 1966): 106–14.

2. Vern Terpstra and Kenneth David, *The Cultural Environment of International Business*, 3rd ed. (Cincinnati, OH: South-Western Publishing, 1991). The seven components of culture presented are those listed in this source.

3. Raymond G. Gordon Jr., *Ethnologue: Languages of the World*, 15th ed. (Dallas, TX: SIL International, 2005), http://www.ethnologue.com/.

4. Ibid.

5. Roger E. Axtell, *Gestures: The Do's and Taboos of Body Language Around the World* (Hoboken, NJ: Wiley, 1998).

6. Zeynep Gurhan-Canli and Durairaj Maheswaran, "Cultural Variations in Country of Origin Effects," *Journal of Marketing Research* 3 (3) (2000): 309–17.

7. Terpstra and David, *The Cultural Environment of International Business*, 106.

8. Lee, "Cultural Analysis in Overseas Operations."

9. Ibid.

DISCUSSION QUESTIONS

1. Describe cultural imperatives, cultural electives (adiaphora), and cultural exclusives.

2. What is the self-reference criterion (SRC)? Describe its impact in cross-border marketing.

3. Describe the differences between culturally congruent, culturally disparate, and culturally distinct strategies.

5

C **hapter 5** addresses the concept of cultural sensitivity and how essential it is in the development of an international marketing strategy. It argues about the cultural knowledge that a marketer must have in order to be successful in the given market. It helps the reader understand the different cultural environments and the different strategies available for success. The chapter offers insights into likely challenges and threats that the marketer may face, such as the self-reference criterion (SRC). It also offers strategies on how to avoid such challenges or threats. Discussion issues include *enculturation*, *acculturation*, *factual knowledge*, *cultural education*, *cultural awareness*, *language*, and *communication semantics*. The chapter also discusses the impact of social relationships in individualistic and collectivistic cultures. The discussion leads to identifying world regions as being individualistic or collectivistic. The importance of *cultural imperatives*, *cultural electives*, *or adiaphora*, and *cultural exclusives* is discussed, and the inevitability of cultural change is emphasized.

Cross-Cultural Issues in Consumer Behavior

5.1

Sharon Shavitt, Angela Y. Lee, and Carlos J. Torelli

Culture, Risk Taking, and Impulsivity

Another area of interest related to goals and self-regulation is how culture influences people's attitudes toward risk and the way they make risky choices. Based on the literature reviewed in the previous section, one would expect that members of collectivist cultures, who tend to be prevention-focused, would be more risk averse than members of individualist cultures, who tend to be promotion-focused (A. Y. Lee et al., 2000). In particular, individuals who are promotion-focused are inclined to adopt an eagerness strategy, which translates into greater openness to risk, whereas those who are prevention-focused are inclined to adopt a vigilant strategy, which usually translates into more conservative behaviors (Crowe & Higgins, 1997). Consider an array of options: Options that have greater potential upsides are likely to also come with greater potential downsides, whereas options with smaller potential downsides are often those with smaller potential upsides. Thus, when choosing between a risky alternative with greater upsides and downsides and a conservative alternative with smaller downsides and upsides, individuals who pay more attention to positive outcomes (i.e., the promotion-focused) would favor the risky option, whereas those who focus more on negative outcomes (i.e., the prevention-focused) would favor the conservative option. These different attitudes toward risk are consistent with findings that promotion-focused participants emphasize speed at the expense of accuracy in different drawing and proofreading tasks and that the reverse is true for those with a prevention focus (Förster, Higgins, & Bianco, 2003).

However, empirical investigations examining how people with distinct cultural self-construals make decisions involving risks have produced mixed results. For instance, Mandel (2003) observed that participants primed with an interdependent versus independent self-construal were more likely to choose a safe versus a risky option when choosing a shirt to wear to a family gathering or when playing truth or dare. However, these same participants were more likely to choose the risky option when making a decision regarding a lottery ticket or a parking ticket. Along similar lines, Hsee and Weber (1999) presented Chinese and Americans with safe versus risky options in three decision domains—financial (to invest money in a savings account or in stocks), academic (to write a term paper on a conservative topic so that the grade would be predictable or to write the paper on a provocative topic so the grade could vary), and medical (to take a pain reliever with a moderate but sure effectiveness or one with a high variance of effectiveness). They found that Chinese were more risk-seeking in the financial domain than their American counterparts, but not in the academic and medical domains. Taken together, these results suggest that while individuals with a dominant interdependent self-construal are more risk averse than those with a dominant independent self-construal in general, they are less risk averse when their decision involves financial risks.

To account for the findings that Chinese were more risk-seeking in the financial domain, Weber and Hsee (Weber & Hsee, 1998, 2000) proposed that members of collectivist cultures can afford to take greater financial risks because their social network buffers them from financial downfalls. That is, individuals' social networks serve as a cushion that could protect them should they take risks and fall; and the wider their social network, the larger the cushion. Because people in collectivist cultures have larger social networks to fall back on relative to those in individualist cultures, they are more likely to choose seemingly riskier options because their perceived risks for those options are smaller than the perceived risks for people in individualist cultures. In one study, Weber and Hsee (1998) surveyed American, German, Polish, and Chinese respondents about their perception of the riskiness of a set of financial investment options and their willingness to pay for these options. They found that their Chinese respondents perceived the risks to be the lowest and paid the highest prices for the investments, whereas American respondents perceived the investments to be most risky and paid the lowest prices for them. Once risk perception was accounted for, the cross-cultural difference in risk aversion disappeared. Consistent with this cushion hypothesis, Mandel (2003) showed that the difference between independent and interdependent participants' risky financial choices is mediated by the size of their social network—the larger their social network, the more risk-taking participants were.

Hamilton and Biehal (2005) suggest that this social network cushioning effect among the interdependents may be offset by their self-regulatory goals. They find that those primed with an independent self-construal tend to prefer mutual funds that are more risky (i.e., more volatile) than do those primed with an interdependent self-construal; and this difference is mediated by the strength of their regulatory goal in that risky preferences are fostered by promotion goals and discouraged by prevention goals.

It is worth noting that both Mandel (2003) and Hamilton and Biehal (2005) manipulated self-construal but found opposite effects of self-construal on risky financial decisions. Whereas an interdependent self-construal may bring to mind a larger social network that serves as a safety net and hence changes risk perceptions, the associated prevention focus also prompts people to be more vigilant and hence lowers the threshold for risk tolerance.

Interestingly, Briley and Wyer (2002) found that both Chinese and American participants whose cultural identity was made salient (vs. not) were more likely to choose a compromise alternative (i.e., an option with moderate values on two different attributes) over more extreme options (i.e., options with a high value on one attribute and a low value along a second attribute) when choosing between such products as cameras, stereo sets, or computers. When presented with the task of picking two pieces of candy, cultural identity-primed participants were also more likely to pick two different candies than two pieces of the same candy. To the extent that choosing the compromise alternative or picking one of each candy reduces the risk of social embarrassment and postchoice regret, the authors presented the results as evidence that individuals who think of themselves as part of a larger collective (i.e., those with an interdependent mindset) are more risk averse, independent of national culture. More systematic investigations of how culture and self-construal affect consumers' risky decision making await future research.

Besides having an influence on the individual's attitude toward risks, culture also plays an important role in the individual's self-regulation of emotions and behaviors. Because the maintenance of harmony within the group often relies on members' ability to manage their emotions and behaviors, collectivist cultures tend to emphasize the control and moderation of one's feelings and actions more so than do individualistic cultures (Potter, 1988; Russell & Yik, 1996; Tsai & Levenson, 1997). Indeed, it has been reported that members of collectivist cultures often control their negative emotions and display positive emotions only to acquaintances (Gudykunst, 1993). Children in these societies are also socialized to control their impulses at an early age (Ho, 1994).

It follows that culture would play an important role in consumers' purchase behavior by imposing norms on the appropriateness of impulse-buying activities (Kacen & Lee, 2002). When consumers believe that impulse buying is socially unacceptable, they are more likely to refrain from acting on their impulsive tendencies (Rook & Fisher, 1995). Whereas members of individualist cultures are more motivated by their own preferences and personal goals, members of collectivist cultures are often motivated by norms and duties imposed by society. Thus, people with a dominant interdependent self-construal who tend to focus on relationship harmony and group preferences should be better at monitoring and adjusting their behavior based on "what is right" rather than on "what I want." Along these lines, Chen, Ng, and Rao (2005) found that consumers with a dominant independent self-construal are less patient in that they are willing to pay more to expedite the delivery of an online book purchase than those with a dominant interdependent self-construal.

Kacen and Lee (2002) surveyed respondents from Australia, the United States, Singapore, Malaysia, and Hong Kong and found that the relationship between trait buying impulsiveness and actual impulsive buying behavior is stronger for individualists (respondents from Australia, the United States) than for collectivists (respondents from Hong Kong, Malaysia, Singapore). Further, they reported a positive relationship between respondents' independent self-construal and impulsivity among the individualists, but not among the collectivists. These results suggest that impulsivity in buying behavior in individualistic societies is more a function of personality than normative constraints, and are consistent with findings that attitude-behavior correlations are stronger in individualistic than collectivistic cultures (Bagozzi, Wong, Abe, & Bergami, 2000; Kashima, Siegal, Tanaka, & Kashima, 1992; J. A. Lee, 2000).

Culture And Persuasive Appeals

Most research on cultural influences on judgment and persuasion has examined the implications of individualism/collectivism or independent/interdependent self-construals. In general, the findings suggest that the prevalence or the persuasiveness of a given type of appeal matches the cultural value orientation of the society. For instance, appeals to individuality, personal benefits, and achievement tend to be more prevalent and persuasive in individualistic compared to collectivistic cultures, whereas appeals to group benefits, harmony, and conformity tend to be more prevalent and persuasive in collectivistic compared to individualistic cultures. Such evidence for "cultural matching" in the nature of appeals has since been followed by studies examining the distinct psychological processes driving persuasion across cultures. These studies suggest that culture can affect how people process and organize in memory product-related information. It can determine the type of information that is weighed more heavily for making judgments (e.g., product attributes versus other consumers' opinions). It can also influence thinking styles and the mental representations of brand information.

Cultural Differences in the Content of Message Appeals

Cross-cultural content analyses of advertisements can yield valuable evidence about distinctions in cultural values. For instance, American advertisers are often exhorted to focus on the advertised brand's attributes and advantages (e.g., Ogilvy, 1985), based on the assumption that consumer learning about the brand precedes other marketing effects, such as liking and buying the brand (Lavidge & Steiner, 1961), at least under high-involvement conditions (Vaughn, 1980). Thus, advertisements that attempt to "teach" the consumer about the advertised brand are typical in the United States, although other types of advertisements are also used.

In contrast, as Miracle (1987) has suggested, the typical goal of advertisements in Japan appears very different. There, advertisements tend to focus on "making friends" with the audience and showing that the company understands their feelings (Javalgi, Cutler, & Malhotra, 1995). The assumption is that consumers will buy once they feel familiar with and have a sense of trust in the company. Because Japan, Korea, and other Pacific Rim countries are collectivist, "high context" cultures that tend toward implicit and indirect communication practices (Hall, 1976), Miracle suggested that the mood and tone of commercials in these countries will be particularly important in establishing good feelings about the advertiser (see also Taylor, Miracle, & Wilson, 1997). Indeed, studies have shown that advertisements in Japan and Korea rely more on symbolism, mood, and aesthetics and less on direct approaches such as brand comparisons than do advertisements in the United States (B. Cho, Kwon, Gentry, Jun, & Kropp, 1999; di Benedetto, Tamate, & Chandran, 1992; J. W. Hong et al., 1987; Javalgi et al., 1995).

This is not to argue that advertisements in collectivist societies use more of a "soft sell" approach in contrast to a "hard sell," information-driven approach in the West. Information content in the advertisements of collectivist cultures can be very high (Tse, Belk, & Zhou, 1989), sometimes even higher than in the United States (J. W. Hong et al., 1987; Rice & Lu, 1988; for a review see Taylor et al., 1997). It is generally more an issue of the type of appeal that the information is supporting.

For instance, a content analysis of magazine advertisements revealed that in Korea, compared to the United States, advertisements are more focused on family well-being, interdependence, group goals, and harmony, whereas they are less focused on self-improvement, ambition, personal goals, independence, and individuality (Han & Shavitt, 1994). However, as one might expect, the nature of the advertised product moderated these effects. Cultural differences emerged strongly only for products that tend to be purchased and used along with other persons (e.g., groceries, cars). Products that do not tend to be shared (e.g., health and beauty aids, clothing) are promoted more in terms of personal, individualistic benefits in both countries.

Paralleling the overall cross-national differences, a content analysis by Kim and Markus (1999) indicated that Korean advertisements, compared to U.S. advertisements, were characterized by more conformity themes (e.g., respect for collective values and beliefs) and fewer uniqueness themes (e.g., rebelling against collective values and beliefs). (For other ad comparisons relevant to individualism/collectivism, see B. Cho et al., 1999; S. M. Choi et al., 2005; Javalgi et al., 1995; Tak, Kaid, & Lee, 1997.)

Recently, studies have extended these cultural conclusions into analyses of Web site content (C.-H. Cho & Cheon, 2005; Singh & Matsuo, 2004). For instance, Cho and Cheon (2005) found that corporate Web sites in the United States and United Kingdom tend to emphasize consumer-message and consumer-marketer interactivity. In contrast, those in Japan and Korea tended to emphasize consumer-consumer interactivity, a pattern consistent with cultural values stressing collectivistic activities that foster interdependence and sociability.

Finally, in studying humorous appeals, Alden, Hoyer, and Lee (1993) found that advertisements from both Korea and Thailand contain more group-oriented situations than those from Germany and the United States. However, it is worth noting that in these studies, evidence also emerged for the value of the vertical/ horizontal distinction previously discussed. Specifically, relationships between the central characters in advertisements that used humor were more often unequal in cultures characterized as having higher power distance (i.e., relatively vertical cultures, such as Korea) than in those labeled as lower in power distance (such as Germany), in which these relationships were more often equal. Such unequal relationships portrayed in the advertisements may reflect the hierarchical interpersonal relationships that are more likely to exist in vertical societies.

Cultural Differences in Judgment and Persuasion

The persuasiveness of appeals appears to mirror the cultural differences in their prevalence. An experiment by Han and Shavitt (1994) showed that appeals to individualistic values (e.g., "Solo cleans with a softness that you will love") are more persuasive in the United States and appeals to collectivistic values (e.g., "Solo cleans with a softness that your family will love") are more persuasive in Korea. Again, however, this effect was much more evident for products that are shared (laundry detergent, clothes iron) than for those that are not (chewing gum, running shoes).

Zhang and Gelb (1996) found a similar pattern in the persuasiveness of individualistic versus collectivistic appeals in an experiment conducted in the United States and China. Moreover, this effect appeared to be moderated by whether the advertised product is socially visible (camera) versus privately used (toothbrush). Finally, Wang and Mowen (1997) showed in a U.S. sample that individual differences in separateness/connectedness self-schema (i.e., the degree to which one views the self as independent of or interconnected with important others) predicts attitudes toward individualistic versus collectivistic ad appeals for a credit card. Thus, cultural orientation and national culture have implications for the effectiveness of appeals. However, such cultural differences are anticipated only for those products or uses that are relevant to both personal and group goals.

Wang, Bristol, Mowen, and Chakraborty (2000) further demonstrated that individual differences in separateness/connectedness self-schema mediate both the effects of culture and of gender on the persuasiveness of individualistic versus collectivistic appeals. Their analysis demonstrated that this mediating role is played by distinct dimensions of separateness/connectedness self-schema for cultural as opposed to gender-based effects.

Cultural differences in persuasion are also revealed in the diagnosticity of certain types of information. For instance, Aaker and Maheswaran (1997) showed that consensus information regarding other consumers'

opinions is not treated as a heuristic cue by Hong Kong Chinese (as it is in the United States, Maheswaran & Chaiken, 1991) but is instead perceived and processed as diagnostic information. Thus, collectivists resolve incongruity in favor of consensus information, not brand attributes. This would be expected in a culture that stresses conformity and responsiveness to others' views. However, cues whose (low) diagnosticity is not expected to vary cross-culturally (e.g., number of attributes presented) elicit similar heuristic processing in the United States and Hong Kong.

Further research indicates that, whereas members of both U.S. and Chinese cultures resolve incongruities in the product information they receive, they tend to do so in different ways (Aaker & Sengupta, 2000). Specifically, U.S. consumers tend to resolve incongruity with an attenuation strategy in which one piece of information is favored over another, inconsistent piece of information. In contrast, Hong Kong Chinese consumers tend to follow an additive strategy in which both pieces of information are combined to influence judgments. This is consistent with the view that East Asians think holistically and take more information into account when making judgments (I. Choi et al., 2003; Nisbett, Peng, Choi, & Norenzayan, 2001).

Cultural Differences in Brand Representations

Recent research points to cultural differences in the mental representation of brand information. Ng and Houston (2006) found that an interdependent view of the self facilitates the accessibility of brand exemplars (i.e., specific products or subcategories), whereas an independent view of the self facilitates the retrieval of brand beliefs (i.e., general descriptive or evaluative thoughts). The authors argue that these results are driven by a tendency by independent consumers to focus on "global beliefs" abstracted from prior product experiences and a tendency by interdependent consumers to focus on contextual and incidental details about the product. The focus of interdependent consumers on contextual variables also led to more favorable evaluations (compared to those of independent consumers) of brand extensions perceived to be used in the same usage occasion as an existing product mix.

Monga and John (2007) provide further insights into the cognitive processes underlying cross-cultural differences in the representation of brand information. They found that priming an interdependent (vs. an independent) self-construal led consumers to perceive a higher degree of fit between a brand extension and the parent brand and to evaluate more positively the brand extension. These findings are attributed to more holistic thinking style, which is oriented toward object-field relationships and is associated with an interdependent view of the self (see Kühnen, Hannover, & Schubert, 2001).

Brands as Symbols of Self and of Culture

Consumers use certain products or brands to express to others their personal values (Richins, 1994). Although the self-expressive function of products may reflect a universal goal, recent research suggests that certain cultures value self-expression more than others do. Moreover, brands and products vary in their likelihood of playing a self-expressive role (see Shavitt, 1990)—that is, some brands are more iconic than others. As a result, such brands may be more likely to carry and activate cultural meanings.

One important aspect of individualism is the expression of inner thoughts and feelings in order to realize one's individuality (Bellah, Madsen, Sullivan, Swidler, & Tipton, 1985). In contrast, in collectivistic cultures expression of one's thoughts is not particularly encouraged. Accordingly, Kim and Sherman (2007) showed that culturally shared assumptions about the function and importance of self-expression impact consumers' judgments. In their studies, European Americans instructed (vs. not) to express their choice of a pen evaluated an unchosen pen more negatively, indicating that they became more attached to the pen they chose. These effects were absent among East Asian Americans. In sum, cultural differences in how people self-expressed through their preferences apparently led to differences in how people felt about their preferences once they were expressed.

Certain brands become consensus expressions of a set of ideas or values held dear by individuals in a given society (Holt, 2004). Consumers associate these brands with the values that are characteristic of the culture (Aaker, Benet-Martinez, & Garolera, 2001). For example, some brands in the United States are associated with ruggedness (e.g., the Marlboro man) and some brands in Japan are associated with peacefulness, and ruggedness and peacefulness are dimensions characteristic of American and East Asian cultures, respectively. To the extent that these brands are associated with knowledge about the culture, they can reach an iconic status and act as cultural reminders (see Betsky, 1997; Ortner, 1973). Encountering such iconic brands can serve as subtle cultural primes that can lead to culturally congruent judgments and behaviors. In line with this reasoning, in a study about the effects of the exposure to American icons on consumers' judgments, Torelli, Chiu, & Keh (2007) found that exposure to iconic brands (e.g., Kellogg's Corn Flakes) led American participants to organize material in memory around cultural themes and to evaluate foreign competitors more negatively.

To the extent that iconic brands can be used to communicate their associated values, consumers can rely on these brands for fulfilling important identity goals. With the advancement of globalization, the marketplace is suffused with images of various iconic brands and products. Continued exposure to iconic products and brands can serve as a cognitive socialization process whereby different cultural values and beliefs are repeatedly activated in consumers' working memory. As Lau-Gesk (2003) pointed out, as the world becomes more culturally diverse and mobile, it is more common for consumers to possess knowledge about the symbols and values of multiple cultures. Thus, J. Zhang (in press) shows that the responses to persuasive appeals by young Chinese consumers resemble those found among bicultural individuals (e.g., East Asians born and raised in the United States). This state of affairs may help to explain why, in rapidly transitioning economies, Westernized appeals are increasingly common. For example, appeals to youth/modernity, individuality/independence, and technology are rather salient in Chinese advertisements (J. Zhang & Shavitt, 2003) as well as frequently employed by current Taiwanese advertising agencies (Shao, Raymond, & Taylor, 1999).

In addition, consumers in developing countries tend to respond favorably to markedly Western products. For instance, in one study of Indian consumers (Batra, Ramaswamy, Alden, Steenkamp, &

Ramachander, 2000), brands perceived as having a nonlocal (Western) country of origin were favored over brands perceived to be local. This effect was stronger for consumers with a greater admiration for the lifestyle in economically developed countries. These cultural-incongruity findings are meaningful because they suggest the important role that advertising can play in reshaping cultural values in countries experiencing rapid economic growth (J. Zhang & Shavitt, 2003). Rather than reflecting existing cultural values, advertising content in those countries promotes new aspirational values, such as individuality and modernity, hence these new values become acceptable and desirable among consumers. Understanding the cognitive implications of multicultural environments for consumers is likely to be a key research topic in cross-cultural consumer psychology for years to come.

REFERENCES

Aaker, J. L., Benet-Martinez, V., & Garolera, J. (2001). Consumption symbols as carriers of culture: A study of Japanese and Spanish brand personality constructs. *Journal of Personality and Social Psychology, 81*(3), 492–508.

Aaker, J. L., & Maheswaran, D. (1997). The effect of cultural orientation on persuasion. *Journal of Consumer Research, 24*(3), 315–328.

Aaker, J. L., & Sengupta, J. (2000). Addivity versus attenuation: The role of culture in the resolution of information incongruity. *Journal of Consumer Psychology, 9*(2), 67–82.

Alden, D. L., Hoyer, W. D., & Lee, C. (1993). Identifying global and culture-specific dimensions of humor in advertising: A multinational analysis. *Journal of Marketing, 57*(2), 64–75.

Bagozzi, R. P., Wong, N., Abe, S., & Bergami, M. (2000). Cultural and situational contingencies and the theory of reasoned action: Application to fast food restaurant consumption. *Journal of Consumer Psychology, 9*(2), 97–106.

Batra, R., Ramaswamy, V., Alden, D. L., Steenkamp, J.-B. E. M., & Ramachander, S. (2000). Effects of brand local and nonlocal origin on consumer attitudes in developing countries. *Journal of Consumer Psychology, 9*(2), 83–95.

Bellah, R. N., Madsen, R., Sullivan, W. M., Swidler, A., & Tipton, S. M. (1985). *Habits of the heart: Individualism and commitment in American life.* New York: Harper & Row.

Betsky, A. (1997). *Icons: Magnets of meaning.* San Francisco: Chronicle Books.

Briley, D. A., & Wyer, R. S., Jr. (2002). The effect of group membership salience on the avoidance of negative outcomes: Implications for social and consumer decisions. *Journal of Consumer Research, 29*(3), 400–415.

Chen, H., Ng, S., & Rao, A. R. (2005). Cultural differences in consumer impatience. *Journal of Marketing Research, 42*(3), 291–301.

Cho, B., Kwon, U., Gentry, J. W., Jun, S., & Kropp, F. (1999). Cultural values reflected in theme and execution: A comparative study of U.S. and Korean television commercials. *Journal of Advertising, 28*(4), 59–73.

Cho, C.-H., & Cheon, H. J. (2005). Cross-cultural comparisons of interactivity on corporate websites. *Journal of Advertising, 34*(2), 99–115.

Choi, I., Dalal, R., Kim-Prieto, C., & Park, H. (2003). Culture and judgement of causal relevance. *Journal of Personality and Social Psychology, 84*(1), 46–59.

Choi, S. M., Lee, W.-N., & Kim, H.-J. (2005). Lessons from the rich and famous: A cross-cultural comparison of celebrity endorsement in advertising. *Journal of Advertising, 34*(2), 85–98.

Crowe, E., & Higgins, E. (1997). Regulatory focus and strategic inclinations: Promotion and prevention in decision-making. *Organizational Behavior and Human Decision Processes, 69*(2), 117–132.

di Benedetto, C. A., Tamate, M., & Chandran, R. (1992). Developing creative advertising strategy for the Japanese marketplace. *Journal of Advertising Research, 32*, 39–48.

Förster, J., Higgins, T. E., & Bianco, A. T. (2003). Speed/accuracy decisions in task performance: Built-in trade-off or separate strategic concerns? *Organizational Behavior and Human Decision Processes, 90*(1), 148–164.

Gudykunst, W. B. (1993). *Communication in Japan and the United States*. NY: State University of New York Press.

Hall, E. T. (1976). *Beyond culture*. Oxford: Anchor.

Hamilton, R. W., & Biehal, G. J. (2005). Achieving your goals or protecting their future? The effects of self-view on goals and choices. *Journal of Consumer Research, 32*(2), 277–283.

Han, S.-P., & Shavitt, S. (1994). Persuasion and culture: Advertising appeals in individualistic and collectivistic societies. *Journal of Experimental Social Psychology, 30*(4), 326.

Ho, D. Y.-F. (1994). Cognitive socialization in Confucian heritage cultures. In P. M. Greenfield & R. R. Cocking (Eds.), *Cross-cultural roots of minority child development* (pp. 285–313). NJ: Lawrence Erlbaum Associates, Inc.

Holt, D. B. (2004). *How brands become icons: The principles of cultural branding*. Cambridge, MA: Harvard Business School Press.

Hong, J. W., Muderrisoglu, A., & Zinkhan, G. M. (1987). Cultural differences and advertising expression: A comparative content analysis of Japanese and U.S. magazine advertising. *Journal of Advertising, 16*(1), 55–62.

Hsee, C. K., & Weber, E. U. (1999). Cross-national differences in risk preference and lay predictions. *Journal of Behavioral Decision Making, 12*(2), 165–179.

Javalgi, R. G., Cutler, B. D., & Malhotra, N. K. (1995). Print advertising at the component level: A cross-cultural comparison of the United States and Japan. *Journal of Business Research, 34*(2), 117–124.

Kacen, J. J., & Lee, J. A. (2002). The influence of culture on consumer impulsive buying behavior. *Journal of Consumer Psychology, 12*(2), 163–176.

Kashima, Y., Siegal, M., Tanaka, K., & Kashima, E. S. (1992). Do people believe behaviours are consistent with attitudes? Towards a cultural psychology of attribution processes. *British Journal of Social Psychology, 31*(2), 111–124.

Kim, H. S., & Markus, H. R. (1999). Deviance or uniqueness, harmony or conformity? A cultural analysis. *Journal of Personality & Social Psychology, 77*(4), 785–800.

Kim, H. S., & Sherman, D. K. (2007). "Express yourself": Culture and the effect of self-expression on choice. *Journal of Personality & Social Psychology, 92*(1), 1–11.

Kühnen, U., Hannover, B., & Schubert, B. (2001). The semantic-procedural interface model of the self: The role of self-knowledge for context-dependent versus context-independent modes of thinking. *Journal of Personality and Social Psychology, 80*(3), 397–409.

Lau-Gesk, L. G. (2003). Activating culture through persuasion appeals: An examination of the bicultural consumer. *Journal of Consumer Psychology, 13*(3), 301–315.

Lavidge, R. J., & Steiner, G. A. (1961). A model for predictive measurements of advertising effectiveness. *Journal of Marketing, 25*(6), 59–62.

Lee, A. Y., Aaker, J. L., & Gardner, W. L. (2000). The pleasures and pains of distinct self-construals: The role of interdependence in regulatory focus. *Journal of Personality and Social Psychology, 78*(6), 1122–1134.

Lee, J. A. (2000). Adapting Triandis's model of subjective culture and social behavior relations to consumer behavior. *Journal of Consumer Psychology, 9*(2), 117–126.

Maheswaran, D., & Chaiken, S. (1991). Promoting systematic processing in low-motivation settings: Effect of incongruent information on processing and judgment. *Journal of Personality & Social Psychology, 61*(1), 13–25.

Mandel, N. (2003). Shifting selves and decision making: The effects of self-construal priming on consumer risk-taking. *Journal of Consumer Research, 30*(1), 30–40.

Miracle, G. E. (1987). Feel-do-learn: An alternative sequence underlying Japanese consumer response to television commercials. In F. G. Feasley (Ed.), *Proceedings of the L.A. Conference of the American Academy of Advertising*. Columbia, SC: The University of South Carolina.

Monga, A. B., & John, D. R. (2007). Cultural differences in brand extension evaluation: The influence of analytic versus holistic thinking. *Journal of Consumer Research, 33*(4), 529–536.

Ng, S., & Houston, M. J. (2006). Exemplars or beliefs? The impact of self-view on the nature and relative influence of brand associations. *Journal of Consumer Research, 32*(4), 519–529.

Nisbett, R. E., Peng, K., Choi, I., & Norenzayan, A. (2001). Culture and systems of thought: Holistic versus analytic cognition. *Psychological Review,* 108(2), 291–310.

Ogilvy, D. (1985). *Ogilvy on advertising.* New York: Vintage Books.

Ortner, S. B. (1973). On key symbols. *American Anthropologist, 75*(5), 1338–1346.

Potter, S. H. (1988). The cultural construction of emotion in rural Chinese social life. *Ethos, 16*(2), 181–208.

Rice, M. D., & Lu, Z. (1988). A content analysis of Chinese magazine advertisements. *Journal of Advertising, 17*(4), 43–48.

Rook, D. W., & Fisher, R. J. (1995). Normative influences on impulsive buying behavior. *Journal of Consumer Research, 22*(3), 305–313.

Russell, J. A., & Yik, M. S. (1996). Emotion among the Chinese. In M. H. Bond (Ed.), *The handbook of Chinese psychology* (pp. 166–188). Hong Kong, China: Oxford University Press.

Shao, A. T., Raymond, M. A., & Taylor, C. (1999). Shifting advertising appeals in Taiwan. *Journal of Advertising Research, 39*(6), 61–69.

Shavitt, S. (1990). The role of attitude objects in attitude functions. *Journal of Experimental Social Psychology, 26*(2), 124–148.

Singh, N., & Matsuo, H. (2004). Measuring cultural adaptation on the Web: a content analytic study of U.S. and Japanese web sites. *Journal of Business Research, 57*(8), 864–872.

Tak, J., Kaid, L. L., & Lee, S. (1997). A cross-cultural study of political advertising in the United States and Korea. *Communication Research, 24,* 413–430.

Taylor, C. R., Miracle, G. E., & Wilson, R. D. (1997). The impact of information level on the effectiveness of U.S. and Korean television commercials. *Journal of Advertising, 26*(1), 1–18.

Torelli, C. J., Chiu, C.-y., & Keh, H. T. (2007). Psychological reactions to foreign cultures in globalized economy: Effects of simultaneous activation of ingroup and outgroup cultures. Manuscript under review.

Tsai, J. L., & Levenson, R. W. (1997). Cultural influences of emotional responding: Chinese American and European American dating couples during interpersonal conflict. *Journal of Cross-Cultural Psychology, 28*(5), 600–625.

Tse, D. K., Belk, R. W., & Zhou, N. (1989). Becoming a consumer society: A longitudinal and cross-cultural content analysis of print ads from Hong Kong, the People's Republic of China, and Taiwan. *Journal of Consumer Research, 15*(4), 457–472.

Vaughn, R. (1980). How advertising works: A planning model. *Journal of Advertising Research, 20*(5), 27–33.

Wang, C. L., Bristol, T., Mowen, J. C., & Chakraborty, G. (2000). Alternative modes of self-construal: Dimensions of connectedness-separateness and advertising appeals to the cultural and gender-specific self. *Journal of Consumer Psychology, 9*(2), 107–115.

Wang, C. L., & Mowen, J. C. (1997). The separateness-connectedness self-schema: Scale development and application to message construction. *Psychology & Marketing, 14*(2), 185–207.

Weber, E. U., & Hsee, C. K. (1998). Cross-cultural differences in risk perception, but cross-cultural similarities in attitudes towards perceived risk. *Management Science, 44*(9), 1205–1217.

Weber, E. U., & Hsee, C. K. (2000). Culture and individual judgment and decision making. *Applied Psychology: An International Review, 49*(1), 32–61.

Zhang, J. (in press). The effect of advertising appeals in activating self-construals: A case of 'bicultural' Chinese X-generation consumers. *Journal of Advertising,* in press.

Zhang, J., & Shavitt, S. (2003). Cultural values in advertisements to the Chinese X-generation: Promoting modernity and individualism. *Journal of Advertising, 32*(1), 23–33.

Zhang, Y., & Gelb, B. D. (1996). Matching advertising appeals to culture: The influence of products' use conditions. *Journal of Advertising, 25*(3), 29–46.

DISCUSSION QUESTIONS

1. How are persuasive appeals affected by different cultures? Explain.

2. How do differences between individualistic and collectivistic values affect appeal persuasiveness?

3. What is holistic style, and how does it relate to an interdependent or collectivistic view of brand information?

4. How do brands or symbols have different impacts on different cultures? Give examples.

6

Chapter 6 discusses select cross-cultural issues in consumer behavior. Within the international market environment, the concern of the marketer is how culture affects consumer behavior; i.e., attitudes, perceptions, purchasing decision making, and consumption behavior. The issue of *risk perception* in different cultures and how consumers in those cultures behave is discussed. The chapter offers insights into how differences in cultures influence *judgment* and *persuasion*. It also discusses the contrast between *individualism* and *collectivism* and how these two cultures affect attitude formation. Cultural differences are also evident in marketing communications whose persuasive appeal may be different, depending on whether the cultural environment is *relationship-oriented* or *agenda-oriented*. For instance, appeals to *individualistic* values are more persuasive in the United States, whereas appeals to *collectivistic* values are more persuasive in an Asian culture. Finally, the chapter discusses the impact of *branding* in individualistic and collectivistic cultures, as well as the role of marketing communications in reshaping cultural values.

Subcultural Segmentation

6.1

Geoffrey Paul Lantos

Background

[...] There is a major trend toward cultural pluralism in that diversity of racial, ethnic, or religious backgrounds is increasingly accepted. Each of the following subcultural groups is also a lifestyle group with unique cultural characteristics. It is important for marketers to understand the unique thinking and behavior patterns of diverse consumer groups.

Bases for Forming Subcultures

The major subcultural segmentation variables are (1) ethnic background (race, nationality, and language); (2) religion; (3) geographic region; and (4) generation or age cohort. In addition, there are many other subcultures frequently targeted by marketers but not reviewed here, including the college market; the gay, lesbian, bisexual, and transgender (GLBT) market; the deaf community; political preference groups; Goth and punk youth; and the physically disabled market.

A few marketers have even formulated or else targeted their own type of microculture. **Consumption subcultures** are groups whose members share an avocational interest and hence a commitment to a particular product category, brand, or consumption activity. Examples include Trekkies or Trekkers (the Star Trek subculture), Harley-Davidson riders, hot-rodders, scrapbookers, karate kids, and skydivers. Pursuing like-minded consumers who spontaneously connect around a product or service is called **tribal marketing**. For example, magazines such as

69

Cooking Light and *Bon Appétit* have sponsored culinary fairs and supper club events.

Major Subcultural Segmentation Considerations

There are six important considerations for subcultural marketers. Later, we will revisit each one for each of the four major variables for subcultural segmentation.

SUBCULTURES SERVE AS A BASIS FOR MARKET SEGMENTATION

Subcultures provide an important foundation for market segmentation in a pluralistic society. While marketers usually describe them with identifiable demographic descriptors, they also understand the lifestyle implications of these variables.

Many subcultures can be further divided into **sub-subcultures**, which are subcultures within subcultures. Therefore, many subcultures can be sub-segmented into smaller, more homogenous groups, each with its own distinctive language, symbols, customs, and other cultural characteristics. For example, the Hispanic (Spanish-language-speaking) subculture can be further segmented by country of origin, such as Mexico, Puerto Rico, or Cuba. Chinese Americans constitute the largest group of Asian Americans. The so-called disabled market consists of three submarkets: adults with disabilities, parents of disabled children, and caretakers such as siblings and grandparents.

Consumers can also be cross-classified by two subcultural segmentation variables, such as baby boomer blacks. Subcultural cross-classification often occurs when geography is used in conjunction with one of the other three subcultural segmentation variables. This is common practice because subcultural segments often cluster geographically. For instance, gays and lesbians congregate in large cities such as San Francisco or New York as well as in Provincetown, Massachusetts. Numerous Mormons live in Utah, many senior citizens reside in Florida, a disproportionate number of Jews

EXHIBIT 6.1 Subcultures Demonstrate Unique Consumer Behavior

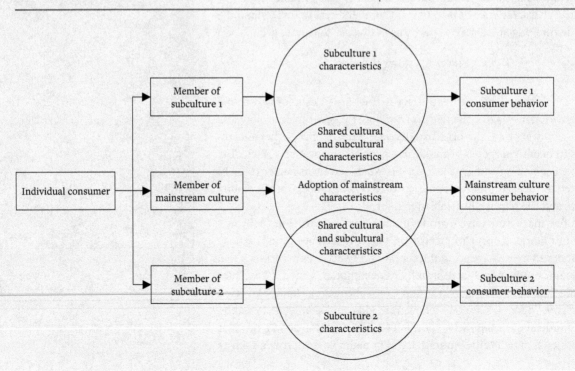

dwell in New York City, and lots of Asian Americans inhabit the West Coast.

MARKETERS SHOULD APPEAL TO SUBCULTURAL CHARACTERISTICS

Marketers must understand and appeal to the norms, values, and other cultural components of a subculture in order to effectively communicate with and appeal to its members. For example, each ethnic, religious, geographic, and age subculture has its own kind of music that can be included in commercials, such as salsa, polka, gospel, bluegrass, and big band.

However, as Exhibit 1 shows, while a person might simultaneously be in one or more micro cultures, he or she is still a member of the core culture. Hence, the individual will exhibit mass market cultural characteristics that do not conflict with those of his or her subculture as well as unique traits of the subculture(s).

To respect the subculture, marketers must avoid violating or offending members' sensitivities along their subcultural characteristics. Unfortunately, advertisers have butchered foreign languages with mistranslations in ethnic markets. This happened when an airline ran an ad that promoted leather seats. The translation was interpreted by Hispanics as either "sit naked" or "fly naked." One of the biggest blunders is to mistranslate advertising copy. The Perdue chicken slogan, "It takes a tough man to make a tender chicken," was wrongly translated into Spanish as, "It takes a sexually excited man to make a chick affectionate." Another was the Coors beer slogan, "Turn it Loose," which in Spanish became, "Suffer from Diarrhea."

Such mistakes usually occur because companies simply use an in-house translator who speaks the language but is not fluent. A more accurate method is the use of **backtranslation**, or having someone fluent in both languages, translate English to the foreign language and then having a second person conversant in both languages translate it back again to English.

Another problem is that the creative idioms so often used in ads do not translate word-for-word into another culture. You cannot talk about "knocking one out of the ballpark" to someone in Albania. Marketers must be familiar with the subculture's special jargon.

A Kraft ad in black magazines featured the headline "You go, Mom!" a play on the black female exclamation, "You go, girl!"

Negative stereotypes of subcultures must be avoided. It is not smart to portray Generation Xers as angst-ridden slackers, devout Christians as dogmatic and bigoted, or all African Americans as musical or athletic. A marketer's best bet is to employ the services of marketing research firms and advertising agencies that specialize in a subcultural market, such as youth researchers and ethnic (multicultural) advertising agencies.

MARKETING TO SUBCULTURES

Generally, subcultures are on the rise, with most growing in absolute size and many expanding relatively as a percentage of the population. Many members of particular subcultures are also achieving upward social mobility—higher incomes, education, and occupational status. They are also gaining political clout, recognition, and visibility.

SUBCULTURES SERVE AS A SPRINGBOARD FOR MAINSTREAM MARKETING

Crossover marketing (**mainstreaming**) involves taking a product originally marketed exclusively to a particular subculture and broadening its appeal to the macroculture. Sports drinks such as Gatorade originated among the consumption subculture of serious athletes and branched out from there. Ethnic foods, such as Mexican burritos, tacos, and even guacamole sauce, are now universally consumed. The U.S. Hispanic-owned food company Goya Foods first targeted the Caribbean immigrant sub-subculture, then branched out to Latin American and Mexican foods. Today, its products are found in mainstream U.S. supermarkets.

SUBCULTURES DEMONSTRATE UNIQUE CBS

Subcultures exhibit unique product and brand preferences, shopping patterns, and media habits. In fact, products are often purchased to make a "statement" about a subculture with which a person identifies. Texans wear ten-gallon hats, string ties, and boots, while Gen Yers enjoy body art, extreme sports, and hopping into a mosh pit at a rock concert.

SUBCULTURES ARE EXPOSED TO SPECIALIZED MEDIA

Specialized media exist to reach subcultural groups through advertising. There are alternative rock radio stations for Gen Yers, *We* magazine for Americans with disabilities, *Latina* magazine for Hispanics, and the Web site Africana.com for African Americans. The social networking site Disaboom.com targets people with disabilities through social networking features like those found on Facebook plus information such as career advice, disability rights, and disability scholarships. Such media appeal to subcultural members who appreciate that marketers are singling out their subculture for attention. Ads run in these formats can be modified to better appeal to subcultural members. These media outlets are cost effective for reaching subcultural niches.

THE FOUR MOST POPULAR SUBCULTURAL BASES

We will now explore the four most common subcultural bases for subcultural segmentation, relating each type of subculture to the six major subcultural considerations outlined earlier.

Ethnic Subcultures

Marketers used to exclusively target the Anglo mainstream culture in the United States (90 percent of the U.S. population in 1950), defined by the U.S. Census Bureau as "non-Hispanic whites." Today, marketers use **multicultural (ethnic, minority) marketing**, which targets groups whose members share subcultural components based on a common race, nationality, or language.

Simply stated, ethnicity is founded on passport or pigment. Definitions of ethnic minorities can be based on one or more of the following: (1) racial groups (white or Caucasian, black or African American, yellow or Asian American, and red or American Indian); (2) nationality groups founded on country of origin (e.g., Asian Americans can come from Korea, Thailand, Japan, China, etc.); and (3) language groups sharing a common mother tongue. For instance, **Hispanics** (**Latinos**) share the Spanish language in either their primary language or the language of an ancestor, but Hispanics can be of various races and nationalities. Although racial and nationality groups are recorded separately by the U.S. Census Bureau, they clearly overlap, and so marketers can use them together to define ethnicity. The top three ethnic groups—African Americans, Hispanic Americans, and Asian Americans—now represent just under one-third (32 percent) of the U.S. population.

The following are the six major ethnic segmentation considerations.

Ethnic Groups Serve as a Basis for Market Segmentation. Clearly, the trend is toward multicultural marketing, both in the United States and in some countries abroad, such as the United Kingdom and Australia. Each of the major ethnic groups can be divided into ethnic sub-subcultures using segmentation variables such as country of origin; language preference (that of the homeland versus the **host culture**—the culture immigrants have adopted); **assimilation**, the process whereby ethnic group members learn and adapt to the values, language, and other cultural characteristics of the host culture, thereby replacing their native subcultural traits; **acculturation**, learning to function within the dominant culture while retaining one's original culture; and **subcultural identification**, the degree to which ethnic group members retain their cultural identity, primarily through socializing institutions such as schools, churches, and neighborhoods. Some ethnic peoples who have lived in the United States their entire lives develop a need to reconnect with their country and culture of origin, a phenomenon marketers call **retro-acculturation**.

Ethnic subcultures tend to cluster geographically, notably in areas of the adopted nation closest to their country of origin (e.g., Asians on the West Coast). Geographic grouping is evident in ethnic neighborhoods within major cities, such as Chinatown, Little Poland, and Little Haiti.

Increasingly, minority individuals, like Tiger Woods, are claiming multiple ethnic identities. Consequently, Mattel launched Barbie's friend Kayla, its first-ever multiethnic doll, designed to be interpreted as Asian, Hispanic, or any combination of various ethnic groups.

Marketers Should Appeal to Ethnic Group Characteristics. The United States has long been referred to as a "cultural melting pot," but this label is outdated. The United States is now viewed as an "ethnic mosaic," a "salad bowl," or an "American rainbow," suggesting acculturation, or assimilation. Members of many subcultural groups bond with each other to maintain their ethnic identities and preserve their cultural traditions and values.

Ethnic consumers, especially those with high subcultural identification, are more responsive to marketing techniques that appeal to their cultural characteristics. For instance, a growing number of retailers are promoting the Hispanic tradition of celebrating Three Kings Day every January 6 as a way to extend the holiday buying season.

It can be hazardous to rely on simple ethnic stereotypes. Too many marketers still spring for cheap laughs, portraying black women as mean, Hispanic men as loose, and Asians as martial artists. Not all blacks bounce basketballs while listening to hip-hop music. Asian Americans do not all live in Chinatown or work in nail salons. In fact, Asian Americans as a group rank highest for median household income, level of education, and business ownership.

Ethnic Subcultures Are Rising. Ethnic groups are increasing in sheer numbers, in purchasing power, and as influencers of urban trends. Growth in numbers is being fueled largely by high immigration and high *fertility rates*, which refers to the average number of babies born to childbearing women during their reproductive years (generally more than two children per family for ethnic groups). Because immigrants tend to be younger and generally have more children, they are becoming a larger part of the nation's younger population. The old are mostly white, and the young are increasingly ethnically diverse. Marketers recognize the shift. Beer ads, for example, are targeted at younger, ethnic people.

The year 2050 is forecast to be the tipping point after which non-Hispanic whites will no longer comprise the majority of the U.S. population. Most ethnic groups are also achieving upward social mobility and more political power and status within the mainstream culture.

Ethnic Groups Serve as a Springboard for Mainstream Marketing. Crossover marketing of minority market products abounds, with notable examples including ethnic foods, music, fashion, and movies. In the case of ethnic minorities, mainstreaming is known as **de-ethnicitization**. Hot sauces and zesty cuisine, including Cajun, Caribbean, and Asian, are going mainstream, driven by burgeoning ethnic groups. Tabasco sauce is hotter than ever! In the early 1990s, sales of salsa, originally a Hispanic and Southern food, surpassed ketchup sales for the first time ever in the United States. Once tucked away in the supermarket's ethnic aisle, tortillas are now familiar to most Americans, and are often called "wraps" to seem more ethnically neutral.

Urban marketing refers to marketing efforts that reflect the trends and attitudes originating in cities, driven by young African American and Hispanic consumers' choices in entertainment and fashion. Coca-Cola, Pepsi-Cola, Dr. Pepper, Reebok, and other advertisers have moved urban music stars, such as Jay-Z and LL Cool J, from targeted ethnic ads to mainstream ads because today's youth are increasingly color-blind and culture blind. Young Americans are especially prone to adopt characteristics of other cultures, a process known as **intraculteralism**. This differs from **multiculturalism**, in which distinct ethnicities are celebrated, and, in the case of *multicultural marketing*, are specifically targeted.

Ethnic Groups Demonstrate Unique CBs. Minority consumers exhibit behavioral patterns at variance from mainstream consumers. Each group has specific product preferences, especially regarding food, clothing, music, and hair and skin care products. For instance, African American consumers seem to enjoy shopping more than the other groups and are more fashion conscious. However, some behavioral distinctions between ethnic and mainstream consumers disappear after controlling for differences in income, education, concentration in central cities, and other socioeconomic indicators. In other words, these demographic factors are better viewed as correlates of certain ethnic CBs than membership in an ethnic group. For example, CB researchers have reported that blacks and Hispanics are more brand loyal than Anglo consumers. However, many ethnic consumers live in areas with restricted retail outlet choices. It is actually geography more than ethnicity that determines brand-switching behavior.

Ethnic Groups Are Exposed to Specialized Media. Specialty media exist for marketers to reach all ethnic groups and, increasingly, many ethnic subgroups. Some of these are ethnic language media. Typically, minority consumers are heavier users of ethnic national TV networks such as BET, Univision, and Telemundo, and local radio stations. Neighborhood media, such as outdoor and transit, also reach geographically concentrated ethnic consumers, who are generally lighter users of print media.

RELIGIOUS SUBCULTURES

Interest in religion, from evangelical Christianity to New Age mysticism, has increased in recent years. This trend is evidenced by best-selling books about religion such as Tim LaHaye and Jerry Jenkins's *Left Behind* series, Pastor Rick Warren's *The Purpose-Driven Life,* Dan Brown's *The Da Vinci Code,* Rhonda Byrne's *The Secret,* and renewed interest in C.S. Lewis's *The Chronicles of Narnia.* Other evidence in popular media includes TV shows such as *Touched by an Angel* and *Joan of Arcadia,* athletes openly praying before a game, Madonna's lovefest with kabbalah, and the public's fascination with paranormal activity and the occult, as evidenced by Harry Potter's escapades.

Religion provides people with important cultural characteristics, notably moral values, beliefs about "big-picture" issues such as sex, family life, and even the meaning of life, and norms, including activities, customs, rituals, and mores.

Religion as a Basis for Market Segmentation. In the United States, the principal organized religious faiths include Protestantism, Catholicism, Judaism, and Islam (the Muslim faith). A number of other religions and religious cults exist with smaller numbers of believers, such as Buddhism and Jehovah's Witnesses.

However, there has been a decline in participation in organized religion. This is primarily because Americans are becoming more pluralistic and individualistic in their religious beliefs. Consequently, most religions contain sub-subcultures, which are by and large defined by conservatism, the extent to which the teachings of the faith are taken literally and seen as the only truth.

Protestantism includes many different denominations, such as Baptist, Methodist, and Lutheran. Each Protestant denomination has branches, such as southern and conservative Baptists. Catholics consist of traditionalists, charismatics, and liberals. Members of the Jewish faith are either Orthodox (ultra-conservative), Conservative, or Reformed.

Each religious subculture and sub-subculture has a demographic profile. For example, within Protestantism, the socioeconomic status of Episcopalians is high, while Methodists are average, and Baptists skew low. One-third of all Baptists are black and one-half of all blacks are Baptist. Catholics are heavily Hispanic, with two-thirds of all Hispanics practicing Catholicism. Each religious subgroup also has subcultural characteristics, such as Orthodox Jews adhering to strict Old Testament dietary regulations and many devout Catholics still abstaining from eating meat on Friday.

Religious groups sometimes cluster geographically. Baptists and Evangelicals congregate in the South's Bible Belt; a disproportionate number of Catholics are found in the Northeast, as well as in areas of high Hispanic concentration; and Jews are most likely to live in New England, especially in urban areas.

Marketers Should Appeal to Religious Groups' Characteristics. Religious values and norms are an important consideration when communicating with religious subcultures, and there are significant distinctions between religious groups. Catholics tend to be more traditional, with a focus on family ties. Protestants still believe in the Protestant work ethic as well as individual responsibility and self-control. Jews stress individual responsibility, education, and achievement. Muslims cling to family norms and hold conservative beliefs regarding drug and alcohol use and sexual permissiveness.

Unfortunately, religious stereotypes persist: Jews are typecast as wealthy, stingy, and shrewd, and Evangelicals are perceived as backwoods buffoons who are self-righteous and hypocritical.

Some Religious Subcultures Are Rising. While the influence of organized religion has waned, religious subcultures remain strong. Growth rates vary widely between the various groups. The Catholic Church attributes most of its growth since the 1970s to the blossoming Hispanic population. Evangelical Christians are a rapidly growing and increasingly influential subculture. The group is characterized by a strong belief in and literal interpretation of the Bible. Muslims, while currently a minority, are the world's fastest-growing religious group.

Religious Subcultures Serve as a Springboard for Mainstream Marketing. Bagels and matzo balls were originally associated with the Jewish subculture but are now mass-marketed. Today, even pagans wear Christian crosses as necklaces. Children's videos featuring Christian fare such as *McGee and Me* and *VeggieTales* are mass marketed. Christian-themed movies include the *Left Behind* series and *The Passion of the Christ.* Also popular are Christian rock artists such as DC Talk, Jars of Clay, Switchfoot, Third Day, and Skillet, and rap/metalists P.O.D.

Religious Subcultures Demonstrate Unique CBs. CB can be influenced strongly by religious convictions. Examples include purchasing products that are associated with the celebration of religious rituals (confirmations and baptisms) and holidays (Christmas as the primary buying season). Religions also have unique symbols and artifacts, such as crosses, doves, fish, and communion cups for Christians, and rainbows, crystals, and unicorns for New Agers.

Religious beliefs and customs dictate the use or nonuse of certain products. Dietary laws for observant Jews mean that pork and shellfish are forbidden. Many Jewish cuisines and cleaning products must be kosher, with "U" and "P" marks on food packaging to indicate that the food meets Jewish dietary laws. However, some kosher products are going mainstream as non-Jews look for these marks as indicators that the food or cleaning product is pure and wholesome. Mormons would make a very poor target for tobacco products, liquor, and items containing caffeine, the consumption of which is forbidden. Because Catholics believe in sex for procreation rather than recreation, practicing Catholics are not a good market for birth control products.

Religious Subcultures Are Exposed to Specialized Media. All major religious groups have specialty media targeting them, notably magazines and radio stations. We see conservative Christians reading *Christianity Today* magazine, watching Christian TV shows such as Pat Robertson's *The 700 Club* and the Trinity Broadcasting Network, listening to former host James Dobson's radio show *Focus on the Family,* and even tuning in to Christian cable channels such as Z Music Television, which plays contemporary Christian music.

REGIONAL SUBCULTURES

Different geographic areas display unique subcultures. Many Americans have a strong sense of regional identification (e.g., New England "Yankees," Southern belles, and Heartlanders). Different geographic areas have their own cultural characteristics, such as language, style of dress, popular foods, and preferred pastimes. Such distinctions are determined by regional characteristics that include ethnic and religious mixes of citizens, climate, and natural resources. Such distinctions suggest that what works in Austin might flop in Boston or what plays in Peoria might not be tops in Texas. Consequently, the trend is toward regional marketing campaigns with decentralized strategic planning and decision making.

Geographic Subcultures as a Basis for Market Segmentation. A common geographic breakout for the United States includes New England, the Northeast or Mid-Atlantic region, the Southeast or South Atlantic, the Midwest, Mountain states, the Southwest, Plains states, the Pacific Northwest, and the Great Plains. Such areas differ demographically: The Northeast is older, largely white, with fewer children; the West is younger and more diverse.

Demographically, regions often overlap with other subcultures. Recall that ethnic groups, religions, and age groups collect geographically. Hispanics dominate large portions of counties in a span of states stretching from California to Texas, African Americans are strongly represented in the South as well as selected urban areas in the Northeast and Midwest, the Asian presence is relatively large and highly concentrated in a few scattered Western counties, and American Indians are concentrated in select pockets of Oklahoma as well as the Southeast, Upper Midwest, and the West. Similarly, many evangelicals populate the Bible Belt and Mormons abound in Utah. Many seniors inhabit Florida and Cape Cod, and many college students can be located in and around Boston and other big cities.

Geographic behavioral differences can also be identified. Southerners, unused to the hurry and crowding of Northeastern cities, tend to consider Northeasterners rude and unfriendly. Northeasterners, unaccustomed to the South's relaxed speech and courtesy, sometimes believe Southerners are slow and stupid.

By targeting regional sub-subcultures, many marketers and retailers practice **micromarketing**, a market segmentation practice varying marketing efforts down to the zip code and neighborhood levels. Kmart stocks each of its stores with fashion, food, and everyday items preferred in each location's community.

Marketers Should Appeal to Regional Characteristics. Values, norms, language, and other cultural indicators vary widely across the nation. Southern culture revolves around the home, family, and church, while southwestern society is more geared toward casual outdoor entertaining, comfortable clothes, and active sports. There are even regional sports cultures, with marketers using local sports heroes in their geographically targeted advertising. Language varies across the country. A submarine sandwich is variously known as a hero, a hoagie, a grinder, a poor boy, a Dagwood, a Giddy Burger, or a Torpedo. Do you prefer tube steaks, wieners, franks, frankfurters, or would you just settle for a hot dog? Radio commercials for Newbury Comics, a New England music store, tap into the local vernacular by promising its patrons a "wicked good time."

Despite the differences, marketers must be wary of negative stereotypes. Most Southerners are not shiftless, redneck Bible thumpers; many New Englanders are not prim, proper, and thrifty; and there are West Coast dwellers who actually are neither beach bums nor surfer dudes.

Some Regional Subcultures Are Rising. The growth trend in the population, jobs, and even political power is moving away from the "frostbelt" and toward the "sunbelt." The balance of population is shifting rapidly from the North and East to the South and West, notably the Mountain states and the Pacific Northwest. The three megastates of California, Texas, and Florida are still growing, albeit at a slower pace than previously. Recently, high growth has been experienced by Arizona, North Carolina, Nevada, and Colorado.

Geographic Subcultures Serve as a Springboard for Mainstream Marketing. Trends in fashions, music, and hot products often originate on the West and East coasts, and then migrate into the Heartland, as happened with Seattle "grunge" music and fashion of the early 1990s. Country music spread from its Southern roots in the 1970s. NASCAR, now the number-two spectator sport (behind the NFL), has rural roots in the Southeast during the outlaw culture of the Prohibition era, when rum-running moonshiners raced one another, using the same hot rods they also employed to evade federal agents.

Regional Subcultures Demonstrate Unique CBs. Product preferences differ from coast to coast. For example, styles of dress vary, with the Southwest being the most casual (to go with their outdoorsy lifestyle) and New England being most conservative.

Regional cuisines vary. Pennsylvania is known for Philly cheese steak, soft pretzels and mustard, shoofly pie, and Pennsylvania Dutch cookery. Louisiana is famous for Cajun cooking and Creole recipes. Southerners love their hominy grits, hush puppies, moon pies, shrimp Creole, collard greens, black-eyed peas, and sweet potato pie. If you shop at a Wal-Mart in Louisiana, you can pick up a bag of fishy-flavored Zapp's Cajun Crawtator potato chips!

Sales figures on certain products skew high in some areas and low in others. Detroit is big on Roller-blades, bowling balls, and popcorn, while Bostonians go for pasta, fish, sailing, and Porsches. People in Concord, New Hampshire, are nuts—they eat a lot of peanuts, mixed nuts, and cashews.

Regionalized Media. Regional media include city, state, and regional magazines; regional newspapers such as the *New York Times* and the *Los Angeles Times;* regional cable news networks such as Northwest Cable News and New England Cable News; and regional editions of most national publications, which feature local as well as national news and advertising. Also, general media preferences vary by locale, with Sunbelt dwellers exposed to less TV and newspapers and more to radio and outdoor media such as billboards.

GENERATIONAL SUBCULTURES (AGE COHORTS): TALKIN' 'BOUT MY GENERATION

A **generation** (**generational cohort, birth cohort, age subculture**) is a group of people born in the same era (typically seventeen to twenty-three years in duration) who have experienced a common social, political, historical, technological, and economic environment as well as a similar significant, defining, or formative life events. Some of the latter are **light-bulb memories**—vivid recollections of significant historical events, such as the space shuttle Challenger explosion of 1986, the 9/11 attacks on the United States, and the Virginia Tech massacre of 2007. Consequently, the members of a generational cohort have much in common regarding values, norms, behaviors, and other cultural characteristics.

Marketers should distinguish three age-related phenomena to help them understand any given age group:

1. **Age effects** (**life cycle effects**). Differences due to age include (a) physical distinctions, such as older people having difficulty seeing and hearing, and (b) psychological differences, such as younger people craving edgy fun and excitement. People in a given age bracket (e.g., teenagers, who are thirteen to nineteen years of age) are known as an **age cohort**, not to be confused with a generational cohort.

2. **Life-stage effects**. Distinctions arising from moving through important personal life events, such as getting a driver's license, going through parenthood, and confronting retirement.

3. **Cohort effects**. Differences due to one's birth year and when one grew up. Early generational experiences shared among cohorts form values and life skills. This explains why in the 1960s, Benny Goodman music was nostalgic for middle-aged adults, whereas in the 1980s and 1990s Beatles and Rolling Stones tunes became sentimental for this same age group. So, it is fallacious to believe that a twenty-year-old living in the dawn of the twenty-first century will think, talk, and act like one living in 1900, 1950, or even 1990.

The following are our six subcultural considerations applied to age cohorts.

1. *Generational Cohorts as a Basis for Market Segmentation.* **Generational marketing** is a segmentation scheme that divides the marketplace on the basis of generational cohorts. The five generations that have attracted marketing attention are as follows:

○ *Pre-Depression Generation (born before 1930).* The **pre-Depression** (**GI**) **generation** grew up in tough times, during the Great Depression and World War II. Many were deprived of material goods and a solid education. They went on to mature during the prosperous 1950s. This group makes up the older end of today's **mature market** (**seniors**), variously defined as people over 50, 55, or 60.

○ *Depression Generation (b. 1930–1946).* The **Depression generation** is sometimes labeled the **silent generation, postwar cohort,** or **bridge generation.** Living as youngsters during the Depression or World War II, they came of age during the 1950s or early 1960s, a period of economic growth and relative social tranquility.

○ *Baby Boom Generation (b. 1946–1964).* The **baby boom generation** (**baby boomers, boomers**) makes up more than 40 percent of the U.S. population. Born during the prosperous years following World War II, they were the offspring of GIs returning from the war to establish families. Boomers came of age amidst mass affluence and social and political upheaval in the 1960s, and stagflation (high inflation and unemployment) in the 1970s. Many were participants in the sexual and drug revolutions of the 1960s, and consequently are sometimes called the "Woodstock" generation (named after the 1969 music festival in Woodstock, New York). They ushered in a radically new set of values concerning gender equality, sexual orientation, premarital sex, and the environment. Demographically, they have high levels of education and income. Many are parents or grandparents in dual-income households.

○ *Generation X (b. 1965–1978).* **Generation Xers** (**Gen X**) were born during what is known as the **baby bust** (because of its small size relative to the baby boom). They are sometimes called **busters, Xers, postboomers, the shadow generation, the MTV generation, thirteeners** (the thirteenth generation produced in America since its founding), and

the Nike generation (after the company's "live-for-the moment" philosophy). The baby bust was the first era during which a large segment of society grew up in either dual-income or single-parent households. Gen Xers came of age during the prosperous 1980s and early 1990s.

Many spent their early years in day care centers and experienced the divorce of their parents while growing up. This led to their acceptance of extended or "alternative" families, which can include stepparents, half-siblings, close friends, and "relationship partners" such as in common-law marriages and same-sex couples. Generation X is slowly replacing the aging boomers in the workplace, and they have the lowest level of loyalty to institutions such as companies, government, and church. It has been suggested that they be renamed "Generation E" because they are entrepreneurial, educated, and e-mail savvy.

○ *Generation Y (b. 1978–2000).* Members of the **Generation Y (Gen Y)** cohort arrived during the so-called **baby boomlet** or the **echo baby boom** (born to parents of the baby boom generation). They are also known as the **Internet generation**, the **Net generation**, or **N-generation** (because many came of age during the birth and early development of the Internet); **millennials** or the **millennium generation** (they were young in the year 2000); and **Generation Next**. They are more diverse racially and ethnically as well as in terms of socioeconomic status than Generation Xers.

This cohort grew up during a booming economy, widespread computer literacy, a technology boom, and unprecedented diversity in the population regarding ethnicity, beliefs, values, and other cultural characteristics. Since they matured in prosperous times and in smaller families with fewer children, they were pampered and are consequently materialistic and self-absorbed. Interestingly, they are also caring, tolerant, and well traveled. They were raised in an era of many social concerns: divorce was common, AIDS was a global epidemic, and international terrorism grew.

Most Gen Yers were raised in dual-income or single-parent households, spent time in day care, and were latchkey kids (they were home alone after school). Consequently, they were responsible for helping out with family shopping during their teen years, resulting in a sophisticated, marketing-savvy generation that is highly skeptical of advertisers and politicians who are not authentic. They will not buy from manufacturers or retailers with dubious environmental or humanitarian records. Having grown up with technology, they use it constantly—for work, leisure, and maintaining relationships. Work-life balance is important to this generation. They are hardworking, entrepreneurial, and candid.

2. *Marketers Should Appeal to Generational Characteristics.* In order to appeal to someone, you must understand them. **Cohort analysis** is a research method used to describe an aggregate of people (usually a birth cohort or marriage cohort) in terms of present as well as future values, attitudes, and lifestyles. These cultural characteristics are formed during an age cohort's "coming of age"—their teen years and early adulthood. Age cohort differences in such characteristics give rise to generation gaps (perhaps they should be called "cohort chasms"!). To appeal to any given age group and avoid these gaps, marketers must strive to understand the target cohort.

People often strive to achieve as adults what they were deprived of as children. For instance, the pre-Depression generation, having grown up in hard economic times, is concerned with material security. Because many members of Generation X matured in unstable homes, they care about establishing secure families.

Marketers must be wary of stereotyping all members of a generation. Those in the older generations despise being portrayed as old, crotchety, senile, frail geezers, especially since many are quite active. Likewise, most Gen Xers resent being pegged as apathetic slackers since many have achieved career success through hard work.

3. *Some Age Cohorts Are Rising.* Generations vary in terms of economic, buying, and political power. Members of the Depression generation hold many positions of power at the top rungs of the corporate and government ladders. The majority of people from the pre-Depression and Depression generations are financially secure. But the baby boomers make up the largest segment of the population and continue to gain in positions of power within business and the government.

4. *Age Subcultures Serve as a Springboard for Mainstream Marketing.* Crossover marketing, which reaches across generations, can occur due to *upward diffusion.* (This also occurs across ethnic groups, crossing over from marketing a given product to a minority to the majority.) Many styles of music, fashion, and video games originate at the lower rungs of the socioeconomic ladder, in this case the younger cohorts, and then trickle upward. Extreme sports such as skateboarding, in-line skating, and motocross or BMX biking originated with the youth of Generations X and Y and became more universally popular. The adoption of "retro" styles by younger generations also illustrates generational crossover.

5. *Generations Demonstrate Unique CBs.* Product preferences vary by generation. For example, musical tastes reflect genres listened to during the teen years through early adulthood. The pre-Depression generation favors big band jazz and the Depression generation likes swing music. TV commercials aimed at baby boomers are replete with oldies and classic rock, while those targeted toward Generations X and Y contain alternative rock and rap.

6. *Specialized Media for Age Cohorts.* Each generation has media targeted directly toward it. For the pre-Depression and Depression generations, there is *AARP: The Magazine* and *50 Plus* magazine. Baby boomers are tuned into VH1, oldies radio stations, and National Public Radio. Baby busters read magazines such as *Spin* and watch Fox network TV shows such as *The Simpsons* and *Family Guy.* Magazines such as *Maxim, Spin,* and

Details, have been developed for Generation Y. Web sites featuring music and online games are popular with both Generations X and Y. These online and wireless-centric consumers live in a different world from those who were raised on print media. Tech-savvy cohorts can be difficult to reach due to the Internet's fragmentation.

Review Questions

1. Explain the relationship between social categories, subcultures, and social classes.

2. What are the four primary bases for subcultural marketing? Cite and describe major groups within each of these segmentation schemes. What other bases are also sometimes used for subcultural marketing?

3. Cite six important subcultural considerations discussed in the exercise and an example of each for all four primary bases of subcultural segmentation.

4. Cite and explain the three important bases for ethnic segmentation.

5. What is the relationship between micromarketing and geodemographic segmentation?

6. What are the three age-related phenomena marketers need to distinguish when practicing generational marketing?

In-Class Applications

Note: When you find advertisements and create your own ads for the following questions, in addition to using ethnic, religious, geographic, and generational subcultures, you are welcome to explore other subcultural groups, such as college students, the physically handicapped, liberal Democrats, surfer dudes, and so on.

1. Describe the subcultural target market for each of the ads in Exhibits 6.2 through 6.7, being as specific and descriptive as possible. Do any ads target either a sub-subculture or two or more subcultures simultaneously? How does each ad

try to appeal to subcultural characteristics? Can any of the ads' appeals be improved in any way?

Are you able to find any examples of crossover marketing or appeals to unique patterns of CB in any of these ads? What kind of medium do you suppose each ad was found in?

2. t is controversial to target certain "vulnerable" groups with "socially irresponsible" products, such as those that are frivolous, i.e., don't satisfy a "genuine" need or else create a "false" problem (e.g., a back scratcher shaped like a paw); those marketed with false claims (weight loss remedies that can help you lose five pounds a day while eating all you want); unhealthy goods (chewing tobacco); potentially dangerous items (handguns and fireworks); or products considered immoral (condoms).

Groups cited as being particularly susceptible to marketing efforts for such products include children, the very elderly, recent immigrants, those of low education, the mentally handicapped, shopaholics, and the recently bereaved. Such people are presumably easily deceived or manipulated, or otherwise more vulnerable to unscrupulous business practices, not fitting the model of the "sovereign" consumer or of the "reasonable person." Therefore, these categories of consumers require extra government protection.

For example, children are considered a vulnerable group. Some believe it is unethical to target this group with advertisements for unhealthy fare such as double cheeseburgers with bacon, large fries, and 64-ounce super-caffeinated cola. The mass marketing of these products may have contributed to childhood obesity. Fast-food restaurants have been unsuccessfully sued for hawking such unhealthy fare.

EXHIBIT 6.2 Betty Crocker Ad

EXHIBIT 6.3 Yankee Magazine Ad

EXHIBIT 6.4 Rosary Ad

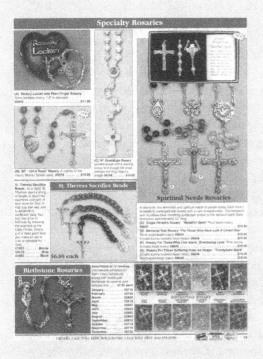

EXHIBIT 6.5 American Family Association Ad

EXHIBIT 6.6 AARP AD

EXHIBIT 6.7 Levi's Ad

Another category sometimes added to the list of "vulnerable" groups is ethnic minorities. Several marketers of "sin" products, such as cigarettes, malt liquor and hard alcohol, and gambling, have come under fire for specifically targeting groups in ethnic neighborhoods, using local media such as flyers and in-store signage.

For example, a billboard for a brand of malt liquor in a black neighborhood in East St. Louis exclaimed, "It'll do the trick." Another said "The power of (brand name)—it works every time," suggesting the product can be used by men to get women drunk. One tobacco company was criticized for selling single cigarettes to African Americans who couldn't afford to buy a whole pack. Critics also point out the large number of liquor stores in Hispanic neighborhoods.

Given that they market such potentially detrimental products to mainstream markets, do you think it is wrong for purveyors of "sin" products to target minorities, especially those of lower income and educational levels living in inner cities? Why or why not? If you believe that such minority marketing is legitimate, should there be stipulations on how the marketing is done? If so, describe.

How do you think marketers justify marketing potentially harmful goods to ethnic minorities?

Do you agree with the marketers or the critics? How do you feel about mainstream marketers such as Chevrolet sponsoring religious concerts or otherwise affiliating themselves with religious groups or events? Should there be separation of church and marketing? Why or why not?

Written Applications

1. Answer Question 1 in the In-Class Applications for four of the ads. If you are a member of any of these subcultures, does the ad appeal to you personally? Why or why not? If you are not a member of any of these subcultures, interview someone who is and get that person's perspective on the advertising's appeal (or lack thereof).

2. Find two additional ads for which you can answer Question 1 in the In-Class Applications. These advertisements can come from either specialized subcultural media or mainstream media that are either targeting one or more particular subcultures or attempting to popularize a subcultural product via crossover marketing.

3. Create an ad for any advertising medium that will appeal to one (or more) subcultures. Answer Question 1 in the In-Class Applications for that ad.

4. Answer Question 2 in the In-Class Applications. In addition to offering your own opinion, solicit the opinion of a member of one of the disadvantaged groups.

DISCUSSION QUESTION

1. Why is subcultural segmentation important to market penetration? Discuss!

REFERENCES

The Barna Group. (2005). "Annual Barna Group Survey Describes Changes in America's Religious Beliefs and Practices." http://www.barna.org/barna-update/article/5-barna-update/181-annual-barna-group-survey-describes-changes-in-americas-religious-beliefs-and-practices (accessed June 16, 2006).

Brown, Mary, and Orsborn, Carol. (2006). *BOOM: Marketing to the Ultimate Power Consumer—The Baby-Boomer Woman*. New York: AMACOM, 2006.

Cimino, Richard, and Lattin, Don. (1999). "Choosing My Religion." *American Demographics*, April, 60–65.

Faura, Juan. (2005). *Hispanic Marketing Grows Up: Exploring Perceptions and Facing Realities*. Ithaca, NY: Paramount Market Publishing.

Gibson, Campbell. (1993). "The Four Baby Booms." *American Demographics,* November, 36–40.

Green, Brent. (2005). *Marketing to Leading-Edge Baby Boomers: Perceptions, Principles, Practices, Predictions,* 2nd ed. Ithaca, NY: Paramount Market Publishing.

Gronbach, Kenneth W. (2008). *The Age Curve: How to Profit from the Coming Demographic Storm.* New York: AMACOM.

Halter, Marilyn. (2000). *Shopping for Identity.* New York: Schocken Books.

Hapoienu, S. L. (1990). "The Rise of Micromarketing." *Journal of Business Strategy,* 1, 37, 37–42.

Harris, Leslie M., ed. (2003). *After Fifty: How the Baby Boom Will Redefine the Mature Market.* Ithaca, NY: Paramount Market Publishing.

Howe, Neil, and Strauss, William. (2000). *Millennials Rising: The Next Great Generation.* New York: Vintage Books.

Katsanis, Lea Prevel. (1994). "The Ideology of Political Correctness and Its Effect on Brand Strategy." *Journal of Product and Brand Management,* 3, 2, 5–14.

Kaufman-Scarborough, Carol. (2000). "Asian-American Consumers as a Unique Market Segment: Fact or Fallacy?" *Journal of Consumer Research,* 17, 2, 249–162.

Korgaonkar, Pradeep K., Karson, Eric J., and Lund, Daulatram. (2000). "Hispanics and Direct Marketing Advertising." *Journal of Consumer Research,* 17, 2, 137–157.

Korzenny, Felipe, and Korzenny, Betty Ann. (2005). *Hispanic Marketing: A Cultural Perspective.* Burlington, MA: Elsevier/Butterworth-Heinemann.

Kosmin, Barry A., and Keysar, Ariela B. (2006). *Religion in a Free Market.* Ithaca, NY: Paramount Market Publishing.

McDaniel, Stephen W., and Burnett, John J. (1991). "Targeting the Evangelical Segment." *Journal of Advertising Research,* 31, 4, 26–33.

Michman, Ronald D. (2003). *Lifestyle Marketing: Reaching the New American Consumer.* Westport, CT: Praeger Publishers.

Miller, Pepper, and Kemp, Herb. (2005). *What's Black About It? Insights to Increase Your Share of a Changing African-American Market.* Ithaca, NY: Paramount Market Publishing.

Morgan, Carol M., and Levy, Doran J. (2002). *Marketing to the Mindset of Boomers and Their Elders.* St. Paul, MN: Attitude Base, The Brewer House.

Moschis, George P., Lee, Euehun, Mathur, Anil, and Strautman, Jennifer. (2000). *The Maturing Marketplace: Buying Habits of Baby Boomers and Their Parents.* Westport, CT: Quorum Books.

Moschis, George P., and Mathur, Anil. (2007). *Baby Boomers and Their Parents: Surprising Findings about Their Lifestyles, Mindsets, and Well-Being.* Ithaca, NY: Paramount Market Publishing.

Mueller, Barbara. (2008). *Communicating with the Multicultural Consumer: Theoretical and Practical Perspectives.* New York: Peter Lang.

Muley, Miriam. (2009). *The 85% Niche: The Power of Women of All Colors—Latina, Black, and Asian.* Ithaca, NY: Paramount Market Publishing.

Napoli, Julie, and Ewing, Michael T. (2001). "The Net Generation." *Journal of International Consumer Marketing,* 13, 1, 21–34.

Nyren, Chuck. (2005). *Advertising to Baby Boomers.* Ithaca, NY: Paramount Market Publishing.

Paul, Pamela. (2001). "Echo Boomerang." *American Demographics,* June, 45–49.

————. (2001). "Getting Inside Generation Y." *American Demographics,* September, 43–49.

Roberts, James A., and Manolis, Chris. (2000). "Baby Boomers and Busters: An Exploratory Investigation of Attitudes Toward Marketing, Advertising, and Consumerism." *Journal of Consumer Marketing,* 17, 6, 481–499.

Rossman, Marlene L. (1994). *Multicultural Marketing.* New York: American Management Association, 153–157.

Schouten, John W., and McAlexander, James H. (1995). "Subcultures of Consumption." *Journal of Consumer Research,* 22, 1, 43–61.

Smith, N. Craig, and Cooper-Martin, Elizabeth. (1997). "Ethics and Target Marketing: The Role of Product Harm and Consumer Vulnerability." *Journal of Marketing,* 61, 3, 1–20.

Strauss, William, and Howe, Neil. (2006). *Millennials and the Pop Culture: Strategies for a New Generation of Consumers in Music, Movies, TV, Internet and Video Games.* Great Falls, VA: Life Course Associates.

Stroud, Dick. (2007). *The Fifty-Plus Market*. London: Kogan Page.

Sturdivant, Frederick D. (1973). "Subculture Theory: Poverty, Minorities, and Marketing." In Scott Ward and Thomas S. Robertson (eds.), *Consumer Behavior: Theoretical Sources*. Englewood Cliffs, NJ: Prentice-Hall, 469–520.

Tharp, Marye C. (2001). *Marketing and Consumer Identity in Multicultural America*. Thousand Oaks, CA: Sage Publications.

Valdés, M. Isabel. (2000). *Marketing to American Latinos (Part 1): A Guide to the In-Culture Approach*. Ithaca, NY: Paramount Market Publishing.

———. (2002). *Marketing to American Latinos (Part 2): A Guide to the In-Culture Approach*. Ithaca, NY: Paramount Market Publishing.

Wolburg, Joyce M. (2005). "Drawing the Line Between Targeting and Patronizing: How 'Vulnerable' Are the Vulnerable?" *Journal of Consumer Marketing*, 22, 5, 287–288.

Yarrow, Kit, and O'Donnell, Jayne. (2009). *Gen Buy: How Tweens, Teens, and Twenty-Somethings Are Revolutionizing Retail*. San Francisco, CA: Jossey-Bass.

Zill, Nicholas, and Robinson, John. (1997). "The Generation X Difference." *American Demographics*, April, 24–33.

Zogby, John. (2008). *The Way We'll Be: The Zogby Report on the Transformation of the American Dream*. New York: Random House.

7

Chapter 7 focuses on one of the most critical areas of cross-national marketing: cross-cultural negotiations. Different cultures attribute different weights or importance to different negotiation stages. For instance, individualistic cultures emphasize technical aspects, whereas in collectivistic cultures, relationships are preeminent. The chapter offers insights into what is important in cross-cultural negotiations and how they can be successful. The concept of *cultural empathy* is pivotal in gaining negotiating advantage over your counterpart in cross-cultural negotiations. The chapter discusses the incidence of *cultural faux pas* and how to avoid blunders. It also lists and discusses the stages in cross-border negotiations and how different cultures use different negotiation styles. The chapter also mentions communication strategies employed during negotiations, team communication, problem solving, and decision making. The importance of achieving integrative negotiations using convergent communication skills is noted.

7.1 Negotiating Cultural Chasms

Michael R. Czinkota and Ilkka A. Ronkainen

We continually refer to the impact of a market's culture on overseas marketing efforts. Even companies in neighboring countries find that cultural, linguistic, or regulatory differences have an effect on every aspect of their business relationships. This is just as important in the negotiation process as it is with the advertising theme, product variations, or anything else. Failure to understand the local culture and to adjust a negotiation style accordingly can lead to negotiation failures. Even the little things make a difference. For example, using a baseball analogy during meetings in Italy, where the national sport is soccer, will fall flat. When in Rome, do as the Romans do.

The two biggest dangers facing global negotiators are parochialism and stereotyping. Americans tend to be guilty of being parochial, thinking that everyone in the international business world will behave as Americans do. While business is more global, it is not necessarily more American. As George Bernard Shaw once said, "England and America are two countries separated by the same language."

Stereotypes are used to explain those behaviors that are not like ours. They can have a positive or negative impact. For example, a negative stereotype about a region's financial stability might lead negotiators to push for a low-risk payment system, whether or not it is necessary. Stereotyping can also lull us into complacency when working with regions that share our native language, as is the case with the U.S., U.K., and Australia. That complacency is not necessarily good.

The negotiating process differs from country to country and is usually different from what Americans are accustomed to. To establish rapport, exchange information, persuade, or make concessions, adjust your style or process when working in an international market. In China, for example, the ideal negotiator is someone already known and respected by a Chinese trading partner. The prevailing business philosophy in China is one of *"guanxi"* (pronounced guan-si). This refers to relationships –particularly those in business –and the expectation that the marketer will look out for and support those with whom there are relationships. Negotiators who understand *guanxi* leverage it by first establishing trust and goodwill with a wide network in the region where they do business. They then go into negotiations either with good *guanxi* with those at the table, or the power of the *guanxi* of those in their network as it extends to the other negotiating party.

At the same time, though, Chinese or Chinese-Americans working on behalf of a company can be at a disadvantage because their Chinese counterparts have higher expectations for these people who understand the local rules. The ideal team for a U.S. company might be a non-Chinese who understands the culture and an ethnic Chinese individual who generates more trust.

In any negotiating situation, if neither party is familiar with the counterpart's culture, engage an outside facilitator.

Understanding the Stages of Negotiation

International business negotiating involves four stages:

1. The offer
2. Informal meetings
3. Formulating the strategy
4. Negotiating

Culture influences which of these stages are most important and how long the process will take, which might be one session or several weeks. In Northern Europe, for example, culture emphasizes the technical, the numerical, and the tested, which leads to a need for careful pre-negotiation preparation. In contrast, Southern European culture favors personal networks, social contexts, and flair, so meetings in the south might take longer, but the decision process might be faster.

The Offer

At the offer stage, both parties assess each other's needs and commitment level. Their goals and the overall atmosphere help establish initial expectations for negotiations. Understanding the goals of the other team helps negotiators identify potential compromises that will create a mutually satisfactory outcome. For example, the other firm might be motivated by a need for more cash or to shelter money. Identifying this upfront can put the marketer in a better position to help both teams meet their goals.

Other expectations or biases come into play at this point, too. For example, if organizations in a particular country have a reputation for a lack of sales persistence or shutting down when the situation grows difficult, a company in another nation might hesitate to do business with companies from that region. When this reluctance is revealed, it can be countered –*if* it is revealed. The other party might be reluctant to be honest and say, "I don't believe you will stay with us when the going gets tough," because such directness might be viewed as impolite. Good negotiators are intuitive, sensing such unspoken objectives and shaping their approaches to address them. Be alert for unspoken issues or agendas and respond accordingly.

Informal Meetings

Informal meetings are held after the seller has made the offer. Designed as get acquainted sessions where both parties can learn more about each other and details of the offer, they often take place in casual settings that are more conducive to relaxed discussion. In regions such as Asia, the Middle East, Southern Europe, and Latin America, these informal meetings can make or break the deal. For business people in these regions, the relationship can be more important than the offer, and it is at this stage that they determine whether they want to work with a company. U.S.

exporters doing business in Kuwait, for example, report that their experience has taught them that establishing a strong business relationship is more important than price in their negotiations in that country.

Impatient marketers who view "handholding" and "schmoozing" as a waste of time are not the best individuals for global negotiations. At the same time, while facilitators can be employed at this stage to move the process forward, there is no substitute for the face-to-face contact that not only helps the marketer gather important market and cultural intelligence, but that also indicates respect for individuals on the other negotiating team.

Formulating the Strategy

Begin formulating a strategy before the offer is made, using the subsequent informal meetings to help sharpen the company's approach and objectives. Strategies should take into account the marketer's priorities, goals, bottom-line requirements, and bargaining positions –and as much of this as the negotiator has learned about the other side during the preliminary and later informal meetings.

Study the behavior and patterns of clients and partners when formulating a strategy. Research has shown, for example, that competitive bargainers are able to take advantage of Americans and Canadians because they are more trusting than other cultural groups. In the case of governmental buyers, too, it is important to understand that government negotiations are different from those in the public sector because government needs or requirements are often different from those in the business sector. Factor all of this into the strategy.

Note, too, that negotiators might not behave as expected, because they might be adapting to the other style. If this happens, be prepared to refine the strategy.

Negotiating

The negotiating approach used will depend on the cultural background and business traditions in the country where the negotiations take place. The competitive and collaborative approaches are the most common. In a competitive strategy, companies are primarily concerned about getting a favorable outcome at the expense of the other party—something of an "I win, you lose" outcome. A collaborative approach focuses on mutual needs, with more of a win–win outcome that capitalizes on the strengths of each group but might involve some compromise on both parts. Anglo Saxons tend to prefer a win–lose approach while Latins opt for the win–win.

There are often difficulties when individuals from high context cultures negotiate with those from low context cultures. Cultures that rely on high context communications tend to observe and learn from nonverbal and verbal cues that supplement what is actually said. People in low context cultures are more literal, expecting others to learn what they need from what is said. High context cultures tend to value the group over individuality, and are more common in Eastern nations and those with less racial diversity. France, Japan, Saudi Arabia, and China are considered to be high context cultures. Low context cultures include those in North America. When these differences are not understood, acknowledged, and taken into account, misunderstandings or confusion can result.

When selecting the location for negotiations, common sense would suggest a neutral location as the fairest option, and this is indeed the choice favored by many, but it is not always an option. In those situations, one becomes the host. When hosting the negotiations on home turf, the host does enjoy that home court advantage with its lower psychological risk because of the familiar surroundings. But being in an unfamiliar location can create culture shock for guests. Add pressure by manipulating the situation with delays or additional demands, and the pressure felt by guests intensifies.

A host looking for the best outcome possible for all parties works to build relationships and reduce stress by putting considerate behavior ahead of speedy timelines. Global travelers understand the challenges presented by jet lag and make certain that they schedule meetings so that their traveling colleagues have time to recover from international travel before negotiating. Early morning breakfast sessions after a colleague crosses multiple time zones is rarely advisable. Some cultures believe it is essential to entertain their guests into the evening, forgetting that those guests might need rest after traveling or perhaps are not accustomed to this approach. This is not an opportunity to wear out the opponent and then take advantage. It is an opportunity to build the connections that will generate a long-lasting business partnership.

Visiting teams are, of course less likely to walk out even when the scheduling or other behavior seems manipulative; as a matter of fact, the pressure is on them to make concessions to achieve an agreement. The advantage of being the visitor, though, is that the visitor has an opportunity to see the counterpart's facilities first-hand and learn more about the operation and the culture.

Negotiations in other Countries

We sometimes have to do things overseas that we would not do at home because what is acceptable and expected in our domestic markets might not work elsewhere—and vice versa. Bridging the cultural chasm is essential for success in negotiations, but it has the potential to offer a much bigger impact than that. The continuing efforts of marketers to understand cultural issues help them identify terminology that is persuasive, but, more than that, these efforts help secure important assimilations of value systems.

Meeting face-to-face generates a global connectedness that helps businesses on a personal level, but helps cultures on a global level. This enhanced "one world" sense can contribute to undermining support for terrorists, who polarize and alienate, rather than unite, world cultures. These suggestions regarding different styles for different regions will help negotiators adjust to the style of the host country.

Learn as much as possible about the other group's traditions and culture first. Ask consultants and local representatives to help identify the critical behaviors or details that can make or break a relationship. For example, in highly structured societies such as those of Korea, people respect age and position, so do the same.

Rituals are important and should be respected. For example, in Asia, a first encounter must include the exchange of business cards. Those who have not packed them should get replacements printed immediately. Add a translation to the back of the card so it can be read in the other group's native language. The exchange of business cards is so important that some airlines offer to print the cards as a service to their business travelers when customers make a reservation for travel to regions where it is a common ritual.

Show respect by reading cards as they are received. Demonstrate the significance of the card's symbolism by holding it with both hands before tucking it carefully away in a protected location, such as an inner jacket pocket, card holder, or wallet.

Use the company's best people. Some companies make the mistake of assigning global negotiation to their less talented players. This could indicate that the organization either is not concerned about the outcome or does not understand the significance of a successful outcome. Because of the importance of business partner relationships and the impact a successful contract has on the company's overall health, the negotiating team should feature a company's top talent.

Use a team. Bringing in specialists will strengthen the company's position and ensure that all points of view get proper attention. Expanding the team also allows less experienced participants to observe and learn more while participating less than they could without the backup. In addition, it helps a company match the firepower of the other group. While Western negotiation teams tend to have just two to four people, Chinese teams might have as many as ten.

Match titles. Negotiators will be more effective in certain regions if they make certain that the "rank" of the most senior member of their team matches the most senior member of the counterpart's team. It can be an important sign of respect. Titles sometimes offer surprising leverage abroad, as well. For example, when meeting the chairman of the U.S. Democratic Party in China, people respond with greater respect than one might expect and certainly with more respect than is offered in the U.S. This is because Mao Tse-tung, the remarkably powerful former leader of the Communist Party in China, was also a party "chairman."

Keep the team's disagreements private. Just as parents work to present a unified front with their children, negotiators need to bring a single voice to the conference room. Team conflicts will exist, of course, but they should be imperceptible and kept out of the negotiating room. Otherwise, the team could be subject to a competitive "divide and conquer" strategy.

Speak the language, even if it is just a few words. In an ideal situation, the negotiator speaks the customer's language fluently. If both teams are using English, but only one team has native English speakers, that team should be careful to avoid jargon and colloquialisms.

Making the effort to learn the language of a potential partner shows commitment, good faith, and sincerity, even if all the team masters is a few greetings or phrases. As international marketing becomes more important, companies will hire people who can speak several languages, particularly those of countries where the company plans to do business. These individuals can become part of the negotiating team, serving as translators when there are language barriers. There are drawbacks associated with using translators or interpreters, though. They impede spontaneity. Their presence can offend an executive who believes he speaks the other language fluently. The companies might be discussing confidential information they do not want to share with an outsider. On the other hand, the fact that they slow things down can provide each team with time to give more thought to what is being said.

Anyone involved with international business will want to learn at least one foreign language. This exposes the learner to new cultures, new thinking, and new ways of doing things—all of which better prepares the marketer for the global marketing experience.

Watch body language, too. Sitting in what might be considered a comfortable position might be interpreted in China as a lack of control over the body and, therefore, a lack of control over the mind.

Find out who has the final decision on the contract. While North American and European negotiators often arrive with the authority to sign a contract, their counterparts in the Far East seldom—if ever—do. Announcing that the negotiators do not have the authority to finalize the contract rarely has a positive effect but can be useful if the goal is to probe the buyer's motives. Verify who has authority and the obstacles the negotiator might face in reaching a decision.

Be patient. In China and certain other countries, negotiations can take three times as long as those in the U.S. and Europe. Showing impatience in certain countries, including Brazil and Thailand, can actually prolong negotiations, not speed them up.

Consider the first offer in context of the culture. U.S. negotiators tend to start the process close to what they believe is a fair offer, while Chinese negotiators are more likely to start with unreasonable demands and a rigid posture.

Understand the negotiating ethics of the region. Being shrewd is valued in some parts of the world but frowned upon elsewhere. While Russian negotiators might frustrate those from Western cultures with last-minute changes or requests for concessions, it is how they do business. Common complaints about ethics in negotiations center around traditional competitive bargaining, false promises, attacking the opponent's network, misrepresentation of position, and inappropriate information gathering.

Do not be afraid of silence. U.S. business people often interpret silence and inaction as negative signs, rushing in to fill the vacuum with premature modifications. Savvy counter-negotiators know to use this ploy to win lower prices or better deals. Japanese negotiators, for example, remain silent because they have learned that by not reacting, they can get their counterparts to offer more favorable terms. The Finns, on the other hand, might sit through a meeting expressionless with their hands folded. This is actually how they show respect and indicate they are listening carefully.

Avoid confrontation. Negotiating partners might view any insistence on answers or an outcome as a threat. In some markets, negotiating is seen as a way of establishing long-term commercial relationships rather than as an event with well-defined winners and losers, so forcing a conclusion can cause problems. Confrontations also might cause a counterpart to lose face, which is considered a particularly serious insult in the Far East.

Keep the big picture in mind. Do not make concessions until all issues have been discussed. Concessions traditionally come at the end of the bargaining. This is especially true when it comes to price. Agreeing on price too soon could lead to pressure to offer too many extras for that price.

Be prepared. A counterpart might reject a price at the outset in the hope of getting an upper hand or obtaining concessions later on. These concessions might include discounts, an improved product, better terms, or other demands that are not in the company's best interest. Prepare for this in advance by knowing as much as possible about the target market and customer, using that knowledge to develop counterproposals.

If a counterpart says better offers are available, request more details on those offers. This lets the marketer provide an informed analysis on why the company's product is superior. Double check competitive prices to see if they do, indeed, reflect market prices. In addition, if a first offer is accepted without comment, check the numbers to make sure there is not a mistake.

Be clear on the final work product. What constitutes a contract might vary from region to region. In many parts of the world, legal contracts are not needed and, in fact, referring to legal counsel might suggest to a counterpart that the relationship is in trouble. In some regions, an oral agreement and a handshake are considered enough, but this approach can leave both parties open to problems. The issue is not that one or the other is not trustworthy. The issue is that unless the agreement is in writing, the parties might not be completely clear on what is expected of each side.

When an agreement is reached, it is critical that both parties leave with a clear understanding of the terms. In some cases, a signed written agreement is enough but in the case of large-scale projects, companies will need a longer document outlining details that include the responsibilities of each party.

The Cultural Faux Pas

There are a number of resources available to help international marketers avoid unpleasant cultural mistakes when traveling overseas. Website ExecutivePlanet.com is a wiki-like resource featuring a country-by-country list of business etiquette guidelines. Use this site or another reference resource to become familiar with the destination country or the mores of the people being entertained. Here are a few examples of potential pitfalls to help those involved appreciate the importance of understanding the culture they are dealing with:

- *Gifts.* It is customary to exchange gifts in Thailand on the second meeting but gift-giving is considered a bribe in China. Avoid black or white wrapping paper in India because both are considered unlucky. Do not offend the gift-giver there by opening a gift in front of them, because that would not be polite, but do give thanks.
- *Names.* Do not use first names with Japanese colleagues. Use their title or their last name and the prefix "san," as in "Czinkota san." It is the equivalent of "Mr." or "Ms." The use of san is not appropriate for spouses or children, though. In Mexico, a business card will include the surname of the individual's father followed by the mother's surname, but it is the father's surname that is used when addressing the individual. This means that Senor Jorge Raul Rodriguez Mendez is Senor Rodriguez, not Senor Mendez.
- *Touching.* Do not hug people in the Netherlands or Russia. And by all means, do not give the German Chancellor a shoulder rub, as former President George Bush did for Angela Merkel during one of his trips abroad. Public displays of affection are verboten in India, too, as actor Richard Gere discovered when he kissed an Indian actress on the cheek several times at a charity event—the government issued a warrant for his arrest on obscenity charges.
- *Hand signs.* In countries such as India, using the left hand for anything is cause for concern, so do not do it. In Indonesia, pounding the fist into the palm of the other hand could be considered an obscene gesture.
- *Social situations.* Do not bring up business topics during social engagements in Australia and Thailand. Leave it to local hosts to decide if business conversations are appropriate. In Australia, make sure that everyone takes a turn at buying a round of drinks. It is not wise to directly reject a social invitation in India. Even if it is not possible to attend, saying "I hope I can be there" is more acceptable. When doing business with a Scot, do not ask personal questions, even though that might be how to begin to establish a relationship with domestic colleagues.
- *Dining out.* In Muslim regions, people believe the left hand is dirty, so using it to eat is inappropriate and disrespectful. In all regions, never refuse

to eat the local delicacy, no matter how unpleasant it might seem.

In the home country, it is wise to approach the negotiation process with as much market intelligence as possible so that the negotiation team is not caught off guard, surprised, or taken advantage of. When negotiating with international partners, the team needs this same information as well as cultural knowledge, awareness, and sensitivity. In international situations, there is greater risk of undermining a position by committing a cultural faux pas but at the same time, counterparts face that risk, too.

FOOD FOR THOUGHT

1. How does your company currently gather data on markets and consumers? How can you improve this process?

2. What are some ways to get to know individuals and consultants who know the state of the market and the competitive environment?

3. Language familiarity is one of the best ways to demonstrate commitment and sincerity. How can your company encourage language learning?

4. What is your company's perspective on concessions? How do you ensure that the big picture is not lost?

FURTHER READINGS

Axtell, Roger. *Essential Do's and Taboos: The Complete Guide to International Business and Leisure Travel.* New York, NY: John Wiley & Sons, 2007.

Jolles, Robert. *The Way of the Road Warrior: Lessons in Business and Life from the Road Most Traveled.* New York, NY: John Wiley & Sons, 2006.

Martin, Jeanette, and Chaney Lillian. *Global Business Etiquette: A Guide to International Communication and Customs.* Westport, CT: Praeger Publishers, 2006.

Requejo, William H. and John Graham. *Global Negotiation.* New York, NY: Palgrave Macmillan, 2008.

ONLINE RESOURCES

Tips for Business Travel Abroad
www.bizmove.com/export/m7i.htm

Going Global: A New Era in Cross-Cultural Communications

www.going-global.com/articles/a_new_era_in_cross-cultural_communications.htm

US-China Business Council: Chinese Business Etiquette
www.uschina.org/info/china-briefing-book/section6a.html

World Biz: Country-specific reports on doing successful business worldwide
www.worldbiz.com/index.php

DISCUSSION QUESTIONS

1. What are the stages of negotiation? Discuss.

2. Why is "bridging the cultural chasm" essential for success in cross-cultural negotiations?

3. What are "cultural faux pas?" Give some examples.

4. Why do different cultures show different negotiation styles?

5. Why does an expert negotiator show convergent communication skills? What does integrative negotiation require?

6. How do different cultures influence the negotiation process? Discuss examples.

7. Why are cultural intelligence, etiquette, protocol, and behavior important in cross-border negotiations?

8

Chapter 8 discusses cross-cultural communications, their impact upon negotiation, and their effect on the selling process. It offers a review of the interpersonal communication process and the impact of culture on the *encoding* and *decoding* processes. The reader will have the opportunity to review the importance of past negotiation experience, individual personal differences of those in the negotiating team, pre-negotiation expectations, inter-team goal compatibility, and the meaning of *trust* to the success of negotiations. The chapter offers insights into the global selling process. For instance, the reader will learn how to *identify sales prospects and qualify them, preparing for presentation and negotiation*. Here, the reader will have the opportunity to use the knowledge acquired in the previous chapters to better understand the impact of different cultures upon communication and decision making.

Selling Across Cultures reviews the selling process in a cross-cultural environment. Issues of *trust, commitment, expectations, exchange*, and other cross-cultural communication elements are discussed and their potential impact noted. The Hofstede model is used to understand the various cultural contexts in which selling may be taking place.

8.1

Cross-Cultural Communication, Negotiation and the Global Selling Process

Earl D. Honeycutt, John B. Ford, and Antonis C. Simintiras

Earl D. Honeycutt, John B. Ford, and Antonis C. Simintiras

T his chapter covers cross-cultural communication, negotiation, and the initial steps of the selling process.

KEY TERMS

- Encoding, Decoding, and Noise.
- Shadowing and Role-playing.
- Sense making and Sense giving.

Introduction

This book is written for the sales manager who will lead a global sales force. Much of the material presented in Chapter 2 [of the original text] details cultural sensitivity and training activities to enhance the sales force's chances of success in the field. This chapter [builds] upon this cultural background

Earl D. Honeycutt, John B. Ford, and Antonis C. Simintiras, "Cross-Cultural Communication, Nego-tiation, and the Global Selling Process I," *Sales Management: A Global Perspective*, pp. 55-71. Copyright © 2003 by Taylor & Francis Group. Reprinted with permission.

by explaining three processes that significantly affect cross-cultural selling. In order for a salesperson to achieve success in sales, it is imperative that he or she understands: (1) how interpersonal communication occurs, (2) the nature of the negotiations process, and (3) the steps involved in the selling process. The smooth functioning of these three processes is complicated by differing cultural backgrounds of the two main players—the prospective buyer and seller. Armed with the cultural knowledge that serves as a fundamental component of this book, proper strategic preparations can be undertaken by the sales manager to ensure their sales force has the necessary knowledge to close the sale. This [reading] presents the first two processes and the initial steps of the selling process. [...]

The Interpersonal Communication Process

The first requirement for success in sales is to insure that the salesperson can effectively communicate with current and potential customers. Of course, the communication of ideas from the sales manager to the salesperson is just as important as communication between the salesperson and potential buyer. The interpersonal communication process, shown in Figure 8.1, begins with an idea in the mind of the person who wants to communicate that idea to another person. That idea must

be translated into a form that enables it to be communicated. This requires the translation of the idea into a series of signs and symbols (language), known as *encoding*, which is used for communication.

These signs and symbols are then transmitted by means of a communication medium (e.g., spoken words, written words). The receiver next attempts to translate the received signs and symbols into an idea, which is called *decoding*. Of course, it is important that the idea received by the potential customer match as closely as possible with the original thought in the salesperson's mind. What makes this a challenge is that during the communication process, *noise* or distortion can significantly affect what is heard and understood by the receiver. Imagine the noise potential when a UK salesperson initially meets with an important Korean customer who has only a limited understanding of the English language. Given this disparity, then add to the communication challenges the distractions that exist in a normal business workplace environment (e.g., manufacturing processes, other conversations, outside noises), and it becomes clear how noise can seriously affect what is actually heard and understood by each party. Now,

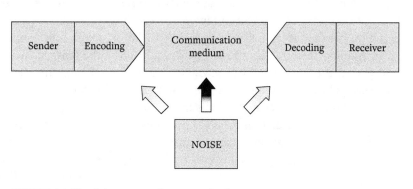

FIGURE 8.1 The interpersonal communication process

Case Vignette   Preparing for Middle East Negotiations

Robert Fraser, a sales manager for a large defense contractor in California, is scheduled to travel to the Middle East next month to discuss sales of aircraft and tanks to the governments of that region. This will be Fraser's first trip to this area of the world and he wants to make a favorable impression. He wonders what type of preparation he should undergo to insure he can successfully interact without offending his hosts.

think about how cultural awkwardness between the buyer and seller can exacerbate the situation.

Fortunately, in an interpersonal context, immediate feedback can be used to clarify the ideas involved in the communication effort. The sender can ask the receiver what they understood was communicated, which permits further explanation or clarification, when necessary. The important role of the salesperson is to insure that he or she understands the language of the potential customer as well as possible so that an accurate meeting of minds occurs.

Often, in cross-cultural settings, inability to understand contextual nuances of the language leads to misunderstandings. When the salesperson calling upon the potential customer is unsure of the language involved, then it is imperative that he or she employs a bilingual interpreter who can assist the two parties in reaching a meaningful agreement. In the event that the salesperson does not know the buyer's language, then just having sales materials written in that language by experts does not ensure that a meeting of the minds will occur, since there is no way for the two parties to effectively seek clarification. Clarification in communication is the key to success, and the interpreter brings a necessary component to the first meetings between buyer and seller. It may be possible, with language training, that later meetings will not require an interpreter, but this may only be viable once a solid relationship has been built between the salesperson and the cross-cultural customer. It is important to remember that cultural awareness [...] provides the salesperson with tools to minimize the impact of noise and distortion during the communication process.

The Negotiation Process

In addition to clarity of communication between the parties, a clear understanding of the negotiation process is integrally important to sales success. When the sales manager understands what is involved in this important process, then he or she can provide helpful training for the salesperson to understand how to arrive at the best position in any negotiation. The negotiation process is shown in Figure 8.2 and each component of the process is discussed below. The first section focuses on the antecedents to negotiation, which include the perspectives the salesperson and prospective buyer bring to the sales negotiation process. The second section involves the negotiation process components, sense making and sense giving, where the parties attempt to process the relevant information. The final section covers the outcomes of the negotiation process.

Antecedents to negotiation

NATIONAL CULTURAL SIMILARITY

One of the most important things the salesperson and prospective cross-cultural customer bring to the negotiation process is their basic national cultural makeup. Chapter 2 [of the original text] discusses national cultural characteristics, and what becomes clear by understanding culture is that the more similar the cultural backgrounds of the parties involved, the greater the chance for understanding and agreement between the parties. Of course, this is made more difficult in the business-to-business sales process; however, if sales teams are utilized, then the more similar the members of the sales team are to those of the prospective buying group, the greater the chance of clear understanding among all parties involved. Intuitively, cultural differences create a potential for misunderstandings and perceived behavioral discrepancies; however, it is the purpose of this book to sensitize the sales manager to culture and its impact and, as a result, minimize the potential for conflict in interactions. This certainly includes the negotiation process. One cautionary note is that the salesperson should not make assumptions about what the cross-cultural customer is thinking or feeling unless both parties are from the same or a similar culture. It is easy to become overconfident and assume that there is complete agreement when in fact there is not. With proper knowledge and preparation, even negotiating parties from widely disparate cultures can reach lasting and beneficial agreements. In such situations preparation and sensitivity are the keys to guiding the other party to a successful outcome.

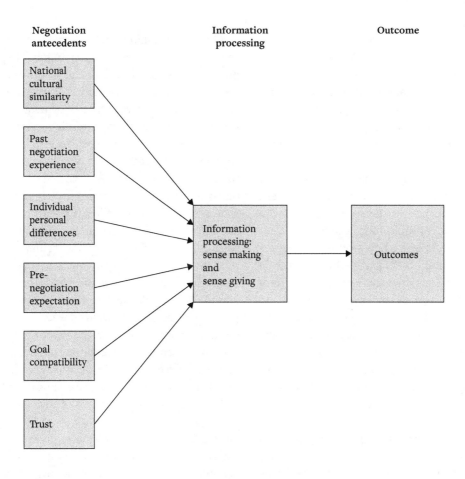

FIGURE 8.2 The cross-cultural negotiation process

PAST NEGOTIATION EXPERIENCE

Research shows that the more experience the salesperson brings to cross-cultural negotiations, the greater their flexibility in dealing with and guiding cross-cultural customers to successful negotiation outcomes. The global sales manager can provide training to compensate for lack of negotiation experience. One training method is to have their most successful and seasoned veterans teach new salespeople what to expect and how to handle themselves during negotiations. This training should be conducted on a periodic basis, by a variety of veteran salespeople that offer suggestions and give help to less experienced salespeople. Other helpful techniques involve: (1) allowing inexperienced salespeople to *shadow* or accompany seasoned veterans to observe how they conduct themselves in different cross-cultural negotiations settings with opportunity for debriefing afterwards or (2) *role playing*, where veterans put trainees through mock negotiations in either or both roles as buyer and seller and subsequently critique them on their handling of different situations. It is particularly helpful to videotape role-play exercises and show the trainees how they did. Trainees also learn a great deal when they watch themselves and hear helpful suggestions from more experienced colleagues or supervisors. Significant improvement is often seen when trainees take part in follow-up role-playing exercises.

INDIVIDUAL PERSONAL DIFFERENCES

While national cultural characteristics and past experience are both important influencers in the negotiation process, other individual personal characteristics are also important. Personal characteristics contribute to each person's individuality and include enduring characteristics like personality, intelligence, and creativity along with such transient characteristics as mood or emotion. The important issue is the ability of the individual to recognize inherent differences and to be sensitive about how they can affect the negotiation process. Even in collectivist cultures, like Japan, where individuality is often suppressed for the betterment of the organization, there are personal traits that can emerge in negotiations and which need to be considered. For example, imagine how traveling for thirty hours or more could affect the negotiating abilities of a Japanese buyer who has come to negotiate a long-term supply contract with your company. The buyer would be tired and potentially in a poor mental state to reach agreement during the sales meeting. It would be best to offer that person the opportunity to sleep and be refreshed before beginning sales negotiation meetings. It is equally important to recognize that in these types of collectivist cultures, individual powers are often minimized for the protection of the group as a whole, which potentially impact the negotiation process in profound ways. A Japanese corporate customer may not have the authority to make the important decisions involved and a series of negotiations may be required before the sales agreement can be successfully reached. One way to effectively deal with personal individual differences is to learn as much as possible about the particular individual before any face-to-face meeting so that their personal actions or mannerisms can be put into the proper context. The more the salesperson knows about the potential customer, the better prepared they will be to recognize differences and avoid situations where these differences could negatively affect personal negotiations. It is also important for the salesperson to be trained to recognize how their own moods or emotions could negatively affect their dealings with others and to avoid conflict before it happens.

PRE-NEGOTIATION EXPECTATIONS

The expectations the parties bring with them also have a significant bearing on the success of the sales negotiation process. Some sizing up of the expectations of each of the parties is necessary so that potential

conflict can be minimized. It is important to remember that compromise is a necessity in most negotiation processes (especially in cultures where negotiations are an important part of daily life). Take for example countries like Italy where the enjoyment of the negotiation process can affect people in their daily lives as when buyers go to street vendors to buy goods. The thrill of the negotiation process in that situation drives the dealings. This suggests that the potential seller needs to plan for compromise so that an initial offer is set artificially high to allow negotiations to proceed and the buyer is given the satisfaction of making personal gains by paying a lower price than was originally proffered. Suppose that the salesperson came to the table with a price that was the lowest that they could offer. Where would the buyer have room to gain any personal satisfaction? Obviously, when the salesperson possesses knowledge about the negotiations expectations of the cross-cultural buyer, the better position they will be in to succeed in negotiations. This requires the salesperson to spend time listening to and possibly acting as a problem solver for the buyer.

GOAL COMPATIBILITY

Another factor that affects the success of the sales negotiation process is the compatibility of the parties' goals. The closer that these goals are in sync with one another, the greater the possibility of reaching a successful agreement. As a result, it becomes imperative for the salesperson to determine the buyer's goals. Careful listening may be the best way to ascertain the nature of not only the buyer's personal goals, but also the goals of their organization. If the negotiations are in a business-to-business context, the goals of the organization normally take precedence over the personal goals of the buyer. Another important point to make is that national culture may have a significant effect on goal compatibility, since buyers from collectivist countries are more focused on the goals of the organization that they represent than their own personal goals.

TRUST

The final antecedent to negotiation is trust. In this case, this means the trust the individual has for the other person or persons involved in the negotiation process. The greater the amount of mutual trust that exists among the negotiating parties, the greater the chance for a successful agreement. Trust focuses on the issue of the integrity among the individuals involved and their perceived benevolence. If integrity is clearly established, and it is believed that the other parties are concerned about the well-being of all involved, then the information that is shared will be relatively free and open, and the negotiation process will work smoothly. Obviously, if the salesperson has had prior dealings with the potential cross-cultural buyer, trust may be easier to establish. However, if there have been no prior dealings, then there will probably be reluctance to openly share relevant information. In this situation, it becomes extremely important for the salesperson to act to build trust as quickly as possible. This can be accomplished through openness, honesty, and a sharing of important information. Providing important information is a sign of trust, and the show of trust on the part of one participant can break down the walls of distrust. If the salesperson has never dealt with the potential buyer, it may be possible to determine trustworthiness by seeking references from others who have had dealings with that individual or group of individuals. The key is to conduct homework ahead of time to find out whatever you can about the other parties involved in the sales negotiation process.

Information variables

The important information-related variables that interplay with each other during the negotiation process are *sense making* and *sense giving*. They capture the actual information conveyance and processing the parties participate in during negotiations. Each is described in detail below.

SENSE MAKING

Sense making involves the way in which an individual assigns meaning to the information presented by one or more parties involved in the sales negotiation process. It is concerned with the attempt to understand the offer being presented or the stand being taken by the other party or parties. The communication process discussed earlier plays an important role, since the effective use of feedback is integral to sense making. When the salesperson has trouble understanding the

logic of the buyer's stance, clarity of logic can be established through further discussion. Sense making is enhanced by clear communication.

SENSE GIVING

Sense giving involves how effectively the individual attempts to communicate the necessary information that allows the other party or parties to make sense of his or her position in the sales negotiation. When any of the negotiating parties withhold information, then it becomes more difficult to assign appropriate meaning to the extended offer. Again, clear cross-cultural communication must occur to effectively give meaning to the recipient of the conveyed information. [...]

Outcomes

Intuitively, an appropriate outcome for the sales negotiation process is a successful agreement. As a result, inability to reach a meeting of minds is an unsuccessful outcome. There, of course, may be a need for further meetings, especially when the individuals negotiating must seek permission from those higher in the organization before finalizing the agreement. The minimum goal of the salesperson for any negotiation should be complete agreement with those involved on exactly where they stand and what needs to be done at that point to successfully complete the process. Leaving things unstated or "up in the air" enhances the chances that there will be no successful outcome to the process. At a minimum, the salesperson should always summarize the stances of the parties and clarify the next steps that will be involved before buyer or buying group members leave the negotiation.

Practical suggestions for improving the sales negotiation process. Given the nature of the sales negotiation process, some practical suggestions will help the sales manager to understand what information must be given to their salespeople to enhance their chances of success in cross-cultural negotiations. First James Sebenius, at Harvard Business School, suggests that it is important for the party entering the negotiation to ascertain: (1) who the real players are in the negotiation and (2) who has the authority to make the necessary decisions.[1] Once such matters are clearly understood, effective strategies for handling negotiations can then be mapped out.

One of the most effective lists of suggestions for what to do and what not to do in cross-cultural negotiations is the following list of "dos" and "don'ts":[2]

Do:
- Know your subject and be well prepared.
- Specify clear objectives and know your bottom line.
- Develop personal relationships but be careful not to be manipulated.
- Seek opportunities for informal get-togethers, since that is where most initial contacts will be made.
- Meticulously follow protocol: cross-cultural parties are often more conscious of status than Americans.
- Understand national sensitivities and do not violate them.
- Assess the flexibility of your opponent and the obstacles he or she faces.
- Understand the decision-making process and build upon your position by taking advantage of each step.
- Pin down details.

Don't:
- Look at everything from your own definition of what determines a rational and scientific viewpoint.
- Press a point when others are not prepared to accept it.
- Look at things from your own narrow self-interest.
- Ask for concessions or compromises that are politically or culturally sensitive.
- Stick to your agenda if the other party has a different set of priorities.
- Use jargon that will confuse the other side.
- Skip authority levels, since you will need middle management to implement the agreement.
- Ask for a decision that you know the other side can't or isn't ready to make.
- Differ with members of your own team in public.

- Stake out extreme positions; be consistent in your approach.

Finally, understanding the communication process, clarity, cultural sensitivity and awareness of how mood and emotion can affect the process increase the chances that meaningful communications will occur, and this enhances the chances for success in reaching a successful sales agreement.

The Global Selling Process

The third important process for success in global sales is the selling process. Clear communications and effective negotiations are necessary once there is a face-to-face meeting between buyer and seller, but the seven steps of the global selling process have been proven in corporate use for generations, and when performed correctly, help the salesperson conclude the sale. The seven steps are: (1) finding customers, (2) preparing, (3) relationship building, (4) product offering, (5) offer clarification, (6) securing the purchase, and (7) maintaining the relationship.

Salespersons follow specific steps that, when successfully implemented, result in prospective or existing customers making a purchase. In the global marketplace, it is necessary for salespersons to follow a more diverse sales process than they might in domestic markets. That is, in a homogeneous domestic market, the salesperson can follow a similar sales process for many of their customers. However, in a multicultural or global market, sales-persons must alter the sales process to account for cultural variations. Depending upon the salesperson–customer relationship, which is formed by cumulative interactions, different amounts of time and effort must be devoted to each process step.

Personal selling is "the" principal promotional tool utilized by the sales firm in the global marketplace. In some cultures, personal selling receives even greater emphasis when local laws restrict advertising and salespersons are inexpensive to employ. For example, in China, a US medical equipment firm hires physicians and nurses to sell to other health care providers.[3] In many developing nations low wages permit the firm to hire and deploy a larger sales force.[4] The first two of the seven steps of the selling process are presented belo [...].

Finding customers

The first step in the sales process, finding customers, consists of two actions: (1) identifying sales prospects and (2) insuring that these potential clients are worthy of additional effort being invested in converting them from prospect to customer. For example, the French firm Cerestar compiled a list of thousands of possible corn starch users in China. Company sales representatives then began to cold call to assess actual customer needs from trading firms, distributors, and representative offices. The sales force found this process to be frustrating because many potential customers were reluctant to talk to strangers and others were bankrupt. In the end, less than 10 percent of the firms on the original list were qualified as potential customers.[5]

IDENTIFYING SALES PROSPECTS

Depending upon the industry and local custom, global salespersons may devote a portion of their work day searching for and contacting new customers. A multitude of reasons explain why a salesperson must find new customers. These include current customers going out of business, relocating, switching to competitors, and even dying! This is why, in certain industries, a salesperson must allocate a significant portion of time to generating new customers. In industrial or business-to-business (B2B) sales, less emphasis is placed upon finding new customers. This is because there are fewer B2B customers, and these accounts have been initially qualified—perhaps by analyzing their SIC code and making a personal visit—and it is rare for new manufacturers to enter the market after the product reaches the maturity stage. However, one global sales manager reports that his job is to enlarge the upper part of the funnel by finding more customers for his sales force to call upon.[6]

In certain sales positions, like insurance, auto sales, and copiers, the customer's needs are temporarily satisfied once the product or service is delivered. It is then possible for the salesperson to "grow" these accounts by having the customer trade up to higher priced or higher quality products/services. In the interim, the salesperson must identify new customers while waiting for existing clients to repurchase. Although there are a large number of sources for finding potential customers, this discussion is meant to be less than complete. Suffice it to say that salespersons have a significant number of methods for finding new customers (see Exhibit 8.1). A few methods employed to locate potential customers are presented in detail below.

Customer recommendations. Satisfied customers can provide the salesperson with a list of his/her friends and colleagues who have a need for the product. In fact, in certain industries it is standard practice for salespersons to ask the customer to provide two or three potential "leads" that might also benefit from purchasing the product represented by the salesperson. The salesperson should not pressure the customer for these names if they are reluctant to offer them and should realize that in certain cultures it is not appropriate behavior to share information about friends or business associates. Most salespersons believe there is no better recommendation than that of a satisfied customer.

Centers of influence. There are influential persons in every community who can recommend potential customers to the salesperson. These leaders—be they civic, religious, or business—should be cultivated for sales leads over breakfast or lunch once or twice a year. The salesperson must be careful not to use the leader's name with the customer unless agreed to by the center of influence. Likewise, the salesperson must be subtle in these meetings and must share information of value in a *"quid pro quo"* relationship with the leader.

Lists. Numerous lists are available for identifying prospective clients. These lists may be as basic as a summary of members of a church, synagogue, or mosque, country club, sports club, property owners' association, or university alumni association. A salesperson must be cautious when utilizing organizational lists so that it is not transparent to the prospects that a salesperson is calling upon group members.

Firms or salespersons can also purchase prospective customer lists from professional agents or firms that derive their data from new product registrations or, in countries where permissible, government databases such as drivers' licenses or voters' lists. These databases may not be current, since in today's highly mobile society people regularly relocate because of

Exhibit 8.1   Methods of finding customers

Over the years, creative sales personnel and managers have established a large number of methods for identifying potential customers.

Methods of locating new customers can be organized into four categories—internal to the firm, external to the firm, promotional sources, and personal sources/actions. Multiple examples of each source are explained briefly below.

INTERNAL SOURCES

- Company records—examine existing records for previous customers or contacts.
- Inactive accounts—former customers who stopped purchasing.
- Junior sales personnel/sales associates—use less costly or new personnel to call or contact potential customers through cold calls or identify through research.
- Telemarketing:
    - Inbound—calls to toll-free numbers requesting information about products. Outbound—calls by sales associates to qualify and establish sales meetings.
- Phone/mail inquiries—inquiries to the firm about products or special offers.
- Caller identification—phone numbers of people who have dialed the firm.
- Other company salespersons—firm salespersons that work in other territories/ products.
- Service department—notification by service manager that product cannot be repaired.
- Credit department—notification that customer is seeking credit approval.
- Surveys—market research information that customer completes
- Current large accounts—potential needs among other departments or divisions.

EXTERNAL SOURCES

- Satisfied customers—ask customer for name of potential customers.
- Endless chain—ask each customer for three to five names; always more than closing ratio.
- Center of influence/community contact—individual in community who can provide information about new firms, managers, or company plans.
- Networking—social relationships that provide business-related information.
- Professional society/civic meetings/social events—opportunities to network and seek information about potential customers.
- Contact agent—external firms that are paid to identify/qualify potential customers.
- Friends and acquaintances—family and friends can suggest potential customers.
- Non-competing salespeople—information shared between salespersonnel from different industries about potential customers that need products from both.
- Salesperson swap meet—special meeting to exchange names between noncompeting salespersons.
- Cultivate visible accounts—make cold calls to visible accounts in territory.
- Chamber of commerce—business organization has membership list of existing and new members.
- Engineering departments of potential customers—technical information about future customer needs.
- Lists:
    - Broker lists—lists of potential customers purchased from list broker.
    - Clubs, universities, companies—membership lists of these groups
    - Computerized databases—databases available from state or credit sources.
- Directories:
    - Industrial directory—directories published by specific industries.
    - Business directory—directories published for specific locations.
    - Local, state, national directories—government-sponsored directories.

PROMOTIONAL SOURCES

- Broadcast media—radio/television commercials with phone number.
- Contests—register to win a free product; nonwinners are potential purchasers.
- Group parties/meetings—meetings of neighbors, church groups, or friends.
- Internet—responses to web site or e-mail messages.
- Media advertising—print advertisements with phone number

- of mail-in postcard.
- Direct Mail—outgoing mail that informs potential customer and provides phone number or contact information for salesperson.
- Trade publication ads—ads in magazine or journal that focuses on industry.
- Shows—shows that exhibit product or introduce new model(s) for one or more companies.
- Trade shows—large shows where all competitors for industry are present.
- Educational seminars—meet-

- ings where new laws or technologies are explained to potential customers. Interested attendees can be identified.
- Sales letters—direct mail signed and sent by salesperson.
- Business-related articles in publications—similar to public relations; a technical article about a new product or an article about a personality that requests individuals wanting to learn more about the product or engineering knowledge to contact the company.

PERSONAL ACTIONS

- Observation—maintaining a watchful eye on new businesses.
- Cold calling—stopping by unannounced and talking to manager/purchaser.
- Spotters/bird dog—agent who sends potential customers to salesperson and, when suc-

- cessful, is paid a commission.
- Business card referral system—similar to spotters; business card given to potential customer, who returns to salesperson for a discount, free gift, etc.
- The itch cycle—contacting former customer just before normal repurchase cycle.

- Orphan adoption—taking over accounts when salesperson leaves firm.
- Technical advancement—contacting customers who have earlier model.
- Claim staking—claiming customers not being serviced by other salespersons.

business transfers or personal choice. In many cultures, citizens are reluctant to provide personal information to market researchers or government agents, so there will not be lists available in these cultures.

Publications. It is possible for the salesperson to learn about new business openings by gathering information from the business section of the newspaper or local business periodicals. In some B2B industries there is a trade journal that publicizes new product introductions, plant openings, and acquisitions/mergers.

Referrals. Potential customers can be referred by company maintenance personnel and sales colleagues. For example, a salesperson from another territory may learn of a need that exists at an office or manufacturing plant located in your territory from his customer. In certain industries, the maintenance manager will notify the salesperson when a customer has requested

maintenance on a product that needs to be replaced. In most cases, these sources pass the salesperson's name or business card to potential customers that make contact with the salesperson.

Advertising-generated. Many industrial firms advertise their products/services and provide either a postcard the reader can use to request additional information or samples. These advertisements also provide avenues for contacting the company in the form of a toll-free phone number, web site, or e-mail address.

QUALIFYING

Once a sufficient number of potential customers is generated, they must be evaluated and prioritized based upon relevant criteria. This step is equally important because not all potential customers qualify for additional sales emphasis, based upon one or more of the following reasons:

- *Money* Can the customer afford to buy the product? Do they have cash, credit, an open account, or an item to trade that results in both the buyer and the seller being better off? In Asia, salespersons monitor the funding status of their customers to insure time is not wasted on customers who do not have the money to purchase.[7]
- *Authority* Does the individual or location the salesperson works at have the authority to purchase? Can they commit or obligate the firm or themselves by signing a purchase order or contract?
- *Need* Does the buyer need the good? In other words, will the buyer or the organization gain utility from purchasing the product/service?
- *Fit* Does the potential buyer's organizational culture fit the culture of the seller? If the buyer's culture is totally divergent from that of the seller, then the ensuing exchange will likely be frustrating and not worth the required effort. One example of a poor fit is when the potential buyer requests that the seller offer a reduced unit price by lowering production standards. Depending upon the importance of the buyer, a decision to conduct business based upon fit will be made by upper management (see Exhibit 8.2).

One expert claims that Chinese salespersons often fail to qualify their customers, because business is still practiced based upon personal relationships or "guan-xi" rather than business potential. This suggests that in certain cultures, the salesperson must be more closely supervised and directed. When customers are to be "qualified," the manager must set clear goals along with a path to achieve those goals.[8] In response, one Chinese manager states that business in China is "still largely unstructured and irrational." A customer that is disqualified today may become a qualified customer tomorrow and then it will be too late to develop a relationship.[9]

If the answer to any one of these four qualification questions—money, authority, need, and fit—cannot be "yes," the salesperson is wasting time by calling upon the prospective buyer. Because an industrial sales call is expensive, firms can ill afford to have their professional sales force calling upon customers who cannot or will not purchase a product. Such behavior misdirects both the time and talent of the sales force. An old American sales proverb is that "a good salesperson can sell ice to an eskimo." However, in today's global market the correct attitude is that a good salesperson has no desire to sell a product to anyone who has no need for the item.

Preparing

Successful salespersons spend significant time preparing for meetings with potential customers. In fact, a professional salesperson devotes time to learn about the qualified prospect, their culture, their organization, product line(s), competitors, and past relationship history between the buyer/seller firms. Today's salesperson must average four or five sales calls before making a sale.[10] In culturally diverse global markets, where it is necessary to get to know the partner well and form long-term relationships, the requisite number of sales calls will be even higher. For example, before major decisions are made in Japan, preliminary meetings are held to discuss what will happen during the decision meeting. In this way both parties know beforehand any controversial issues that may arise, as well as the outcome of the meeting.[11]

During the preparation stage, the salesperson can gain information from existing company files, customer relationship management (CRM) software, the potential customer's web site, and commercial sources such as magazines, newspapers, and commercial sources. Also, when interacting with different cultures it is essential to seek information about the cultural norms and expectations from salespersons and managers who have worked successfully in the culture, from resource books and, as appropriate, from consultants. In most situations, the more that is known about the prospective customer, the greater the probability of identifying and satisfying existing needs and forming a long-term relationship. It should be obvious, based upon the time that must be devoted to this effort, that the salesperson can make this type of commitment only for potentially profitable customers.

Before meeting with the prospect, the salesperson should insure that he or she can correctly pronounce the prospect's name. One technique for gaining

Exhibit 8.2   are all customers a good fit?

When global firms initiate business contacts with new customers, the cultural and economic fit between the two firms should be investigated. Situations encountered in China by global firms aptly illustrate this point. Even with membership in the World Trade Organization (WTO), global firms know that making a sale in China does not mean you will get paid for the goods. As a result, high levels of credit or "accounts receivable," caused by a lack of working capital, are constraining growth in the Chinese marketplace. Global firms now add "receivables" to a long list of difficulties that include fake products, incompetent joint venture partners, protectionism, and government regulations. These problems impact global and domestic firms that conduct business with government-owned enterprises in China.

When government-sponsored firms fail, a chain reaction of events is created: the bankrupt firm cannot pay distributors and distributors are unable to pay their suppliers.

In response, Nike and other global firms restrict or deny credit to problem accounts. While this approach retards growth, Nike believes the economic health of the brand and business are maintained. Asimco, an automotive parts supplier, took a different approach and pays managers a bonus based upon the joint venture's earnings, which are affected negatively by accounts receivable. Some government-run companies pay Asimco through barter, like receiving trucks as payment for parts. This requires Asimco to use the trucks in its business or sell them on the open market. As a result, Asimco sells fewer products in

China and more to other Asian countries. Procter & Gamble and Gillette adopted different approaches to deal with errant payers. Both global firms demand mortgage guarantees, which means that if a debtor fails to pay, their property must be forfeited. Gillette also requires third-party guarantees. Gillette believes the third-party guarantee system is very effective for securing payment. Gillette is also paying closer attention to financial statements, assets, and distribution systems to assess the financial viability of potential customers. Therefore, a global firm would be wise to not conduct business with a firm unless an acceptable fit exists between the buyer and seller.

Source. Trisha Saywell, "Accounts Unreceivable," *Far Eastern Economic Report*, July 6, 2000, 66–8.

---

this knowledge is to call the prospective customer's assistant or company receptionist to confirm the appointment, which insures the salesperson hears and correctly pronounces the prospect's name. One of the authors telephoned a Philippine office to confirm an appointment and pronounced the manager's name in Tagalog, the national language. It was quite a surprise to learn the manager was an American with a Spanish-appearing family name that was pronounced quite differently. Other information about the prospect, such as hobbies, interests, and likes/dislikes, also makes getting acquainted easier and may shed light upon the type of gift the prospect would value.

The salesperson should also anticipate the types of products the prospect will need and how these products will satisfy those needs. The salesperson should possess an accurate understanding of how their products compare with competitors' and why the prospect is purchasing or might prefer a competitive product

instead of the one being offered. In other words, the salesperson should have a plan for approaching the prospect that anticipates questions and concerns that may be raised during the initial meeting(s). Such planning should be repeated for future meetings as well.

Formal presentations should be compiled, using professional software or transparencies as dictated by technology and culture. In developing countries like India, it may be risky to use high-technology equipment for sales presentations.[12] Therefore, global salespersons should prepare transparencies or flip charts as a backup for computer-generated presentations. It is also prudent for the salesperson to practice the formal presentation for important customers in the presence of technical and managerial staff. In so doing, the sales presentation can be reviewed for clarity and technical competence. This process also insures the salesperson's presentation accurately portrays management's point of view.

CHAPTER SUMMARY

Global sales managers must be prepared to provide their global sales force with the necessary tools to ensure sales success. The interpersonal communication process affects the success of communications between the salesperson and their prospective customer. The sales negotiation process is also important, since it affects the ability of the salesperson and the prospective customer to reach an acceptable agreement.

Finally, the seven steps of the personal selling process are important, as they help the salesperson to organize their efforts toward building a meaningful relationship with the prospective customer and produce sales in both the present and the future. This chapter presented the first two of these processes and the steps of the selling process leading up to the initial meeting with the prospective customer.

DISCUSSION QUESTIONS

1. What is the interpersonal communication process, and why is it so important for the global salesperson?

2. What are the different antecedents to negotiation, and how can the global salesperson deal effectively with each?

3. What is the difference between sense making and sense giving, and why are they important in the sales negotiation process?

4. What are some suggestions for things to do and things not to do during the sales negotiation process?

5. What are the seven different steps of the global selling process?

6. What are six different mechanisms for identifying potential customers that could be used by the global salesperson?

7. Why is preparation so important for the global salesperson?

8. How would customer relationship management software be used during the preparation stage by the global salesperson?

References

Sebenius, James K. (2002), "The Hidden Challenge of Cross-border Negotiations," *Harvard Business Review*, March, 76–85.

Herbig, Paul, and Hugh Kramer (1992), "Dos and Don'ts of Cross-cultural Negotiations," *Industrial Marketing Management*, 21, 287–98.

Xu, Gang "Jerry" (2001), E-mail communication in response to questions, July 12.

Terpstra, Vern, and Ravi Sarathy (2000), *International Marketing*, eighth edition, Fort Worth TX: Dryden Press.

Lawrence, Susan V. (2000), "Formula for Disaster," *Far Eastern Economic Review*, October 5, 52–4.

Xu, Gang "Jerry" (2001), E-mail communication in response to questions, July 12.

Xu, Gang "Jerry" (2001), E-mail communication in response to questions, July 12.

Miller, Chip E. (1996), "US Techniques not Best for Chinese Sales Reps," *Marketing News*, November 4, 5.

Xu, Gang "Jerry" (2001), E-mail communication in response to questions, July 12.

Morris, Michael, Leyland Pitt, and Earl Honeycutt (2001), *Business-to-Business Marketing*, Fair Oaks CA: Sage Publications.

Daft, Doug (2000), "Coke's New Formula," *Far Eastern Economic Review*, April 20, 64–5.

Honeycutt, Earl D., Jr., John B. Ford, and Lew Kurtzman (1996), "Potential Problems and Solutions when Hiring a Worldwide Sales Team," *Industrial Marketing Management*, 11:1, 42–54.

Selling Across Cultures

8.2

Anup Soans and Joshua Soans

I n 1991, India opened up its markets to the world economy, bringing a billion people into the global market. They were made up of over 2,000 ethnicities, 1,576 "mother tongues," eight major religions, and thousands of local dietary and religious practices. Multinationals entering the Indian market would have to successfully navigate this cultural jungle to survive and thrive.

The fact that McDonald's, the world's largest seller of beef products, has a thriving business in India, the land of the sacred cow, is proof that cultural differences are only a barrier when a company fails in its due diligence. McDonald's has a strict "no-beef, no-pork" policy in India because the cow is widely worshipped by Hindus and consumption of pork is forbidden in Islam. Instead, the fast-food chain has a variety of vegetarian and chicken dishes in local flavors and is considered to be just as Indian by urbanites as curry and naan. Because of its cultural astuteness the world over, McDonald's has become the poster child for "glocalization"—the art of being global in character but local in spirit.

In her book *111 Ideas to Engage Global Audiences*, Renie McClay says, "there is not a 'there' when learning about other cultures. You don't learn everything about a culture." What businesses do need to factor in when selling across cultures are the "known knowns" and "known unknowns" of cultural behaviors.

A key role for sales managers is to help sellers "translate" their sales process into the language and practices of their customers to be effective. A simple Inter-net search on "selling to different cultures" will bring up several pages of useful information. Some important questions to ask when selling to different cultures are:

Anup Soans and Joshua Soans, "Selling Across Cultures," *The Art of Modern Sales Management*, ed. Renie McClay, pp. 65-73. Copyright © 2013 by Association for Talent Development (ATD). Reprinted with permission.

- How much time on average does it take to build trust and relationships with customers?
- How important are references and which references will carry more weight?
- How direct can you be with your questioning and probing?
- How strongly can you push the advantages and benefits of your product or service?
- How strongly can you push for a commitment from the customer?

Self-Awareness for the Seller

Knowledge of one's own cultural preferences and tendencies is the starting point for understanding and appreciating those of others. There are many ways to do this. A formal understanding of culture is always useful (and quite interesting!) if you have the time.

Since the pioneering work of Geert Hofstede in the 1970s, much work has been done on mapping out the cultural tendencies of countries and social groups using Hofstede's parameters of power distance, individualism, uncertainty avoidance, masculinity, and long-term orientation.

- Power distance is the degree to which social hierarchy is accepted and expected to be adhered to.
- Individualism is the degree to which individual behavior and responsibility is emphasized versus collective or group behavior and responsibility.
- Uncertainty avoidance measures a society's preference for regularity and systems versus ambiguity.
- Masculinity is the degree to which a society is imbued with "masculine" values like competition and heroism versus "feminine" values like cooperation and modesty.
- Long-term orientation can be interpreted as a society's preference for absolute truths and tradition (doing the right thing in the short run) at the

cost of contextual aptness versus a preference for practicable and amicable solutions with a focus on long-term stability and relationships.

A recent addition to these five parameters is indulgence versus restraint. The former stands for a society that encourages the basic human drives for pleasure and fun and the latter for societies that privilege stoicism and self-control. Even a bare minimum understanding of where one's own culture scores on these parameters can be an eye-opener. The Hofstede Centre website is a good place to start for those who want to better understand the cultural dimensions listed above and see how different countries compare.

Accounting for the Hofstede's dimensions while selling across cultures might seem like a daunting task, but like any skill, mastery is a function of awareness and practice. This is an area sales managers need to learn and excel and then they can help their sales teams to do the same.

For example, Americans doing business in Japan (as in many countries), need to adjust their normal selling practices. Expecting to close a deal with one or maybe two sales calls is not a reasonable expectation. You will build trust by repeatedly getting to know them, likely including social events for the purpose of getting to know each other. They are not just buying your product; they are buying the company and the individuals they will be working with.

In Latin America you gain favor with a referral from someone the prospect respects, so your network becomes vitally important there.

Alfredo Castro was teaching a sales workshop in Brazil to 12 directors from the same company, half from Brazil and half from Europe and Asia. The Brazilians had powerful narratives for engaging the other person in sales dialogue. They established a strong emotional connection and provided great reasons for doing business together. It was a very different approach from the Europeans and Asians, but they had to admit it had a positive impact on doing business and getting a "yes" from their customers.

Tips for Sellers

- Use Hofstede's Dimensions to clearly map out your cultural preferences and those of your customers and see how they compare.
- Which are the areas where your cultural preferences and the preferences of your customer are likely to be at odds?
- Culture aside, do your personality traits favor any of the above mentioned cultural preferences?

For example, are you someone who prefers order and regularity in your business dealings or are you comfortable with ambiguity and open-endedness? Are these traits in sync with the cultural tendencies of the customer (a strength to be played up) or are they at odds (a weakness to be mindful about)?

- Is there someone from the local culture whom you can trust? Is

that person familiar with your culture or better still, you? You might want to play out a critical scenario with him or her. There are also many professional service providers who can perform this role.

These questions are great for discussing in sales meetings, with new salespeople, and with veterans who are selling to a new geography or culture.

Be Clear and Forthright About Your Core Values

It is easy to fall prey to cultural relativism when doing business globally. Knowledge of what constitutes one's core beliefs and the role they play in the success of the enterprise undertaken will help avoid that pitfall. Sticking to core beliefs in the face of local opposition might look like short-changing oneself. But in the long run that always makes good business sense.

When Indian pharmaceutical companies started mushrooming after the Indian Patent Act of 1970 was passed, they demonstrated a knack for cutting corners in order to undercut the more well-established multinational companies (MNCs). Bribing doctors to buy prescriptions was one method employed. MNCs, known to maintain high standards of ethics and professionalism, soon joined the race. Today there is widespread activism and government crackdowns on these practices and MNCs can no longer claim the moral high ground. As a result, they have lost what used to be a unique selling proposition in attracting customers and professional talent.

Some values like precision, egalitarianism, diversity, and humanism are worth holding onto even when doing business across cultures. Most cultures respect

and reward some form of these values and the differences are often in how rather than what.

Sellers should:

- Identify or reaffirm the core values of the company, service, or product.
- Ask: "How do the core values differ from the peripheral ones?" For example, for a car manufacturer, passenger safety and precision engineering would be core values because they ensure that passengers stay safe and cars don't break down. Passenger comfort might be a peripheral value, as not all cultures demand comfort while driving.
- Ask: "What are the areas where conflicts may arise on account of differing values?"
- Ask: "How might these conflicts be resolved?" This might demand a compromise and can be tricky. Take gender for example. Many South Asian cultures may strongly enforce gender roles even in the corporate sphere. Does a company that values egalitarianism object to perceived injustice or simply choose to accept it?

Watch for clues from the client on managing conflict. For some countries, harmony is the most important thing. They do not hit tough topics head on verbally. Watch for verbal nuances and body language.

The Difference Between Culture and Personality

There is a fine line between cultural sensitivity and cultural stereotyping. Remember that culture describes a group of individuals, and personality describes the individual. Behavioral manifestations of cultural tendencies take place through filters of personality, economic background, education, and experience. Just because a country scores low on power distance in its culture, does not mean everyone you meet there will take kindly to backslapping bonhomie.

At best, knowledge of cultural mores can help one avoid more egregious faux pas, especially in a group setting. In India, for example, including a vegetarian menu at any social function involving food is an absolute must. However, assuming that everyone avoids meat is equally false.

Once aware about cultural themes that are particularly sensitive in nature, when it comes to individuals, the best thing to do is ask. Make it clear that you come from a different cultural setting, that you are aware of the cultural importance of a particular action, and ask how the person in question would prefer that action be performed.

Managing time will vary in different countries. In America, it is common to make appointments and expect the schedule to go as planned. America and Germany are two examples of being time focused versus being event focused. Showing up on time for appointments is important because time is seen as a precious commodity (time is money) and it is respectful to others to manage time well and in an organized, linear manner. Southern European and Arab countries take a different view of time. They are more event focused. For them the meeting or event is what is important, the precise starting time is less important. Many Asian cultures have an even different view—time is cyclical, as in the sun rising and setting daily for millions of years. It is not seen as a scarce commodity. Their view of time affects how they make decisions, careful and not in a hurry. Sales managers should be careful when planning their schedule globally—overscheduling can be a detriment; if one appointment goes long, it can mess up the rest of the day. When you are 20 minutes away from the next appointment it is easier to manage and reschedule.

Research and conversations with your trusted local contact will help when getting to know a new culture. A very important place sales managers can add value is by helping salespeople to view sales as educating the client versus just as persuading them to buy. Helping the client to identify their business issue and presenting a solution (or options) to solve that problem will lead to building credibility and trust.

Summing It Up

Culture is a lens through which people make sense of the world. Wearing another's lens or walking the proverbial mile in another's shoes will cause some discomfort at first, but those who master the process stand to reap huge gains.

Some businesses learn this the hard way. Like when Italian automaker Fiat entered the Indian market. Their promotions focused mainly on the superior

Tips for Sellers

- Get to know your counterpart beforehand—a light back-and-forth over email or on the phone will be insightful prior to meeting in person.
- Stay aware and in tune to your customer during interactions. Watch for nonverbal feedback.
- When in doubt, ask.

engineering of their cars. Others, like Hyundai and Ford, embraced strong Indian values like family-based decision making. Their promotions adopted uniquely Indian slogans and were aimed at families rather than individuals.

Ford and Hyundai were rewarded with a thriving business in India, whereas Fiat was relegated to the bottom of the pyramid—a sad state of affairs for one of the world's finest car makers. As marketing and sales functions work together to understand values and cultures their country connection can be strengthened and improved.

ACTION PLAN

- Assess the strengths of your team for cross-border selling. Create a development plan for those who need additional knowledge or skills on the topic.
- Leverage strong team members and other resources to share additional information. Share successful examples of culturally sensitive transactions in sales meetings to demonstrate the importance.
- Set up alignment meetings to ensure the existing sales process is consistent with how your company wants to do business with different countries. Recommend adjustments as needed to incorporate respect, sales cycle, local business acumen, and values.

REFERENCES

"Dimensions." The Hofstede Centre. http://geert-hofstede.com/dimensions.html.

"International Sales Training—Developing a Cross-Cultural Sales Process." (2010).

Tack International. www.tack.co.uk/blog/?tag=selling-to-different-cultures.

McClay, R. (2013). *111 Ideas to Engage Global Audiences*. Learniappe Publishing.

ABOUT THE AUTHORS

Anup Soans is the editor of *MedicinMan*, India's first magazine for field force excellence in pharmaceutical sales. He is the author of three books for pharma field force professionals and a facilitator of learning and development programs at India's top pharma companies. He conducts skill development and field force engagement programs that bring an alignment between employee aspirations and organizational objectives.

Joshua Soans has a master's degree in development studies from IIT Madras and is the executive editor of *MedicineMan*.

DISCUSSION QUESTIONS

1. Why are global knowledge and cultural sensitivity important in cross-border sales?

2. What are encoding, decoding, and noise in communications?

3. Sales reps try to qualify customers as "effective." What does this mean?

9

Chapter 9 reviews the components of the international promotional mix and how such promotional mixes are used to communicate to international consumers. It also discusses the international communication process, the channels of communication, *encoding*, *decoding*, *noise*, and other elements of communication. Furthermore, it reviews and discusses the complexities of international advertising strategy; for instance, the strategies of *adaptation* and *standardization* and how their use may be affected by the culture of the foreign market.

Local Brands vs. Worldwide Brands discusses the options available to the international marketer. That is, should a marketer use one brand name or multiple? The strategy of brand standardization is also discussed. Examples of company brands and their strategies are offered and reviewed.

The International Promotional Mix

9.1

Dana-Nicoleta Lascu

The components of the **international promotional mix** are international advertising, international sales force management, international sales promotion, and public relations and publicity **(see Figure 9.1)**. Companies use the promotional mix to communicate with international consumers about their products and services. In the process of expanding internationally, companies are faced with numerous challenges to their plans for communicating with the world's consumers. Many of the challenges are attributed to differences in culture. [...] Understanding the norms, motivations, attitudes, interests, and opinions of the target market is crucial to company success in marketing to and communicating with different cultures around the globe. Companies also must be prepared to handle the challenges presented by the local media, local advertising infrastructure, and the different layers of government regulating all aspects of communication with the target market.

[...]

FIGURE 9.1 The International Promotional Mix

International Advertising

International Salesforce Management

International Sales Promotion

Public Relations and Publicity

The International Communication Process

The **international communication process** involves using the entire promotional mix to communicate with the final consumer (**see Figure 9.2**). Regardless of the elements of the promotional mix involved, the communication essentially has the same format. The international sponsor (**sender**), usually represented by an advertising agency, encodes the sponsor's message into words and images. The message is then translated into the language of the target market and transmitted through a **channel of communication,** or medium, to the international consumer in the target market (**receiver**). The medium may be a **nonpersonal medium:**

Alternatively, the channel may be a **personal medium:**

- A salesperson calling on a supplier or a door-to-door salesperson calling on consumers
- A **telemarketer** calling on consumers (telemarketing)
- A trade show, where one can address questions to an individual who is knowledgeable about the product

The international consumer (receiver) receives the message and decodes it into meaning. Ideally, the meaning of the decoded message should be identical to the meaning of the encoded message. However, **noise**—all the potential interference in the communication process, particularly noise attributed to cultural differences—can impede communication. During the

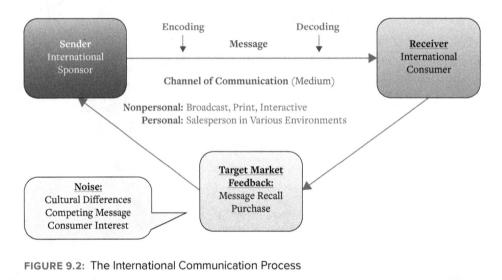

FIGURE 9.2: The International Communication Process

- A **print medium,** such as a newspaper, magazine, billboard, pamphlet, or a point-of-purchase display
- A **broadcast medium,** such as television and radio
- An **interactive medium,** such as a website or a computer terminal on the retailer's premises

message transmission and delivery processes, noise can interfere with proper message reception. The sponsor (sender) collects and relies on information regarding the effectiveness of the message (**feedback**) to evaluate the success of the promotional campaign. Such information may be provided by sales data or by advertising research evaluating message recall rates.

Each step of the international communication process presents challenges to the message sponsor beyond those encountered when marketing to home-country consumers. First, when **encoding** the message, the source determines whether the attitudes, interests, and motivations of consumers in the international target market are different from those in the home-country target market. Manufacturers of Peugeot bicycles in France selling their product in Belgium and the United States need to be aware that consumer motivations behind the purchase differ. In Belgium, the main purpose of using the Peugeot bicycle is transportation. Major cities have bicycle paths on the sidewalks, and pedestrians and automobiles are not allowed to block them. Bicycle paths also have their own signals at intersections. In the countryside, paths, in parallel with the main roads or highways, are reserved for bicycles. A Belgian consumer who purchases a Peugeot bicycle wants a product that is reliable and can perform optimally, regardless of weather. Communication about the product, then, should stress durability, reliability, and quality. In the United States, a Peugeot bicycle is used primarily for recreation. Communication about the product is more likely to be successful if it focuses on a weekend recreational activity and on performance.

Similarly, Pizza Hut in the United States and the United

FIGURE 9.3 Lucky Strike's cigarettes' English message for German-speaking consumers: "iSmoke" —plays on the statement "I Smoke" and on the name of the trendy iPhone.

Kingdom is a staple family restaurant for busy families who do not have time to cook. Pizza Hut advertising focuses on deals for the entire family. In Poland, Pizza Hut is the in-place for dinner accompanied by techno music before consumers descend to the downstairs disco in the city of Wroclaw. It is also the place for a business lunch near Warsaw's prestigious Marriott hotel, located strategically between stores selling haute couture. Consequently, communication about Pizza Hut in Poland should not limit itself to a family focus.

When encoding the message, one must ensure that the message is appropriately translated. In the process of translating the message, one should note that language is closely related to advertising strategy. For example, English requires less space in print and less airtime for broadcast advertising. This is one of the reasons it is widely used in advertising (**see Figure 9.3**). Translated into German, Dutch, or French, the headline, body copy, and tag line require more space for a print or online advertisement and more airtime for a broadcast ad.

From product name to the entire marketing communication, all must be monitored to ensure that the meanings intended are the meanings conveyed. There is an explosion of naming consultancies, set up as offshoots of advertising agencies, which develop brand names that are intended to work worldwide. Because consumers travel everywhere, it is important that brand names are consistent in any country where they are sold.[1] From names such as Vaux-hall's Nova automobile, meaning "no go" in Spanish, to airlines claiming that one will fly "naked" (as opposed to "sitting on leather") in first class, companies have made many mistakes when communicating with international consumers.

Sending the message through the appropriate channel is often a challenge. The media infrastructure might be such that the most appropriate medium cannot be successfully used. In countries where mail is less reliable, such as India and Mali, it is advisable not to send direct mail containing samples. In other countries where the mailing system is reliable, such as Saudi Arabia, mail might not constitute a traditional medium for sending samples, and a direct mail package might be perceived as suspicious. In Rwanda and Burundi, for the last several decades, radio has been the primary broadcast medium; however, international brands are rarely advertised on this medium. To reach the mass market in these two countries, the primary appropriate communication medium has been the billboard. Furthermore, it is preferable that the advertisement has few words and relies on pictorials to convey the message because many target consumers are illiterate. However, the Internet is inching toward a 10 percent penetration rate in the two countries, and digital marketing might be a viable alternative for communicating with consumers in these countries in the near future.

The different channels of communication, the programming itself, and noise, as well as audience inattention—another form of noise—could negatively affect the decoding process, such that the target consumer does not fully comprehend the communication. To lessen the impact of these communication impediments, companies do the following:

- Conduct research to evaluate the message in multiple international environments.
- Evaluate the effectiveness of the communication in attracting target market attention, using recall tests and other memory-based procedures.
- Evaluate the effectiveness of the communication in getting consumers to purchase the product.

The company then uses this research to modify the message or to design future communication strategies.

The Advertising Strategy

Standardization versus Adaptation in Creating Message Strategies

One of the most important decisions of firms designing their international promotional mix is whether to standardize (globalize) their promotional strategy (**standardization of the advertising strategy**), to adapt their promotional mix to each country or market (**adaptation of the advertising strategy**), or to create local campaigns. Practitioners are divided on this issue. Sponsors, as well as advertising agencies, agree that using a standardized strategy worldwide presents substantial advantages. This is most obvious from a cost perspective: Costs are reduced considerably if companies do not need to duplicate the creative effort and the resultant communication campaign in each market. In addition, as product life cycles shrink, companies are pressured to accelerate worldwide rollout of new products. Developing communication strategies for each market would delay launch.[2] Moreover, world consumers are developing common product preferences and increasingly share similar frames of references with regard to products and consumption because they are exposed to the same sources of influence (broadcast and print media, in particular, as well as blockbuster films and tourists, among others).

High-profile advertisers, including Mercedes-Benz, Hewlett-Packard, Walt Disney, and Coca-Cola, have started, or announced plans to start, worldwide ad campaigns. Some of these marketers have previously eschewed global campaigns or have gone back and forth between local and regional approaches. Now, however, there is clearly a shift in the strategy of multinational firms. Standardization versus adaptation decisions come down to a battle between marketing and sales—marketing emphasizes a global approach, whereas sales insists on being local.[3]

Typically, marketers end up in between, with a consistent overall image, but tailoring the ads for perceived local differences. McDonald's, in the earlier example, has been using this strategy since 2003, with its theme "I'm lovin' it."[4] The campaign, however, adapts to appeal to local markets, assuring consumers that McDonald's products are local.

Other companies whose brand identities had become fragmented through regional or country-specific advertising have also moved toward global campaigns. Coca-Cola, for example, has moved to unify its advertising under the theme, "The Coke side of life." Or, companies can have a unique regional theme that appeals to a broad market segment. For example, Coca-Cola removed its logo from its soda cans in the Muslim world during Ramadan in 2015, to encourage people not to judge one another. Its labels then read "Labels are for cans, not for people."

The auto industry, which has for many years rejected adopting global campaigns, has also changed its strategy at the insistence of local sales branches. Mercedes hired the advertising agency BBDO to develop a single global ad campaign for its new C-Class. Hewlett-Packard rolled out its first global advertising campaign for its personal computer division, and Disney started a global campaign for its theme parks. This approach makes sense, as it costs less for one ad agency to create a single global ad campaign than it does for multiple agencies to create separate campaigns. Moreover, new technology makes it easier to adapt a global campaign for individual markets, and procurement officials know this, putting further pressure on agencies to cut costs. Most big marketing campaigns now include a substantial online presence, and the enormous popularity of social networking and video-sharing web services means ads and videos quickly zip across borders.[5]

Mercedes-Benz introduced the new C-Class using a comprehensive integrated marketing campaign, with the slogan "C-for Yourself," developed by the advertising agency BBDO France. The campaign attempted to convince customers based on the world of qualities of the new C-Class sedan, its design, comfort, agility, and safety. Interestingly, Mercedes decided that all communication measures for the C-Class should be geared toward direct contact with customers and

potential buyers. Specifically, magazines and newspapers with high circulation featured ads inviting customers to test-drive the sedan.[6]

In Germany, a 30-/40-second television commercial was launched on all prominent public and commercial stations, featuring the Formula 1 world champion race-car driver Fernando Alonso. At the end of the ad, Alonso, who drives for the Vodafone McLaren Mercedes Formula 1 team, symbolically hands over the keys to a new C-Class to the audience at home, inviting them to test-drive the vehicle. Mercedes coupled this campaign with the more local "Exclusive Driving Experience" campaign, which allowed 80 consumers from all over Europe to experience the C-Class. In Barcelona, participants drove an off-road course—and King Juan Carlos of Spain and representatives of founding partner Mercedes-Benz attended the event. Vacationers at Robinson Club Resorts and Westin Hotels & Resorts facilities in Germany, Austria, Scotland, Italy, Spain, Portugal, and Greece were also offered the opportunity to test drive the new C-Class. In addition to its traditional advertising strategies, Mercedes combined direct communication at driving events with interactive films on the Internet. The online presentation at www.mercedes-benz.com/c-class allowed viewers to select the vehicle of their choice and see it displayed against realistic backdrops. The site also offered several interactive films featuring individuals describing details of the new C-Class as they took the vehicle for a drive.[7]

Differences between countries, however, might render standardization a challenge, or even impossible. The following are barriers to advertising standardization:

- The communication infrastructure is one barrier. A particular medium might be inappropriate or not available for advertising.
- International advertising agencies might not serve a particular market.
- Consumer literacy level constitutes another major barrier. Consumers might not be able to read the body copy of the advertisement, so the information conveyed to the consumer should be visual.
- Legal restrictions and industry self-regulation might also impede standardization: Comparative advertising is not permitted in many countries, whereas, in others, such as Korea, Confucianism forbids the public criticism of others.[8]
- Values and purchase motivations differ across countries and cultures [...]. Targeting consumers with a campaign that stresses the good life, exemplified by driving a luxury car and having a blonde on one's side, might be inappropriate in countries where consumers are living a subsistence existence and just as improper in highly developed, cultured environments. Consumers from collectivist cultures will also question the values suggested by such ads. The decision of whether to standardize is most often contingent on the degree of cultural similarity between the sponsor and the target market. Standardization of communication is recommended when similarity exists between senders and receivers in the communication process.
- Attitudes toward the product or service country of origin create another barrier. Especially in environments where there is some level of hostility toward the United States and its economic and cultural dominance, it might be best not to have an advertising campaign that stresses the product's country of origin.

The elements of the promotional mix—particularly advertising[9]—are especially difficult to standardize because communication is language- and culture-specific.

Budgeting Decisions for International Advertising Campaigns

Companies use the following approaches to advertising spending decisions. *Objective-and-Task Method:* Companies using the **objective-and-task method** first identify advertising goals in terms of communication goals such as target audience reach, awareness, comprehension, or even purchase. As a next step, research is conducted to determine the cost of achieving the respective goals. Finally, the necessary sum is allocated for the purpose.

This method is the most popular one used by multinational corporations in the process of deciding on their advertising budgets because it takes into consideration the firms' strategies. A comprehensive international study suggests that this method is more frequently used by firms from Canada and Singapore and less frequently by Swedish and Argentinean firms.[10]

Percent-of-Sales Method: The **percent-of-sales method** determines the total budget allocated to advertising based on past or projected sales. This method is difficult to adopt for firms entering new markets, which are more likely to benefit from budgeting methods such as competitive parity or objective and task. The problem with this method is that it causes advertising expenditures to decline as sales decline, whereas, at this point, the company should increase advertising spending.

For firms that have been in a particular international market for some time, this method is used by almost half of the respondents in a study on transnational advertising practices. This study found that the percent-of-sales method is most popular in Brazil and Hong Kong and less popular in Germany.[11]

Historical Method: Firms using the **historical method** base their advertising budget on past expenditures, usually giving more weight to more recent expenditures. The percent-of-sales method uses the historical method as a first step, if the percentages allocated to advertising are based on past, rather than projected, sales. This method is not recommended for firms that operate in unstable economic, political, or competitive environments.

Competitive-Parity Method: The **competitive-parity method** uses competitors' level of advertising spending as benchmarks for a firm's own advertising expenditure. This approach is not recommended for a firm entering a new market and whose brands are not known locally. Moreover, this method suggests that a firm's goals and strategies are identical with those of competitors, which, most likely, is not the case.

Executive-Judgment Method: In the **executive-judgment method,** executive opinion is used in determining the advertising budget. A third of the responding firms queried in the above-mentioned study reported relying on executive judgment.

All-You-Can-Afford Method: Most small and medium-sized enterprises entering a new market do not have the large budgets of multinational corporations. The **all-you-can-afford method** best suits the financial limitations of these firms. Unfortunately, this approach completely ignores strategic considerations.

ENDNOTES

1. Sam Solley, "Developing a Name to Work World-wide," Marketing, December 21, 2000, p. 27.
2. William Wells, John Burnett, and Sandra Moriarty, *Advertising: Principles and Practice*, Seventh Edition, Upper Saddle River, NY: Pearson, 2006.
3. Eric Pfanner, "On Advertising: Passport to Success?" International Herald Tribune, August 6, 2006, online edition.
4. Knowledge@Wharton, "McDonald's Sets Out to Conquer the World by Changing Its Image," October 22, 2003, accessed at http://knowledge.wharton.upenn.edu/article/mcdonalds-sets-out-to-conquer-the-world-by-changing-its-image/ on January 5, 2016.
5. Eric Pfanner, "On Advertising: Passport to Success?" International Herald Tribune, August 6, 2006, online edition.
6. "C-for Yourself": Mercedes-Benz launches integrated marketing campaign for the new C-Class, Stuttgart, March 19, 2007, Official Press Release, www.mercedes-benz.com/c-class, accessed on October 12, 2012.
7. Ibid.
8. Michel Laroche, V. H. Kirpalani, and Rene Darmon, "Determinants of the Control of International Advertising by Headquarters of Multinational Corporations," Revue Canadienne de l'Administration, Vol. 16, No. 4, December 1999, pp. 273–290.
9. Zahna Caillat and Barbara Mueller, "Observations: The Influence of Culture on American and British Advertising: An Exploratory Comparison of Beer Advertising," Journal of Advertising Research, Vol. 36, No. 3, May/June 1996, pp. 79–88.
10. Nicolaos E. Synodinos, Charles F. Keown, and Lawrence W. Jacobs, "Transnational Advertising Practices: A Survey of Leading Brand Advertisers in Fifteen Countries," Journal of Advertising Research, Vol. 29, No. 2, April/ May 1989, pp. 43–50.
11. Ibid.

9.2 Local Brands vs. Worldwide Brands

Sak Onkvisit and John J. Shaw

When the manufacturer decides to put its own brand name on the product, the problem does not end there if the manufacturer is an international marketer. The possibility of having to modify the trademark cannot be dismissed. The international marketer must then consider whether to use just one brand name worldwide or different brands for different markets or countries. To market brands worldwide and to market worldwide brands are not the same thing.

A single, worldwide brand is also known as an *international, universal,* or *global* brand. A Eurobrand is a slight modification of this approach, as it is a single product for a single market (i.e., the European Union and the other Western European countries), with an emphasis on the search for intermarket similarities rather than differences.

For a brand to be global or worldwide, it must, by definition, have a commonly understood set of characteristics and benefits in all of the countries where it is marketed. Coca-Cola is a global brand in the sense that it has been successful in maintaining similar perceptions across countries and cultures. However, most other brands do not enjoy this kind of consistency, thus making it debatable whether a global brand is a practical solution.

A worldwide brand has several advantages. First, it tends to be associated with status and prestige. Second, it achieves maximum market impact overall while reducing advertising costs because only one brand is pushed. Bata Ltd, a Canadian shoe marketer and retailer in 92 countries, found out from its research that consumers generally thought Bata to be a local concern, no matter the country surveyed. The company thus decided to become an official sponsor of World Cup soccer in order to enhance Bata's international stature. For Bata and others, it is easier to achieve worldwide exposure for one brand than it is for multiple local brands. Too many brands create confusion and fragmentation.

Third, a worldwide brand provides a convenient identification, and international travelers can easily recognize the product. There would be no sense in creating multiple brands for such international products as *Time* magazine, American Express credit-card, Diner's Club credit-card, Shell gasoline, and so on.

Finally, a worldwide brand is an appropriate approach when a product has a good reputation or is known for quality. In such a case, a company would be wise to extend the brand name to other products in the product line. This strategy has been used extensively by General Electric Co. In another case, 3M Company perceived commonalities in a consumer demographics and market development worldwide; in response, it devised a "convergence marketing" strategy to develop global identity for its Scottish brand of electronic recording products, whose design prominently displays the Scottish name and a globe-like logo.

Global consumer culture positioning (GCCP) is a positioning tool which suggests one pathway through which a brand can be perceived by consumers as "global." GCCP is a construct which associates a brand with a widely understood and recognized set of symbols that constitute an emerging global consumer culture. A significant number of advertisements employ GCCP (instead of positioning the brand as a member of a local or specific foreign consumer culture).[1]

As noted by *Business Week* in 2005, most companies with the biggest increase in brand value operate as single brands everywhere. A single worldwide identity offers efficiency, consistency, and impact.[2]

The use of multiple brands, also known as the *local* or *individual* approach, is probably much more common than many people realize. Discover Financial Services, while using the Discover name in the U.S.A., issues a consumer credit-card in England under the Morgan Stanley Dean Witter. In the case of Unilever, its fabric softener is sold in ten European countries under seven names. Due to decentralization, the multinational firm allows country managers to choose names, packages, and formulas that will appeal to local tastes. More recently, the company, while keeping local brand names, has been gradually standardizing packaging and product formulas.

There are several reasons for using local brands. First, developing countries resent international brands because the brands' goodwill is created by an advertising budget that is much greater than research and development costs, resulting in no benefit derived from research and development for local economies. In addition, local consumers are forced to pay higher prices for advertising and goodwill, benefiting MNCs but hindering the development of local competitive capacity. Such resentment may explain why India's ministries, responding to domestic soft drink producers' pressure, rejected Pepsi's 35 percent Pepsi-owned joint venture. Some governments have considered taxing international brands or limiting the use of such brands, as in the case of South Korea, which has considered placing restrictions on foreign trademarks intended for domestic consumption.

Second, when the manufacturer is unable to ensure uniform product quality across countries or when it wants to vary its quality level for different countries, it should consider local brands. Shanghai Automotive Industry Corp. is a joint-venture partner of both General Motors Corp. and Volkswagen AG, and it has rolled out cars under its own brand. Honda Motor Co. will start selling cars with its Chinese partner (Guangzhou Automobile Group Co.) under a new brand in 2010, becoming the first foreign car manufacturer to develop an original brand in China. The first few models will be derived from existing Honda cars and will likely be priced below $10,000, targeting the low end of the market. The new brand will allow it to penetrate China's growing market for low-cost cars without diluting its image. Toyota, in contrast, has no plans to establish a new brand in China.[3]

Third, when an existing brand is difficult to pronounce, a new brand may be desirable. Sometimes, consumers avoid buying a certain brand when it is difficult pronounce because they want to avoid the embarrassment of a wrong pronunciation.

Fourth, a local brand is more easily understood and more meaningful for local consumers. By considering foreign tastes and preferences, a company achieves a better marketing impact. Post-it note pads made by 3M are marketed as Yellow Butterflies in France. Grey, an international advertising agency, worked with Playtex to create appropriate names for Playtex's brassières in different languages. The result was Wow in England and Traumbugel (dream wire) in Germany. Translation can also make a brand more meaningful. This approach is sometimes mistaken for a single-brand approach when in fact a new brand is created. Close-Up (toothpaste) was translated as Klai-Chid (literally meaning "very close") in Thailand; the translation retained the meaning and the logo of the brand as well as the package design.

Fifth, a local brand can avoid a negative connotation. Pepsi introduced a non-cola under the Patio name in America but under the Mirinda name elsewhere due to the unpleasant connotation of *patio* in Spanish.

Sixth, some MNCs acquire local brands for quick market penetration in order to save time, not to mention money, which would otherwise be needed to build the recognition for a new, unknown brand in local markets. Renault would have been foolish to abandon the AMC (American Motors) name after a costly acquisition. Thus, Renault 9, for example, became AMC Alliance in the U.S.A. Chrysler subsequently bought AMC from Renault, one reason being AMC's coveted Jeep trademark.

Seventh, multiple brands may have to be used, not by design but by necessity, due to legal complications. One problem is the restrictions placed on the use of certain words. Diet Coke in countries that restrict the use of the word *diet* becomes Coke Light. Anti-trust problems can also dictate this strategy. Gillette, after acquiring Braun A.G., a German firm, had to sign a consent decree not to use the name in the U.S. market until 1985. The decree forced Braun to create the Eltron brand, which had little success.

Eighth, and perhaps the most compelling reason for creating new local brands, is because local firms may have already used the names that multinational firms have been using elsewhere. In such a case, to buy the right to use the name from a local business can prove

expensive. Unilever markets Sure antiperspirant in the United Kingdom but had to market test the product under the Trust name in the U.S.A., where Sure is Procter & Gamble's deodorant trademark.

In an interesting case, Anheuser-Busch bought the American rights to the Budweiser name and recipe from the brewer of Budweis in Czechoslovakia; Budejovicky Budvar Narodni Podnik, the Czech brewer, holds the rights in Europe. Operating from the town of Ceske Budejovice, known as Budweis before the First World War, this brewer claims exclusive rights to the Budweiser name in the United Kingdom, France, and several European countries. Courts have ruled that both companies have the right to sell in the United Kingdom, but Anheuser-Busch has to use the Busch name in France and the corporate name in other parts of Europe.

Budejovicky Budvar NP, owned by the Czech government, has argued that the Budweiser name has been associated with beer made in the Ceske Budejovice area since about 1265. Anheuser Busch, on the other hand, has pointed out that it began using the name in 1876 but that Budejovicky Budvar was not founded until 1895. Anheuser Busch applied for several EU-wide trademarks in 1996, and most of them were granted over Budvar's objections. In 2007, a European Union court rejected Budvar's appeals.[4]

Ninth, a local brand may have to be introduced due to price control. This problem is especially acute in countries with inflationary pressures. Price control is also one reason for the growth of the so-called gray marketers, as the phenomenon contributes to price variations among countries for the same product. Thus, instead of buying a locally produced product or one from an authorized distributor/importer, a local retailer can buy exactly the same brand from wholesalers in countries where prices are significantly lower. A manufacturer will have a hard time prohibiting importation of gray market goods, especially in EU countries where products are supposed to be able to move freely. Parallel trading can be minimized by having different national brands rather than just a worldwide brand.

As mentioned earlier, brand standardization is a common strategy. Companies tend to brand globally but advertise locally. Interestingly, although the McDonald's logo is one of the most recognizable trademarks in the world, McDonald's has changed its advertising logo just for Quebec, perhaps the only market in the world receiving this special treatment. The most well-known logo in Quebec is J'M. This is a play on "j'aime" which means "I love" in French.

The strategy of using a worldwide brand is thus not superior (or inferior) to using multiple local brands. Each strategy has its merits and serves its own useful functions. This is where managerial judgment comes in. Unilever, for example, considers consumer responses to a particular brand mix. It uses an international brand for such products as detergents and personal products because common factors among countries outweigh any differences. Food products, however, are another story. Food markets are much more complex due to variations in needs and responses to different products. The southern half of Europe mainly uses oil for cooking rather than margarine, white fats, or butter. The French more than the Dutch consider butter to be an appropriate cooking medium. German homemakers, when compared to British homemakers, are more interested in health and diet products. Soup is a lightweight precursor to the main dish in Great Britain but can almost be a meal by itself in Germany. Under such circumstances of preferential variations, the potential for local brands is greatly enhanced.

It is interesting to note that local brands may sometimes be viewed as foreign brands. As in the case of pizza, which is a foreign product category in India, consumers experience local brands as foreign brands. It is thus reasonable to believe that hamburgers, a staple item in the U.S.A., will also be viewed as a foreign product in Asia and Latin America. Fried chicken, on the other hand, is probably more common (i.e., not foreign) among the various cultures.[5]

Any domestic market is unlikely to be homogeneous, and there is room for both international and local brands. There is empirical evidence to show that consumers buying imported brand clothing have lifestyle and shopping orientations that differ from those who prefer domestic brand clothing.[6]

While it is often assumed that an international brand is more prestigious than a local brand, this assumption must be carefully assessed. After all, local brands have their own strengths and are perceived in a favorable manner with regard to several aspects. Local brands tend to generate more awareness, trust, value, and image of reliability and being "down to earth."[7] Compared to global brands, local brands are not necessarily inferior. Foreign brands' market shares are driven by their superior core advantages. Conversely, the market shares of domestic brands are significantly affected by their local advantages.[8]

When creating local brand names in the multilingual international market, companies have three translation methods to consider: phonetic (i.e., by sound), semantic (i.e., by meaning), and phonosemantic (i.e., by sound plus meaning). The effectiveness of translation depends on the emphasis of the original English name and the translation method previously used for brand names within the same category. When the phonetic naming method is used, brand name evaluations are more favorable for names that emphasize an English word than for those names that emphasize a Chinese word.[9]

NOTES

1. Dana L. Alden, Jan-Benedict E.M. Steenkamp, and Rajeev Batra, "Brand Positioning Through Advertising in Asia, North America, and Europe: The Role of Global Consumer Culture," *Journal of Marketing* 63 (January 1999): 75–87.

2. "Global Brands," *Business Week,* August 1, 2005, 86–94.

3. "Honda Will Create Brand for China's Auto Market," *Wall Street Journal,* July 19, 2007.

4. "EU Court Upholds Anheuser Trademarks," *Wall Street Journal,* June 13, 2007.

5. Giana M. Eckhardt, "Local Branding in a Foreign Product Category in an Emerging Market," *Journal of International Marketing* 13 (No. 4, 2005): 57–79.

6. Cheng-Lu Wang, Noel Y.M. Siu, and Alice S.Y. Hui, "Consumer Decision-making Styles on Domestic and Imported Brand Clothing," *European Journal of Marketing* 38 (Nos 1/2, 2004): 239–52.

7. Isabelle Schuiling and Jean-Noel Kapferer, "Real Differences Between Local and International Brands: Strategic Implications for International Marketers,"

Journal of International Marketing 12 (No. 4, 2004): 97–112.

8. Gerald Yong Gao *et al.*, "Market Share Performance of Foreign and Domestic Brands in China," *Journal of International Marketing* 14 (No. 2, 2006): 32–51.

9. Shi Zhang and Bernd H. Schmitt, "Creating Local Brands in Multilingual International Markets," *Journal of Marketing Research* 38 (August 2001): 313–25.

DISCUSSION QUESTIONS

1. Why do international marketers face challenges in their communications to their foreign market?

2. What is the impact of "noise" in international communications? That is, what is its source?

3. Why should the international marketer, when encoding their message, pay attention to the consumers' attitudes, interests, and motivations? Discuss.

4. How might sending the message through a channel be a challenge? Discuss.

5. What might be the impediments to decoding a message? How might such impediments be mitigated?

6. How can an international marketer decide to adapt or standardize their communication message? Discuss the criteria under which adaptation or standardization would make sense.

7. What are the barriers to advertising standardization? When could an advertiser standardize?

8. Discuss the budgeting methods in use in marketing communications, such as Objective-and-Task, Percent-of-Sales, Historical, Competitive-Parity, Executive-Judgment, and All-You-Can-Afford.

9. What is the difference between a local brand and a worldwide or global brand?

10. Under what circumstances are local brands or global brands superior to each other?

11. Why do global brands customize their offering locally? Give an example.

12. How does product quality uniformity affect a decision to use a local versus a global brand?

10

Chapter 10 focuses on the importance of **Emerging Markets**, also known as developing or industrializing economies. It looks into the economic status of such markets and discusses their impact on their regional, as well as global, economies. The chapter describes the traits and characteristics of the emerging markets and their distinct contribution to the developed economies. As such, the economic relationship between developed and emerging markets is discussed and its impact on international trade is emphasized.

The Political and Regulatory Environment addresses the political economy in a cross-cultural environment. Specifically, it discusses the various political systems, institutional influence, political risks, nationalization versus socialization, and politically motivated risks, such as *domestication*, *expropriation*, *confiscation*, and related issues. It identifies the dynamics of the political system that may contribute or enhance political risk. This section also reviews the dominant legal systems of the world, namely, *common law*, *code law*, and *theocratic law* and how these different legal systems impact cultural values and markets.

10.1 Understanding Emerging Markets

Economy and Culture

Marcus Goncalves and Finn Majlergaard

An Overview of Emerging Markets

As economic globalization has brought down trade and investment barriers and has connected far-reaching countries in an integrated global supply chain—and emerging markets seem to be converging with the world's "rich industrial countries"—distinguishing these economies from developed markets may seem to matter less than before.

Well, we disagree. One fundamental premise of this book is that businesses still need to distinguish emerging markets—collectively from developed markets and individually from each other. In addition, international business professionals need to understand the cultural aspects of each of these countries and regions, so that they are able to leverage the cultural diversity of these markets.

It is important, therefore, that we stabilize the term emerging market. What is it, or better yet, what is it not? Economists at the International Finance Corporation, within the World Bank, coined the term, emerging markets, in 1981, when the group was promoting the first mutual fund investments in developing countries. Since then, references to emerging markets have become ubiquitous in the media, foreign policy and trade debates, investment fund prospectuses, and multinationals' annual reports.

Defining Emerging Markets

These groups of emerging economies are not easy to define. Although the World Bank coined the term *emerging countries* more than a quarter of a century ago, it only started to become a household term in the mid-1990s.[1] After the debt crises of the 1980s, several of these rapidly developing economies gained access to international financial markets, while they had liberalized their financial systems, at least far enough to enable foreign investors broad access into their markets.[2] From a small group of nations in East Asia, these groups of emerging economies have gradually grown to include several countries in Latin America, Central and Eastern Europe, the Middle East, as well as a few countries in Africa. The leading groups today are the ASEAN (Association of South East Asian Nations); the BRICS (Brazil, Russia, India, China, and South Africa); the CIVETS (Colombia, Indonesia, Vietnam, Egypt, Turkey, and South Africa); and the MENA (Middle East and North Africa) groups, in addition to what Jim O'Neil calls the N-11, or next-eleven emerging economies [...].

The definitions of the term, however, still vary widely, often reduced to the unhelpful tautology that emerging markets are "emerging" because they have not "emerged." To understand emerging markets, we need to consider carefully the ways in which they are emerging and the extent to which they are genuine markets. Although this is not the objective of this book,[3] we provide here an overview of such markets and also a subset of them, known as frontier markets, before we can endeavor into the real aim of the book: leveraging its cultural diversity for business advantage.

Emerging markets are not distinctly different from other markets; rather, they are simply starting from a lower base and rapidly catching up. Indicators such as the growing numbers of emerging market-based companies listed on the New York Stock Exchange or the growing ranks of billionaires from emerging markets listed annually by the *Forbes Magazine* can well illustrate this trend.

A good general acceptable definition we would propose is that emerging markets are countries in which their economies are progressing toward becoming advanced, as shown by some liquidity in local debt and equity markets and the existence of some form of market exchange and regulatory body.

Emerging markets generally do not have the level of market efficiency and strict standards in accounting and securities regulation to be on par with advanced economies, as we would find in the United States, Europe, and Japan, but emerging markets will typically have a physical financial infrastructure including banks, a stock exchange, and a unified currency.

Such criteria are important features of many emerging markets, but they do not delineate the underlying characteristics that predispose an economy to be emerging, nor are they particularly helpful for businesses that seek to address the consequences of emerging market conditions. We see these features of emerging markets as symptoms of underlying market structures that share common, important, and persistent differences from those in developed economies.

Emerging Markets' Economic Dynamics

Emerging markets, without a doubt, have been on a tear over the past decade. BRICS countries powered the high growth rate in those economies, despite volatility. However, that growth has slowed down in recent years, coming to a screeching halt in 2013, mainly due to fears of an economic slowdown in China and that the Federal Reserve would taper its bond-buyback program, limiting investments in emerging markets.

These markets have been the source of global economic growth for quite some time now, with far-reaching effects on the rest of the world, in particular on advanced economies. It is not news that emerging markets have become the sweethearts of the financial press and a favorite talking point of governments, foreign trade advisers, and corporations worldwide. Although these markets were best known in the past as a commodity paradise, or the place to go for natural resources, cheap labor, or low manufacturing costs, emerging markets today are positioned for growth. Its rapid population development, growing middle class, and sustained economic development are making many international investors and corporations look to emerging markets with new lenses.

In the past decade, the emerging markets have been growing at a much faster pace than the advanced economies. Consequently, its participation in the global gross domestic product (GDP), global trade, and foreign direct investment (FDI), particularly in the global financial markets, has significantly increased as well. Such trends, according to a study conducted by the Banco de Espana's analysts Orgaz, Molina, and Carrasco (2011), are expected to continue for the next few years. The global economic crises have actually fostered relevant changes to the governance of the global economy, particularly with the substitution of the G8 with the G20 group as a leading international forum in the development of global economic policies.

Economic theorists corroborate this point by arguing that free FDI across national borders is beneficial to all countries, as it leads to an efficient allocation of resources, which raises productivity and economic growth everywhere. Although in principle this is often the case, at this time, for emerging markets, the situation is a bit different, as it is much more apparent now when we look at country indicators from sources such as the International Monetary Fund (IMF) or World Bank that large capital inflows can create substantial challenges for policy makers in those market economies.

After the global financial crisis of 2008 to 2009, net private capital flows to emerging markets surged and have been volatile since then, raising a number of concerns in those recipient economies. As advanced economies issued robust monetary stimuli to revive their sluggish economies, emerging markets faced an overabundance of foreign investments amid strong recoveries. Hence, policy tensions rapidly ensued between these two groups of economies. As strong FDI, mainly private net capital, was injected into emerging markets' economies, both in pre- and post-global financial crisis periods, policy makers in those emerging economies reacted by actually reversing the flow of capital back into advanced market economies, often in an effort to control local currency appreciation, and fend off the export of inflation from advanced economies into these markets.

Therefore, we are all witnessing a rapid development in the global trade landscape, one that hitherto was dominated by advanced economies, with trading policies developed typically by members of the G8 group of nations. Meanwhile, some members of the G8 group are beginning to lose its influence to emerging economies, as a result of profound changes that the global markets are undergoing. One of the most important changes, henceforth, the consequences of which still remain to be understood fully, is the growing role of the G20 countries as new policy makers for international trade and fast-developing emerging markets.

When studying emerging markets today, it is important to understand how the global economy is changing, an attempt to understand what the world will look like tomorrow, five years from now, a decade from now, and how it will impact each of us. The weight of the emerging markets is already significant and being felt throughout the advanced economies and it is likely to expand further. Governance of the global economy organizations as discussed later in this chapter, cannot disregard the implications of the rise of the emerging markets on the world economy, some of which are already evident.

The ASEAN Bloc Influence

Many emerging market countries that had previously posed no competitive threat to advanced economies do so now. The financial crisis that started in mid-1997 in Southeast Asia, which resulted in massive currency depreciations in a number of emerging markets in that region, also spilled over to many other emerging nations as far as Latin America and Africa. However, such crisis since then has subsided, as these same regions were the first to recover from the latest crisis of 2008. The intense currency depreciation in Asia during the late 1990s has positioned the region in a more competitive landscape across global markets.

According to an OECD (Organization for Economic Cooperation and Development) report,[4] although these emerging market economies in Asia have experienced massive exchange rate depreciations, as depicted in Table 10.1,[5] they have also reinforced their absolute cost advantages, given the increasing importance of these economies in world trade. Countries such as

TABLE 10.1 Changes in Asian emerging market economies' exchange rates since mid-1997*

	Percentage		
	vis-à-vis U.S. dollar	vis-à-vis Japanese Yen	vis-à-vis Deutsehemark
China	0	13	5
Chinese Taipei	−15	−3	−10
Hong Kong, China	0	13	5
Indonesia	−76	−73	−75
Korea	−10	−32	−37
Malaysia	−32	−22	−28
Philippines	−32	−24	−29
Singapore	−11	1	−7
Thailand	−40	−32	−37

*Changes between 1 July 1997 and 18 March 1998.

Thailand, Indonesia, and South Korea, which were impacted the most during the 1990s are now emerging market leaders, representing a major shift in the global competitive landscape, which we believe is a trend that will only continue to strengthen as these countries grow in size, establish dominance, and seek new opportunities beyond their traditional domestic and near-shore markets.

Meanwhile, advanced economies in the G7 group are still struggling with indebtedness. The United States continues to deal with debt ceiling adjustments to cope with its ever-increasing government debt while the eurozone is far from solving its own economic problems. Conversely, despite inevitable risks and uncertainties, Southeast Asia registered solid economic growth in 2012 and continues to be on an upward trajectory for the foreseeable future, as China's economy stabilizes and higher levels of FDI are pouring in.

The ASEAN is an organization of countries located in the Southeast Asian region that aims to accelerate economic growth, social progress, and cultural development among its members and to promote regional peace. The region has undergone a period of substantial resurgence after the 1997 to 1998 Asian financial crisis, and has been playing second fiddle to more industrialized economies in Asia-Pacific, which manage to attract the majority of capital inflows. What we have seen since the financial crisis, however, is that ASEAN has been showcasing its ability to recover and advance its position within global markets.

As of 2012, the ASEAN bloc comprises 10 member states including Brunei Darussalam, Cambodia, Indonesia, Laos People Democratic Republic (PDR), Malaysia, Myanmar, Philippines, Singapore, Thailand, and Vietnam, as depicted in Figure 10.1.

Studies carried out by the Asian Development Bank Institute (Cheewatrakoolpong, Sabhasri, and Bunditwattanawong 2013) suggest that the emergence of international production networks in East Asia results from market-driven forces such as vertical specialization and higher production costs in the home countries and institutional-led initiatives, such as free trade agreements. For instance, the region has experienced significant growth in the trade of parts and components since the 1990s, especially with China, one of the important major assembly bases. In addition, the decline

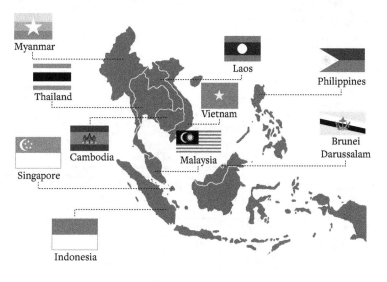

FIGURE 10.1 List of ASEAN member countries as of 2012

Source: ASEAN.[6]

in the share of parts and components trade in several members of the ASEAN bloc, such as Indonesia and Thailand, indicates the increasing importance of the bloc countries as assembly bases for advanced economies such as Japan, and its multinational enterprises. China and Thailand are becoming important auto parts assembly bases for Japan and other advanced economies, attracting foreign investments into those countries, raising their GDP and contributing more to the emergence of international production networks than just free trade agreements. Figure 10.2 provides a list of ASEAN members and their respective GDP, as well as a comparison with major G7 member states, with the exception of China, also included for comparison.

Of course, the ASEAN region has had its fair share of risks and challenges, which unfortunately are not going away as its politicians, like politicians everywhere, occasionally cave in to populist measures—as a matter of fact, since the crisis of 2008, these populist measures have been present in both the advanced economies and emerging markets, with only the level of intensity as the single variant. However, ASEAN's deep commitment to macroeconomic stability, open trade, business-friendly policies, and regional cooperation has created the foundation for steady growth in those regions.

This is also true for many emerging market nations around the globe and in particular the BRICS. Nonetheless, the ASEAN region remains among the most attractive destinations for foreign investors who are running out of options in other emerging markets due to its relative political and macroeconomic stability, low levels of debt, and integration in East Asian production networks. In addition, open trade and investment policies are giving the region a distinct advantage over other emerging markets around the world. As depicted in Figure 10.3, these countries have been growing at an average rate above 6 percent (in 2012) a year, with Indonesia and the Philippines exceeding GDP forecasts. Thailand, hit with devastating floods in 2011, has now recovered and is in full swing to achieve higher than expected GDP growth. The same goes for Malaysia, which has enjoyed the benefits of an expansionary election budget.

According to Arno Maierbrugger, from Investvine,[7] the ASEAN economy will more than double by 2020, with the nominal GDP of the regional bloc increasing from US$2 trillion in 2012 to US$4.7 trillion. The global research firm, IHS,[8] argues that Vietnam and Myanmar are expected to reach a nominal GDP of US$290 billion and US$103 billion, respectively, by 2020, while Indonesia is expected to reach a projected nominal GDP of about US$1.9 trillion. The report also says that, overall, emerging markets in Asia are expected to be the fastest growing in the world and will continue to expand. It is estimated that GDP growth of emerging markets would

Rank	Country	Population in millions		GDP Nominal millions of USD		GDP Nominal per capita USD		GDP (PPP) millions of USD		GDP (PPP) per capita USD	
—	World	7,013.42		71,707,302		10,200		83,140,055		11,850	
—	European Union	502.56		16,584,007		32,518		16,092,525		32,021	
—	United States	314.18		15,684,750		49,922		15,684,750		49,922	
—	China	1,354.04		8,227,037		6,076		12,405,670		9,162	
—	Japan	127.61		5,963,969		46,736		4,627,891		36,266	
—	ASEAN	615.60	100.0	2,305,542	100.0	3,745	100.0	3,605,602	100.0	5,857	100.0
—	South Korea	50.01		1,155,872		23,113		1,613,921		32,272	
1	Indonesia	244.47	39.7	878,198	38.1	3,592	95.9	1,216,738	33.7	4,977	85.0
2	Thailand	64.38	10.5	365,564	15.9	5,678	151.6	651,856	18.1	10,126	172.9
3	Malaysia	29.46	4.8	303,527	13.2	10,304	275.1	498,477	13.8	16,922	288.9
4	Singapore	5.41	0.9	276,520	12.0	51,162	1,366.1	326,506	9.1	60,410	1,031.4
5	Philippines	95.80	15.6	250,436	10.9	2,614	69.8	424,355	11.8	4,430	75.6
6	Vietnam	90.39	14.7	138,071	6.0	1,528	40.8	320,677	8.9	3,548	60.6
7	Myanmar	63.67	10.3	53,140	2.3	835	22.3	89,461	2.5	1,405	24.0
8	Brunei	0.40	0.1	16,628	0.7	41,703	1,113.5	21,687	0.6	54,389	928.6
9	Cambodia	15.25	2.5	14,241	0.6	934	24.9	36,645	1.0	2,402	41.0
10	Laos	6.38	1.0	9,217	0.4	1,446	38.6	19,200	0.5	3,011	51.4

FIGURE 10.2 List of ASEAN countries' GDP

Source: IMF Global Outlook 2012 estimates.

exceed that of developed countries in 2020, continuing to expand thereafter.

Internal macroeconomic policies and structural reforms in the ASEAN region will continue to drive growth in the foreseeable future. The Philippines and Myanmar should see higher GDP growth as a result of earnest government efforts to improve economic governance. Myanmar, after 50 years of self-imposed isolation, fear, and poverty, has now rejoined the international community, attracting fresh foreign investments, which should yield significant growth dividends.

In 2013, two parallel efforts toward trade integration, the ASEAN-driven Regional Comprehensive Economic Partnership (RCEP) and the U.S.-driven Trans-Pacific Partnership (TPP), began vying for traction beyond the ASEAN bloc. Currently, the TPP is certainly more advanced but faces important challenges before it can come to closure. Discussions on the RCEP have only just begun and also face significant obstacles, but progress could accelerate if agreement on the basic parameters is reached soon. Although both of these trade agreements should be able to coexist, they not only include a set of advanced economies to the mix, which can be very beneficial to those countries, but also represent different philosophies as to how economic integration should be achieved.

The risk to emerging markets in the ASEAN bloc and the advanced economies' partnership in trade, as in TTP, are the mounting tensions in the South China Sea, with China facing off against Vietnam and the Philippines. ASEAN's diplomatic attempts to defuse the conflict have only succeeded in raising them even further. It is important now that under a new chair in Brunei, ASEAN countries find ways to settle their internal differences, agree quickly on a code of conduct for the South China Sea, and engage China early in the process so that it becomes an important stakeholder in its implementation, and most importantly, international trade.

Despite geopolitical risks in the region, one of the major catalysts for ASEAN's accelerated growth is its relative low specialized labor costs. While estimates of absolute cost levels in the manufacturing sector are not fully available, data from OECD and the IMF suggest that over the 1975 to 1996 period, China (including Taipei) and South Korea, in particular, were able to maintain significantly lower levels of specialized labor costs than any other industrialized countries for which data exist. It is important to note, as argued by Durand, Madaschi, and Terribile (1998), the fact that while in the past, these potential competitive advantages deriving from nominal exchange rate depreciations often tended to be eroded by rising inflation, there is a widespread sentiment that recent global economic and in-country financial policy developments might have reinforced the absolute cost advantage that emerging markets might have already compared to OECD countries, which makes these markets even more competitive internationally.

Such arguments are reinforced by the fact that, in principle, competitiveness is normally correlated with companies, which can gain and lose market

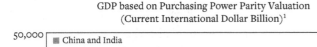

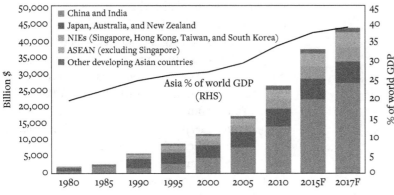

FIGURE 10.3 Asian economic GDP growth based on purchasing power parity (PPP)

Source: International Monetary Fund, World Economic Outlook, October 2012; Austrade.

[1]An international dollar has the same purchasing power over GDP as the U.S. dollar has in the United States.

shares, and eventually even go out of business; the same cannot be said for countries. As P. Krugman (1996) argues,[9] countries cannot go out of business and therefore we should not care about competing countries. Nonetheless, in our opinion, countries still need to be concerned with shifts in market shares, since such shifts may indicate changes in the composition of country output and in the living standards of that nation. Hence, it is likely that labor cost levels in most other emerging market economies in the ASEAN bloc are also lower, and we would emphasize much lower, than in other nations, particularly advanced economies, as depicted in Table 10.2.

We believe that leading emerging markets will continue to drive global growth. Estimates show that 70 percent of world growth over the next decade, well into 2020 and beyond, will come from emerging markets, with China and India accounting for 40 percent of that growth. Such growth is even more significant if we look at it from the PPP perspective, which, adjusted for variation, the IMF forecasts that the total GDP of emerging markets could overtake that of advanced economies

as early as 2014. Such forecasts also suggest that FDI will continue to find its way into emerging markets, particularly the ASEAN bloc for the time being, and also into the fast-developing MENA bloc, as well as Africa as a whole, followed by the BRIC and CIVETS. In all, however, the emerging markets already attract almost 50 percent of FDI global inflows and account for 25 percent of FDI outflows.

Between now and 2050, the world's population is expected to grow by 2.3 billion people, eventually reaching 9.1 billion. The combined purchasing power of the global middle classes is estimated to more than double by 2030 to US$56 trillion. Over 80 percent of this demand will come from Asia. Most of the world's new middle class will live in the emerging world, and almost all will live in cities, often in smaller cities not yet built. This surge of urbanization will stimulate business but put huge strains on infrastructure.

The BRICS Bloc Influence

The BRIC countries are composed of Brazil, Russia, India, and China. Jim O'Neill, a retired former asset manager at Goldman and Sachs, coined the acronym back in 2001 in his paper entitled *Building Better Global Economic BRICs*.[10] The acronym has come into widespread use as a symbol of the apparent shift in global economic power away from the developed G7 economies toward the emerging markets. When we look at the size of its economies in GDP terms, however, the order of the letters in the acronym changes, with China leading the way (second in the world), followed by Brazil (sixth), India (ninth), and Russia (10th).[11] Since 2010, however, despite the lack of support from leading economists participating at the Reuters 2011 Investment Outlook Summit,[12] South Africa (28th) joined the BRIC bloc, forming a new acronym dubbed BRICS.[13]

It has been difficult to project future influences of the BRICS on the global economy. While some research suggests that this bloc might overtake the G7 economies by 2027,[14] other more modest forecasts, such as Goldman Sachs, argue that, while the BRICS are developing rapidly, their combined economies could eclipse the combined economies of the current richest

TABLE 10.2 Relative levels of unit labor costs in manufacturing

	1985	1990	1996
United States	100	100	100
Japan	74	116	169
Germany[a]	71	144	166
France	96	154	163
Italy	60	114	101
United Kingdom	100	158	148
Canada	84	118	102
Australia	98	118	145
Belgium	75	135	156
Denmark	97	205	218
Korea	29	51	58
Netherlands	65	122	120
Spain	49	108	100
Sweden	82	158	160
Chinese Taipei	41	70	70

[a]**West Germany.**
Source: OECD calculations based on 1990 PPPs. For details on the methodological aspect, see OECD (1993).

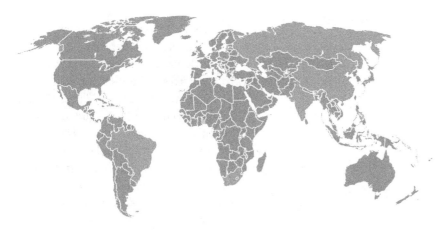

FIGURE 10.4 The BRICS countries: Brazil, Russia, India, China, and South Africa

president of Russia, scorns "the irresponsibility of the system that claims leadership," while Luiz Inácio Lula da Silva, former president of Brazil, in an interview with *Newsweek* magazine during the G20 Summit in London, said that the United States bears the brunt of responsibility for the crisis, and for fixing it.[17]

countries of the world only by 2050.[15] In his recent book titled *The Growth Map: Economic Opportunity in the BRICs and Beyond*,[16] O'Neil corrects his earlier forecast by arguing that the BRICS may overtake the G7 by 2035. Such forecast represents an amazing accomplishment considering how disparate some of these countries are from each other geographically and how different their culture and political and religious systems are. Figure 10.4 illustrates the BRICS geographical locations on the globe.

Notwithstanding these uncertain economic forecasts, researchers seem to agree that the BRICS are having a major impact on their regional trading partners, more distant resource-rich countries, and in particular advanced economies. The ascent of these formerly impoverished countries is gaining momentum, and their confidence is evident not only in utterances such as those of former Chinese premier Wen Jiabao when he stated in 2009 that China had "loaned huge amounts of money," to the United States, warning the United States to "honor its word" and "ensure the safety of Chinese assets," but of other leaders as well. Vladimir Putin, as the fourth

No doubt, there is a lot of global macroeconomics synergy behind the BRICS, and the performance indicators are backing it up. As of 2012, these countries accounted for over a quarter of the world's land mass and more than 46 percent of the world's population,[18] as depicted in Figure 10.5, although still only accounting for 25 percent of the world GDP.[19] Nonetheless, by 2020, this bloc of countries is expected to account for nearly 50 percent of all global GDP growth.

Since its formation, it is clear that the BRICS have been seeking to form a *political club*. According to a Reuter article, the BRIC bloc has strong interest in converting "their growing economic power into greater geopolitical clout."[20] Granted, the BRICS bloc does not represent a political coalition currently capable of

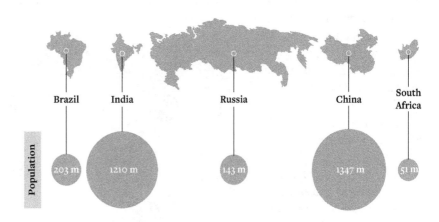

FIGURE 10.5 BRICS account for almost 50 percent of the world population

Source: Population Reference Bureau.

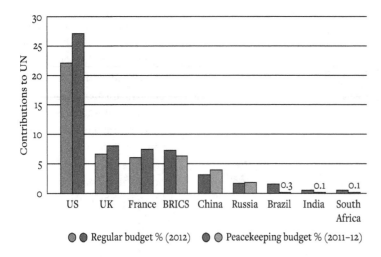

FIGURE 10.6 BRICS have increased their participation and contribution to UN budgets

playing a leading geopolitical role on the global stage, over the last decade, the BRICS has come to symbolize the growing power of the world's largest emerging economies and their potential impact on the global economic and, increasingly, political order.

All BRICS countries are current members of the United Nations (UN) Security Council. Russia and China are permanent members with veto power, while Brazil, India, and South Africa are nonpermanent members currently serving on the council. Furthermore, the BRICS, combined, hold less than 15 percent of voting rights in both the World Bank and the IMF, yet, their economies are predicted to surpass the G7 economies in size by 2032, which can only strengthen their position at the UN, IMF, and the World Bank.

As depicted in Figure 10.6, BRICS have stepped up their participation at the UN by donating large sums of money to its regular and peacekeeping budgets. Russia has gone ahead and led the bloc by holding the first BRIC summit back in June 2009 in Yekaterinburg, issuing

a declaration calling for the establishment of an equitable, democratic, and multipolar world order.[21] Since then, according to the *Times*,[22] the BRICS have met in Brasília (Brazil) in 2010, in Sanya (China) in 2011, and in New Delhi (India) in 2012.

In recent years, the BRICS have received increasing scholarly attention. Brazilian political economist Marcos Troyjo and French investment banker Christian Déséglise founded the BRIC Lab at Columbia University, a forum examining the strategic, political, and economic consequences of the rise of BRIC countries, especially by analyzing their projects for power, prosperity, and prestige through graduate courses, special sessions with guest speakers, Executive Education programs, and annual conferences for policy makers, business and academic leaders, and students.[23]

The CIVETS Bloc Influence

The CIVETS acronym, which includes Colombia, Indonesia, Vietnam, Egypt, Turkey, and South Africa countries, as illustrated in Figure 10.7, was coined by Robert Ward, global director of the Global Forecasting Team of the Economist Intelligence Unit in late 2009.[24]

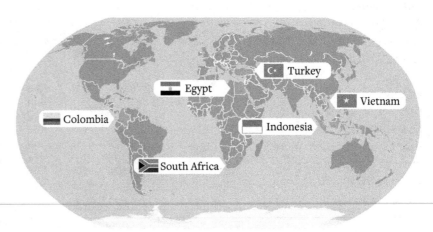

FIGURE 10.7 The CIVETS bloc

It was then further circulated by Michael Geoghegan, president of the Anglo-Chinese HSBC bank, in a speech to the Hong Kong Chamber of Commerce in April 2010. These groups of countries are predicted to be among the next emerging markets to quickly rise in economic prominence over the coming decades for their relative political stability, young populations that focus on education, and overall growing economic trends. Geoghegan compared these countries to the civet, a carnivorous mammal that eats and partially digests coffee cherries, passing a transformed coffee bean that fetches high prices.

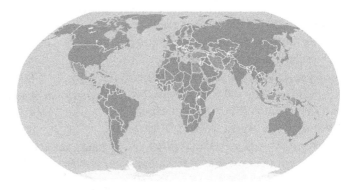

FIGURE 10.8 The Next-Eleven (N-11) countries

The CIVETS bloc is about 10 years younger than the BRICS with similar characteristics. All of these bloc countries are growing very quickly and have relatively diverse economies, which offer a greater advantage over the BRICS for not depending so heavily on foreign demands. They also have reasonably sophisticated financial systems, controlled inflation, and soaring young populations with fast-rising domestic consumption.[25]

Geoghegan argued in 2010 that emerging markets would grow three times as fast as developed countries that year, suggesting that the center of gravity of the world growth and economic development was moving toward Asia and Latin America.[26] All the CIVETS countries except Colombia and South Africa are also part of O'Neil's *Next Eleven* (N-11) countries, as depicted in Figure 10.8: Bangladesh, Egypt, Indonesia, Iran, Mexico, Nigeria, Pakistan, the Philippines, Turkey, South Korea, and Vietnam. These countries are believed to have a high chance of becoming, along with the BRICS, the world's largest economies in the 21st century.[27]

Some critics argue that the CIVETS countries have nothing in common beyond their youth populations. What does Egypt have in common with Vietnam? Data also suggest that, on the negative side, liquidity and corporate governance are patchy, while political risk remains a factor, as seen with Egypt in the past few years.

The MENA Countries

According to the World Bank,[28] the bloc, commonly known as MENA countries, covers an extensive region, extending from Morocco to Iran and including the majority of both the Middle Eastern and Maghreb

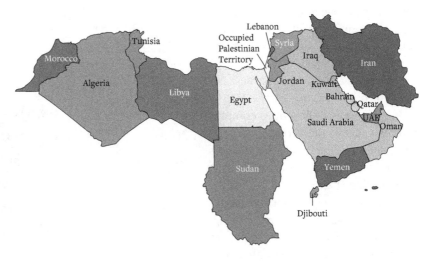

FIGURE 10.9 The MENA countries (dark shade) and other countries often considered as part of the bloc (lighter shade)

Source: GreenProfit.

countries. The World Bank argues that due to the geographic ambiguity and Eurocentric nature of the term *Middle East*, people often prefer to use the term WANA (West Asia and North Africa)[29] or the less common NAWA (North Africa–West Asia), as argued by Paz, Tourre, and Planton.[30] As depicted in Figure 10.9, MENA countries include Algeria, Bahrain, Djibouti, Egypt, Iran, Iraq, Israel, Jordan, Kuwait, Lebanon, Libya, Malta, Morocco, Oman, Qatar, Saudi Arabia, North and South Sudan, Syria, Tunisia, United Arab Emirates (UAE), Yemen, West Bank, and Gaza.

The MENA bloc, known as WANA or NAWA (we will be using MENA throughout this book), is an economically diverse region that includes both the oil-rich economies in the Gulf and countries that are resource scarce in relation to population, such as Egypt, Morocco, and Yemen. According to the Middle East Strategy at Harvard (MESH) project at the John Olin Institute for Strategic Study at Harvard University, the population of the MENA region, as depicted in Table 10.3, at its least extent, is roughly 381 million people, about 6 percent of the total world population. At its greatest extent, its population is roughly 523 million.

Two years after the *Arab Spring* commenced, many nations in the MENA region are still undergoing complex political, social, and economic transitions. Economic performance indicators were mixed in 2012, while most of the oil-exporting countries grew at healthy rates; the same is not true for oil importer ones, which have been growing at a sluggish pace. These differences did narrow in 2013, however, due to the scaling back of hydrocarbon production among oil exporters and a mild economic recovery among oil importers. In all, many of these countries are confronted with the

TABLE 10.3 MENA's population size and growth: 1950, 2007, and 2050

Country and region	Population in thousands			Ratio of population	
	1950	2007	2050[a]	2007/ 1950	2050/ 2007
Middle East and North Africa (MENA)	103,836	431,587	692,299	4.2	1.6
MENA–Western Asia	51,452	215,976	332,081	4.2	1.5
Iran	16,913	71,208	100,174	4.2	1.4
Iraq	5,340	28,993	61,942	5.4	2.1
Israel	1,258	6,928	10,527	5.5	1.5
Jordan	472	5,924	10,121	12.5	1.7
Lebanon	1,443	4,099	5,221	2.8	1.3
Palestinian Territory	1,005	4,017	10,265	4.0	2.6
Syria	3,536	19,929	34,887	5.6	1.8
Turkey	21,484	74,877	98,946	3.5	1.3
Arabian Peninsula	8336	58,544	123,946	7.0	2.1
Bahrain	116	753	1,173	6.5	1.6
Kuwait	152	2,851	5,240	18.7	1.8
Oman	456	2,595	4,639	5.7	1.8
Qatar	25	841	1,333	33.6	1.6
Saudi Arabia	3,201	24,735	45,030	7.7	1.8
United Arab Emirates	70	4,380	8,521	62.9	1.9
Yemen	4,316	22,389	58,009	5.2	2.6
Northern Africa	44,099	157,068	236,272	3.6	1.5
Algeria	8,753	33,858	49,610	3.9	1.5
Egypt	21,834	75498	121,219	3.5	1.6
Morocco	8,953	31,224	42,583	3.5	1.4
Libya	1,029	6,160	9,683	6.0	1.6
Tunisia	3,530	10,327	13,178	2.9	1.3

[a]Projected.
Source: UN Population Division, *World Population Prospects: The 2006 Revision* (2007; http://esa. un.org/, accessed April 10, 2007): table A.2.

immediate challenge of re-establishing or sustaining macroeconomic stability amid political uncertainty and social unrest, but the region must not lose sight of the medium-term challenge of diversifying its economies, creating jobs, and generating more inclusive growth.

The region's economic wealth over much of the past quarter century has been heavily influenced by two factors: the price of oil and the legacy of economic policies and structures that had emphasized a leading role for the state. With about 23 percent of the 300 million people in the MENA living on less than US$2 a day, however, empowering poor people constitutes an important strategy for fighting poverty.

Modest growth is anticipated, however, across the region. According to the IMF (IMF Reports 2013), subdued growth in MENA oil importers is expected to improve in 2013, although such growth is not expected to be sufficient to even begin making sizable inroads into the region's large unemployment problem. The external environment continues to be a challenge and to exert pressure on international reserves in many oil-importing countries among the MENA bloc. In addition, sluggish economic activity with trading partners, mostly advanced economies, in particular the eurozone area, is holding back a quicker recovery of exports, while elevated commodity prices continue to weigh on external balances in countries that depend on food and energy imports. Tourist arrivals, which have decreased significantly since the terrorist attacks on the United States in 2001, are gradually rebounding, but remain well below pre-2011 levels, before the global recession set in.

According to a new study reported in the Dubai-based *Khaleej Times*,[31] however, the sunny region and its associated countries could solar power the world three times over. If such projections ever become reality, poverty may have a chance to be eradicated in the region. Countries that move fast, the study suggests, could have the competitive advantage. MENA countries, especially ones located on the Arabian Peninsula, as well as others like Jordan, Lebanon, and Israel, are well positioned to take the lead in this industry. These countries are no strangers to the notion of solar energy. As the *Khaleej Times* article points out, the countries in the MENA region have the "greatest potential for solar regeneration"

supplying 45 percent of the world's energy sources possible through renewable energy. Renewable energy sources of interest in this region include Abu Dhabi's Masdar City as well as its hosting of the World Renewable Energy Agency headquarters.

Funding for these projects may pose an issue. FDI, according to the IMF, (IMF Reports 2013) is expected to remain restrained, lower than that in other emerging markets and advanced economies. Moreover, growing regional economic and social spillovers from the conflict in Syria are expected to add to the complexity of MENA's economic environment. While oil-exporting countries, mainly in the Gulf Cooperation Council (GCC), face a more positive outlook, there is still the risk of a worsening of the global economic outlook, particularly with advanced economies, which are major consumers of oil. Should this occur, oil exporter nations within MENA will likely face serious economic pressures. A prolonged decline in oil prices, rooted in persistently low global economic activity, for instance, could run down reserve buffers and result in fiscal deficits for the region.

Notwithstanding, the latest IMF's World Economic Outlook[32] projections suggest that economic performance in the MENA bloc will remain mixed. According to Qatar National Bank Group (QNB Group),[33] this dual

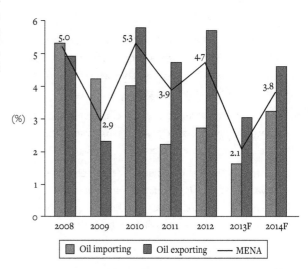

FIGURE 10.10 MENA's real GDP growth rates

Source: IMF data and QNB group forecasts.

speed development should continue over the next few years, with the GCC countries as the driving force for growth in the MENA region and the main source of investment and financing. As shown in Figure 10.10, the group forecasts MENA's economy to grow 2.1 percent in 2013 and 3.8 percent in 2014. Note in Figure 10.10 that the overall forecast disguises a significant difference in performance between oil exporters, including the GCC countries, and oil importers. The 2012 restrained growth of 2.7 percent in MENA oil importers is expected to fall to 1.6 percent in 2013 and recover to 3.2 percent in 2014, which will not suffice in creating enough jobs to reduce these countries' large unemployment rates. Meanwhile, oil exporters' healthy growth rates are projected to moderate this year to 3.0 percent as they scale back increases in oil production amid modest global energy demand. Continued large infrastructure investment is expected to lead to a rise in economic growth to 4.5 percent in 2014.

In addition, the MENA countries in transition continue to face political uncertainty with the challenge of delivering on the expectations for jobs and fostering economic cohesion, which also deters growth. In particular, the Syrian crisis has had a strong negative impact on growth in the Mashreq region—the region of Arab countries to the east of Egypt and north of the Arabian Peninsula, such as Iraq, Palestine–Israel, Jordan, Kuwait, Lebanon, and Syria—which has a large size of refugees straining the fiscal resources of countries like Iraq, Jordan, Lebanon, and Turkey to a lesser extent. A notable example we cite is that more than 800,000 Syrian refugees who have already entered Lebanon, about 19 percent of the population, have had a substantial impact on the already weak fiscal position of the Lebanese budget. Equally damaging have been the setbacks of the political transitions as well as the escalation of violence in Libya, Egypt, and Tunisia, which have further deterred much-needed economic reforms and deterred FDI.

Looking ahead, MENA countries will continue on their path of economic transition owing primarily to the benign GCC outlook, which will continue to act as the locomotive for regional growth. That said, caution must be given to the external environment in oil-importing countries, which remains volatile, with spillovers from the Syria conflict. Finally, as important as it is now to focus on maintaining economic stability, it is critical for MENA governments not to lose sight of the fundamental medium-term challenge of modernizing and diversifying the region's economies, creating more jobs, and providing fair and equitable opportunities for all.

NOTES

1. The term was coined in 1981 by Antoine W. van Agtmael of the International Finance Corporation of the World Bank, http://www.investopedia.com/articles/03/073003.asp (accessed October 29, 2013).

2. According to the International Monetary Fund's glossary at http://www.imf.org/external/np/exr/glossary/index.asp (accessed on October 29, 2013).

3. We recommend that you check Goncalves et al.'s book *Advanced Economies and Emerging Markets: Perspective for Globalization*, 2014, from the same publisher, for a comprehensive discussion of this theme.

4. http://www.oecd.org/eco/outlook/2088912.pdf

5. *Source*: http://www.oecd.org/eco/outlook/2088912.pdf

6. http://www.asean.org/asean/asean-member-states

7. http://investvine.com/aseans-gdp-to-double-by-2020/ (accessed October 29, 2013).

8. http://www.ihs.com/products/Global-Insight/industry-economic-report.aspx?ID=106594726

9. Krugman, P. 1996. *Pop Internationalism*. Cambridge, MA: The MIT Press.

10. Kowitt, B. June 17, 2009. "For Mr. BRIC, Nations Meeting a Milestone." CNNMoney.com (accessed October 26, 2013).

11. According to United Nations 2011 ranking.

12. Reuters 2011 Investment Outlook Summit, London and New York, December 6–7, 2010.

13. According to an article on South Africa Info titled "New era as South Africa joins BRICS." SouthAfrica.info, June 19, 2012.

14. Foroohar, R. 2009. "BRICs Overtake G7 By 2027." *Newsweek*, March 20. http://www.newsweek.com/brics-overtake-g7-2027-76001 (accessed March 17, 2013).

15. "Brazil, Russia, India, and China (BRIC). "Investopedia." Archived from the original on May 21, 2008. http://www.investopedia.com/terms/b/bric.asp (accessed April 12, 2008).

16. Published by Penguin Group, December 2011.

17. Foroohar, R. 2009. "BRICs Overtake G7 By 2027." *Newsweek,* March. http://www.newsweek.com/brics-overtake-g7-2027-76001 (accessed April 12, 2009).

18. Young, V. 2006. "Macquarie Launches Australia's First BRIC Funds." *Investor Daily*, November. http://www.investordaily.com.au/25542-macquarie-launches-australias-first-bric-funds (accessed May 23, 2007).

19. Haub, C. April 2012. "The BRIC Countries." Population Reference Bureau. http://www.prb.org/Publications/Articles/2012/brazil-russia-india-china.aspx (accessed December 5, 2012).

20. Faulconbridge, G. June 8, 2008. "BRICs Helped by Western Finance Crisis: Goldman." Reuters. St. Petersburg, Russia. http://www.reuters.com/article/2008/06/08/us-russia-forum-bric-idUSL071126420080608 (accessed July 12, 2012).

21. Mortished, C. 2008. "Russia Shows Its Political Clout by Hosting BRIC summit." *The Times* (London). http://www.thetimes.co.uk/tto/business/markets/russia/article2143017.ece (accessed May 12, 2012).

22. Halpin, T. 2009. "Brazil, Russia, India and China Form Bloc to Challenge U.S. Dominance." http://www.timesonline.co.uk/tol/news/world/us_and_americas/article6514737.ece (accessed March 23, 2011).

23. http://www.sipa.columbia.edu/news_events/announcements/BRICLab04132011.html

24. According to an article titled "BRICS and BICIS." 2009. *The Economist Magazine*, November 26. http://www.economist.com/blogs/theworldin2010/2009/11/acronyms_4

25. According to an article titled "BRICS and BICIS." 2009. *The Economist Magazine*, November 26. http://www.economist.com/blogs/theworldin2010/2009/11/acronyms_4

26. According to an article titled "BRICS and BICIS." 2009. *The Economist Magazine*, November 26. http://www.economist.com/blogs/theworldin2010/2009/11/acronyms_4

27. O'Neil, J. December 1, 2005. "How Solid Are the BRICS." Goldman Sachs' Global Economics Paper No. 134. http://www.goldmansachs.com/our-thinking/archive/archive-pdfs/how-solid.pdf (accessed November 14, 2012).

28. According to the World Bank definition of MENA countries. http://web.worldbank.org/WBSITE/EXTERNAL/COUNTRIES/MENAEXT/0,,menuPK:247619~pagePK:146748~piPK:146812~theSitePK:256299,00.html (accessed November 1, 2013).

29. http://www.worldbank.org/html/cgiar/newsletter/april97/8beltagy.html

30. Paz, S., M. Tourre, and S. Planton. October 10, 2003. "North Africa-West Asia (NAWA) Sea-Level Pressure Patterns and Their Linkages with the Eastern Mediterranean (EM) Climate." Wiley Online Library. http://onlinelibrary.wiley.com/doi/10.1029/2003GL017862/abstract (accessed November 1, 2013).

31. Saseendran, S. 2013. "Shaikh Mohammed Inaugurates Solar Power Park Phase-1." *Khaleej Times* (Dubai-based), October 23. http://www.khaleejtimes.com/kt-articledisplay-1.asp?xfile=data/nationgeneral/2013/October/nationgeneral_October299.xml&section=nationgeneral (accessed November 4, 2013).

32. http://www.imf.org/external/pubs/ft/weo/2013/01/ (accessed November 2, 2013).

33. QNB Group. October 14, 2012. "Economic and International Affairs." http://www.qnb.com.qa/cs/Satellite/QNBFrance/en_FR/AboutQNB/CorporateSocial-Responsibility/enEconomicandnationalAff (accessed November 2, 2013).

REFERENCES

Cheewatrakoolpong, K., C. Sabhasri, and N. Bundit-wattanawong. February 2013. "Impact of the ASEAN Economic Community on ASEAN Production Networks." ADBI, no. 409. http://papers.ssrn.com/sol3/papers.cfm?abstract_id=2222459 (accessed March 12, 2013).

Durand, M., C. Madaschi, and F. Terribile. 1998. "Trends in OECD Countries' International Competitiveness: The Influence of Emerging Market Economies." OECD Economics Department Working Paper, No. 195.

IMF Reports. May 2013. "Middle East and North Africa: Defining the Road Ahead." Regional Economic Outlook Update, Middle East and Central Asia Department. http://www.imf.org/external/pubs/ft/reo/2013/mcd/eng/pdf/mcdreo0513.pdf (accessed November 2, 2013).

Orgaz, L., L. Molina, and C. Carrasco. 2011. In El Creciente Peso de Las Economias Emergentes en La Economia Y Gobernanza Mundiales. Los Países BRIC." Documentos Ocasionales Numero 1101, Banco de Espana Eurosistema. http://www.bde.es/f/webbde/SES/Secciones/Publicaciones/PublicacionesSeriadas/DocumentosOcasionales/11/Fich/do1101.pdf (accessed December 12, 12).

BIBLIOGRAPHY

Economist's Staff Writers. 2009. "BRICS and BICIS." *The Economist*, November 26, 2009. http://www.economist.com/blogs/theworldin2010/2009/11/acronyms_4 (accessed November 9, 2012).

Halpin, T. 2009. "Brazil, Russia, India and China Form Bloc to Challenge U.S. Dominance." http://www.timesonline.co.uk/tol/news/world/us_and_americas/article6514737.ece (accessed March 23, 2011).

Haub, C. April 2012. "The BRIC Countries." Population Reference Bureau. http://www.prb.org/Publications/Articles/2012/brazil-russia-india-china.aspx (accessed December 05, 2012).

IMF. April 2013. "World Economic Outlook." http://www.imf.org/external/pubs/ft/weo/2013/01/weodata/index.aspx (accessed April 12, 2013).

O'Neill, J. 2001. "Building Better Global Economic BRICs." Global Economics Paper No. 66, Goldman Sachs. http://www.goldmansachs.com/our-thinking/archive/archive-pdfs/build-better-brics.pdf (accessed December 17, 2011).

O'Neill, J. 2011. *The Growth Map: Economic Opportunity in the BRICs and Beyond*. New York: Penguin Group.

The Political and Regulatory Environment

10.2

Betty Jane Punnett

P olitical risk is generally defined to include three major categories: forced divestment, unwelcome regulations, and interference in operations.

Forced Divestment

Forced divestment means that a government requires that a company give up its assets against its will. The government may acquire the company's assets itself, or it may force the company to give up the assets to other parties. At worst, a government may confiscate the assets of a company with no compensation. This is unusual except where there is clear evidence of wrongdoing on the company's part. The Cuban takeover of foreign companies in 1960 is often considered a confiscation, because the companies received no compensation for their assets; however, the Cuban government maintains that it offered compensation that was not accepted by the companies. More often the government forces a sale of assets, either to the government itself or to other local interests. Forced divestment may focus on one company when a government expropriates the assets, or it may entail the nationalization of an entire industry. In these cases, payment is made for assets, but in this situation, many companies believe their assets are substantially undervalued and that they are unfairly compensated. Sometimes payment is made in the local currency, which may not be readily convertible, or in government bonds, which are not negotiable and subject to foreign exchange risk. Again, companies consider this to be unfair treatment.

Types of Political Risk

The risk associated with the political environment is essentially the likelihood that a government will take actions that have an unexpected, negative impact on a firm. These actions can include:

- government confiscation of a firm's property with no compensation to the firm;

- government expropriation of a firm's property for compensation to be determined by the government;

- government acquisition of a firm's property for a sum determined by an objective third party;

- government imposition of taxes on foreign firms;

- government passage of regulations that make it difficult for foreign firms

---

to operate efficiently and effectively;

- government encouragement of negative attitudes toward a particular firm or foreign firms in general; and

- government spearheading and supporting a buy-local campaign that discriminates against foreign firms.

The impact of forced divestment can be substantial for a company or industry, and the risks must therefore be assessed carefully. The likelihood of forced divestment is, however, relatively low. The period from 1970 to 1977 was a period when a substantial number of forced divestments took place around the world; a reported high of nearly seventy such acts took place in 1975 (Minor 1990), still a relatively small number. From 1980 to the present there have been few forced divestments. In contrast, privatization has been more common in this period. Governments have returned assets to former owners or sought private sector buyers (often foreign) for government-owned companies.

Forced divestment or nationalization is most often undertaken by a host government against a foreign company, either because the company is seen as having a negative impact on the host, or because the host believes it can run the company for its own benefit. Interestingly, in 2008, the UK government announced that it would nationalize the Northern Rock Bank, a UK bank, because of the problems the bank had suffered due to bad loans associated with the U.S. subprime loans. The UK government had provided substantial financing to stop a run on the bank in late 2007. The government claimed that nationalization was necessary to save the bank, but shareholders did not agree.

While the impact of forced divestment is substantial, it is a one-time event. Unwelcome regulations can be of more ongoing concern for many companies, as discussed in the following section.

Unwelcome Regulations

Governments can impose new restrictions that affect a firm's ability to operate effectively and profitably in a particular location. Unwelcome regulations include new taxes, local ownership or management requirements, reinvestment provisions, limits on size or location, and foreign exchange restrictions. If these regulations are expected, then managers can make decisions to deal with them. The risk occurs because they are often unexpected. Decisions made without taking the restrictions into account may no longer be appropriate when the restrictions are imposed. In contrast to forced divestment, governments do not usually reimburse firms for losses in profits resulting from the imposition of regulations, so it is particularly important for managers to assess and manage these events.

Generally, new and unwelcome regulations are imposed either to raise revenues for the government (e.g., new taxes) or to encourage particular aspects of development (e.g., local ownership). If managers invest in understanding a government's priorities, they are more likely to be able to predict government regulations. For example, if the government is concerned with unemployment, it may impose local employment requirements; if it wants to establish a broadly based industrial complex, it may require local sourcing and technology development; if improving local management skills is important, it will likely want training for local managers. If managers can predict likely regulations, they can plan for them. Managers can also choose to be proactive and implement plans to help achieve development objectives, thus building an image as a good corporate citizen.

Unwelcome regulations were prevalent in the 1970s but have become less common in the 1990s. Many countries around the world have recently sought to promote themselves as good places to do business, and thus to attract foreign investors. Along with this has been a decrease in regulations. There are still many regulations, however, and, as noted previously, firms are likely to be examined more closely in the coming years. Terrorism, conflicts, poverty, and apparently unethical corporate activities are all likely to result in increased attempts to control business activities.

In addition to unwelcome regulations, governments can interfere in company activities in a variety of more subtle ways as outlined in the following section.

Interference in Operations

Interference in operations refers to a government action that makes it difficult for a firm to operate effectively. This includes government support and encouragement of unionization, negative comments about foreigners and foreign businesses, and discriminatory support of local businesses. Governments may engage in such activities for a variety of reasons. They may believe that a foreign firm is detrimental to local development and thus that opposing the foreign firm will increase the government's popularity. In some circumstances, anti-foreign sentiment might allow the government to remain in power. In other situations, anti-foreign sentiments are based on historical events. The Japanese occupation of Korea before and during World War II means that Japanese firms are not always welcomed in Korea. American firms may find the South Korean environment friendlier.

This type of political risk is particularly difficult to assess and manage because it is often motivated by current political sentiment and can occur in different and subtle forms. Forced divestment and unwelcome regulations have an immediate and identifiable impact on operations. The activities described as interference with operations may be less obvious and the related effects unclear. Yet while not immediately obvious, the effects can nevertheless have a major impact over time (through lost sales, increased costs, difficult labor relations, and so forth). Managers should therefore consider this aspect of political risk to be as important as the other two.

Understanding the reasons for various types of political activity enables managers to assess the likelihood of a particular activity occurring and to devise ways to manage such occurrences.

Assessment and Management of Political Risk

Assessment of political risk is a relatively informal activity in many companies, although some companies have detailed systems of political risk assessment and management in place. For example, the following systems have been described (Punnett and Ricks 1997):

- At Xerox, each managing director of a major foreign affiliate prepared a quarterly report listing the ten most salient political issues in the local environment. These issues were analyzed in terms of their implications for Xerox, and alternative action plans for dealing with them were prepared. These reports went to the operating vice president and the director of international relations at the company headquarters, who considered the combined implications of all the reports. Decisions about responses to political events were made by the operating vice president and director of international relations, incorporating the managing directors' recommendations. These decisions were incorporated into the company's annual plans.
- At Chemical Bank, political spreadsheets were completed for each location. Significant political issues and actors were identified for each location, and the actors were evaluated in terms of their stands on issues, their power to enforce a stand, and their degree of concern about it. Overall, this was used to provide a rating for a given location and details regarding political issues of concern. The spreadsheets were completed by local managers and reviewed at headquarters.
- The Royal Bank of Canada used a ranking method to gauge the relative risk in different countries (according to Bertrand 1990). The ranking was based on economic, business, and political issues. Economic issues included the economic structure and resources (including natural resources), recent economic trends and policies, foreign debt and liquidity, and short- and long-term economic outlook. Business issues included the quality and skills of the labor pool and business leaders, the legislative environment (including rules for ownership and taxation), and the financial strength and competitiveness of the country's top companies. Political issues included the quality and stability of the government, as well as social factors such as the impact

of special interest groups, civil unrest, and relationships with its neighbors, major powers, and Canada. Once the bank had all the data, it ranked countries from 0 (worst) to 100 (best). At least once a year the bank's Country Review Committee reviewed all countries in which the bank did business.

Sophisticated political risk analysis systems are computer based and incorporate a wide variety of country and company data. Concerns about terrorism and Internet security are likely to lead to a greater emphasis on political risk analysis in many companies. The following discussion considers sources of information on political risk, factors that suggest risk, and approaches for managing risk.

Sources of Information

Information for political risk assessment comes from external and/or internal sources. External sources include banks, accounting firms, consultants, trade officials, and country risk services. A variety of these organizations publish books on individual countries that include a political analysis. The CIA (Central Intelligence Agency) Factbooks and The *Economist* Intelligence Units are two well-known sources of country information. In addition, organizations such as Business International and Business Environmental Risk Intelligence specialize in assessing and rating country risk. Each source provides a somewhat different viewpoint, and managers will want to utilize several. These external sources of information are a good starting point, but they focus on the country only.

In order to assess political risk validly, managers need to consider their company and the country in question. This means that internal sources of information are as important as external. Managers with substantial company history and international experience, employees who have lived or worked in a particular country, as well as regional and local managers can all provide somewhat different perspectives. Combining these provides a rounded look at any situation. Larger companies have staff departments that specialize in political risk assessment and

management, but smaller companies generally rely on a more informal process.

Factors Affecting Political Risk

The degree of political risk that a company faces is a function of both the country where business takes place and the particular company and its type of business. For example, for most companies, political risk would increase in times of civil unrest. For a company that provides negotiations services, which are valued by both sides in the civil unrest, the situation is the reverse. This is clearly the case of companies providing security in Iraq during the war. This is an extreme example, but serves to illustrate the point that what is risky for one company may be neutral or safe for another. There are certain characteristics of countries and companies that generally suggest increased political risk, and these are discussed in the following sections. It is the job of the international manager to apply these generic concepts to the specifics of the company's situation.

COUNTRY CHARACTERISTICS

Generally, instability is associated with increased risk. Instability implies uncertainty, which implies risk. Instability and uncertainty imply political risk from a business perspective because the government may behave in unexpected ways. Characteristics such as type of government, level of economic development, and stability of social and political systems make a country more or less risky. For most companies, frequent government changes, an unstable economy, and social upheavals increase the business risk associated with a particular location. War, revolution, and terrorism increase personal and property risks, as well as business risk. When a gap exists (as is the case in many less-developed countries) between what people expect (particularly in terms of material goods) and what they have access to, the population may be hostile toward foreigners, who seem to be better off than locals; this also increases the degree of political risk, as the governments will be conscious of this hostility.

Although instability, war, and terrorism imply increased risk for many companies, it is also true that some companies benefit from them and a fair number are not affected. At the extreme, a company whose business is selling guns or training executives to counter terrorism benefits from situations that most companies would seek to avoid. A company that provides material goods at a low cost might be attracted to a location where the expectations/reality gap is high. Other companies are involved in businesses that are not particularly affected by changes in government, the economy, or society—for example, a company that manufactures cardboard boxes might fall into this category—and therefore they can to some extent ignore these instabilities.

INDUSTRY AND COMPANY CHARACTERISTICS

Certain industries appear to be more subject to government activity than others. This is usually because these industries are seen as being important to a country's welfare and development, and the government therefore wants to maintain control over them. An interesting ongoing issue is the attempt to control Internet access by a variety of countries, such as the People's Republic of China, Myanmar, North Korea, and various Arab countries experiencing civil unrest. In addition, industries that are highly visible to the local population are important to governments in maintaining political control. Extractive industries (e.g., petroleum, mining), those that use natural resources (e.g., agriculture, tourism), as well as infrastructure (e.g., banking, insurance, railroads, airlines, communication) and defense are all seen as important and are highly visible. Historically, these have been most subject to government intervention, sometimes to the point of nationalization.

The makeup of a company also affects the degree of risk that it faces—factors such as ownership, management, technology, and size may mean that a company faces more or less risk in a particular country. It is quite possible that there could be two companies operating in the same foreign country and the same industry with one facing substantial political risk and the other very little.

If a company is seen as a good corporate citizen by the government and the host county population, then it is less likely to face political intervention. Local ownership, local management, good employee relations, use of local suppliers, contribution to development goals, and provision of appropriate technology are all characteristics of good corporate citizenship and tend to lower the likelihood of government intervention.

In contrast, a foreign company can also make government intervention difficult by controlling critical aspects of the local business outside the host country. Control of technology, needed resources, distribution systems, markets, and so on makes the subsidiary dependent on the parent and means that it is hard for the government to intervene effectively.

These two sides of the vulnerability to political risk picture lead to two distinct risk management strategies, which have been described as defensive and integrative (Gregory 1989). Although based on research some twenty years ago, these approaches are still applicable in general terms; however, their specific application will be influenced by technological developments. Essentially, defensive strategies focus on maintaining control and power with the parent company, while integrative strategies aim to develop a positive local image for the company. The investor needs to examine the political situation in the host country to select the appropriate strategy.

DISCUSSION QUESTIONS

1. What is an emerging market or big emerging market (BEM)? Give examples.

2. What are the traits or characteristics of emerging markets? Discuss.

3. Why are emerging markets important to the global economy? Discuss.

4. What are the distinct contributions of emerging markets to the developed economies? Discuss.

5. What is political risk?

6. What are expropriation, domestication, and confiscation? Discuss the differences.

7. How can an international marketer assess and manage political risk? Discuss.

8. What are the factors that affect political risk? Discuss.

REFERENCES

Bertrand, K. 1990. "Politics Pushes the Marketing Foreground." *Business Marketing* (March): 51–55.

Gregory, A. 1989. "Political Risk Management." In *International Business in Canada*, ed. A. Rugman, 310–329. Scarborough, Ontario: Prentice-Hall Canada.

Minor, M. 1990. "Changes in Developing Country Regimes for Foreign Direct Investment." Monograph. Columbia: University of South Carolina Press.

Punnett, B.J., and D. Ricks. 1997. *International Business*. Cambridge, MA: Blackwell.

11

Chapter 11 discusses strategies for global value creation. The three generic strategies discussed in the chapter are *adaptation*, *aggregation (standardization)*, and *arbitrage (exploiting economic differences)*. The first two strategies define the difference between the traditional marketer who employs a multi-domestic strategy—that is, differentiation—and the contemporary global marketer who seeks to maximize cost efficiencies through standardization. The third strategy, *arbitrage*, capitalizes on the differences between individual economies as it focuses on benefiting from optimum buying or selling. A discussion follows regarding which one strategy a company should use and under what circumstances. The impact of the company's experience with globalization, as well as the intensity of and exchange in, the global environment will shed light into the type of strategy most advisable. The chapter lists numerous examples of companies that have employed these generic strategies.

11.1 Generic Strategies for Global Value Creation

Cornelis A. de Kluyver

I n this chapter, we introduce three generic strategies for creating value in a global context—*adaptation*, *aggregation*, and *arbitrage*—and a number of variants for each.[1] This conceptualization was first introduced by Pankaj Ghemawat in his important book *Redefining Global Strategy* and, as such, is not new. In the next chapter, we extend this framework, however, by integrating these generic strategies with the proposition that global strategy formulation is about changing a company's business model to create a global competitive advantage.

Ghemawat's "AAA" Global Strategy Framework

Ghemawat so-called AAA framework offers three generic approaches to global value creation. *Adaptation* strategies seek to increase revenues and market share by tailoring one or more components of a company's business model to suit local requirements or preferences. *Aggregation* strategies focus on achieving economies of scale or scope by creating regional or global efficiencies; they typically involve standardizing a significant portion of the value proposition and grouping together development and production processes. *Arbitrage* is about exploiting economic or other differences between national or regional markets, usually by locating separate parts of the supply chain in different places.

Adaptation

Adaptation—creating global value by changing one or more elements of a company's offer to meet local requirements or preferences—is probably the most widely used global strategy. The reason for this will be readily apparent: some degree of adaptation is essential or unavoidable for virtually all products in all parts of the world. The taste of Coca-Cola in Europe is different from that in the United States, reflecting differences in water quality and the kind and amount of sugar added. The packaging of construction adhesive in the United States informs customers how many square feet it will cover; the same package in Europe must do so in square meters. Even commodities such as cement are not immune: its pricing in different geographies reflects local energy and transportation costs and what percentage is bought in bulk.

Ghemawat subdivides adaptation strategies into five categories: *variation, focus, externalization, design,* and *innovation* (Figure 11.1).

Variation strategies not only involve making changes in *products and services* but also making adjustments to *policies, business positioning,* and even *expectations for success.* The *product* dimension will be obvious: Whirlpool, for example, offers smaller washers and dryers in Europe than in the United States, reflecting the space constraints prevalent in many European homes. The need to consider adapting *policies* is less obvious. An example is Google's dilemma in China to conform to local censorship rules. Changing a company's overall *positioning* in a country goes well beyond changing products or even policies. Initially, Coke did little more than "skim the cream" off big emerging markets such as India and China. To boost volume and market share, it had to reposition itself to a "lower margin–higher volume" strategy that involved lowering price points, reducing costs, and expanding distribution. Changing *expectations* for, say, the rate of return on investment in a country, while a company is trying to create a presence is also a prevalent form of variation.

Adaptation	Aggregation	Arbitrage
Variation		*Performance Enhancement*
Focus: Reduce Need for Adaptation		
Externalization: Reduce Burden of Adaptation	*Economies of Scale*	*Cost Reduction*
Design: Reduce Cost of Adaptation	*Economies of Scope*	*Risk Reduction*
Innovation: Improve on Exixting Adaptation		

FIGURE 11.1 AAA strategies and their variants.

A second type of adaptation strategies uses a *focus* on particular *products, geographies, vertical stages* of the value chain, or *market segments* as a way of reducing the impact of differences across regions. A *product* focus takes advantage of the fact that wide differences can exist *within* broad product categories in the degree of variation required to compete effectively in local markets. Ghemawat cites the example of television programs: action films need far less adaptation than local newscasts. Restriction of *geographic* scope can permit a focus on countries where relatively little adaptation of the domestic value proposition is required. A *vertical* focus strategy involves limiting a company's direct involvement to specific steps in the supply chain while outsourcing others. Finally, a *segment* focus involves targeting a more limited customer base. Rather than adapting a product or service, a company using this strategy chooses to accept the reality that without modification, their products will appeal to a smaller market segment or different distributor network from those in the domestic market. Many luxury good manufacturers use this approach.

Whereas focus strategies overcome regional differences by narrowing scope, externalization strategies transfer—through *strategic alliances, franchising, user adaptation,* or *networking*—responsibility for specific parts of a company's business model to partner companies to accommodate local requirements, lower cost, or reduce risk. For example, Eli Lilly extensively uses *strategic alliances* abroad for drug development and testing. McDonald's growth strategy abroad uses *franchising* as well as company-owned stores. And software companies heavily depend on both *user adaptation and networking* for the development of applications for their basic software platforms.

A fourth type of adaptation focuses on *design* to reduce the cost of, rather than the need for, variation. Manufacturing costs can often be achieved by introducing design *flexibility* so as to overcome supply differences. Introducing standard production *platforms*

and *modularity* in components also helps to reduce cost. A good example of a company focused on design is Tata Motors, which has successfully introduced a car in India that is affordable to a significant number of citizens.

A fifth approach to adaptation is *innovation*, which, given its crosscutting effects, can be characterized as improving the effectiveness of adaptation efforts. For instance, IKEA's flat-pack design, which has reduced the impact of geographic distance by cutting transportation costs, has helped that retailer expand into 3 dozen countries.

Minicase 11.1   McDonald's McAloo Tikki[2]

When Ray Kroc opened his first McDonald's in Des Plaines, Illinois, he could hardly have envisioned the golden arches rising 5 decades later in one of the oldest commercial streets in the world. But McDonald's began dreaming of India in 1991, a year after opening its first restaurant in China. The attraction was obvious: 1.1 billion people, with 300 million destined for middle-class status.

But how do you sell hamburgers in a land where cows are sacred and 1 in 5 people are vegetarian? And how do you serve a largely poor consumer market that stretches from the Himalayas to the shores of the Indian Ocean? McDonald's executives in Oak Brook struggled for years with these questions before finding the road to success.

McDonald's has made big gains since the debut of its first two restaurants in India, in Delhi and Mumbai, in October 1996. Since then, the fast-food chain has grown to more than 160 outlets. The Indian market represents a small fraction of McDonald's $24 billion in annual revenues. But it is not insignificant

because the company is increasingly focused on high-growth markets. "The decision to go in wasn't complicated," James Skinner, McDonald's chief executive officer, once said. "The complicated part was deciding what to sell."

At first, McDonald's path into India was fraught with missteps. First, there was the nonbeef burger made with mutton. But the science was off: mutton is 5% fat (beef is 25% fat), making it rubbery and dry. Then there was the french fry debacle. McDonald's started off using potatoes grown in India, but the local variety had too much water content, making the fries soggy. Chicken kabob burgers? Sounds like a winner except that they were skewered by consumers. Salad sandwiches were another flop: Indians prefer cooked foods.

If that was not enough, in May 2001, the company was picketed by protesters after reports surfaced in the United States that the chain's fries were injected with beef extracts to boost flavor—a serious infraction for vegetarians. McDon-

ald's executives in India denied the charges, claiming their fries were different from those sold in America.

But the company persevered, learned, and succeeded. It figured out what Indians wanted to eat and what they would pay for it. It built, from scratch, a mammoth supply chain—from farms to factories—in a country where elephants, goats, and trucks share the same roads. To deal with India's massive geography, the company divided the country into two regions: the north and east, and the south and west. Then it formed 50-50 joint ventures with two well-connected Indian entrepreneurs: Vikram Bakshi, who made his fortune in real estate, runs the northern region; and Amit Jatia, an entrepreneur who comes from a family of successful industrialists, manages the south.

Even though neither had any restaurant experience, this joint-venture management structure gave the company what it needed: local faces at the top. The two entrepreneurs also brought money: before the first restaurant opened, the partners invested $10 million into building a workable supply chain, establishing distribution centers, procuring refrigerated trucks, and finding production facilities with adequate hygiene. They also invested $15 million in Vista Processed Foods, a food processing plant outside Mumbai. In addition, Mr. Jatia, Mr. Bakshi, and 38 staff members spent an entire year in the Indonesian capital of Jakarta studying how McDonald's operated in another Asian country.

Next, the Indian executives embarked on basic-menu research and development (R&D). After awhile, they hit on a veggie burger with a name Indians could understand: the McAloo Tikki (an "aloo tikki" is a cheap potato cake locals buy from roadside vendors).

The lesson in the McDonald's India case: local input matters. Today, 70% of the menu is designed to suit Indians: the Paneer Salsa Wrap, the Chicken Maharaja Mac, the Veg McCurry Pan. The McAloo, by far the best-selling product, also is being shipped to McDonald's in the Middle East, where potato dishes are popular. And in India, it does double duty: it not only appeals to the masses; it is also a hit with the country's 200 million vegetarians.

Another lesson learned from the McDonald's case: vegetarian items should not come into contact with nonvegetarian products or ingredients. Walk into any Indian McDonald's and you will find half of the employees wearing green aprons and the other half in red. Those in green handle vegetarian orders. The red-clad ones serve nonvegetarians. It is a separation that extends throughout the restaurant and its supply chain. Each restaurant's grills, refrigerators, and storage areas are designated as "veg" or "non-veg." At the Vista Processed Foods plant, at every turn, managers stressed the "non-veg" side was in one part of the facility, and the "vegetarian only" section was in another.

Today, after many missteps, one can truly imagine the ghost of Ray Kroc asking Indians one of the greatest questions of all time—the one that translates into so many cultures: "You want fries with that?" Yes, Ray, they do.

Aggregation

Aggregation is about creating *economies of scale or scope* as a way of dealing with differences (see Figure 11.1). The objective is to exploit similarities among geographies rather than adapting to differences but stopping short of complete standardization, which would destroy concurrent adaptation approaches. The key is to identify ways of introducing economies of scale and scope into the global business model without compromising local responsiveness.

Adopting a *regional* approach to globalizing the business model—as Toyota has so effectively done—is probably the most widely used aggregation strategy. As discussed in the previous chapter, *regionalization* or *semiglobalization* applies to many aspects of globalization, from investment and communication patterns to trade. And even when companies do have a significant presence in more than one region, competitive interactions are often regionally focused.

Examples of different *geographic* aggregation approaches are not hard to find. Xerox centralized its purchasing, first regionally, later globally, to create a substantial cost advantage. Dutch electronics giant Philips created a global competitive advantage for its Norelco shaver product line by centralizing global production in a few strategically located plants. And the increased use of global (corporate) branding over product branding is a powerful example of creating economies of scale and scope. As these examples show, geographic aggregation strategies have potential application to every major business model component.

Geographic aggregation is not the only avenue for generating economies of scale or scope. The other, nongeographic dimensions of the CAGE framework [...]—*cultural, administrative, geographic*, and *economic*—also lend themselves to aggregation strategies. Major book publishers, for example, publish their best sellers in but a few languages, counting on the fact that readers are willing to accept a book in their second language (*cultural* aggregation). Pharmaceutical companies seeking to market new drugs in Europe must satisfy the regulatory requirements of a few selected countries to qualify for a license to distribute throughout the EU (*administrative* aggregation). As for *economic* aggregation, the most obvious examples are provided by companies that distinguish between developed and emerging markets and, at the extreme, focus on just one or the other.

Minicase 11.2 Globalization at Whirlpool Corporation[3]

The history of globalization at the Whirlpool Corporation—a leading company in the $100-billion global home-appliance industry—illustrates the multitude of challenges associated with globalizing a business model. Whirlpool manufactures appliances across all major categories—including fabric care, cooking, refrigeration, dishwashing, countertop appliances, garage organization, and water filtration—and has a market presence in every major country in the world. It markets some of the world's most recognized appliance brands, including Whirlpool, Maytag, KitchenAid, Jenn-Air, Amana, Bauknecht, Brastemp, and Consul. Of these, the Whirlpool brand is the world's top-rated global appliance brand and ranks among the world's most valuable brands. In 2008, Whirlpool realized annual sales of approximately $19 billion, had 70,000 employees, and maintained 67 manufacturing and technology research centers around the world.

In the late 1980s, Whirlpool Corporation set out on a course of growth that would eventually transform the company into the leading global manufacturer of major home appliances, with operations based in every region of the world. At the time, Dave Whitwam, Whirlpool's chairman and CEO, had recognized the need to look for growth beyond the mature and highly competitive U.S. market. Under Mr. Whitwam's leadership, Whirlpool began a series of acquisitions that would give the company the scale and resources to participate in global markets. In the process, Whirlpool would establish new relationships with millions of customers in countries and cultures far removed from the U.S. market and the company's roots in rural Benton Harbor, Michigan.

Whirlpool's global initiative focused on establishing or expanding its presence in North America, Latin America, Europe, and Asia. In 1989, Whirlpool acquired the appliance business of Philips Electronics N.V., which immediately gave the company a solid European operations base. In the western hemisphere, Whirlpool expanded its longtime involvement in the Latin America market and established a presence in Mexico as an appliance joint-venture partner. By the mid-1990s, Whirlpool had strengthened its position in Latin America and Europe and was building a solid manufacturing and marketing base in Asia.

In 2006, Whirlpool acquired Maytag Corporation, resulting in an aligned organization able to offer more to consumers in the increasingly competitive global marketplace. The transaction created additional economies of scale. At the same time, it expanded Whirlpool's portfolio of innovative, high-quality branded products and services to consumers.

Executives knew that the company's new scale, or global platform, that emerged from the acquisitions offered a significant competitive advantage, but only if the individual operations and resources were working in concert with each other. In other words, the challenge is not in buying the individual businesses—the real challenge is to effectively integrate all the businesses together in a meaningful way that creates the leverage and competitive advantage.

Some of the advantages were easily identified. By linking the regional organizations through Whirlpool's common systems and global processes, the company could speed product development, make purchasing increasingly more efficient and cost-effective, and improve manufacturing utilization through the use of common platforms and cross-regional exports.

Whirlpool successfully refocused a number of its key functions to its global approach. Procurement was the first function to go global, followed by technology and product development. The two functions shared much in common and have already led to significant savings from efficiencies. More important, the global focus has helped reduce the number of regional manufacturing platforms worldwide. The work of these two functions, combined with the company's manufacturing footprints in each region, has led to the development of truly global platforms—products that share common parts and technologies but offer unique and innovative features and designs that appeal to regional consumer preferences.

Global branding was next. Today, Whirlpool's portfolio ranges from global brands to regional and country-specific brands of appliances. In North America, key brands include Whirlpool, KitchenAid, Roper by Whirlpool Corporation, and Estate. Acquired with the company's 2002 purchase of Vitromatic S.A., brands Acros and Supermatic are leading names in Mexico's domestic market. In addition, Whirlpool is a major supplier for the Sears, Roebuck and Co. Kenmore brand. In Europe, the company's key brands are Whirlpool and Bauknecht. Polar, the latest addition to Europe's portfolio, is the leading brand in Poland. In Latin America, the brands include Brastemp and Consul. Whirlpool's Latin American operations include Embraco, the world's leading compressor manufacturer. In Asia, Whirlpool is the company's primary brand and the top-rated refrigerator and washer manufacturer in India.

Arbitrage

A third generic strategy for creating a global advantage is *arbitrage* (see Figure 11.1). Arbitrage is a way of exploiting differences, rather than adapting to them or bridging them, and defines the original global strategy: buy low in one market and sell high in another. Outsourcing and offshoring are modern day equivalents. Wal-Mart saves billions of dollars a year by buying goods from China. Less visible but equally important absolute economies are created by greater differentiation with customers and partners, improved corporate bargaining power with suppliers or local authorities, reduced supply chain and other market and nonmarket risks, and through the local creation and sharing of knowledge.

Since arbitrage focuses on exploiting differences between regions, the CAGE framework [...] is of particular relevance and helps define a set of substrategies for this generic approach to global value creation.

Favorable effects related to country or place of origin have long supplied a basis for *cultural arbitrage*. For example, an association with French culture has long been an international success factor for fashion items, perfumes, wines, and foods. Similarly, fast-food products and drive-through restaurants are mainly associated with U.S. culture. Another example of cultural arbitrage—real or perceived—is provided by Benihana of Tokyo, the "Japanese steakhouse." Although heavily American—the company has only one outlet in Japan out of more than 100 worldwide—it serves up a theatrical version of teppanyaki cooking that the company describes as "Japanese" and "eatertainment."

Legal, institutional, and political differences between countries or regions create opportunities for *administrative* arbitrage. Ghemawat cites the actions taken by Rupert Murdoch's News Corporation in the 1990s. By placing its U.S. acquisitions into holding companies in the Cayman Islands, the company could deduct interest payments on the debt used to finance the deals against the profits generated by its newspaper operations in Britain. Through this and other similar actions, it successfully lowered its tax liabilities to an average rate of less than 10%, rather than the statutory 30% to 36% of the three main countries in which it operated: Britain, the United States, and Australia. By comparison, major competitors such as Disney were paying close to the official rates.[4]

With steep drops in transportation and communication costs in the last 25 years, the scope for *geographic* arbitrage—the leveraging of geographic differences—has been diminished but not fully eliminated. Consider what is happening in medicine, for example. It is quite common today for doctors in the United States to take X-rays during the day, send them electronically to radiologists in India for interpretation overnight, and for the report to be available the next morning in the United States. In fact, reduced transportation costs sometimes create new opportunities for geographic arbitrage. Every day, for instance, at the international flower market in Aalsmeer, the Netherlands, more than 20 million flowers and 2 million plants are auctioned off and flown to customers in the United States.

As Ghemawat notes, in a sense, all arbitrage strategies that add value are "economic." Here, the term *economic* arbitrage is used to describe strategies that do not directly exploit *cultural*, *administrative*, or *geographic differences*. Rather, they are focused on leveraging differences in the costs of labor and capital, as well as variations in more industry-specific inputs (such as knowledge) or in the availability of complementary products.[5]

Exploiting differences in labor costs—through outsourcing and off-shoring—is probably the most common form of economic arbitrage. This strategy is

Minicase 11.3   Indian Companies Investing in Latin America? To Serve U.S. Customers?[6]

Indian investment in Latin America is relatively small but growing quickly. Indian firms have invested about $7 billion in the region over the last decade, according to figures released by the Latin American division of India's Ministry of External Affairs in New Delhi. The report projects that this amount will easily double in the next few years.

As India has become a magnet for foreign investment, Indian companies themselves are looking abroad for opportunities, motivated by declining global trade barriers and fierce competition at home. Their current focus is on Latin America, where hyperinflation and currency devaluation no longer dominate headlines.

Like China, India is trying to lock up supplies of energy and minerals to feed its rapidly growing economy. Indian firms have stakes in oil and natural gas ventures in Colombia, Venezuela, and Cuba. In 2006, Bolivia signed a deal with New Delhi-based Jindal Steel and Power, Ltd., which plans to invest $2.3 billion to extract iron ore and to build a steel mill in that South American nation.

At the same time, Indian information technology companies are setting up outsourcing facilities to be closer to their customers in the West. Tata Consultancy Services is the leader, employing 5,000 tech workers in more than a dozen Latin American countries.

Indian manufacturing firms, accustomed to catering to low-income consumers at home, are finding Latin America a natural market. Mumbai-based Tata Motors, Ltd., has formed a joint venture with Italy's Fiat to produce small pickup trucks in Argentina. Generic drug makers, such as Dr. Reddy's, are offering low-cost alternatives in a region where U.S. and European multinationals have long dominated.

The Indian government has carefully positioned India as a partner, rather than a rival out to steal the region's resources and jobs, a common worry about China. Mexico has been particularly hard-hit by China's rise. The Asian nation's export of textiles, shoes, electronics, and other consumer goods has cost Mexico tens of thousands of manufacturing jobs, displaced it as the second-largest trading partner with the United States, and flooded its domestic market with imported merchandise. In 2006, Mexico's trade deficit with China was a record $22.7 billion, but China has invested less than $100 million in the country since 1994, according to the Bank of Mexico.

Mexico's trading relationship with India, albeit small, is much more balanced. Mexico's trade deficit with India was just under half a billion dollars in 2006, and Indian companies have invested $1.6 billion here since 1994—or about 17 times more than China—according to Mexico's central bank.

Some of that investment is in basic industries and traditional *maquiladora* factories making goods for export. For example, Mexico's biggest steel plant is owned by ArcelorMittal. Indian pharmaceutical companies, too, are finding Latin America to be attractive for expansion. Firms including Ranbaxy Laboratories, Ltd., Aurobindo Pharma, Ltd., and Cadila Pharmaceuticals, Ltd., have sales or manufacturing operations in the region.

widely used in labor-intensive (garments) as well as high-technology (flat-screen TV) industries. Economic arbitrage is not limited to leveraging differences in labor costs alone, however. Capital cost differentials can be an equally rich source of opportunity.

Which "A" Strategy Should a Company Use?

A company's financial statements can be a useful guide for signaling which of the "A" strategies will have the greatest potential to create global value. Firms that heavily rely on branding and that do a lot of advertising, such as food companies, often need to engage in considerable adaptation to local markets.

Those that do a lot of R&D—think pharmaceutical firms—may want to aggregate to improve economies of scale, since many R&D outlays are fixed costs. For firms whose operations are labor intensive, such as apparel manufacturers, arbitrage will be of particular concern because labor costs vary greatly from country to country.

Which "A" strategy a company emphasizes also depends on its globalization history. Companies that start on the path of globalization on the supply side of their business model, that is, that seek to lower cost or to access new knowledge, first typically focus on aggregation and arbitrage approaches to creating global value, whereas companies that start their globalization history by taking their value propositions to foreign markets are immediately faced with adaptation challenges. Regardless of their starting point, most companies will need to consider all "A" strategies at different points in their global evolution, sequentially or, sometimes, simultaneously.

Nestlé's globalization path, for example, started with the company making small, related acquisitions outside its domestic market, and the company therefore had early exposure to adaptation challenges. For most of their history, IBM also pursued an adaptation strategy, serving overseas markets by setting up a mini-IBM in each target country. Every one of these companies operated a largely local business model that allowed it to adapt to local differences as necessary. Inevitably, in the 1980s and 1990s, dissatisfaction with the extent to which country-by-country adaptation curtailed opportunities to gain international scale economies led to the overlay of a regional structure on the mini-IBMs. IBM aggregated the countries into regions in order to improve coordination and thus generate more scale economies at the regional and global levels. More recently, however, IBM has also begun to exploit differences across countries (arbitrage). For example, it has increased its work force in India while reducing its headcount in the United States.

Procter & Gamble's (P&G) early history parallels that of IBM, with the establishment of mini-P&Gs in local markets, but it has evolved differently. Today, the company's global business units now sell through market development organizations that are aggregated up to the regional level. P&G has successfully evolved into a company that uses all three "A" strategies in a coordinated manner. It adapts its value proposition to important markets but ultimately competes—through global branding, R&D, and sourcing—on the basis of aggregation. Arbitrage, while important—mostly through outsourcing activities that are invisible to the final consumer—is less important to P&G's global competitive advantage because of its relentless customer focus.

From A to AA to AAA[7]

Although most companies will focus on just one "A" at any given time, leading-edge companies—such as General Electric (GE), P&G, IBM, and Nestlé, to name a few—have embarked on implementing two, or even all three of the "A"s. Doing so presents special challenges because there are inherent tensions between all three foci. As a result, the pursuit of "AA" strategies, or even an "AAA" approach, requires considerable organizational and managerial flexibility.

Pursuing Adaptation and Aggregation

P&G started out with a focus on adaptation. Attempts to superimpose aggregation across Europe first proved difficult and, in particular, led to the installation of a matrix structure throughout the 1980s, but the matrix proved unwieldy. So, in 1999, the then CEO, Durk Jager, announced another reorganization whereby global business units (GBUs) retained ultimate profit responsibility but were complemented by geographic market development organizations (MDOs) that actually managed the sales force as a shared resource across GBUs. The result was disastrous. Conflicts arose everywhere, especially at the key GBU-MDO interfaces. The upshot: Jager departed after less than a year in office.

Under his successor, A. G. Lafley, P&G has enjoyed much more success, with an approach that strikes a better balance between adaptation and aggregation and that makes allowances for differences across general business units and markets. For example, the pharmaceuticals division, with distinct distribution channels, has been left out of the MDO structure. Another example: in emerging markets, where market development challenges are huge, profit responsibility continues to rest with country managers.

Aggregation and Arbitrage

VIZIO, founded in 2002 with only $600,000 in capital by entrepreneur William Wang to create high quality, flat panel televisions at affordable prices, has surpassed established industry giants Sony Corporation and Samsung Electronics Company to become the top flat-panel high definition television (HDTV) brand sold in North America. To get there, VIZIO developed a business model that effectively combines elements of aggregation and arbitrage strategies. VIZIO's contract manufacturing model is based on aggressive procurement sourcing, supply-chain management, economies of scale in distribution.

While a typical flat-screen television includes thousands of parts, the bulk of the costs and ultimate performance are a function of two key components: the panel and the chipset. Together, these two main parts account for about 94% of the costs. VIZIO's business model therefore focuses on optimizing the cost structure for these component parts. The vast majority of VIZIO's panels and chipsets are supplied by a handful of partners. Amtran provides about 80% of VIZIO's procurement and assembly work, with the remaining 20% performed by other ODMs, including Foxconn and TPV Technology.

One of the cornerstones of VIZIO's strategy is the decision to sell through wholesale clubs and discount retailers. Initially, William Wang was able to leverage his relationships at Costco from his years of selling computer monitors. VIZIO's early focus on wholesale stores also fit with the company's value position and pricing strategy. By selling through wholesale clubs and discount stores, VIZIO was able to keeps its prices low. For VIZIO, there is a two-way benefit: the prices of its TVs are comparatively lower than those from major manufacturers at electronics stores, and major manufacturers cannot participate as fully as they would like to at places like Costco.

VIZIO has strong relationships with its retail partners and is honored to offer them only the most compelling and competitively priced consumer electronics products. VIZIO products are available at valued partners including Wal-Mart, Costco, Sam's Club, BJ's Wholesale Club, Sears, Dell, and Target stores nationwide along with authorized online partners. VIZIO has won numerous awards including a number-one ranking in the *Inc.* 500 for "Top Companies in Computers and Electronics," *Good Housekeeping*'s "Best Big-Screens," *CNET*'s "Top 10 Holiday Gifts," and *PC World*'s "Best Buy," among others.[8]

Arbitrage and Adaptation

An example of a strategy that simultaneously emphasizes arbitrage and adaptation is investing heavily in a local presence in a key market to the point where a company can pass itself off as a "local" firm or "insider." A good example is provided by Citibank in China. The company, part of Citigroup, has had an intermittent presence in China since the beginning of the 20th century. A little more than 100 years later, in 2007, it was one of the first foreign banks to incorporate locally in China. The decision to incorporate locally was motivated by the desire to increase Citibank's status as an "insider"; with local incorporation, the Chinese government allowed it to extend its reach, expand its product offerings, and become more closely engaged with its local customers in the country.

China's decision in 2001 to become a member of the World Trade Organization (WTO) was a major factor in Citibank's decision to make a greater commitment to the Chinese market. Prior to China' joining the WTO, the banking environment in China was fairly restrictive. Banks such as Citibank could only give loans to foreign multinationals and their joint-venture partners in local currency, and money for domestic Chinese companies could only be raised in offshore markets. These restrictions made it difficult for foreign banks to gain a foothold in the Chinese business community.

Once China agreed to abide by WTO trading rules, however, banks such as Citibank had significantly greater opportunities: they would be able to provide local currency loans to blue-chip Chinese companies and would be free to raise funds for them in debt and equity markets within China. Other segments targeted by Citibank included retail credit cards and home mortgages. These were Citibank's traditional areas of expertise globally, and a huge potential demand for these products was apparent.

Significant challenges remained, however. Competing through organic growth with China's vast network of low-cost domestic banks would be slow and difficult. Instead, in the next few years, it forged a number of strategic alliances designed to give it critical mass in key segments. The first consisted of taking a 5% stake in China's ninth-largest bank, SPDB, a move that allowed Citibank to launch a dual-currency credit card that could be used to pay in *renminbi* in China and in foreign currencies abroad. In the following years, Citibank steadily increased its stake to the maximum 20% allowed under Chinese law and significantly expanded its product portfolio.

In June 2007, Citibank joined forces with Sino-U.S. MetLife Insurance Company, Ltd., to launch an investment unit-linked insurance product. In July of 2008, the company announced the launch of its first debit card. Simultaneously, it signed a deal with China's only national bankcard association, which allowed Citibank's debit cardholders to enjoy access to the association's vast network in China. The card would provide Chinese customers with access to over 140,000 ATMs within China and 380,000 ATMs in 45 countries overseas. Customers could also use their debit cards with over 1 million merchants within China and in 27 other countries. Today, Citibank is one of the top foreign banks operating in China, with a diverse range of products, eight corporate and investment bank branches, and 25 consumer bank outlets.[9]

Developing an AAA Strategy

There are serious constraints on the ability of any one company to use all three "A"s simultaneously with great effectiveness. Such attempts stretch a firm's managerial bandwidth, force a company to operate with multiple corporate cultures, and can present competitors with opportunities to undercut a company's overall competitiveness. Thus, to even contemplate an "AAA" strategy, a company must be operating in an environment in which the tensions among adaptation,

aggregation, and arbitrage are weak or can be overridden by large-scale economies or structural advantages, or in which competitors are otherwise constrained. Ghemawat cites the case of GE Healthcare (GEH). The diagnostic imaging industry has been growing rapidly and has concentrated globally in the hands of three large firms, which together command an estimated 75% of revenues in the business worldwide: GEH, with 30%; Siemens Medical Solutions (SMS), with 25%; and Philips Medical Systems (PMS), with 20%. This high degree of concentration is probably related to the fact that the industry ranks in the 90th percentile in terms of R&D intensity.

These statistics suggest that the aggregation-related challenge of building global scale has proven particularly important in the industry in recent years. GEH, the largest of the three firms, has consistently been the most profitable, reflecting its success at aggregation through (a) economies of scale (e.g., GEH has higher total R&D spending than its competitors, but its R&D-to-sales ratio is lower), (b) acquisition prowess (GEH has made nearly 100 acquisitions under Jeffrey Immelt before he became GE's CEO), and (c) economies of scope (the company strives to integrate its biochemistry skills with its traditional base of physics and engineering skills; it finances equipment purchases through GE Capital).

GEH has even more clearly outpaced its competitors through arbitrage. It has recently become a global product company by rapidly migrating to low-cost production bases. By 2005, GEH was reportedly more than halfway to its goals of purchasing 50% of its materials directly from low-cost countries and locating 60% of its manufacturing in such countries.

In terms of adaptation, GEH has invested heavily in country-focused marketing organizations. It also has increased customer appeal with its emphasis on providing services as well as equipment—for example, by training radiologists and providing consulting advice on postimage processing. Such customer intimacy obviously has to be tailored by country. And, recently, GEH has cautiously engaged in some "in China, for China" manufacture of stripped-down, cheaper equipment, aimed at increasing penetration there.

Pitfalls and Lessons in Applying the AAA Framework

There are several factors that companies should consider in applying the AAA framework. Most companies would be wise to *focus on one or two of the "A"s*—while it is possible to make progress on all three "A"s, especially for a firm that is coming from behind, companies (or, more often to the point, businesses or divisions) usually have to focus on one or, at most, two "A"s in trying to build competitive advantage. Companies should also *make sure the new elements of a strategy are a good fit organizationally.* If a strategy does embody substantially new elements, companies should pay particular attention to how well they work with other things the organization is doing. IBM has grown its staff in India much faster than other international competitors (such as Accenture) that have begun to emphasize India-based arbitrage. But quickly molding this work force into an efficient organization with high delivery standards and a sense of connection to the parent company is a critical challenge: failure in this regard might even be fatal to the arbitrage initiative. Companies should also *employ multiple integration mechanisms.* Pursuit of more than one of the "A"s requires creativity and breadth in thinking about integration mechanisms. Companies should also *think about externalizing integration.* Not all the integration that is required to add value across borders needs to occur within a single organization. IBM and other firms have shown that some externalization can be achieved in a number of ways: joint ventures in advanced semiconductor research, development, and manufacturing; links to, and support of, Linux and other efforts at open innovation; (some) outsourcing of hardware to contract manufacturers and services to business partners; IBM's relationship with Lenovo in personal computers; and customer relationships governed by memoranda of understanding rather than detailed contracts. Finally, companies should *know when not to integrate.* Some integration is always a good idea, but that is not to say that more integration is always better.

POINTS TO REMEMBER

1. There are three generic strategies for creating value in a global context: *adaptation, aggregation,* and *arbitrage.*

2. *Adaptation* strategies seek to increase revenues and market share by tailoring one or more components of a company's business model to suit local requirements or preferences. *Aggregation* strategies focus on achieving economies of scale or scope by creating regional or global efficiencies. These strategies typically involve standardizing a significant portion of the value proposition and grouping together development and production processes. *Arbitrage* is about exploiting economic or other differences between national or regional markets, usually by locating separate parts of the supply chain in different places.

3. Adaptation strategies can be subdivided into five categories: *variation, focus, externalization, design,* and *innovation.*

4. Aggregation strategies revolve around generating *economies of scale or scope.* The other nongeographic dimensions of the CAGE framework [...]—*cultural, administrative, geographic,* and *economic*—also lend themselves to aggregation strategies.

5. Since arbitrage focuses on exploiting differences between regions, the CAGE framework also defines a set of substrategies for this generic approach to global value creation.

6. A company's financial statements can be a useful guide for signaling which of the "A" strategies will have the greatest potential to create global value.

7. Although most companies will focus on just one "A" at any given time, leading-edge companies such as GE, P&G, IBM, and Nestlé, to name a few, have embarked on implementing two, or even all three, of the "A"s.

8. There are serious constraints on the ability of any one company to simultaneously use all three "A"s with great effectiveness. Such attempts stretch a firm's managerial bandwidth, force a company to operate with multiple corporate cultures, and can present

competitors with opportunities to undercut a company's overall competitiveness.

9. Most companies would be wise to (a) focus on one or two of the "A"s, (b) make sure the new elements of

a strategy are a good fit organizationally, (c) employ multiple integration mechanisms, (d) think about externalizing integration, and (e) know when not to integrate.

NOTES

1. This chapter draws substantially on Ghemawat (2007b).
2. Mucha and Scheffler (2007, April 30).
3. http://www.whirlpoolcorp.com/about/history.aspx
4. Ghemawat (2007a), chap. 6.
5. Ghemawat (2007a), chap. 6.
6. Dickerson (2007, June 9).
7. This discussion draws on Ghemawat (2007b), Chapter 7.
8. http://www.vizio.com/
9. Citibank's Co-Operative Strategy in China (2009).

DISCUSSION QUESTIONS

1. What are the strategies of the Global Strategy Framework; i.e., adaptation, aggregation, and arbitrage?
2. How are the generic strategies of adaptation, aggregation, and arbitrage used?
3. How do these generic strategies affect value creation?
4. Under what conditions or criteria might adaptation be more appropriate than aggregation?
5. What would you say are the constraints for a company in using adaptation?
6. Under what circumstances are adaptation and aggregation superior to each other?

REFERENCES

Citibank's co-operative strategy in China: The Renminbi debit card. (2009). Case 09/412C, Poon Kam Kai Series. Asia Case Research Center, University of Hong Kong.

Dickerson, M. (2007, June 9). Latin America attracting investors from India: Similarities in consumer bases help make the region a natural market. *Los Angeles Times*.

Ghemawat, P. (2007a). Why the world isn't flat. *Foreign Policy, 159*, 54–60.

Ghemawat, P. (2007b). Redefining global strategy: Crossing borders in a world where differences still matter. Harvard Business School Press, Boston.

Muccha, T., & Scheffler, M. (2007, April 30), Outsurcing, Inc. Retrieved from http://www.chicagobusiness.com/

12

C **hapter 12** discusses the various **Foreign Market Entry Strategies** that the contemporary international marketer may choose from. The criteria that guide the selection of an appropriate entry strategy are reviewed, and the impact of those different entry strategies is assessed. For instance, export-import strategy is unique for a domestic marketer who aspires to become international. It is a useful strategy even for a seasoned international marketer. Licensing, franchising, international joint ventures, and other partnering relationships are reviewed and their appropriateness is analyzed. Foreign direct investment (FDI) strategies such as acquisition and greenfield are discussed, and their impact on the foreign government and economy is assessed. The criteria for selecting the strategy of a wholly owned subsidiary are discussed and the strategy's impact assessed. The concept of free or foreign trade zones (FTZs) is reviewed; their impact on international trade and their use are discussed. Finally, the chapter is enriched with a great number of examples of companies that have used these foreign market entry strategies.

Foreign Market Entry Strategies

12.1

Sak Onkvisit and John J. Shaw

A merchant, it has been said very properly, is not necessarily the citizen of any particular country. It is in great measure indifferent to him from what places he carries on his trade; and a very stifling disgust will make him move his capital, and together with the industry which it supports, from one country to another.

Adam Smith

Chapter outline

- Marketing strategy: raging Bull
- Foreign direct investment (FDI)
- Exporting
- Licensing
- Management contract
- Joint venture
- Manufacturing
- Assembly operations
- Turnkey operations
- Acquisition
- Strategic alliances
- Analysis of entry strategies
- Free trade zones (FTZs)
- Conclusion
- Case 9.1 Taylor Candy Company and the Caribbean market

Marketing strategy   Raging Bull

Chaleo Yoovidhya, the founder of T.C. Pharmaceutical Co. in Thailand, developed several decades ago a formula for Krating Daeng, an energy drink. The brand is a huge success in Thailand, predominantly among blue-collar workers (e.g., truckers, laborers).

Then came Dietrich Mateschitz, an Austrian salesman of a cosmetics company that was represented in Thailand by the Yoovidhya family. The salesman was intrigued by Krating Daeng and obtained a license to make it in Austria. Krating Daeng became Red Bull, a literal translation. Yoovidhya and Mateschitz formed Red Bull GmbH, each taking a 49 percent stake. Yoovidhya's son got the other 2 percent. Red Bull was marketed in Austria in 1987 before charging into Hungary, its first foreign market, in 1992.

Energy drinks, heavy on caffeine and sugar (seven teaspoons in a can), are particularly popular among young Americans. The number of young drinkers more than doubled in three years to some 7.6 million teens. Red Bull aggressively gives a sample of its product at sporting events and on campuses. In the U.S.A., the company's marketing teams use dance halls, disc jockeys, alternative sports venues, and cab drivers to promote the brand. They may drive Red Bull cars (with a large Red Bull can mounted on the back) to hand out samples. Red Bull is the sponsor of some 500 extreme athletes. Its fleet of Flying Bulls show planes can be seen at air shows all over the world.

Red Bull's sleek blue-and-silver cans have become a standard package for the product category. Many other competitors imitate the shape and colors of the can. Over 500 new energy drinks were introduced worldwide in 2006.

Unlike the way it is marketed in its motherland (Thailand), Red Bull is promoted aggressively as a trendy product associated with extreme sports. In the U.S.A., the product is highly popular with high-school and college students. At about $2 for an 8-ounce can, Red Bull is pricey, but the price does not deter students from drinking it.

Red Bull has become a global success. With a sales volume of more than one billion cans a year in 83 countries, Red Bull commands 70 percent of the world's energy drink market—in spite of a slew of imitators that compete by offering lower prices or greater quantity per can. The worldwide success is enough to propel Yoovidhya to the top of Thailand in terms of wealth. In the process, he has joined the world's billionaires as ranked by *Forbes* magazine.

Sources: "Red Bull Tycoon Joins Elite Club," *Bangkok Post*, March 1, 2003; "Energy Drinks Hook a Generation," *San José Mercury News*, November 13, 2006; and "Hansen Natural Charging at Red Bull with a Brawny Energy Brew," *Business Week*, June 6, 2005, 74–7.

Purpose of chapter

Red Bull has demonstrated a practical way to enter foreign markets. Likewise, Heineken has not entered all markets with a one-track mind and a single-entry method. Even a large multinational corporation, with all its power, still has to adapt its operating methods and formulate multiple entry strategies. The dynamic nature of many overseas markets makes it impossible for a single method to work effectively in all markets.

This chapter is devoted to a coverage of the various market entry strategies. Some of these techniques—such as exporting, licensing, and management contracts—are indirect in the sense that they require no investment overseas. Other techniques, however, require varying degrees of foreign direct investment. These foreign direct investment methods range from joint-venture to complete overseas manufacturing facilities, with such strategies as assembly operations, turnkey operations, and acquisition falling somewhere in between. These strategies do not operate in sequence, and any one of them may be appropriate at any time. In addition, the use of one strategy in one market does not rule out the use of the other strategies elsewhere. The methods vary in terms of risk accepted and, to a certain extent, the degree of commitment to the foreign market.

Another purpose of this chapter is to discuss the advantages and disadvantages associated with each method of market penetration. Factors that have an impact on the appropriateness of entry methods are covered in order to provide guidelines for the selection of market entry strategies. The chapter ends with an examination of free trade zones, which can be used to complement most entry strategies.

Foreign Direct Investment (FDI)

To enter a foreign market, a company needs to consider the risk–reward ratio. To minimize risk, the firm may try to enter the foreign market indirectly in the sense that it tries to minimize its foreign direct investment and physical presence abroad. Some of the indirect market entry strategies include exporting, licensing, and management contract. By trying to play it relatively safe, the reward potential is also reduced accordingly.

To maximize a profit potential while tolerating a higher degree of risk, a marketer may want to consider FDI. Economists usually advocate a free flow of capital across national borders because capital can then seek out the highest rate of return. Owners of capital can diversify their investment, while governments will be less able to pursue bad economic policies. In addition, a global integration of capital markets spreads best practices in corporate governance, accounting rules, and legal traditions.

However, some critics point out that free capital flows are driven by speculative and short-term considerations. Empirical evidence, however, shows that FDI flows are more stable than all other forms of capital (portfolio and other investment flows). In fact, FDI flows are a stabilizing factor even during a financial crisis. The stability is due to the fact that FDI focuses on positive longer term sentiment about a recipient country. In addition, physical investment in plant and equipment cannot be easily reversed.[1] Empirical evidence indicates that FDI benefits developing host countries.[2]

Figures 12.1 shows that the CEE-10 countries (EU members in Central and Eastern Europe) have attracted large FDI inflows, and Figure 12.2 shows the surging inflows of FDI to emerging market countries. One indisputable fact is that developed countries are both the largest recipients and sources of FDI. The

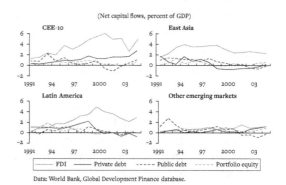

Data: World Bank, Global Development Finance database.

FIGURE 12.1 CEE-10 and FDI inflows

Source: IMF Survey (November 20, 2006, 334). © International Monetary Fund. *IMF Survey* (www. imf.org/imfsurvey).

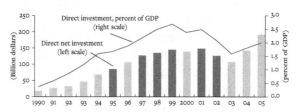

Note: Includes countries in the Emerging Markets Bond Index, India, and Czech Republic. Darker bars indicate the years of financial crisis: 1995–Mexico; 1997–Korea and Thailand; 1998–Brazil, Indonesia, Philippines, Russia, and Ukraine; 1999–Ecuador; 2001–Argentina and Turkey; 2002–Uruguay.

FIGURE 12.2 Emerging markets and FDI inflows

Source: "Why FDI may not be as Stable as Governments Think," *IMF Survey* (January 29, 2007, 26). © International Monetary Fund. *IMF Survey* (www.imf.org/imfsurvey).

phenomenon is dominated by the triad of the European Union, the U.S.A., and Japan. Over the past few decades, the share of the triad in total world inward FDI flows and stocks has been about 60 to 70 percent, with a shift in the direction of the EU and away from Japan. As a matter of fact, the EU commands almost half of global inward and outward flows and stocks. It is encouraging that developing countries have made a gain as recipients of FDI, as evidenced by their share in total world inflows rising from 20 percent in 1978 to 1980 to 35 percent in 2003 to 2005. Unfortunately for African countries, their share has fallen.[3]

Certain countries have managed to attract large amounts of FDI. The U.S.A. is the world's top recipient of FDI. In the case of Africa, to attract FDI, African countries have relied on their natural resources, locational advantages, and targeted policies. Above all, the countries that are successful in attracting FDI have certain traits: political and macroeconomic stability and structural reforms. "Strong, pro-democracy political leadership that has embraced policies to overcome social and political strife and a firm commitment to economic reform are key factors linked with sizable FDI inflows."[4] Therefore, even those countries that lack natural resources or location advantages can still attract foreign investors by adopting sound economic policies within an open political environment. Figure 12.3 shows that Cyprus has been successful in attracting a number of multinational corporations to locate their operations there.

Countries may be classified in terms of their FDI potential and performance. According to the United Nations Conference on Trade and Development, there are four groups: (1) front-runners (e.g., Australia, Bahamas) that have high FDI potential/high FDI performance, (2) above potential (e.g., Albania, Angola) due to low FDI potential/high FDI performance, (3) below potential (e.g., Algeria, Argentina) due to high FDI potential/low FDI performance, and (4) underachievers (e.g., Bangladesh, Benin) that have low FDI potential/low FDI performance.[5] Based on the Inward FDI Performance Index, the top five countries are Azerbaijan, Brunei Darussalam, Hong Kong, Estonia, and Singapore.

Russia, one of the so-called BRIC (Brazil, Russia, India, and China) economies, has grown significantly

as a market. Not surprisingly, Russia attracted a record $16.7 billion in FDI in 2005. Consumer-related sectors did very well. Coca-Cola Co. spent $600 million to acquire Russian fruit-juice market Multon, while Dutch brewer Heineken spent $750 million in acquisitions. Nestlé has so far invested $500 million, and its $120 million instant-coffee factory was its first international greenfield investment for two decades.[6]

Corruption has a negative impact on FDI. From the ethics standpoint, foreign investors generally avoid corruption because it is morally wrong. From the economic standpoint, investors prefer not to have to manage such costly risks.[7] A recent study, however, found that host-country corruption was not viewed as a significant market barrier. Instead, the negative effect of corruption was in the form of a discount on local takeover synergies. A deterioration in the corruption index by 1 point on a 10-point scale resulted in a reduction of 21 percent of local targets' premiums.[8]

Exporting

Exporting is a strategy in which a company, without any marketing or production organization overseas, exports a product from its home base. Often, the exported product is fundamentally the same as the one marketed in the home market.

The main advantage of an exporting strategy is the ease in implementing the strategy. Risks are minimal because the company simply exports its excess production capacity when it receives orders from abroad. As a result, its international marketing effort is casual at best. This is very likely the most common overseas entry approach for small firms. Many companies employ this entry strategy when they first become involved with international business and may continue to use it on a more or less permanent basis.

The problem with using an exporting strategy is that it is not always an optimal strategy. A desire to keep international activities simple, together with a lack of product modification, make a company's marketing strategy inflexible and unresponsive.

The exporting strategy functions poorly when the company's home-country currency is strong. In the

FIGURE 12.3 Cyprus and FDI

1970s, the Swiss franc was so strong that Swiss companies found it exceedingly difficult to export and sell products in the U.S. market. Swiss companies had to resort to investing abroad in order to reduce the effects of the strong franc. During the first term of the Reagan administration, the U.S. dollar had also gained an extremely strong position. U.S. firms not only found it extremely difficult to export U.S. products but they also had to contend with a flood of inexpensive imports that became even more inexpensive as the dollar became stronger. A currency can remain strong over a stretch of several years, creating prolonged difficulties for the country's exports. Continuing the long-term trend, the Japanese yen surged 20 percent against the U.S. dollar in early 1995 and greatly harmed Japanese exporters.

Austria represents a small but open economy that requires international exchange. Based on a study of the effects of determinants on export performance, the most promising predictors of export performance are firm size, management's motives to internationalize, and use of the differentiation strategy.[9]

One study of Portuguese small and medium-sized exporters found a crucial role of past performance on their commitment to exporting.[10] Another study of small and medium-sized exporters found that decision-makers' cosmopolitanism influenced export initiation. These decision-makers often learned of foreign opportunities through their existing social ties—rather than through formal scanning and market research. The findings were consistent across different industrial settings.[11] In addition, a study of export behavior found a negative relationship between the psychic distance index and firms' actual selection of export markets.[12]

One study measured the export-entrepreneurial orientation construct so as to derive a high versus low export-entrepreneurial taxonomy. While Nigerian firms in the study perceive domestic environmental problems, high export-entrepreneurial firms appear to be better able to adapt and subsequently exhibit a higher tendency to initiate exporting. In addition, high export-entrepreneurial firms are more proactive and innovative in developing exporting while being less averse to exporting risks.[13]

It should be noted that research in international exchange tends to focus on the perspective of exporters. A more complete understanding requires an inclusion of the perspective of importers in the dyad. Based on a study of 36 exporter–importer dyads operating in four countries, the best-performing dyads exhibited a maintenance of close relationships by people on either side.[14]

Licensing

When a company finds exporting ineffective but is hesitant to have direct investment abroad, licensing can be a reasonable compromise. Licensing is an agreement that permits a foreign company to use industrial property (i.e., patents, trademarks, and copyrights), technical know-how and skills (e.g., feasibility studies, manuals, technical advice), architectural and engineering designs, or any combination of these in a foreign market. Essentially, a licensor allows a foreign company to manufacture a product for sale in the licensee's country and sometimes in other specified markets.

Examples of licensing abound. Some 50 percent of the drugs sold in Japan are made under license from European and U.S. companies. *Playboy* used to take licensed materials from France's *Lui* for its *Oui* magazine, which was distributed in the U.S. market. *Playboy*'s more common role, however, is that of a licensor, resulting in nine *Playboy* foreign editions. *Penthouse* magazine, likewise, has Japanese and Brazilian versions under license in addition to those in Spain, Australia, and Italy. German-speaking countries account for *Penthouse*'s largest overseas edition. As of 2006, Starbucks has more than 13,000 stores worldwide and is opening seven new stores each day. Out of the total number, more than 5,000 are licensed locations. Retail store licensing accounts for 45 percent of the company's specialty revenue of $1.2 billion.[15]

Licensing is not only restricted to tangible products. A service can be licensed as well. Chicago Mercantile Exchange's attempt to internationalize the futures market led it to obtain licensing rights to the Nikkei stock index. The exchange then sublicensed the Nikkei index to the SIMEX for trade in Singapore in 1986.

In spite of a general belief that FDI is generally more profitable and thus the preferred scheme, licensing offers several advantages. It allows a company to spread out its research and development and investment costs, while enabling it to receive incremental income with only negligible expenses. In addition, granting a license protects the company's patent and/or trademark against cancellation for nonuse. This protection is especially critical for a firm that, after investing in production and marketing facilities in a foreign country, decides to leave the market either temporarily or permanently. The situation is especially common in Central and South America, where high inflation and devaluation drastically push up operating costs.

There are other reasons why licensing should be used. Trade barriers may be one such reason. A manufacturer should consider licensing when capital is scarce, when import restrictions discourage direct entry, and when a country is sensitive to foreign ownership. The method is very flexible because it allows a quick and easy way to enter the market. Licensing also works well when transportation cost is high, especially relative to product value. Although Japan banned all direct investment and restricted commercial loans in South Africa, Japan's success there was due to licensing agreements with local distributors.

A company can avoid substantial risks and other difficulties with licensing. Most French designers, for example, use licensing to avoid having to invest in a business. In another example, Disney gets all of its royalties virtually risk-free from the $500 million Tokyo Disneyland theme park owned by Keisei Electric Railway and Mitsui. The licensing and royalty fees as arranged are very attractive: Disney receives 10 percent of the gate revenue and 5 percent of sales of all food and merchandise. Moreover, Disney, with its policy of using low-paid young adults as park employees, does not have to deal with the Japanese policy of lifetime employment.

An owner of a valuable brand name can greatly benefit from brand licensing. In addition to receiving royalties from sales of merchandise bearing its name or image, the trademark owner receives an intangible benefit of free advertising which reinforces the brand's image. Another benefit is that the brand is extended into new product categories in which the trademark owner has no expertise. Coca-Cola, for example, has licensed its brand name to more than 3000 products which are marketed by 200 licensees in 30 countries.

Recognizing the value of the licensing approach as well as the contributions of licensees in European countries, McDonald's has made a strategic adjustment. In Europe, the share of restaurants that are directly owned by McDonald's will decline from the current 30 percent to 20 or 25 percent. Compared to directly owned restaurants there, franchise outlets achieve better profit margins. However, outside of Europe and the U.S.A., the company plans to rely on its own know-how. McDonald's wants to grow in Russia and other regions with its directly owned restaurants since the business there has only recently been established.[16]

Nevertheless, licensing has its negative aspects. With reduced risk generally comes reduced profit. In fact, licensing may be the least profitable of all entry strategies.

It is necessary to consider the long-term perspective. By granting a license to a foreign firm, a manufacturer may be nurturing a competitor in the future—someone who is gaining technological and product knowledge. At some point, the licensee may refuse to renew the licensing contract. To complicate the matter, it is anything but easy to prevent the licensee from using the process learned and acquired while working under license. Texas Instruments had to sue several Japanese manufacturers to force them to continue paying royalties on its patents on memory chips.

Another problem often develops when the licensee performs poorly. To attempt to terminate the contract may be easier said than done. Once licensing is in place, the agreements can also prevent the licensor from entering that market directly. Japanese laws give a licensee virtual control over the licensed product, and such laws present a monumental obstacle for an investor wishing to regain the rights to manufacture and sell the investor's own product.

Inconsistent product quality across countries caused by licensees' lax quality control can injure the reputation of a product on a worldwide basis. This possibility explains why McDonald's goes to extremes in supervising operations, thus ensuring product quality and consistency. McDonald's was successful in court in preventing a franchisee from operating the franchises in France because the franchisee's quality was substandard. Anheuser-Busch, likewise, requires all licensees to meet the company's standards. The licensees must agree to import such ingredients as yeast from the U.S.A.

Even when exact product formulations are followed, licensing can still sometimes damage a product's image—that is, psychologically. Many imported products enjoy a certain degree of prestige or mystique that can rapidly disappear when the product is made locally under license. The Miller brewery became aware of this perception problem when it started brewing Lowenbrau, a German brand, in Texas.

In some cases, a manufacturer has no choice at all about licensing. Many developing countries force patent holders to license their products to other manufacturers or distributors for a royalty fee that may or may not be fair. Canada, owing to consumer activism, is the only industrialized nation requiring compulsory licensing for drugs.

Licensing, in spite of certain limitations, is a sound strategy that can be quite effective under certain circumstances. Licensing terms must be carefully negotiated and explicitly treated (see Figure 12.4). In general, a license contract should include these basic elements: product and territorial coverage, length of contract, quality control, grantback and cross-licensing, royalty rate and structure, choice of currency, and choice of law.

When licenses are to be granted to European firms, a firm must consider the anti-trust rules of the EU, specifically Article 85 of the Rome Treaty. This article prohibits those licensing terms (with some exemptions) that are likely to adversely affect trade between EU countries. Such arrangements as price fixing, territorial restrictions, and tie-in agreements are void.

A prudent licensor does not "assign" a trademark to a licensee. It is far better to specify the conditions under which the mark can or cannot be used by the licensee. From the licensee's standpoint, the licensor's trademark is valuable in marketing the licensed product only if the product is popular. Otherwise, the licensee would be better served by creating a new trademark to protect the marketing position in the event that the basic license is not renewed.

Licensing should be considered a two-way street because a license also allows the original licensor to gain access to the licensee's technology and product. This is important because the licensee may be able to build on the information supplied by the licensor. Unlike American firms, European licensors are very interested in grantbacks and will even lower the royalty rate in return for product improvements and potentially profitable new products. Thus, an intelligent practice is always to stipulate in a contract that licenses for new patents or products covered by the return grant are to be made available at reasonable royalties.

Finally, the licensor should try not to undermine a product by overlicensing it. For example, Pierre Cardin diluted the value of his name by allowing some 800 products to use the name under license. Subsequently, he created Maxim's as the second brand for restaurants, hotels, and food items. Similarly, fashion legend Yves Saint Laurent put his name (YSL) on numerous products ranging from baseball caps to plastic shoes. A luxury brand can lose its cachet when it has too much exposure. Gucci Group paid $1 billion for YSL's ready-to-wear and perfume businesses and quickly moved to restore the brand's image. Production, marketing, and distribution were overhauled. Even though YSL's licensing agreements contributed 65 percent of YSL's revenues, Gucci Group decided to walk away from revenues for the sake of the brand's luxury image. In three months, 11 franchised stores were bought back, and a ready-to-wear factory in Tours was sold. Overall, Gucci terminated 152 of 167 licenses to stop the brand's slide in quality and reputation. Some critics believed that Gucci paid too much for YSL by underestimating how far the brand has fallen.[17]

Neither extreme of overlicensing nor underlicensing is desirable. Underlicensing results in potential profit being lost, whereas overlicensing leads to a weakened market through overexposure. Overlicensing can increase income in the short run, but it may in the long run mean killing the goose that laid the golden egg. Some of the risks associated with licensing are suboptimal choice, opportunism, quality, production, payment, contract enforcement, and

FIGURE 12.4 Licensing strategy

marketing control. The methods to manage such risks include planning, licensee selection, compensation choices, ongoing relationship, contract specification, and organization of the licensing function.[18]

Management Contract

In some cases, government pressure and restrictions force a foreign company either to sell its domestic operations or to relinquish control. In other cases, the company may prefer not to have any FDI. Under such circumstances, the company may have to formulate another way to generate the forfeited revenue. One way to generate revenue is to sign a management contract with the government or the new owner in order to manage the business for the new owner. The new owner may lack technical and managerial expertise and may need the former owner to manage the investment until local employees are trained to manage the facility.

Management contracts may be used as a sound strategy for entering a market with a minimum investment and minimum political risks. Club Med, a leader in international resort vacations, is frequently wooed by developing countries with attractive financing options because these countries want tourism. Club Med's strategy involves having either minority ownership or none at all, even though the firm manages all the resorts. Its rationale is that, with management contracts, Club Med is unlikely to be asked to leave a country where it has a resort.

Management contract is a common strategy in the hotel business. Accor SA, a French hotel giant, for example, has purchased a large stake in Zenith Hotels International.[19] Zenith itself manages nine hotels in China and one hotel in Thailand without owning them, and most of its hotels do not carry the Zenith name. Accor's acquisition is an attempt to catch up in China with Bass PLC, the parent of Holiday Inn. It hopes to use Zenith's connections and experience to land more management contracts. Accor's Sofitel brand also has a hotel in China. In the U.S.A., the Motel 6 chain is also operated by Accor.

Joint Venture

The joint venture is another alternative a firm may consider as a way of entering an overseas market. A joint venture is simply a partnership at corporate level, and it can be domestic or international. For the discussion here, an international joint venture is one in which the partners are from more than one country.

Similar to a partnership formed by two or more individuals, a joint venture is an enterprise formed for a specific business purpose by two or more investors sharing ownership and control. Time Warner Entertainment and Taiwan Pan Asia Investment Company, for instance, have formed a joint venture in Taiwan called Tai Hua International Enterprise Co. Ltd. for the purpose of providing products and services to Taiwan's emerging cable TV industry. The U.S.-based McDonald's owns 50 percent of McDonald's Holdings in Japan.

One recent joint venture involves Advanced Micro Devices (AMD) and Fujitsu to replace a previous joint venture (Fujitsu–AMD Semiconductor Ltd.). The previous joint venture allowed the partners jointly to develop flash memory chips. The arrangement was for them to have separate sales forces and geographic territories while competing against each other in selling these jointly developed chips in Europe. Unlike the previous 50–50 joint venture, AMD owns 60 percent of the new company (called FASL LLC), while Fujitsu owns the rest. The three manufacturing plants in Japan, owned by the former joint venture, are folded into the new venture. With the new joint venture, both partners combine all sales, research, engineering, and marketing.[20]

Joint ventures, like licensing, involve certain risks as well as certain advantages over other forms of entry into a foreign market. In most cases, company resources, circumstances, and the reasons for wanting to do business overseas will determine if a joint venture is the most reasonable way to enter the overseas market. According to one study, firms tend to use joint ventures when they enter markets that are characterized by high legal restrictions or high levels of investment risks.[21]

Marketers consider joint ventures to be dynamic because of the possibility of a parent firm's change in mission or power [...]. There are two separate overseas investment processes that describe how joint ventures tend to evolve. The first is the "natural," nonpolitical investment process. In this case, a technology-supplying firm gains a foothold in an unfamiliar market by acquiring a partner that can contribute local knowledge and marketing skills. Technology tends to provide dominance to the technology-supplying firm. As the technology partner becomes more familiar with the market, it buys up more or all equity in the venture or leaves the venture entirely. A contributor of technology, however, is not likely to reduce its share in a joint venture while remaining active in it. The second investment process occurs when the local firm's "political" leverage, through government persuasion, halts or reverses the "natural" economic process. The foreign, technology-supplying partner remains engaged in the venture without strengthening its ownership position, the consequence being a gradual takeover by the local parties.[22]

There are several reasons why joint ventures enjoy certain advantages and should be used. One benefit is that a joint venture substantially reduces the amount of resources (money and personnel) that each partner must contribute.

Frequently, the joint-venture strategy is the only way, other than through licensing, that a firm can enter a foreign market. This is especially true when wholly owned activities are prohibited in a country. Centrally planned economies, in particular, usually limit foreign firms' entry to some sort of cooperative arrangement. China has made it quite clear that only those automakers with long-term commitments will be allowed to assemble foreign models with local partners. Foreign manufacturers must agree to have less than 50 percent control of the joint ventures.

Sometimes *social* rather than legal circumstances require a joint venture to be formed. When Pillsbury planned to market its products in Japan, it considered a number of options, ranging from exporting and licensing to the outright purchase of a Japanese company. Although foreign ownership laws had been relaxed, Pillsbury decided to follow traditional business custom in Japan by seeking a good partner. It thus got together with Snow Brand to form Snow-Brand/Pillsbury.

Joint ventures often have social implications. The familial and tightly knit relationship between suppliers and middlemen is prevalent in many countries. In Japan, this relationship is known as *keiretsu*, which

Legal Dimension 12.1 From Russia—without love

Russia has the world's largest reserves of natural gas, and the country is No. 6 in oil. In 2003 BP PLC put $8 billion into TNK–BP, a 50–50 joint venture between BP and three Russian billionaires. As noted by the CEO in 2007, the Russian joint venture TNK–BP Ltd. "has been a very profitable investment." BP's share in TNK–BP amounts to one-fifth of BP's global reserves, a quarter of its production, and almost one-tenth of its global profits. Unfortunately, the investment environment and political climate have drastically changed. President Vladimir Putin has made clear his desire for Russian control of energy resources and control

over large energy companies. The desire appears to be achieved at the expense of Western investors.

Russia has threatened to cancel TNK–BP's license for Kovykta because BP and its partners did not meet production targets. Putin questioned how the Russian shareholders in Kovykta managed to acquire their stakes in the 1990s. Interestingly, Russian regulators indicated that license issues could be resolved if Gazprom, the state-controlled gas monopoly, could enter into the project. Kovykta may hold nearly as much natural gas as Canada. Facing pressure from the Kremlin, BP has agreed to sell its majority stake.

It would cede its holdings in a $20 billion Russian natural-gas project to state-controlled gas monopoly OAO Gazprom. TNK–BP would sell its 62.7 percent stake in the Kovykta field for almost $1 billion.

Earlier, Russian regulators threatened to shut down the Sakhalin-2 energy project due to alleged environmental violations. As a result, Royal Dutch Shell PLC found it necessary to sell control of the project to Gazprom.

Source: "BP Set to Leave Russia Gas Project," *Wall Street Journal*, June 22, 2007.

means that family-like business groups are linked by cross-ownership of equity. Such customs and business relationships make it difficult for a new supplier to gain entry. Even in the event that the new supplier is able to secure some orders, the orders may be terminated as soon as a member of the family is able to supply the product in question. A joint venture thus provides an opportunity for the foreign supplier to secure business orders through the back door.

A joint venture can also simultaneously work to satisfy social, economic, and political circumstances since these concerns are highly related. In any kind of international business undertaking political risks always exist, and a joint venture can reduce such risks while it increases market opportunities. In this sense, a joint venture can make a difference between securely entering a foreign market or not entering at all. Many American firms seek Saudi partners to establish joint ventures so that they can deal effectively with Saudi Arabia's political demands.

Joint ventures are not without their shortcomings and limitations. First, if the partners to the joint venture have not established clear-cut decision-making policy and must consult with each other on all decisions, the *decision-making process* may delay a necessary action when speed is essential. Partners' commitment to a joint venture is a function of the perceived benefits of the relationship. Conflict, on the other hand, reduces efficiency and the perceived benefits.

When two individuals or organizations work together, there are bound to be *conflicts* due to cultural problems, divergent goals, disagreements over production and marketing strategies, and weak contributions by one or the other partner. Although the goals may be compatible at the outset, goals and objectives may diverge over time, even when joint ventures are successful. Dow–Badische was set up in the U.S.A. with BASF providing the technology to make chemical raw materials and fibers and Dow supplying the marketing expertise. A split eventually occurred despite good profits when BASF wanted to expand the fiber business—Dow felt that the venture was moving away from Dow's mainstream chemical business. BASF ultimately bought out Dow and made the business its wholly owned subsidiary.

Another potential problem is the matter of *control*. By definition, a joint venture must deal with double management. If a partner has less than 50 percent ownership, that partner must in effect allow the majority partner to make decisions. If the board of directors has a 50–50 split, it is difficult for the board to make a decision quickly or at all. Dow's experience with its Korea Pacific Chemical joint venture illustrates this point. When prices plunged, the joint venture lost $60 million. To stem the loss, Dow wanted to improve efficiency but was opposed by its Korean partner. The government-appointed directors boycotted board meetings and a decision could not be reached. Both sides eventually ended up bringing lawsuits against each other.

There are four types of partitioning of management control: split management control, shared management, multinational-enterprise-partner-dominant management, and local-partner-dominant management. In the case of international joint ventures in Korea, the split control approach is superior to the others. As a result, multinational corporations and their local partners should split control by matching particular activities with the firm-specific advantages.[23]

There are several factors that may determine whether a company wants to take equity ownership in international joint ventures. These source country factors are exchange rate, cost of borrowing, export capability, and management orientation. Based on a study of 8078 international joint ventures in China, parent firms are more likely to take equity ownership when they are from a source country with a strong currency, low cost of borrowing, strong export capability, and high uncertainty avoidance.[24]

It is interesting to note that, while cultural differences indeed affect international joint-venture performance, culture distance stems more from differences in organizational culture than from differences in national cultures. A survey of Indian executives and their partners from other countries confirmed this relationship.[25]

With regard to performance, based on a study of 1335 Japanese joint ventures in 73 countries (excluding Japan), there is no significant relationship between the number of joint-venture partners and the performance of the venture.[26] According to another study involving a cross-sectional sample of more than 700 joint ventures, three sponsor categories may be identified: (1) partners from developed countries, (2) partners from newly industrialized countries, and (3) partners from developing countries. These categories result in U.S. firms' differential market performance.[27] In addition, partners' cooperation strongly affects performance in equity joint ventures, especially when market uncertainty is present.[28]

The "softer" (behavioral) side of international joint ventures needs to be considered. There are five stages of formation (need determination, partner search, partner selection, negotiations, and operations), four dimensions of trust (personal, competence, contractual, and goodwill), and three dimensions of commitment (intentions-based, contractual, and affective). The knowledge of these stages and dimensions can improve chances of success.[29] In addition, tie strength, trust, and shared values and systems play a role in the transfer of tacit knowledge, especially for mature international joint ventures.[30]

Manufacturing

The manufacturing process may be employed as a strategy involving all or some manufacturing in a foreign country. The success of Ford Motor Co. in Russia has to do with the company's major commitment to the market. In 1999, Ford spent $150 million on the first foreign-owned automobile factory. The plant opened in 2002. Production has been climbing as Russian consumers step up purchases of automobiles. Local manufacturing has made it possible for Ford to keep prices down. Ford is able to sell its Focus sedans for about $3000 less than similarly equipped imports which have to deal with a 25 percent duty.[31]

Central Europe has gained attention as a manufacturing base for companies that want to enter the EU. The former Soviet bloc countries that are now the new members of the EU offer wages that are just a fraction of those in Western Europe, and they are eager to attract FDI so as to create jobs. Taiwan's Foxconn Technology Co. and Chinese electronics manufacturer Sichuan Changhong have received 10-year tax holidays in the Czech Republic. Another benefit is that manufacturing in the EU lets foreign manufacturers avoid the 14 percent tariff imposed on television sets made in China.[32]

One kind of manufacturing procedure, known as **sourcing**, involves manufacturing operations in a host country, not so much to sell there but for the purpose of exporting from that company's home country to other countries. This chapter is concerned more with another manufacturing objective: the goal of a manufacturing strategy may be to set up a production base inside a target market country as a means of invading it. There are several variations on this method, ranging from complete manufacturing to contract manufacturing (with a local manufacturer) and partial manufacturing.

From the perspective of the host countries, it is obvious as to why they want to attract foreign capital. Although job creation is the main reason, there are several other benefits for the host country as well. Foreign direct investment, unlike other forms of capital inflows, almost always brings additional resources that are very desirable to developing economies. These resources include technology, management expertise, and access to export markets.

There are several reasons why a company chooses to invest in manufacturing facilities abroad. One reason may involve gaining access either to raw materials or to take advantage of resources for its manufacturing operations. As such, this process is known as *backward vertical integration*. Another reason may be to take advantage of lower labor costs or other abundant factors of production (e.g., labor, energy, and other inputs). Hoover was able to cut its high British manufacturing costs by shifting some of its production to France. The strategy may further reduce another kind of cost—transportation. British publishing firms have begun to do more printing abroad because they can save 25 to 40 percent in production and shipping costs. Figure 12.5 shows how the Galician Institute for Economic Promotion has attracted more than 10,000 companies to do business in Galicia, Spain.

Manufacturing in a host country can make the company's product more price-competitive because the company can avoid or minimize high import taxes, as well as other trade barriers. Honda, with 68 percent of its car sales coming from exports and 43 percent from the U.S. market, has a good reason to be sensitive to trade barriers. In order to avoid future problems of this nature,

FIGURE 12.5 Doing business in Spain

it set up plants in Ohio. Likewise, Honda has committed itself to the market in China and will even work with its partner to create a new brand just for this market.[33]

A manufacturer interested in manufacturing abroad should consider a number of significant factors. The important incentives include: freedom of intercompany payments and dividend remittances, import duty concessions, tax holidays, and guarantees against expropriation.

From the marketing standpoint, *product image* deserves attention. Although Winston cigarettes are made in Venezuela with the same tobaccos and formula as the Winston cigarettes in the U.S.A., Venezuelans still prefer the more expensive U.S.-made Winston. Philip Morris and R.J. Reynolds faced this same problem in Russia when setting up manufacturing plants there. Unilever had a similar problem when it began manufacturing locally in Nepal where people prefer Indian-made products.

Competition is an important factor, since to a great extent competition determines potential profit. Another factor is the resources of various countries, which should be compared to determine each country's comparative advantage. The comparison should also include production considerations, including production facilities, raw materials, equipment, real estate, water, power, and transport. Human resources, an integral part of the production factor, must be available at reasonable cost.

Manufacturers should pay attention to absolute as well as relative changes in *labor costs*. A particular country is more attractive as a plant's location if the wages there increase more slowly than those in other countries. The increase in labor costs in Germany led GM's Opel to switch its production facilities to Japan and led Rollei to move its production to Singapore. Several Japanese firms have been attracted by a low wage rate in Mexico, a rate even lower than the hourly pay in Singapore and South Korea. A manufacturer must keep in mind, however, that labor costs are determined not only by compensation but also by productivity and exchange rates. Mexico's labor costs, already extremely low, become even lower if the peso is weak, but this advantage is offset somewhat because Mexican workers are relatively unskilled and thus produce more defective products.

The *type of product* made is another factor that determines whether foreign manufacturing is an economical and effective venture. A manufacturer must weigh the economies of exporting a standardized product against the flexibility of having a local manufacturing plant that is capable of tailoring the product to local preferences.

Taxation is another important consideration. Countries commonly offer tax advantages, among other incentives, to lure foreign investment. Puerto Rico does well on this score. In addition, there are no exchange problems since the currency is the U.S. dollar.

Just as important as other factors is the *investment climate* for foreign capital. The investment climate is determined by geographic and climatic conditions, market size, and growth potential, as well as by the political atmosphere. As mentioned earlier, political, economic, and social motives are highly related, and it is hardly surprising that countries, states, and cities compete fiercely to attract foreign investment and manufacturing plants.

Multinational corporations have been investing more and more overseas, with Asia and Latin America as their prime targets. It should be pointed out that the importance of cheap, unskilled labor in attracting manufacturing investment has been diminishing. Because of technology development in products and processes, there is a greater need for human skill in product manufacturing. Therefore, developing countries that can successfully influence plant location decisions will be those that have more highly skilled labor at relatively low wages.

Assembly Operations

An assembly operation is a variation on a manufacturing strategy. According to the U.S. Customs Service, "Assembly means the fitting or joining together of fabricated components." The methods used to join or fit together solid components may be welding, soldering, riveting, gluing, laminating, and sewing.

In this strategy, parts or components are produced in various countries in order to gain each country's comparative advantage (see Figure 12.6).

Mercedes-Benz excellence means more than just outstanding cars.

As the world automobile industry celebrates the 100th anniversary of the automobile, the Mercedes-Benz three-pointed star has achieved universal recognition as a symbol of undisputed technological advancement and excellence.

This high standard of excellence applies also to Mercedes-Benz trucks throughout America. The three-pointed star gives assurance that Mercedes-Benz trucks provide value:

- Proven product reliability
- A full range of 126-250 HP engines for both tractors and straight trucks to handle the most demanding jobs
- The only guaranteed parts-availability program in the industry
- 18-months unlimited warranty
- A nationwide dealer network for support
- American craftsmanship: Mercedes-Benz trucks are assembled in a modern, state-of-technology plant in Hampton, Virginia, by workers whose record for quality is the finest anywhere.

The Mercedes-Benz three-pointed star stands for excellence of each and every Mercedes-Benz truck in America. The majority of parts and components for these trucks are sourced from Mercedes-Benz do Brasil, the largest producer of trucks over six tons in the southern hemisphere.

Mercedes-Benz do Brasil S.A.

FIGURE 12.6 Assembly operations

Source: Mercedes-Benz do Brasil S.A.

Capital-intensive parts may be produced in advanced nations, and labor-intensive assemblies may be produced in a less developed country, where labor is abundant and labor costs are low. This strategy is common among manufacturers of consumer electronics. When a product becomes mature and faces intense price competition, it may be necessary to shift all of the labor-intensive operations to less developed countries.

An assembly operation also allows a company to be price-competitive against cheap imports, and this is a defense strategy employed by U.S. apparel makers against such imports. As far as pattern design and fabric cutting are concerned, a U.S. firm can compete by using automated machines, but sewing is another matter altogether, since sewing is labor-intensive and the least-automated aspect of making the product. To solve this problem, precut fabrics can be shipped to a low-wage country for sewing before bringing them back for finishing and packaging. Warnaco and Interco save on aggregate labor costs by cutting fabrics in the U.S.A. and shipping them to plants in Costa Rica and Honduras to be sewn. The duties collected on finished products brought back are low.

Assembly operations also allow a company's product to enter many markets without being subject to tariffs and quotas. The extent of freedom and flexibility, however, is limited by local product-content laws. South American countries usually require that more than 50 to 95 percent of components used in products be produced domestically. Note that as the percentage of required local content increases, the company's flexibility declines and the price advantage erodes. This is so because domestic products can be sheltered behind tariff walls, and higher prices must be expected for products with a low percentage of local content.

In general, a host country objects to the establishment of a screwdriver assembly that merely assembles imported parts. If a product's local content is less than half of all the components used, the product may be viewed as imported, subjected to tariffs and quota restrictions. The Japanese, even with joint ventures and assembly operations in Europe, keep local content in foreign production facilities to a minimum while maximizing the use of low-cost Japanese components. British Leyland's Triumph Acclaim is one such example. Made in the United Kingdom under license from

Honda, Acclaim contained over 55 percent of Japanese parts. Italy considered Acclaim to be a Japanese, not a European car. Since the EU's rule of thumb seemed to be at least 45 percent local content, Italy asked the European Commission to decide what percentage of local content a product must have to be considered "made in Europe." An assembly manufacturing operator must therefore carefully evaluate the tradeoff between low-cost production and the process of circumventing trade barriers.

Turnkey Operations

A turnkey operation is an agreement by the seller to supply a buyer with a facility fully equipped and ready to be operated by the buyer's personnel, who will be trained by the seller. The term is sometimes used in fast-food franchising when a franchisor agrees to select a store site, build the store, equip it, train the franchisee and employees, and sometimes arrange for the financing. In international marketing, the term is usually associated with giant projects that are sold to governments or government-run companies. Large-scale plants requiring technology and large-scale construction processes unavailable in local markets commonly use this strategy. Such large-scale projects include building steel mills; cement, fertilizer, and chemical plants; and those related to such advanced technologies as telecommunications.

Owing to the magnitude of a giant turnkey project, the winner of the contract may expect to reap huge rewards. Thus, it is important that the turnkey construction package offered to a buyer is an attractive one. Such a package involves more than just offering the latest technology, since there are many other factors important to less developed countries in deciding on a particular turnkey project. Financing is critical, and this is one area in which U.S. firms are lacking. European and Japanese firms are much more prepared to secure attractive financing from their governments for buyers. Another factor for consideration involves an agreement to build a local plant. All equipment must be installed and tested to make certain that it functions as intended. Local personnel must be trained to run the operation, and after-sale services should be contracted for and made available for the future maintenance of the plant.

Acquisition

When a manufacturer wants to enter a foreign market rapidly and yet retain maximum control, direct investment through acquisition should be considered [...]. The reasons for wanting to acquire a foreign company include product/geographical diversification, acquisition of expertise (technology, marketing, and management), and rapid entry. For example, Renault acquired a controlling interest in American Motors in order to gain the sales organization and distribution network that would otherwise have been very expensive and time-consuming to build from the ground up. After being outbid in 1994 when Forstmann Little & Co. bought Ziff-Davis Publishing, a company well known for its *PC Magazine* and other computer-related publications, Japan's Softbank Corp. was finally able to acquire the publisher a year later, albeit at a much higher price ($2.1 billion). The deal made the Japanese software company the world's largest computer magazine publisher and the largest operator of computer trade shows including Comdex.

Acquisition is viewed in a different light from other kinds of foreign direct investment. A government generally welcomes foreign investment that starts up a new enterprise (called a **greenfield** enterprise), since that investment increases employment and enlarges the tax base. An acquisition, however, fails to do this since it displaces and replaces domestic ownership. Therefore, acquisition is very likely to be perceived as exploitation or a blow to national pride—on this basis, it stands a good chance of being turned down. There was a heated debate before the United Kingdom allowed Sikorsky, a U.S. firm, to acquire Westland, a failing British manufacturer of military helicopters. That episode caused the Thatcher government to halt its negotiation with Ford concerning the acquisition of British Leyland's Austin-Rover passenger-car division. A greenfield project, while embraced by the host country, implies gradual market entry.

When host states and investors bargain over the terms of investment in sensitive sectors of the economy, there are political and economic tensions. Private ownership is positively related to greenfield investment (vs. divestiture) and joint venture (vs. wholly owned) projects.[34]

Although greenfield is a favored investment from the perspective of a host country, it is necessary to assess both the short-term and long-term benefits of this type of investment. A merger or acquisition merely involves ownership change, while greenfield FDI adds productive capital and employment—at least over the short term. However, after the initial period, it is difficult to assess the impact on host countries based on entry mode.[35]

A special case of acquisition is the **brownfield** entry mode. This mode occurs when an investor's transferred resources dominate over those provided by an acquired firm. In addition, this hybrid mode of entry requires the investor to extensively restructure

Cultural Dimension 12.1 How to make a successful acquisition

Jack Welch, the highly successful and former CEO of General Electric, lists the "six sins" of mergers and acquisitions. First, any "merger of equals" sounds good in theory but is a mess in practice. Second, the cultural fit of the two partners is as important as (if not more so than) a strategic fit. Third, run away from a "reverse hostage" situation when an acquirer makes so many concessions to the point that the acquired company will be in charge. Fourth, "be not afraid" as boldness is necessary and sensible for integration. Fifth, avoid the "conqueror syndrome" by installing own people everywhere in the new territory. Sixth and finally, "don't pay too much."

Source: Jack Welch and Suzy Welch, "The Six Sins of M&A," *Business Week*, October 23, 2006, 148.

Ethical Dimension 12.1 — In the name of free trade: dying for profits

It is an undeniable fact that cigarette smoking kills 4.9 million people every year. Once young people start smoking, many will be hooked for life. If cigarettes are a brand new product that is introduced to the market for the very first time, it is doubtful whether any governments could allow this harmful product to be marketed. A case can be made that cigarettes should be classified as an illegal drug.

Health officials all over the world have been prodding their governments to discourage smoking as well as the marketing of cigarettes. After all, health costs are enormous. While the U.S.A. has forced tobacco firms to curtail their marketing activities in the U.S. market, it seems to have taken the opposite approach abroad. While the U.S. cigarette market is now a mature or even declining one, such overseas markets as China and Russia are very attractive. The Chinese and Russian markets are big, and people there are not as concerned about the health issues. There is no question that cigarettes are a highly profitable industry and that American tobacco firms have dominated markets worldwide. But should the U.S.A. push to open up markets abroad for American cigarettes by using free trade as an excuse? The Bush administration has even tried to interfere with international controls on tobacco by opposing the Framework Convention on Tobacco Control.

The World Health Organization has spent three years working out an agreement with 171 countries to control the spread of smoking-related diseases. The treaty bans tobacco advertising, except where such a ban would be in conflict with national laws. The treaty additionally imposes a substantial tax on tobacco products and mandates warning labels on cigarette packages. Strangely, the U.S.A., citing free speech, seems to be more concerned with the welfare of the tobacco industry, which happened to give $6.4 million to the 2002 campaign chests of Republican candidates. But then the Bush administration has rejected a global warming agreement, an international criminal court, and a treaty on women's rights.

Japan Tobacco Inc. acquired Britain's Gallaher Group PLC in 2006 for $14.7 billion. Gallaher's brands include Benson & Hedges and Silk Cut. Because of health concerns in the U.S.A., coupled with falling tobacco sales in Japan, Japan Tobacco is seeking profits in fast-growing economies that do not have strict smoking-related regulations. Gallaher's largest factory in Moscow produces 65 billion cigarettes. The combined entity will have almost 35 percent of the hugely profitable Russian market. The market share in neighboring Kazakhstan will be 50 percent.

Sources: "Deadly Export," *San José Mercury News*, May 21, 2002; "Tobacco Treaty Changes Sought," *San José Mercury News*, April 30, 2003; "U.S. Feeds the World's Tobacco Habit," *San José Mercury News*, May 4, 2003; and "Japan Tobacco Makes Big Bet," *Wall Street Journal*, December 18, 2006.

the acquired company so as to assure fit between the two organizations. This is not uncommon in emerging markets, and the extensive restructuring may yield a new operation that resembles a greenfield investment. As such, integration costs can be high. Still, brownfield is a worthwhile strategy to consider when neither pure acquisition nor greenfield is feasible.[36]

Due to the sensitive nature of acquisition, there are more legal hurdles to surmount. In Germany, the Federal Cartel Office may prohibit or require divestiture of those mergers and acquisitions that could strengthen or create market domination. As in the case of Nestlé's acquisitions of U.S. companies in quick succession, it paid $10.3 billion in cash for Ralston Purina Co. (a pet-food powerhouse), over $2.6 billion in stock for a controlling stake in Dreyer's Grand Ice Cream Inc. (the largest U.S. maker of ice cream), and another $2.6 billion for Chef America Inc. Nestlé had to spend almost a year convincing American regulators to let it acquire Dreyer's Grand Ice Cream. The U.S. Federal Trade Commission blocked the proposed deal because the takeover would eliminate brand and price competition for such premium brands as Häagen Dazs and Godiva.

We know we don't control the price of gas, but we can innovate to reduce the need. That's why we're building cars that can go 500 miles on a single tank and producing 250,000 E-85 ethanol vehicles this year. We even have 12 vehicles that get 30 mpg or more.* At Ford, innovation is the guiding compass of everything we do.

Bill Ford, Chairman and CEO
Ford Motor Company

DRIVING AMERICAN INNOVATION

*Based on EPA estimated hwy mpg.   ford.com/innovation

FIGURE 12.7 Ford's acquisitions and brands

Nestlé, Dreyers, and Unilever control 98 percent of superpremium ice cream sales in the U.S.A.

There does not appear to be any sign that mergers and acquisitions are abating. Vivendi paid $2.09 billion to Bertelsmann in 2006 to acquire the BMG Music Publishing Group which has the world's largest collection of music catalogs and songs.[37] Barclays decided to acquire ABN Amro in 2007 for 67 billion euros.[38]

Several of Ford Motor Co.'s premium brands are a result of acquisitions (see Figure 12.7), and they include Volvo (1999), Jaguar (1989), and Aston Martin (1987). A 2000 acquisition was a payment of nearly $3 billion to BMW Group for the British-born Land Rover line of sport-utility vehicles. BMW acquired Rover Group Ltd. in 1995 and lost $1.25 billion on this investment over five years. To cut the loss, BMW sold Rover Group's Rover and MG brands to a British investment group and Land Rover to Ford.

The value of a currency may either reduce or increase the costs of an acquisition. A buyer whose home currency is getting weaker will see its costs go up but will benefit if its currency becomes stronger. As in the case of Hoechst, a German chemical giant, it bid $7.2 billion for the U.S.-based Marion Merrell Dow Inc. and was able to save at least $250 million because the value of the dollar plunged in the meantime.

International mergers and acquisitions are complex, expensive, and risky. The problems are numerous: finding a suitable company, determining a fair price, acquisition debt, merging two management teams, language and cultural differences, employee resentment, geographic distance, and so on. Acquirers must thus exercise due diligence. Sometimes, it may be better to walk away from a deal. The reasons for exiting from a deal include: high price, no agreement on governance issues, no synergies, poor quality of management, environmental issues, ethical reasons, no strategic fit, detection of significant unrecorded/undisclosed liability, potential problem with anti-trust laws, and uncertainty about legal/tax aspects.[39]

Quite often, the future synergies due to vertical integration are elusive. Unicord PLC, a large fish processor located in Thailand, paid $280 million to acquire Bumble Bee Seafood Inc., a San Diego tuna canner. The acquisition was a failure, and the founder of Unicord committed suicide in 1995 as lenders sought payment.

Japan's Bridgestone Corp. paid $2.6 billion to acquire money-losing Firestone Tire & Rubber Co. and lost $1 billion in the first five years after the acquisition while enduring a bitter and lengthy strike. Overall, foreign acquirers pay almost twice as much as domestic buyers would. The U.S. market in particular, due to its market size, tends to force foreign acquirers to pay a premium price.

Major differences in national culture hurt foreign acquisition performance if the acquirer tightly integrates the acquired unit, but performance is enhanced if there is a limited degree of post-acquisition integration.[40] The parties should also consider a performance-contingent payout structure to mitigate risk of adverse selection. There is evidence that firms lacking acquisition experience rely on contingent payouts when purchasing targets in high-technology and service industries. There is a tendency to avoid contingent payouts in host countries which have problems with investor protection and legal enforceability.[41] In any case, pre-acquisition experience of both target and a multinational enterprise is important.[42]

Country differences in intellectual property rights protection can affect the choice of market entry. When protection is not secure, companies choose R&D joint ventures over contractual partnerships.[43]

According to a study by *Business Week* and Mercer Management Consulting Inc. of 150 deals worth at least $500 million, mergers and acquisitions do not benefit stockholders. When judged by stock performance in relation to Standard & Poor's industry indexes, about half of the 150 deals harmed shareholder wealth, while another one-third hardly contributed anything. Yet, in spite of the high failure rate for cross-border acquisitions, more and more international deals can be expected. A followup study showed that transatlantic mergers had a better chance to succeed—far better than the usual success ratio of American domestic or intra-European deals. One contributing factor is that such deals tended to expand geographic reach, reducing the need to cut costs by disruptively merging overlapping operations. In addition, because of the hassles of having to pass the scrutiny of anti-trust regulators on both sides of the ocean, companies choose to pursue only the most promising prospects.[44]

Strategic Alliances

As discussed, to gain access to new markets and technologies while achieving economies of scale, international marketers have a number of organization forms to choose from: licensing, partially owned or wholly owned subsidiaries, joint ventures, and acquisitions. A relatively new organizational form of market entry and competitive cooperation is **strategic alliance**. This form of corporate cooperation has been receiving a great deal of attention as large multinational firms still find it necessary to find strategic partners to penetrate a market.

There is no clear and precise definition of strategic alliance. There is no one way to form a strategic alliance. An alliance may be in the areas of production, distribution, marketing, and research and development. America Online is a good example of strategic alliances. In 2000, America Online and Bertelsmann AG formed a global alliance to expand the distribution of Bertelsmann's media content and electronic commerce properties over America Online's interactive brands worldwide. As an example of R&D alliances, Sony and Philips ally to compete with another alliance led by Toshiba in developing DVDs.

Strategic alliances may be the result of mergers, acquisitions, joint ventures, and licensing agreements. Joint ventures are naturally strategic alliances, but not all strategic alliances are joint ventures. Unlike joint ventures which require two or more partners to create a separate entity, a strategic alliance does not necessarily require a new legal entity. As such, it may not require partners to make arrangements to share equity. Instead of being an equity-based investment, a strategic alliance may be more of a contractual arrangement whereby two or more partners agree to cooperate with each other and utilize each partner's resources and expertise to penetrate a particular market.

Airlines are a good example of the international nature of strategic alliances. Almost all major airlines have joined one of the three strategic groups: Star, SkyTeam, and Oneworld. The SkyTeam group consists of Delta, Air France, Aeromexico, Alitalia, Czech Airlines, and Korean Air. Oneworld has American, British Airways, Aer Lingus, Cathay Pacific, Finnair, Iberia, Japan Airlines, LanChile, and Qantas. The Star alliance, the largest group, comprises United, Air Canada, Air New Zealand, ANA, Austrian, British Midland, Lauda, Lufthansa, Mexicana, Scandinavian, Singapore, Thai, Tyrolean, and Varig. Turkish Airlines was accepted in 2006 as the 21st member. While the alliances vary in size and degree of integration, most of them have code sharing by offering seats on a partner's flights. In addition, passengers earn frequent-flier points on their home carrier when flying with the alliance members. These members also provide reciprocal access to their airport lounges.

Companies enter into alliance relationships for a variety of reasons. Those in the emerging Latin American economies are similar to their counterparts in many other nations in terms of their motivations. In general, through alliances with foreign partners, they seek resource acquisition, competitive posturing, and risk/cost reduction.[45] While companies have paid attention to the hard side of alliance management (e.g., financial issues and other operational issues), the soft side also requires attention. The soft side has to do with the management of relationship capital in an alliance. Relationship capital focuses on the socio-psychological aspects of the alliance, and the two important areas of relationship capital are mutual trust and commitment.[46]

Analysis of Entry Strategies

To enter a foreign market, a manufacturer has a number of strategic options, each with its own strengths and weaknesses. Many companies employ multiple strategies. IBM has employed strategies ranging from licensing, joint ventures, and strategic alliances on the one hand to local manufacturing and subsidiaries on the other hand. Likewise, McDonald's uses joint ventures in the Far East while licensing its name without putting up equity capital in the Mid-East. Walt Disney Co. has a 39 percent stake in Euro Disney while collecting management and royalty fees which amount to $70 million a year.

One would be naive to believe that a single entry strategy is suitable for all products or in all countries. For example, a significant change in the investment climate can make a particular strategy ineffective even though it worked well in the past. There are a number of characteristics that determine the appropriateness of entry strategies, and many variables affect which strategy is chosen. These characteristics include political risks, regulations, type of country, type of product, and other competitive and market characteristics.

Viacom Inc. appears to take culture into account in deciding on entry strategies. In the case of its MTV channel, the company generally does not have partners, but in the case of its Nickelodeon channel, the firm has made an effort to have local partners. It is difficult to tell Europeans that they should have the same cultural underpinnings inherent in American children's programming. Although children may watch programming from other countries, they are more inclined to watch their own programs.

Markets are far from being homogeneous, and the type of country chosen dictates the entry strategy to be used. In free-enterprise economies, an MNC can choose any entry strategy it deems appropriate. In controlled economies, the options are limited. Until recently, the most frequent trade entry activity in controlled economies was exporting, followed by licensing for Eastern Europe.

Market entry strategies are also influenced by *product type*. A product that must be customized or that requires some services before and after the sale cannot easily be exported to another country. In fact, a service or a product whose value is largely determined by an accompanied service cannot be practically distributed outside of the producing country. Any portion of the product that is service-oriented must be created at the place of consumption. As a result, service-intensive products require particular modes of market entry. The options include management contract to sell service to a foreign customer, licensing so that another local company (franchisee) can be trained to provide that service, and local manufacturing by establishing a permanent branch or subsidiary there.

A product that is basically a *commodity* may require local production in order to reduce labor and shipping costs. For a *value-added or differentiated product*, a firm can depend on the exporting mode because of the higher profit margin. Furthermore, local manufacturing may destroy the product's mystique and thus diminish a previously existing market.

There are two schools of thought that explain how multinational corporations select ownership structures for subsidiaries. The first has to do with what the firm wants, and MNCs want structures that minimize the transaction costs of doing business abroad (e.g., whole ownership). Factors affecting what the firm wants include the capabilities of the firm, its strategic needs, and the transaction costs of different ways of transferring capabilities. The second school of thought, related to what the firm can get, explains that what it wants may differ from what it can get (e.g., joint venture). In this case, ownership structures are determined by negotiations, whose outcomes depend on the relative bargaining power of the firm and that of the host government.

In practice, American manufacturers prefer joint ventures in the Far East because of legal and cultural barriers. Regarding how American manufacturers want to enter the European Union market, the preferred methods of entry are: joint venture, sales representative, branch/subsidiary, and distribution facility.

A company's entry choice of joint ventures versus wholly owned subsidiaries may be influenced by its competitive capabilities as well as market barriers. In the case of Japanese investors entering the U.S. market, they choose joint ventures when facing high market barriers. But they prefer to establish wholly owned subsidiaries when they possess competitive capabilities. These ownership decisions are influenced more by marketing variables than by technological factors. One caveat: the results vary across industries (low technology vs. high technology) and products (consumer products vs. industrial products).[47] The costs of organizing a business in transition economies influence entry mode choice. Host-country institutions have an impact because underdeveloped institutions drive up costs of establishing wholly owned ventures.[48]

Institutional isomorphism seems to exist as later entrants often use the entry mode patterns established by earlier entrants. In addition, this behavior exists within a firm as companies exhibit consistency in their entry mode choices across time.[49]

In the case of China, a company's timing of entry is associated with non-equity modes, competitors' behavior, and lower levels of country risk. Firms cannot delay their entry when the competitors are moving in.

In addition, a firm's entry is accelerated if a non-equity mode of entry is chosen. Favorable risk conditions (locational features), likewise, accelerate entry timing. In addition, corporate size facilitates early entry. A firm of good size is able to muster resources, extend support among the related products sectors, and capitalize on economies of scale. This is consistent with the resource-based arguments that early entrants differ from late entrants in terms of resources and capabilities.[50]

One study focuses on conflicting results which show that cultural distance is associated with wholly owned modes in some studies and with joint ventures in other studies. The evidence shows that, for Western firms investing in Central and Eastern Europe, investment risk moderates the relationship between cultural distance and entry mode selection. Firms entering culturally distant markets that are low in investment risk prefer cooperative modes of entry. However, if such culturally distant markets pose high investment risk, wholly owned modes of entry are preferred.[51] Conversely, although cultural distance is routinely used as an independent variable that supposedly influences performance and entry mode choice, it is conceivable that the relationship may be reversed. A case can be made that cultural distance is a dependent variable because entry mode and performance may affect the perceived distance.[52]

With regard to Spanish FDI in Latin America, cultural affinity is the most important factor in the selection of the destination.[53] A review of 26 studies reveals that the nationality of companies affects entry mode decisions. The effect, however, varies due to some cultural and economic factors.[54] The effect of cultural distance is not straightforward. While it is negatively related with international diversification for high-technology industries, the relationship is positive for other industries. For U.S.-based multinationals, there is a strong negative association between cultural distance and entry mode choice.[55] Logically, multinationals need to conform to the institutional environment of the host country. Therefore, FDI should be utilized when there is minimal institutional distance between the home-country and host-country environments.[56]

It may make sense to differentiate between hard- and soft-service firms. Hard-service suppliers can learn from the experience of manufacturing companies going abroad. Soft services, however, are unique because of the importance of interaction between soft-service suppliers and their clients. Based on a study of 140 Swedish service firms, soft-service firms are likely to prefer a high control entry mode to a low control entry mode.[57]

Free Trade Zones (FTZs)

When entering a market, a company should go beyond an investigation of market entry modes. Another question that should be asked is whether a free trade zone (FTZ) is involved and needs consideration. The decisions concerning market entry and FTZs are somewhat independent. An FTZ can be used regardless of whether the entry strategy is exporting or local manufacturing.

An **FTZ** is a secured domestic area in international commerce, considered to be legally outside a country's customs territory. It is an area designated by a government for the duty-free entry of goods. It is also a location where imports can be handled with few regulations, and little or no customs duties and excise taxes are collected. As such, goods enter the area without paying any duty. The duty would be paid only when goods enter customs territory of the country where an FTZ is located.

Variations among FTZs include freeports, tariff-free trade zones, airport duty-free arcades, export-processing zones, and other foreign grade zones. FTZs are usually established in countries for the convenience of foreign traders. The zones may be run by the host government or by private entities. FTZs vary in size from a few acres to several square miles. They may be located at airports, in harbor areas, or within the interior of a country (e.g., Salt Lake City). In addition to the FTZs (general-purpose zones), there are also subzones throughout the U.S.A. Subzones are special-purpose facilities for companies unable to operate effectively at public zone sites.

One popular misconception about FTZs is that they are used basically for warehousing. Although goods can be stored for an unlimited length of time in an FTZ, any gain from doing so is small when compared to the alternative of a bonded warehouse, which allows temporary storage without duty. Actually, the future of FTZs lies in manufacturing (product manipulation), not storing.

FTZs offer several important benefits, both for the country and for companies using them. One benefit is job retention and creation. When better facilities and grants are provided to attract MNCs, FTZs can generate foreign investment and jobs. For example, the Buffalo, New York, FTZ was able to attract a Canadian automobile assembly operation and a Japanese camera importer to establish operations there. China has set up special economic zones (SEZs) for manufacturing, banking, exporting and importing, and foreign investment. Figure 12.8 mentions Macedonia's incentives as well as its free economic zones.

Some countries, for political reasons, are not able to open up their economies completely. Instead they have set up **export-processing zones**, a special type of FTZ, in order to attract foreign capital for manufacturing for export.

The benefits of FTZ use are numerous. Some of these benefits are country-specific in the sense that some countries offer superior facilities for lower costs (e.g., utilities and telecommunications). Other benefits are zone-specific in that certain zones may be better than others within the same country in terms of tax and transportation facilities. Finally, there are zone-related benefits that constitute general advantages in using an FTZ. Some of the zone-related benefits are: lower theft rate, lower insurance costs, delay of tax payment, and reduction of inventory in transit.

FTZs provide a means to facilitate imports. Imported merchandise may be sent into FTZs without formal customs entry and duty payment until some later date. Both foreign and domestic goods can be moved into FTZs and remain there for storage, assembling, manufacturing, packaging, and other processing operations. Goods that were improperly marked or cannot meet standards for clearance may be remarked and salvaged. Moreover, goods may be cleaned, mixed, and used in the manufacturing of other products. One Swiss cosmetics company imports in bulk and employs U.S. labor to repackage its goods for retailing. In fact, importers can even display and exhibit merchandise and take orders in FTZs without securing a bond. For retailers, benefits derived by using FTZs include the sorting, labeling, and storing of imports.

FTZs not only facilitate imports but can also facilitate export and re-export, though the gain from this practice is small when compared to the alternatives of duty drawback and temporary import bond. Still, domestic goods can be taken into an FTZ and are then returned free of quotas and duty, even when they have been combined with other articles while inside the zone. Sears uses the New Orleans FTZ to inspect foreign cameras it subsequently ships to Latin America. Seiko Time corporation of America opened a 200,000-square-foot facility in the New Jersey FTZ to store and ship watches to Canada and Latin America. One European medical supply firm that makes kidney dialysis machines use German raw materials and American labor in a U.S. FTZ for assembly purposes, and then exports 30 percent of the finished product to Scandinavia.

Conclusion

If a company wants to avoid FDI when marketing in foreign markets it has a number of options. It can export its product from its home base, or it can grant a license permitting another company to manufacture and market its product in a foreign market. Another option is to sign a contract to sell its expertise by managing the business for a foreign owner.

If the firm is interested in making foreign direct investment, it can either start its business from the ground up or acquire another company. The acquisition, however, may receive a less than enthusiastic response from the foreign government. If the company decides to start a new business overseas, it must consider whether a sole venture or joint venture will best suit the objective. Sole ventures provide a company with better control and profit, whereas joint ventures reduce risk and utilize the strengths of a local partner. Regardless of whether a sole venture or joint venture is used, the company must still decide whether local production is going to be complete or partial (i.e., assembly). Finally, foreign sales to governments often take the form of giant turnkey projects that require the company to provide a complete package, including financing, construction, and training.

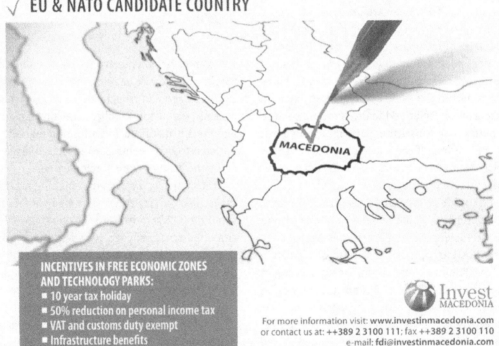

FIGURE 12.8 Macedonia's incentives and free economic zones

Once a particular market is chosen, management needs to decide on the market entry strategy. In addition, the company should consider the feasibility of operating all or some of its international business in a free trade zone, since such a zone can complement many of the market penetration options.

A word of caution is in order. Compared to the other aspects of international business, market entry strategies (especially joint ventures) have received disproportionate attention. Unfortunately, contradictory results abound. These contradictions should not come as a surprise. After all, many of these studies have employed different measurement methods, variables, countries, industries, and sample sizes. For example, one study focused on entry forms of five small Norwegian computer software firms,[58] while another study focused on 4000 market entry decisions of Japanese multinationals.[59]

Each market entry strategy has its own unique strengths and weaknesses. In most circumstances the strategies are not mutually exclusive. A manufacturer may use multiple strategies in different markets as well as within the same market. No single market penetration is ideal for all markets or all circumstances. The appropriateness of a strategic option depends on corporate objectives, market conditions, and political realities.

CASE 12.1

Taylor Candy Company and the Caribbean Market

Jun Onishi, Hirosaki University, Japan

Taylor Candy Company is a small, family-owned candy company located in the southern Florida area. When it was originally established in 1957, it sold candy only in that area. Over the years, its candy bars have grown in popularity and are now distributed throughout the southeastern U.S.A.

Its most popular product is the Coco-Loco bar, which has a toasted coconut outside with a crisp peanut crunch inside. Because coconuts are not grown in the U.S.A., this candy bar is marketed as an "exotic, island treat." The wrapper shows palm trees and a thatch-roofed beach bungalow, emphasizing this image. The advertisements for the product feature someone relaxing on a tropical beach, eating the candy bar. Market research shows that most of the consumers of this candy bar

are working and in the lower-middle class, making lower-than-average to average incomes. Consumers interviewed said that the candy bar's flavor is the main reason why they purchased it, but they also indicated that they were influenced by the tropical image. Some consumers said that, since they could not afford to vacation on a tropical island, eating the candy bar made them feel as if they were on an island. A large percentage of consumers also indicated that they were influenced by the company's aggressive anti-littering and pro-recycling stance.

At this point in time, attempts to distribute the candy bar in the U.S.A. outside of the southeastern region have not been successful due primarily to competition from other, longer established companies with a similar line-up of candy. Several years ago, the company looked into the possibility of dis-

tributing its candy in the Caribbean area, but several factors discouraged the company from distributing the product there. These factors included the high cost of transportation, poor transportation and distribution infrastructure within the islands, corrupt governments, and uncertain demand.

Recently, Tom Taylor, Director of Marketing, was vacationing in the Bahamas and discovered that a small general store near a popular tourist resort was selling one of his candy bars. Tom asked the owner of the store about where he got the candy bars. The owner told him that he had a friend who flew between Miami and the Bahamas on business several times a year and who always brought a big box of the candy bars as a favor. In exchange, the owner, who knows many local officials, helped the businessman with his local deals. He said that the store always sold out of the candy bar within a few days, mainly to tourists, but also to the middle- and upper-class locals.

Taylor decided that the fact that the store always sold out of the Coco-Loco bar within a few days indicated a high potential demand. However, he wanted to be sure that this demand was not strictly local. So he did some research to find out what kind of demand there might be for candy bars in the Caribbean. He found that very few U.S. candy companies exported to the Caribbean, which indicated that there was not a high demand. However, additional research indicated that Caribbean people were fond of sweets. Chocolate, which originated in Central America, was very popular in the Caribbean and was used in many desserts. He found a website with recipes which showed that many Caribbean cakes, pastries, and pies were made using fruits, rum, chocolate, spices, and lots of sugar.

Based on this information, Taylor decided that there might be demand for Taylor Candy Company candy bars. He decided to gather updated information on other factors that had previously led the company to decide against trying to distribute to the Caribbean. He discovered that transportation costs between Florida and the islands had decreased considerably over the past few years. He also learned that the local transportation and distribution infrastructures had improved on the largest and most populated islands.

He also researched several websites to obtain current information on the political situation in the region. He discovered that there was still little true democracy and that a great deal of corruption still existed, but that, in general, things had become more politically stable with a higher degree of political and economic freedom. While he did not think that it would be a good idea to try to do business in a country that was extremely corrupt or unstable, he thought that there could be some Caribbean countries which would have an acceptable political and social environment.

Taylor decided that the idea of exporting to the Caribbean was worth exploring; so he discussed it with the President of the company. They decided that they should consider several additional factors.

First, they thought it would be important to identify the islands that would be the best target markets in terms of being able to support sufficient demand. They reasoned that the best islands would be those with either high numbers of tourists or those with large local populations and relatively high average incomes. They decided that a country would have to have either a population of at least 100,000 people, an average income of at least US$5000, or a total national tourism income of at least US$100 million per year to support significant sales. Any country meeting at least one of these requirements would also have to be politically stable.

The second item considered was whether they could price the candy bars for the local market and make a profit on those islands where they were not going to depend on sales from tourists. They knew that even the islands with the highest average local incomes would have average incomes far lower than incomes in the U.S.A. The shop in the Bahamas where he had found the candy bars selling at a very low price was due to the merchant being a friend of the owner who gave him the candy bars free in exchange for favors.

Third, they knew that, to make a worthwhile profit, they would have to ship the candy bars in sufficiently large quantities every couple of months. Thus, there would have to be a local distributor who could handle those quantities of candy stock and keep the product fresh for approximately two months. They also knew that the climate in the Caribbean was hot and humid, and that it would be necessary to keep the stock in a climate-controlled warehouse and distribute it to each store in small amounts.

The fourth factor that was considered was whether there were any cultural factors that might affect sales. They of course knew the story about Chevrolet's failure to market the Nova in Latin America because "nova" means "no go" in Spanish and the story about Coca-Cola's name in China sounding like "bite the wax tadpole." Would it be possible that the name "Coco-Loco" would have some meaning in a local language that would be strange or offensive to someone in that market? Could consumers be suspicious of the ingredients within the product because of the name? Taylor felt more confident by comparison with English-speaking countries where the company's products were sold.

They were also concerned about general attitudes within the population toward the U.S.A. and American products. Would there be any anti-American sentiment which could discourage people from buying their candy bars? Could they be perceived as a luxury item even though they were priced to be affordable? In 1997, a lawsuit was initiated against Co-co-Loco by an Indian businessman who claimed that the trade name 'Coco-Loco' was registered as the product name of his company. After a lengthy trial, Taylor Candy Company won this suit since the court held that the registration was valid only in India, but this incident created a negative image of the company among Indians.

Because of their close location to the U.S.A., there are ambivalent feelings among Caribbean people toward American products. A stable political environment is also an important criterion for Taylor Candy Company. A disruptive political incident by Cambodians in 2003 against Thailand reminded Taylor of the importance of having political stability.

The sixth item that was given consideration was the environ-mental issue. In the U.S.A., Taylor Candy Company pursues a strict policy of environmental protection. The production process is set up to minimize energy usage and waste generation. The company also tries to promote anti-littering and recycling of candy bar wrappers in their advertisements. They know that this is an important concern with many of their customers in the U.S.A., and the company wants to maintain its reputation as a pro-environmental company. The company felt so strongly about this issue that it decided to market in the Caribbean only if consumers there would be receptive to its anti-littering and pro-recycling promotional messages. Taylor Candy Company goes so far as to include notices on candy bar wrappers asking people to recycle the wrappers.

Finally, the company considered the possibility of a decrease in tourism travel by Americans due to the terrorist attacks on the World Trade Center and the Pentagon on September 11, 2001. They knew that a very large percentage of tourism revenue in the Caribbean came from the U.SA. If tourism to the Caribbean area significantly decreased, they felt that this would have a negative effect on sales to tourists.

Taylor collected additional information on population, average income, and average annual tourism expenditures for several Caribbean countries (see Table 12.1). The company then reviewed the information he had previously collected on the politics and culture of each of the above countries. All of the Caribbean countries have predominantly black populations, with varying percentages of white (mainly Spanish, French, or British ancestry), East Indian, and mixed-race minorities.

Some of Taylor's observations about the various countries included the following: Haiti is nominally a democracy, but there is a long history of political and social violence that is still continuing. An organization that rates the level of political freedom of various countries, on a scale of 1 (completely free) to 15 (no freedom), gave Haiti a 9.

TABLE 12.1 Country Statistics

Country	Population	Purchasing power parity (U.S.$)	Tourism expenditure (million U.S.$)
Haiti	7,000,000	1800	58
Dominican Republic	8,600,000	5700	1755
Jamaica	2,700,000	3700	1100
Trinidad and Tobago	1,200,000	9500	105
Guyana	700,000	4800	38
Suriname	435,000	3400	17
Bahamas	298,000	15,000	1450
Belize	257,000	3200	84
Grenada	89,000	4400	60
Antigua	67,000	8200	257

Antigua is a member of the British Commonwealth and is also nominally a democracy. However, one political party has control of the media and a monopoly on patronage, making it effectively a one-party state. Antigua was given a freedom score of 7.

The Dominican Republic is also a nominal democracy, but there have been numerous charges of election fraud. The government is very conservative and has strong links to the military.

The Dominican Republic and Suriname also have a history of military governments, but recently have had elections. Both of these countries were given a freedom score of 6.

Jamaica is considered a working democracy, with a freedom score of 5, but there is much social violence in the country. Jamaica also has a small East Indian minority within its population.

Guyana has multiple parties with elections that appear to be fair. However, the current government, led by a Marxist prime minister, has been in power for a long period of time. It was given a freedom score of 4. It also has a small East Indian minority.

The Bahamas is a multi-party democracy and was given a freedom score of 3. However, since the opposition party does not generally win elections there is very little change in government. The government is considered by some to be very corrupt. It has a small East Indian minority.

Trinidad, Belize, and Grenada are among the most successful democracies in the Caribbean, with respective freedom scores of 3, 2, and 3. Trinidad has a large East Indian population. A recent coup attempt in that country by dissatisfied Muslims was successfully put down. Belize has had successful elections in which the government has changed hands without violence. Grenada has strong ties to the U.S.A.

In researching cultural factors that influence acceptance of the candy bar, Taylor found that the word "loco" means "crazy" in Spanish and that "coco" might suggest "cocaine".

Taylor also read an article about the effect of the terrorist attacks on tourism in the Caribbean area. The article stated that tourism had been adversely affected. One of the effects of the attacks was that many cruise lines were selling cabins at drastically reduced prices, well below the price at which Caribbean hotels could compete. However, cruise lines still account for only 7 percent of tourism revenue in the Caribbean. He wondered that, if so many of the Caribbean countries were so heavily dependent on the tourism industry for economic prosperity and if tourism travel suddenly declined, some countries might not be suitable target markets for Taylor Candy Company to export its products to those countries.

QUESTIONS

1. Briefly explain these market entry strategies: exporting, licensing, joint venture, manufacturing, assembly operations, management contract, turnkey operations, and acquisition.

2. What is cross-licensing or grantback?

3. What are the factors that should be considered in choosing a country for direct investment?

4. What is an FTZ? What are its benefits?

DISCUSSION ASSIGNMENTS AND MINICASES

1. Since exporting is a relatively risk-free market entry strategy, is there a need for a company to consider other market entry strategies?

2. Can a service be licensed for market entry purposes?

3. In spite of the advantages of free trade zones, most companies have failed to utilize them effectively.

What are the reasons? Can anything be done to stimulate interest?

4. One of the most celebrated joint ventures is NUMMI (New United Motor Manufacturing, Inc.), a joint venture between General Motors and Toyota. It seems surprising that the two largest competitors would even think of joining forces. GM is the number one manufacturer

in the U.S.A. as well as in the world. Toyota, on the other hand, is number one in Japan and number two worldwide. NUMMI is a 50–50 joint venture with the board of directors split equally between the two companies. Initially, the venture was to manufacture the Toyota-designed subcompact, and the name chosen for the car was Nova. At present, the plant manufactures Toyota Tacoma, Toyota Corolla, and Toyota Voltz. What are the benefits each partner may expect to derive from the NUMMI joint venture? Do you foresee any problems?

5. Each year, foreign companies generate some $10 billion in capital and 300,000 new jobs for the U.S. economy. As may be expected, U.S. politicians, states, and local governments have aggressively competed for foreign direct investment. Discuss the business of attracting foreign corporations from the viewpoints of both the companies and states. What are the matters of concern to companies which they will take into consideration when making their location decisions? What are the incentives which states can offer to lure businesses to locate in a particular state?

NOTES

1. "Why FDI May Not Be As Stable As Governments Think," *IMF Survey*, January 29, 2007, 26–7.
2. Prakash Loungani and Assaf Razin, "How Beneficial Is Foreign Direct Investment for Developing Countries?" *Finance & Development*, June 2001, 6–9.
3. United Nations Conference on Trade and Development, *World Investment Report* 2006.
4. "FDI in Africa: Why Do Select Countries Do Better?" *IMF Survey*, March 25, 2001, 91–2.
5. *World Investment Report 2006: FDI from Developing and Transition Economies*, UNCTAD, 2006, 17.
6. "Shoppers Gone Wild," *Business Week*, February 20, 2006, 46–7.
7. Mohsin Habib and Leon Zurawicki, "Corruption and Foreign Direct Investment," *Journal of International Business Studies* 33 (Second Quarter 2002): 291–307.
8. Utz Weitzel and Sjors Berns, "Cross-border Takeovers, Corruption, and Related Aspects of Governance," *Journal of International Business Studies* 37 (November 2006): 786–806.
9. Artur Baldauf, David W. Cravens, and Udo Wagner, "Examining Determinants of Export Performance in Small Open Economies," *Journal of World Business* 35 (No. 1, 2000): 61–75.
10. Luis Filipe Lages and David B. Montgomery, "Export Performance As an Antecedent of Export Commitment and Marketing Strategy Adaptation: Evidence from Small and Medium-sized Exporters," *European Journal of Marketing* 38 (Nos 9/10, 2004): 1186–214.

11. Paul Ellis and Anthony Pecotich, "Social Factors Influencing Export Initiation in Small and Medium-Sized Enterprises," *Journal of Marketing Research* 38 (February 2001): 119–30.
12. Paul A. Brewer, "Operationalizing Psychic Distance: A Revised Approach," *Journal of International Marketing* 15 (No. 1, 2007): 44–66.
13. Kevin I.N. Ibeh and Stephen Young, "Exporting as an Entrepreneurial Act—An Empirical Study of Nigerian Firms," *European Journal of Marketing* 35 (No. 5, 2001): 566–86.
14. Ashley Lye and R.T. Hamilton, "Search and Performance in International Exchange," *European Journal of Marketing* 34 (No. 1, 2000): 176–89.
15. "Starbucks to Grow 'a Latte,'" *San José Mercury News*, October 29, 2006.
16. "McDonald's in [800m Push to Lift Profile Across Europe," *Financial Times*, August 21, 2007.
17. "Saint Laurent's Newest Look," *Business Week*, July 31, 2000, 82, 84; and "Making Over YSL Is No Stroll Down the Catwalk," *Business Week*, January 28, 2002, 54.
18. Sandra Mottner and James P. Johnson, "Motivations and Risks in International Licensing: A Review and Implications for Licensing to Transitional and Emerging Economies," *Journal of World Business* 35 (No. 2, 2000): 171–88.
19. "Accor Buys Zenith Stake to Life China Exposure," *The Asian Wall Street Journal*, January 4, 2001.

20. "AMD to Form New Venture with Fujitsu," *San José Mercury News*, March 31, 2003; and "Fujitsu, AMD Expand Venture," *San José Mercury News*, April 1, 2003.

21. Keith D. Brouthers, "Institutional, Cultural and Transaction Cost Influences on Entry Mode Choice and Performance," *Journal of International Business Studies* 33 (Second Quarter 2002): 203–21.

22. Linda Longfellow Blodgett, "Partner Contributions as Predictors of Equity Share in International Joint Ventures," *Journal of International Business Studies* 22 (No. 1, 1991): 63–78.

23. Chang-Bum Choi and Paul W. Beamish, "Split Management Control and International Joint Venture Performance," *Journal of International Business Studies* 35 (May 2004): 201–15.

24. Yigang Pan, "Equity Ownership in International Joint Ventures: The Impact of Source Country Factors," *Journal of International Business Studies* 33 (Second Quarter 2002): 375–84.

25. Vijay Pothukuchi *et al.*, "National and Organizational Culture Differences and International Joint Venture Performance," *Journal of International Business Studies* 33 (Second Quarter 2002): 243–65.

26. Paul W. Beamish and Ariff Kachra, "Number of Partners and JV Performance," *Journal of World Business* 39 (May 2004): 107–20.

27. Hemant Merchant, "The Structure–Performance Relationship in International Joint Ventures: A Comparative Analysis," *Journal of World Business* 40 (February 2005): 41–56.

28. Yadong Luo and Seung Ho Park, "Multiparty Cooperation and Performance in International Equity Joint Ventures," *Journal of International Business Studies* 35 (March 2004): 142–60.

29. Chris Styles and Lisa Hersch, "Executive Insights: Relationship Formation in International Joint Ventures: Insights from Australian–Malaysian International Joint Ventures," *Journal of International Marketing* 13 (No. 3, 2005): 105–34.

30. Charles Dhanaraj *et al.*, "Managing Tacit and Explicit Knowledge Transfer in IJVs: The Role of Relational Embeddedness and the Impact on

Performance," *Journal of International Business Studies* 35 (September 2004): 428–42.

31. "They've Driven a Ford Lately," *Business Week*, February 26, 2007, 52.

32. "Made in China—Er, Veliko Turnovo," *Business Week*, January 8, 2007, 43.

33. "Honda Will Create Brand for China's Auto Market," *Wall Street Journal*, July 19, 2007.

34. Jonathan P. Doh, Hildy Teegen, and Ram Mudambi, "Balancing Private and State Ownership in Emerging Markets' Telecommunications Infrastructure: Country, Industry, and Firm Influences," *Journal of International Business Studies* 35 (May 2004): 233–50.

35. *World Investment Report 2006*, 17.

36. Klaus E. Meyer and Saul Estrin, "Brownfield Entry in Emerging Markets," *Journal of International Business Studies* 32 (Third Quarter 2001): 575–84.

37. "Vivendi Plans to Pay $2.09 Billion to Buy BMG," *San José Mercury News*, September 7, 2006.

38. "Barclays to Acquire Dutch Bank ABN Amro," *San José Mercury News*, April 24, 2007.

39. Philippe Very and David M. Schweiger, "The Acquisition Process as a Learning Process: Evidence from a Study of Critical Problems and Solutions in Domestic and Cross-Border Deals," *Journal of World Business* 36 (No. 1, 2001): 11–31.

40. Arjen H. L. Slangen, "National Cultural Distance and Initial Foreign Acquisition Performance: The Moderating Effect of Integration," *Journal of World Business* 41 (June 2006): 161–70.

41. Jeffrey J. Reuer, Oded Shenkar, and Roberto Ragozzino, "Mitigating Risk in International Mergers and Acquisitions: The Role of Contingent Payouts," *Journal of International Business Studies* 35 (January 2004): 19–32.

42. Klaus Uhlenbruck, "Developing Acquired Foreign Subsidiaries: The Experience of MNEs in Transition Economies," *Journal of International Business Studies* 35 (March 2004): 109–23.

43. Jeffrey J. Reuer, Oded Shenkar, and Roberto Ragozzino, "Mitigating Risk in International

Mergers and Acquisitions: The Role of Contingent Payouts," *Journal of International Business Studies* 35 (January 2004): 19–32.

44. "Mergers: Will They Ever Learn?", *Business Week*, October 30, 1995, 178; and "Is the European Grass Greener?", *Business Week*, January 29, 2001, 28.

45. Masaaki Kotabe *et al.*, "Strategic Alliances in Emerging Latin America: A View from Brazilian, Chilean, and Mexican Companies," *Journal of World Business* 35 (No. 2, 2000): 114–32.

46. John B. Cullen, Jean L. Johnson, and Tomoaki Sakano, "Success Through Commitment and Trust: The Soft Side of Strategic Alliance Management," *Journal of World Business* 35 (Fall 2000): 223–40.

47. Shih-Fen S. Chen and Jean-François Hennart, "Japanese Investors' Choice of Joint Ventures versus Wholly-owned Subsidiaries in the U.S.: The Role of Market Barriers and Firm Capabilities," *Journal of International Business Studies* 33 (First Quarter 2002): 1–18.

48. Klaus E. Meyer, "Institutions, Transaction Costs, and Entry Mode Choice in Eastern Europe," *Journal of International Business Studies* 32 (Second Quarter 2001): 357–67.

49. Jane W. Lu, "Intra- and Inter-organizational Imitative Behavior: Institutional Influences on Japanese Firms' Entry Mode Choice," *Journal of International Business Studies* 1 (First Quarter 2002): 19–37.

50. Vibha Gaba, Yigang Pan, and Gerardo R. Ungson, "Timing of Entry in International Market: An Empirical Study of U.S. Fortune 500 Firms in China," *Journal of International Business Studies* 33 (First Quarter 2002): 39–55.

51. Keith D. Brouthers and Lance Eliot Brouthers, "Explaining the National Cultural Distance Paradox," *Journal of International Business Studies* 32 (First Quarter 2001): 177–89.

52. Oded Shenkar, "Cultural Distance Revisited: Towards a More Rigorous Conceptualization and Measurement of Cultural Differences," *Journal of International Business Studies* 32 (Third Quarter 2001): 519–35.

53. José I. Galan and Javier Gonzalez-Benito, "Distinctive Determinant Factors of Spanish Foreign Direct Investments in Latin America," *Journal of World Business* 41 (June 2006): 171–89.

54. Ulrike Mayrhofer, "International Market Entry: Does the Home Country Affect Entry-mode Decisions?", *Journal of International Marketing* 12 (No. 4, 2004): 71–96.

55. Laszlo Tihanyi, David A. Griffith, and Craig J. Russell, "The Effect of Cultural Distance on Entry Mode Choice, International Diversification, and MNE Performance: A Meta-analysis," *Journal of International Business Studies* 36 (May 2005): 270–83.

56. Len J. Trevino and Franklin G. Mixon Jr., "Strategic Factors Affecting Foreign Direct Investment Decisions by Multinational Enterprises in Latin America," *Journal of World Business* 39 (August 2004): 233–43.

57. Anders Blomstermo, D. Deo Sharma, and James Sallis, "Choice of Foreign Market Entry Mode in Service Firms," *International Marketing Review* 23 (No. 2, 2006): 211–29.

58. Oystein Moen, Morten Gavlen, and Iver Endresen, "Internationalization of Small, Computer Software Firms: Entry Forms and Market Selection," *European Journal of Marketing* 38 (Nos 9/10, 2004): 1236–51.

59. Christine M. Chan, Shige Makino, and Takehiko Isobe, "Interdependent Behavior in Foreign Direct Investment: The Multi-level Effects of Prior Entry and Prior Exit on Foreign Market Entry," *Journal of International Business Studies* 37 (September 2006): 642–65.

DISCUSSION QUESTIONS

1. What is Foreign Direct Investment (FDI)? When is it used? Discuss.

2. What is a Greenfield investment? What is an acquisition? Discuss their impacts.

3. Discuss the various foreign market entry strategies. Under what conditions are they used?

4. What are the pros and cons of the various foreign market entry strategies? Discuss.

5. Why is choosing the right foreign market entry strategy critical in international marketing? Discuss.

6. What is a Foreign Trade Zone (FTZ)? What is a Free Trade Zone (FTZ)?

7. How are FTZs used? Discuss.

8. Why are FTZs important in international marketing and international trade? Discuss.

13

C hapter 13 discusses three topics.

Economic Integration, the topic of economic and regional integration, as well as the various types of trade agreements. It reviews the stages of integration, beginning with the incipient stage of free trade area (FTA) and ending with the last stage, political union (PU). Special attention is given to the development of the European Union (EU), its birth, and its evolution. Furthermore, this topic explores the various institutions of EU, such as the European Monetary Institution (EMI) and the European Central Bank (ECB), and it reviews the challenges that the EU has been facing; for instance, the 2010 European Sovereign Debt Crisis.

Growth and Direction of International Trade discusses the determinants of trade; for instance, the underpinnings of exporting/importing. It reviews the impact of the World Trade Organization (WTO) and emphasizes the differences between multilateral trade agreements (MTAs) and regional trade agreements (RTAs).

Countertrade and its importance in today's globalizing environment are noted. The reasons for its development are discussed, and credence is given to the argument that countertrade should be an integral part of a company's comprehensive international trade policy. Conditions and criteria that are present in, and conducive to, countertrade are reviewed. The various types of countertrade and their relevant conditions under which they are used are discussed.

13.1 Economic Integration

Nader H. Asgary, Dina Frutos-Bencze, and Masswood V. Samii

Types of Trade Agreements

Economic integration has been an important dimension of international trade and investment. The different levels of economic integration (see Figure 13.1) between countries are the following:

- **Bilateral trade agreement:** This type of trade agreement is either between two nations, between a nation and a trading bloc, or between two trading blocs. The objective of a bilateral agreement is to give the parties involved a favored trading status between each other. The following are examples of bilateral trade agreements: the Mexico–Israel free trade agreement and the Japan–Singapore free trade agreement.
- **Free trade area (FTA):** In this case, countries abolish all tariffs on goods among them, while maintaining an individual external tariff against non-FTA economies. Tariffs or quotas are eliminated on most or all of the products. Countries normally establish a time period to implement the changes. One of the most well-known examples of a free trade area is the North American Free Trade Agreement (NAFTA), comprised of Canada, Mexico, and the United States that came into effect in 1994. Other examples are the South Asia Free Trade Agreement (SAFTA), the Common Market for Eastern and Southern Africa (COMESA), and the ASEAN Free Trade Area (AFTA), which is the free trade zone among the Association of Southeast Asian Nations (ASEAN). A very common practice in FTAs is the establishment of "rules of origin," which consists of

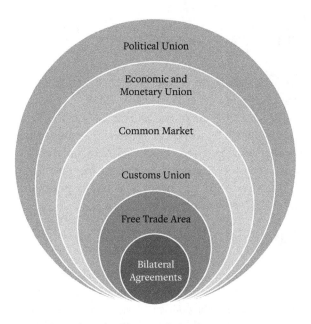

FIGURE 13.1 Levels of integration.

- **Economic and monetary union:** The EMU is a common market with a shared currency. The largest EMU right now is the Euro-zone, which consists of a group of European Union members who have adopted the euro as the official currency. In addition to that, members also share the same economic policy, meaning that key macroeconomic decisions are no longer taken by each individual country, but are centralized. In the case of the European Union, the European Central Bank (ECB) is responsible for the monetary policy in the area.

- **Political union:** This is the maximum level of integration among countries and occurs when a group of states adopts not only common economic and monetary practices, but also a common political policy. One of the examples is the United Arab Emirates (UAE).

identifying where the product comes from with the objective of avoiding duty evasion through re-exportation of products.

- **Customs union:** The major difference between a FTA and a customs union is the fact that in addition to eliminating internal tariffs among members, countries also have common tariffs against nonmembers. Unlike the FTA, where every country keeps their own external tariffs, in this case countries agree on a common external trade policy. A well-known customs union is the Mercado Común del Sur (or Mercosur in Spanish), which means Southern Common Market. Mercosur consists of Argentina, Brazil, Paraguay, Uruguay, and Venezuela.

- **Common market:** In this case, in addition to the characteristics of a customs union, there is also free mobility of factors of production (land, labor and capital) among the members of the common market. The objective is that the movement of those factors is free inside of the area. The European Union, which officially became a single market in 1996 with the signature of the Maastricht Treaty, is the most well-known and established common market.

Winners and Losers from Economic Integration

There are sociocultural, political, and economic changes associated with economic integration. The static effects and, to a lesser extent, the dynamic effects caused by increasing levels of integration among economies are the most common effects studied.

Static effects refer to the shift in the allocation of resources from less efficient economies to more efficient ones. Dynamic effects refer to the overall growth experienced by an economy due to the accessibility to a new, larger market share and factors of input.

It is believed that static effects take place when one of the following two situations occurs:

- **Trade creation:** This is the overall positive effect on trade caused by higher levels of economic integration. It occurs when there is an increase in the amount of trade as a result of shifts in resource allocation. In this case, production moves to more efficient participants in the common trade area, replacing other less efficient producers, for reasons of comparative advantage.

Free trade implies no protection for national producers. Therefore, companies that before joining a trade agreement were facing difficulties with exporting to other "protected" countries can now do so without any problem or tariffs. Increased efficiency in production leads to higher demand and, consequently, to more trade and economic growth. The downside part of trade creation is for those companies whose demand declines as a consequence of comparative advantage. In a nonprotected environment they will have to learn how to compete with more efficient producers, who might be using factors of production less costly or in a more efficient way.

- Trade diversion: This might be considered the main drawback of economic integration, although it also leads to economic growth for the member countries. Trade diversion occurs when trade shifts from nonmember participants to member countries as a result of the elimination of trade barriers. In this case, the shift might be occurring not because the member countries are more efficient than the nonmembers, but because the nonexistence of trade barriers makes it cheaper to import within the free trade zone. The immediate loser in trade diversion is, obviously, the nonmember country, since it is losing market share at the expense of member participants. However, in reality there is an overall loss for all participants, since trade diversion means that less efficient products are being traded, contrary to what the theory of comparative advantage states.

For example, when NAFTA was created there were concerns that trade diversion would happen as a consequence of the trade agreement, shifting exports and imports from nonmember countries to NAFTA members. However, later studies have demonstrated that there has not been a significant trade diversion (Fukao, Okubo, & Stern, 2003). For instance, Mexico's exports from 1991 to 2001 to non-NAFTA markets increased as much as its exports to the United States and Canada.

The European Union

The need for the European Union (EU) stemmed from the devastation created during World War II. Political leaders realized they could accomplish a lot more and more quickly by working together to improve their economies. The cooperation has increased over the years, and the member countries are more and more intertwined with each other. This brings advantages as well as some challenges.

The Treaty of Maastricht

The Maastricht Treaty, signed in 1992, called for the establishment of a European economic, monetary, and political union. The political union involves a common European citizenship. It also involves joint foreign, defense, immigration, and policing policies. Harmonization of social policy on workers' issues was another goal of the treaty. Some countries such as France and Germany want closer European integration. Others, such as the United Kingdom and Denmark want less centralized control.

The European Monetary Union (EMU) is an umbrella term for the group of policies aimed at converging the economies of members of the European Union to adopt the euro (single currency). The term Eurozone is used interchangeably. The European Monetary System (EMS) is the system set up to create exchange rate stability in Europe, and the European Currency Unit (ECU) is a composite or basket of currencies in the EMS where each country's value is weighted according to economic strength and other factors.

Convergence Criteria

There are minimum criteria that a country must achieve prior to admittance to the EMU. The requirements are:

- Inflation must be held to within 1.5% of the rate of the top three countries.
- Long-term interest rates need to be controlled to within 2% of the interest rate of the top three countries with the lowest interest rates.

- The currency must be stabilized. For at least 2 years, the country needs to keep the currency fluctuations within the normal fluctuation margins of the European Exchange Rate Mechanism.
- The budget deficit, as a percent of Gross Domestic Product (GDP), must be less than or equal to 3% GDP. GDP is the value of production that occurs within a country's borders whether done by domestic or foreign factors of production.
- The public debt as a percent of GDP must be less than or equal to 60% GDP.

Key EU Institutions
European Monetary Institute (EMI)

This is the predecessor to the European Central Bank (ECB). It was established on January 1, 1994, to assist with the transition needed to meet the requirements of the Maastricht Treaty. It helped create the framework for a smooth transition to a single currency. Another function of the EMI was to assist with the legal framework needed so that people would have faith in existing contracts and that legal documents would remain valid under the new system. In its later stages, the EMI provided the infrastructure for business to continue between the member countries. Furthermore, it provided common standards (such as operating times, settlement times, etc.) for transactions to continue as the members moved toward the common currency. The EMI was dissolved when the ECB was formed.

European System of Central Banks (ESCB)

The ESCB consists of the European Central Bank (ECB) and the National Central Banks (NCB) of the 25 member countries. The ESCB functions to set monetary policy, perform foreign exchange transactions, offer a payment transaction system, and hold the foreign reserves of the member countries.

European Central Bank (ECB)

The ECB was formed on July 1, 1998, with the purpose of setting monetary policy and managing the exchange rate system. Other functions, added in 1999, are to coordinate the central bank activities of its member countries and to set monetary policy.

Major Problems

A major problem is the instability in currency values. As mentioned previously, in order to join the EMU, countries must minimize the fluctuations in their currency as compared to the euro. This has been a challenge for many potential members.

Another major obstacle is the inability to meet the required criteria, especially debt related criteria. Germany, France, and Italy have violated the budget deficit requirements for the past several years. As a result of this, the EU has not enforced the fines that were originally called for under these circumstances. There have been calls for reform of the requirements.

Governments struggle to make the needed social cuts that are required to meet the economic criteria for membership. These potential budget cuts for social services such as pensions, health care, and education are highly unpopular and implementing them can prove extraordinarily difficult.

Agricultural subsidiaries are another issue. This issue became more pressing as 10 new members joined in 2004. They have more employment dependent on agriculture than the other member countries. It will be expensive to get the farms of these countries up to the standards required by the Common Agricultural Policy (CAP).

The vastly different economies of EU members have different threats to their economies. For example, France and Germany, with slow growth and high unemployment rates, need low interest rates to hold down inflation and stimulate the economy. The United Kingdom and Denmark, on the other hand, have faster growth rates and low unemployment. They need higher interest rates to slow down the economy. Many of the new members have very high levels of unemployment. This conflicts with the actions of the European Central Bank whose objective is to keep inflation under control. This creates problems for some of the member countries that do not have control over their fiscal or monetary policy.

The 2010 European Sovereign Debt Crisis

The European sovereign crisis illustrates the financial, economic, and political interconnectedness of Europe. In early 2010, fears of a sovereign debt crisis concerning Greece, Ireland, Italy, Portugal, and Spain developed. Concerns about rising government deficits and debt levels across the globe, together with a wave of downgrading of European government debt, created alarm in financial markets. The debt crisis had been mostly centered on Greece, but it had repercussions throughout the region and beyond.

In May of 2010, the Eurozone countries and the International Monetary Fund agreed to a €110 billion loan for Greece, conditional on the implementation of harsh Greek austerity measures. Europe's finance ministers approved a comprehensive rescue package worth almost a trillion dollars aimed at ensuring financial stability across Europe by creating the European Financial Stability Facility (BBC News, 2010).

Causes of the Greek Government Funding Crisis

The Greek economy was one of the fastest growing in the Eurozone during the 2000s. A strong economy and falling bond yields allowed the government of Greece to run large structural deficits. After the introduction of the euro, Greece was initially able to borrow due to the lower interest rates government bonds could command. The global financial crisis that began in 2008 had a particularly large effect on Greece because two of the country's largest industries, tourism and shipping, were badly affected by the downturn with revenues falling 15% in 2009.

Without a bailout agreement, there was a possibility that Greece would have been forced to default on some of its debt. A default would most likely have taken

the form of restructuring where Greece would pay creditors only a portion of what they were owed, perhaps 50% or 25%. This would have effectively removed Greece from the euro, as it would no longer have collateral with the European Central Bank. It would also destabilize the Euro Interbank Offered Rate, which is backed by government securities. However, the overall effect of a probable Greek default would itself have been small for the other European economies. Greece represents only 2.5% of the Eurozone economy. The more severe danger was that a default by Greece would cause investors to lose faith in other Eurozone countries. This concern was also focused on Portugal and Ireland, all of which have high debt and deficit issues. Italy also has a high debt, but its budget position is better than the European average, and it is not considered amongst the countries most at risk.

The crisis was seen as a justification for imposing fiscal austerity on Greece in exchange for European funding, which would lower borrowing costs for the Greek government. The negative impact of tighter fiscal policy could offset the positive impact of lower borrowing costs, and social disruption could have

FIGURE 13.2 Greece, Italy, Portugal and Spain with Ireland with United Kingdom.

a significantly negative impact on investment and growth in the longer term.

Many questions can be asked and debated about this case. Here are a few questions:

What are the effects of the Greek crisis on the value of the euro? What are the effects of the crisis on Spain, Portugal and Italy? What is their effect on the rest of the Eurozone? What are the challenges that the EU is facing? What are the potential solutions? What is its implication for the rest of the world? What are the impacts of globalization on regionalization?

REFERENCES

BBC News. (2010). EU ministers offer 750bn-euro plan to support currency. Retrieved August 16, 2014, from http://news.bbc.co.uk/2/hi/business/8671632.stm

Fukao, K., Okubo, T., & Stern, R. M. (2003). An econometric analysis of trade diversion under NAFTA. *The North American Journal of Economics and Finance*, *14*(1), 3–24.

13.2 Growth and Direction of International Trade

Belay Seyoum

Determinants of Trade

Why do some countries export or import more than others? Several studies have been conducted to establish major factors that influence exports. The trade and exchange-rate regime (import tariffs, quotas, and exchange rates), presence of an entrepreneurial class, and efficiency-enhancing government policy, as well as secure access to transport (and reasonable transport costs) and marketing services are considered to be important influential factors of export behavior (Fugazza, 2004; Kaynak and Kothavi, 1984). A study on the nature, composition, and determinants of Singapore's technology exports suggests that the country's open trade and investment regime and development-oriented economic policy have been the key factors in enhancing the country's exports. Singapore's economy has shown continued and remarkable growth in exports for more than thirty years, with only two brief and mild recessions in the mid-1970s and mid-1980s. Its total trade as a proportion of GDP remains one of the highest in the world, approximately 416 percent in 2012 (WTO, 2013). A recent study on the determinants of export performance underlines the importance of foreign direct investment (FDI) and the general quality of the institutional framework. FDI contributes to capital formation and helps promote the development and export of knowledge-based industries (Fugazza, 2004).

Much of the research literature on imports underlines the importance of high per capita incomes, price of imports, and the exchange rate in determining import levels (Lutz, 1994). For developing countries, however, determinants of import demand also include factors such as government restrictions on imports and availability of foreign exchange. A study examining the factors influencing import demand in Pakistan from 1959 to 1986 found that the policy of devaluation and raising tariffs was not significant in reducing imports except in the case of imports of machinery and equipment (Sarmand, 1989).

Volume and Direction of Trade

In 1990, the world reached a milestone when the volume of international trade in goods and services measured in current dollars surpassed $4 trillion. By 2012, the volume of exports of goods and services was more than four times the 1990 levels, approaching $19 trillion. The dollar value of total world trade in 2012 was greater than the gross national product of every nation in the world including the United States. Another measure of the significance of world trade is that one fourth of everything grown or made in the world is now exported.

The rapid increase in the growth of world trade after World War II can be traced to increased consumption of goods and services as more people joined the middle class in many countries of the world. Trade liberalization, at both the regional and the international level, has created a global environment that is conducive to the growth and expansion of world trade. New technologies such as computers, telecommunications, and other media also assisted in the physical integration of world markets.

Small countries tend to be more dependent on international trade than larger ones because they are less able to produce all that they need. Larger countries (in terms of population) import fewer manufactured goods on a per capita basis because such countries tend to have a diversified economy that enables them to produce most of their own needs. This is exemplified by the case of the United States, Japan, India, and China, which have low import propensities compared to countries such as Belgium or the Netherlands.

Merchandise trade currently accounts for about four fifths of world trade. The top 10 exporters accounted for just over one half of world merchandise exports (China, United States, Germany, Japan, Netherlands, France, South Korea, Italy, Russia, and Belgium) (Table 13.1). Merchandise trade includes three major sectors: agriculture, mining, and manufactures. Trade in manufactured goods has been the most dynamic component of world merchandise trade. In 2012, the value of world merchandise exports was estimated at $18 trillion (U.S.) compared to that of $4 trillion (U.S.) for services (WTO, 2013).

Industrial market economies account for the largest part of world trade. Trade among these countries is estimated to be approximately 52 percent of global merchandise trade. Over the past few decades, one observes shifting patterns of trade as evidenced by a steady growth in the role of developing countries especially that of emerging economies and increasing levels of trade among developing nations.

Important Developments in Trade
Multilateral and Regional Trade Agreements

- After the implementation of the Uruguay Round, members of the World Trade Organization (WTO) launched a subsequent round in Doha, Qatar, in 2001 to further reduce trade barriers. The focus of this round has been on the reduction of trade-distorting agricultural subsidies provided by developed countries and the introduction of equitable trade rules for developing nations. The negotiations are at a complete stalemate with no prospect of success in spite

TABLE 13.1 Leading Exporters and Importers of Merchandise and Commercial Services, 2011 ($ billions)

Merchandise exporters	Value	Merchandise importers	Value	Service exporters	Value	Service importers	Value
China	1898	United States	2266	United States	581	United States	395
United States	1480	China	1743	United Kingdom	274	Germany	289
Germany	1472	Germany	1254	Germany	253	China	237
Japan	823	Japan	855	China	182	United Kingdom	170
Netherlands	661	France	714	France	167	Japan	166
France	596	United Kingdom	638	Japan	142	France	143
South Korea	555	Netherlands	599	Spain	140	India	124
Italy	523	Italy	557	India	137	Netherlands	118
Russia	522	South Korea	524	Netherlands	134	Ireland	114
Belgium	477	Hong Kong	511	Singapore	129	Italy	114

Source: WTO, 2012

of considerable progress on specific issues. In a multipolar world, there are a number of power centers and a proliferation of national interests that erode international consensus across many areas. This is going to impede the development of international trade rules and standards and undermine the role of the WTO as a forum for trade negotiations.

- The current irreconcilable deadlock in the Doha Round has provided additional motivation for countries to engage in bilateral and regional trade agreements. Bilateral and regional agreements require less time to negotiate and provide opportunities for deeper trade policy integration. The United States, for example, has recently launched trade agreements with Asia and European countries (the Trans-Pacific partnership for Asia and the Transatlantic Trade and Investment Partnership with Europe). Many developing countries also perceive such agreements to be the most feasible means for gaining market access as the prospects for completing the Doha negotiations seem more remote. The share of trade among bilateral and regional trade partners is likely to grow in the next few decades.

- Many scholars believe that such bilateral/regional agreements are inferior to the multilateral, nondiscriminatory approach of the WTO. Bilateral/regional trade arrangements discriminate against nonmembers and create a maze of trade barriers that vary for every exporting country: rules of origin, tariff schedules, nontariff barriers such as quotas, and so on. There are concerns that such agreements also work in favor of powerful nations that will sneak in reverse preferences such as protection of intellectual property rights or labor standards.

Global Trade Imbalances

- The U.S. current account deficit reached 5 percent of GDP in the last quarter of 2012. Imports exceed exports by about $780 billion (2012). At the same time, the East Asian economies (including Japan) held about $6.1 trillion (U.S.) in official foreign exchange reserves out of a global total of $9.2 trillion in 2012. China's foreign currency reserves alone was estimated at $3.31 trillion (U.S.) by the end of 2012. The Southeast

Asian countries' heavy reliance on exports as a way of sustaining domestic economic growth, weak currencies, and high savings rates has resulted in unsustainable global imbalances. Global imbalances cannot diminish without, inter alia, reducing such excess savings through currency adjustments and/or increased imports in the surplus countries.

- Export-led growth in surplus countries feeds (and is dependent on) debt-led growth in deficit countries. It is impossible for all countries to run surpluses, just as it is impossible for all to run deficits. A country's trade balance is a reflection of what it spends minus what it produces. In surplus countries, income exceeds their spending, so they lend the difference to countries where spending exceeds income, accumulating international assets in the process. Deficit countries are the flip side of this. They spend more than their income, borrowing from surplus countries to cover the difference, in the process accumulating international liabilities or debts.

- So long as trade deficits remain modest and economies invest the corresponding capital inflows in ways that boost productivity growth, such imbalances are sustainable. But the imbalances we see today are of a different character. First, they are much bigger. The most egregious is that between China and the United States, where China is running a huge trade surplus with the United States ($334 billion in 2012). Many of the other imbalances are between countries of broadly similar levels of economic development, such as those between members of the euro zone or that between Japan and the United States.

- Trade imbalances lead to destabilizing capital flows between economies. For example, the global financial crises of 2007 and the subsequent euro-zone crisis were basically the result of capital flows between countries. Overleveraged banks amplified the problem, but the underlying cause was outflows of capital from economies with excess savings in search of higher returns. The deficit countries that attracted large-scale capital inflows struggled to find productive uses

for them: rather than boosting productivity, the inflows pumped up asset prices and encouraged excessive household borrowing.

Developing Countries in World Trade

- There has been a steady growth in the role of developing countries in world trade. Between 1995 and 2011, the share of developed nations (value share) in world merchandise trade declined from 69 to 52 percent while that of developing nations increased from 29 percent to 48 percent. Over this period, China's share alone increased from 2.6 percent to 11 percent. The share of Latin America and the Caribbean also increased from 4.5 percent to 6.2 percent.

- China joined the WTO in 2001. Within three years, its exports doubled, and the country is now the world's largest merchandise exporter ($1.9 trillion in 2011) and second largest importer of goods ($1.74 trillion in 2011).

- Only a few developing nations have managed to climb up the value chain and diversify their export base to cater to the expanding global market. About 83 percent of the increase in the share of developing countries' total trade (1995–2010) accrued to a small number of emerging economies: the BRICs (Brazil, Russia, India, and China), Mexico, and South Korea. India, China, and South Korea accounted for about one third of world exports and about two thirds of developing-country exports in 2011.

- Such shifting patterns of trade and the increased demand for primary commodities from rapidly growing economies have strengthened South-South (trade among developing countries) trade and economic cooperation. South-South trade increased at a rate of 14 percent per year (1995–2010) compared to the world average of 9 percent. During the same period, merchandise exports from the developing countries to the developed nations increased by 10 percent per year.

Transportation and Security

- About 60 percent (by value) of total world merchandise trade is carried by sea. In volume terms, 75 percent of world merchandise trade is carried by sea, whereas 16 percent is by rail and road (9 percent by pipeline and 0.3 percent by air). Increases in fuel prices could act as a disincentive to exports by raising transportation costs. In air transportation (which is more fuel sensitive than shipping), rising oil prices could severely damage trade in time-sensitive products such as fruits and vegetables and parts in just-in-time production. Faster economic growth in emerging economies is also putting pressure on the limited supply of other raw materials such as copper and coal.

- World air cargo traffic has grown during the past decade due to increased trade in high-value-low-weight cargo, globalization, and associated just-in-time production and distribution systems.

- In light of increasing threats of terrorism, countries have put in place procedures to screen cargo across the entire supply chain. There is an overall attempt to facilitate international trade without compromising national security.

CHAPTER SUMMARY

Major benefits of international trade	To acquire a variety of goods and services, to reduce cost of production, to increase incomes and employment, to learn about advanced technical methods used abroad, and to secure raw materials.
Determinants of trade	*Major determinants of exports:* Presence of an entrepreneurial class, access to transportation, marketing, and other services, exchange rates and government trade and exchange rate policies. *Major determinants of imports:* Per capita income, price of imports, exchange rates, government trade and exchange rate policies, and availability of foreign exchange.
Value and volume of trade	1. World trade approached $19 trillion (U.S.) in 2012. 2. Services trade accounts for about 19 percent of total trade. 3. Merchandise trade accounts for 81 percent of world trade. 4. The industrial market economies account for 52 percent of world merchandise trade.
Major developments in trade	1. The absence of any meaningful progress in the Doha negotiations of the WTO. 2. Proliferation of bilateral and regional trade agreements. 3. Growing role of developing countries in world trade. 4. The increasing U.S. current account deficit and global imbalances. 5. Fast economic growth in many countries and pressure on limited resources. 6. Business adjustment to security costs after 9/11.

REVIEW QUESTIONS

1. Discuss the importance of international trade to national economies.
2. What are the major determinants of exports? Why do some countries trade more than others?
3. What is the volume of trade?
4. What are some of the major developments in trade over the past two decades?
5. What are the implications of the increasing U.S. trade deficit for global production and exports?

6. What is the reason behind the increase in common markets and free-trade areas over the last few decades?

7. What are the limitations of export led growth?

8. Why are small countries more dependent on international trade than larger ones?

REFERENCES

Fugazza, M. (2004). *Export Performance and Its Determinants: Supply and Demand Constraints.* Study no. 26. Geneva: UN Conference on Trade and Development.

Kaynak, E., and Kothavi, V. (1984). Export behavior of small and medium-sized manufacturers: Some policy guidelines for international marketers. *Management International Review,* 24: 61–69.

Lutz, J. (1994). To import or to protect? Industrialized countries and manufactured products. *Journal of World Trade,* 28(4): 123–145.

Sarmand, K. (1989). The determinants of import demand in Pakistan. *World Development,* 17: 1619–1625.

World Trade Organization (2013). *International Trade Statistics.* Geneva: WTO.

WORLD WIDE WEB SOURCES

Growth of International Trade/Trade Data/ Developments

http://www.wto.org/english/news_e/pres13_e/pr688_e.htm

http://www.census.gov/foreign-trade/balance/c4239.html#2013

http://unctad.org/en/pages/PublicationWebflyer.aspx?publicationid=210

13.3 Countertrade

Johny K. Johansson and
Michael T. Furick

Countertrade is the term for transactions in which all or part of the payment is made in kind rather than cash. The practice has been known as "barter trade" throughout recorded history, and often involves a great deal of negotiations, patient persuasion and "haggling." The practice has a long tradition in the Orient, especially the countries around the Silk Road between Xian in China and the cities in Eastern Mediterranean, including Tyre in Lebanon and Istanbul (then Constantinople) in Turkey (Exhibit 13.1).

The primary moving force behind countertrade has been a shortage of hard currencies available to developing countries, in particular those lacking a strong export sector to generate foreign earnings. In addition, the failure of the globally integrated financial markets to support the stability of domestic currencies has made countertrade again appear as a viable alternative payment.

It is useful to distinguish between five kinds of countertrade:[1]

- barter,
- compensation deals,
- counter-purchase,
- product buy-back, and
- offset.

Selection from Johny K. Johansson and Michael T. Furick, "Global Pricing," *The New Global Marketing: Local Adaptation for Sustainability and Profit*, pp. 391-395, 401-403. Copyright © 2018 by Cognella, Inc. Reprinted with permission.

EXHIBIT 13.1 Inside the Grand Bazaar in Istanbul. The Grand Bazaar is one of the largest and oldest covered markets in the world, with 61 covered streets and over 3,000 shops. The tradition of negotiating prices over a cup of tea or coffee is still alive in many emerging countries.
Copyright © 2015 by Shutterstock/ Christian Mueller.

The World Trade Organization estimates that 15 percent of the $5.62 trillion in international trade is conducted on a non-cash basis. Commercial arrangements involving bartering across countries involve as many as 450,000 businesses with 10 percent annual growth.[3] Hundreds of companies and websites now exist to help with international barter transactions including The International Barter Alliance, a trade group.

There is a darker side to counter trade. As an example, in December 2016, Paris-based International Council on Museums (Icom) issued a list and report on ancient manuscripts and historic religious items looted by extremists in the west African country of Mali. The fear is that these antiquities will be sold via barter in non-cash transac- tions to avoid alerting the world banking community and police.

Barter

Barter is the oldest form of countertrade. It is the direct exchange of goods between two trading partners. For barter to make economic sense, the seller must be able to dispose of the goods received in payment. To assist companies that engage in barter trading and cannot count on such arrangements, several barter houses have been established, primarily in Europe, where many of the exchanges are negotiated.

A famous barter transaction involving consumer goods was Pepsi-Cola's entry into the Soviet Union (see box, "Bartering Russian Vodka for Pepsi Cola").

Compensation Deals

Compensation deals are a type of countertrade that involves the exports of goods in one direction but the payment back is usually split into at least two parts. The first part of the payment is in cash by the importer in the usual manner and for the rest of the payment the original exporter makes an obligation to purchase some of the buyer's goods. Essentially the payment is made in both cash and goods. In one case GM sold locomotives to former Yugoslavia for $12 million and was paid in cash plus Yugoslavian machine tools valued at approximately $4 million. The introduction of the cash portion is to make the deal more attractive to the seller, and most companies faced with the possibility of a countertrade agreement will in fact insist that at least some portion of the bill be settled

BOX: Bartering Russian Vodka for Pepsi Cola[2]

One of the classic countertrade cases was Pepsi-Cola's entry into the Soviet Union back in 1972. At that time the Soviets did not have access to much hard currency since the Cold War was severely limiting trade outside the Soviet bloc and the oil that today accounts for much of Russia's foreign exchange was considered a strategic good and not exported.

The American president at that time, Richard Nixon, had been an attorney at Pepsi-Cola and had maintained a close relationship with Donald Kendall, Pepsi's CEO. Kendall convinced Nixon that a trade relationship between Soviet Russia and the United States would help ease tensions, and what better symbol of this relationship than selling Pepsi-Cola to the Russians? For the opportunity to become the first Western consumer product sold in the Soviet Union, Pepsi would be willing to consider any countertrade offer.

Pepsi-Cola's relationship with the Soviet Union actually dated back to 1959 when then Soviet leader Nikita Khrushchev was photographed sipping Pepsi-Cola at an American national exhibition in Moscow. But it was on a visit to Soviet Russia in 1971 that President Nixon proposed to his Soviet counterpart President Leonid Brezhnev

that Pepsi-Cola be allowed to build a bottling plant and sell its cola in the Russian market. The proposal was accepted and as a quid pro quo the Russians of- fered Pepsi the exclusive American distribution rights for the number one Russian drink, Stolichnaya vodka.

Exchanging cola for vodka was an offer that PepsiCo executives could not refuse. A $2 billion land- mark countertrade agreement was reached in 1972 to exchange Pep- si-Cola concentrate for the rights to sell Stolichnaya vodka in the Unit- ed States. Pepsi-Cola's first Soviet bottling plant opened in 1974 and soon 22 plants were turning out the concentrate. Fortunately for Pepsi, Stolichnaya became the best-sell- ing imported vodka in the United States for the first 10 years of the agreement and is still near the top of the vodka market.

At the time Pepsi managers had few alternatives for entering a closed market that lacked a fully convertible hard currency. Soviet officials were unwilling to part with any foreign exchange reserves, so a barter arrangement appealed to both sides. The difficulty, as in any other barter agreement, was being able to independently assess the value of the goods or services in- volved. Compounding this assess- ment was Pepsi's inability over the

agreement's first 15 years to utilize any modern marketing techniques in the Russian market, since tele- vision advertisements, radio com- mercials, and supermarket promo- tions with entertainment celebrities or top athletes were all unavailable to the soft drink giant.

However, once the Berlin Wall fell in 1989 and the Russian market opened up, the Pepsi head start proved a handicap. Rather than gaining first-mover advantages, the brand seemed old and tainted by the old regime. Although Coca-Cola took some time to develop its Rus- sian distribution network, it seemed only a matter of time before Pepsi would be overtaken. By 1994 Pepsi still had 60 percent of the Russian market compared to Coke's 38 per- cent. However, an estimated $500 investment in Russia vaulted Coke to a 51 percent share in 1996 ver- sus Pepsi's 44 percent, and Coke has been leading ever since. As of 2013, Coca-Cola had double the market share of Pepsi (36 percent vs. 18 percent, respectively) in the carbonated soft drink category in Russia.

Pepsi had some consolation in that its entry into a traditional Russian category Kvass, a local fermented drink, is successful. Its "Russian Gift" brand is in the num- ber three spot, ahead of Coca-Cola.

in cash. As in the case of barter, the goods portion of the payment has to be sold in a third market, and the additional transaction costs should logically be added to the original amount invoiced.

Counter-Purchases

Counter-purchases represent the most typical ver- sion of the countertrade. Here two contracts are usually negoti- ated: one to sell the product (the initial agree- ment) at an agreed-upon cash price, and a second to buy goods from the purchaser at an amount equal to the bill in the initial agreement. This type of contract simply represents one way for the buyer to reuse valuable foreign currency and force exports and is usually introduced relatively late in the exchange negotiations. In practice the seller gets its money and then has a limited period of time (usually 6 to 12 months) before its purchases from the country must be completed. In some of these cases the second contract is sold (at a steep discount) to a third party (a barter house, for example), but this is not always easy. For a classic example, McDonnell Douglas, the American aircraft manufacturer now merged with Boeing, once had to buy and then resell ham from China in order to sell a few of its aircraft there.

Product Buy-Backs

In **product buy-backs** both the seller and buyer agree to accept payment in goods rather than cash and these usually come in two types. In one type of product buy-back agreement the seller accepts a certain amount of the output as full or partial payment for the goods sold. Alternatively, the seller can agree to buy back some of the output at a later date. Levi Strauss is accepting Hungarian-made jeans (bearing its brand name) in partial payment for setting up a jeans factory outside Budapest. Another Western company has established a tractor plant in Poland and agreed to buy back a certain number of Polish-built tractors as part of the deal.

Offset Deals

In **offset deals**, the seller contracts to invest in local production or procurement to partially offset the sale price. In aircraft, for example, it is not uncommon for a national airline buying airplanes to demand that the manufacturer procure certain components, parts, or supplies in the buyer's country, or invest in some assembly operation there. This helps justify the purchase price paid to the manufacturer from cash-strapped nations.

Business Evaluation

For the seller evaluating a countertrade proposal, the following points are important to consider:

1. Is this the only way the order can be secured?
2. Can the received goods be sold?
3. How can we maximize the cash portion?
4. Does the invoiced price incorporate extra transaction costs?
5. Are there any import barriers to the received goods (so that we will have trouble disposing of the goods at home, say)?
6. Could there be currency exchange problems if we try to repatriate the earnings from sales in a third country?

If these issues receive a positive evaluation, countertrade might be a useful alternative. When the opposite happens, the firm might be better off curbing its appetite for foreign sales.

PRICE AND POSITIONING

Before settling on a final price, the targeted positioning needs to be considered. Positioning as a premium brand, for example, necessarily involves a premium price, typically meaning a higher than average competitive price. For bottom-of-the-pyramid products, where low prices are necessary, a premium brand cannot be used. For most multinationals, there are several brands and models and versions in their product lines, and it is important for positioning purposes, that they reflect different price points. Price will not be the only positioning tool even in poor markets, but it will be the clearest and most important one.

Customers will often attribute high quality to a product with high price. They assume that it costs more to produce a high-quality product, and thus its price will be higher. This is commonly known as the **price–quality relationship.**

Although much research confirms this bias, research has also shown that this price–quality relationship varies in strength by products category. It is strong, for example, for many durable products, but weaker for daily consumables and supermarket items.[4]

The price–quality relationship is also weakened in markets protected by trade barriers and taxes. In such markets imported products will usually show an artificially high price (because of the price escalation due to tariffs and nontariff barriers and entry taxes), and thus a high price signals an imported product, not necessarily a high-quality product.

Because of price escalation from high tariffs and taxes, some imports will make no inroads against established domestic brands. An example is the situation in an emerging market such as China where taxes and nontariff barriers have made markets "dualistic," with a domestic and an import segment. The majority of the market falls to the domestic producers, between whom competition is intense, while the imports garner a small fringe segment of the market, whose primary buying appeal is not "quality" but "status." But with prices of luxury brands in China at 50 percent or more above prices elsewhere, it is hardly surprising that many Chinese travel abroad to go shopping.[5]

SELECTED REFERENCES

"China's addiction to luxury goods," *The Economist explains*, Apr 29th 2014.

"Cola Wars In Russia (Part 1)," *Trefis.com*, Dec.19, 2013.

Hollie, Pameal, "Pepsico Renews Deal with Russians," *New York Times*, May 22, 1985, p. D5.

Lelyveld, Michael, "Innovation Is the Key to Keep Vodka Flowing to U.S. Shores," *Journal of Commerce*, July 29, 1993, p. 2C.

Li, Hao, Ping Zhao, Yan Wang and Gao Wang, "A Qualitative Research of *Tuangou*: Modes, Characteristics and Roles of the New E-Business Model," *International Symposium on Information Engineering and Electronic Commerce*, IEEE Computer Society, 750–53, 2009.

Parks, Michael, "For Pepsi, Road to Moscow Was a Trip Back in Time," *Washington Post*, July 6, 1988, p. A1.

Seyoum, Belay, *Export-Import Theory, Practices, and Procedures*, 3rd ed. London: Routledge, 2013.

Zeithaml, Valarie A., "Consumer Perceptions of Price, Quality, and Value: A Means-End Model and Synthesis of Evidence," *Journal of Marketing*, Vol. 52, No. 3 (July 1988), pp. 2–22.

ENDNOTES

1. Seyoum, 2013, ch. 12, offers a good discussion of countertrade options.
2. Sources: Hollie, 1985; Lelyveld, 1993; Parks, 1988; "Cola Wars In Russia," 2013.
3. For an overview, see Zeithaml, 1988.
4. See "China's addiction to luxury goods," 2014.
5. See Li, Zhao, Wang, and Wang, 2009.

DISCUSSION QUESTIONS

1. What is regional economic integration? Give some examples.

2. Identify the five (5) phases that pertain to regional economic integration. Discuss those.

3. What are the pros and cons to regional economic integration?

4. What is trade diversion? Give an example.

5. What are the reasons for countertrade?

6. What are the different types of countertrade? Discuss their differences.

7. What is switch trading?

8. Why might regional economic integration create or divert trade?

9. What are bilateral, trilateral, or multilateral trade agreements? What institution promotes such agreements?

10. Discuss the evolution of the European Union (EU).

11. What was the impact of the Maastricht Treaty on the European Union?

12. What are the Maastricht Treaty's convergence criteria?

13. What was the 2010 European Sovereign Debt crisis about?

14. Discuss the cause of the Greek sovereign debt crisis that led the country into managed bankruptcy.

15. What are the reasons for international trade? That is, why does international trade exist?

16. What is free trade? What is protectionism? Argue their impact on the economy.

SECTION II

Cases

- **Corruption** (definition, cultural diagnosis, managing)
- **Letter of Credit** (securing trade transactions & exchange)
- **Retailing** (challenges of global retailers in culturally sensitive markets)
- **Segmentation** (culture-oriented segmentation of foreign markets)
- **Negotiations** (cross-cultural negotiations/impact of *individualism* and *collectivism*)
- **Entry strategies** (toward an optimum foreign market entry strategy)

Introduction

The book's listed topics are accompanied by cases that have been carefully selected to impart critical information to the reader and offer experiential knowledge on the functioning of an increasingly globalizing environment. The underlying core value of every case is *how the cultural environment of foreign markets* affects the level of success of international marketers.

Admittedly, there is a multitude of topics, which may potentially affect the success of international marketing operations. However, the selection of these cases was guided by the extent to which *culture* may affect the success of a marketing program. Largely, culture is the last barrier that globalization must overcome, and the critical determinant of international marketing success, given that marketing methodology applied is the same whether the given marketing project concerns a domestic market or an international one.

As a result, the interfacing of the chapters noted and the cases will guarantee a solid understanding of not only the contemporary global environment but it will also cultivate the reader's critical thinking of how marketers may succeed in their cross-border marketing activities.

The cases selected cover areas that are considered fundamental to international marketing operations. Specific operational issues that are embedded in international marketing activities, and which these cases discuss, include:

Can 7-Eleven® Succeed in Germany?

Jutta Ulrich and Kenichi Minami

Introduction

Robin Carter searched her dictionary for a good German word for the term "convenience store." Having studied international management and completed several courses in German business language, she was not satisfied using the term *"Convenience-Laden"* that she had seen used. Then she started to think back to her year as an exchange student in Freiburg, Germany, and how she had to hurry to get her shopping done before all the stores closed at 6 p.m. For some years now, stores had been open until 8 p.m. in Germany, and shopping habits had started to change along with the relaxed shopping hours. In 2003, the German government once again began the discussion of a proposal allowing stores to remain open even longer.

With a glance at her resumé, her new supervisor at 7-Eleven had instructed Robin to prepare a report for the next meeting of the project group "7-Eleven in Germany" analyzing language and cultural issues that might influence the decision whether or not to enter the German market. Had the shopping behavior changed enough in Germany for acceptance of the concept of American-style convenience stores? Would the German openness to adapting foreign words and concepts into their language and other cultural factors support a business decision to enter the German market? As Robin began to write her report, she wondered whether even the name "7-Eleven" might have to be changed.

7-Eleven®, Inc.

The convenience store concept was born in 1927 when an enterprising ice dock employee of the Southland Ice Company in Dallas, Texas, began to sell milk, bread, and eggs on Sundays and evenings after grocery stores had closed.[1] Customers quickly accepted this new service, and the concept became a strong competitive advantage for the company's Tote'm stores, changed to 7-Eleven in 1946 to reflect the stores' new hours of operation. By 2003, nearly 5,800 7-Eleven and other convenience stores were operated and franchised by the company in the U.S. and Canada, and 7-Eleven was a leader in convenience retailing with more than 24,000 stores worldwide and approximately six million customers per day. The stated goals of the company include "meeting the needs of busy shoppers by providing a broad selection of fresh, high-quality products and services at everyday fair prices, along with speedy transactions and a clean, safe, and friendly shopping environment." The company has been successful overseas, especially in Asian countries such as Japan, Taiwan, South Korea, and Thailand. 7-Eleven Japan operates more than 9,000 stores in Japan and Hawaii under an area license agreement granted initially in 1971.

There were a small number of licensed stores in European countries such as Sweden, Spain, Nor-way, Denmark, and Turkey, but the number of locations was only 2% of that in Asian countries (see Appendix 1). Despite the increasing demand for convenience stores in Germany, 7-Eleven had not entered the German convenience retailing market before 2003. Competition was intense, margins slim, and the hours of store operation limited by law to daytime hours, Monday through Saturday. With continuing changes in the retail environment, however, 7-Eleven might want to reassess its opportunities for entering the German market.

The Food Retailing Environment in Germany

With 82 million people and the largest economy in Europe, Germany was the leading food and beverage market in Europe. Products from within Germany and other EU countries dominated the shelves of stores, mainly due to the duty-free movements of goods and geographical advantages among the EU countries.[2] Although there were stringent food laws and regulations with regard to packaging and labeling, there were excellent opportunities for entry by companies from non-EU countries, since the German government actively encouraged foreign investment in Germany.[3] International firms must, however, take into consideration all regulations regarding advertising, packaging, and store operations since German law treats international and German firms alike.

In addition, retailers were affected by local labor laws. Labor costs were high, due to the relatively high standard of living and also mandatory benefits. Part-time employment was becoming more widespread, but pressure was high on employers to provide full-time positions with benefits. All employers in Germany paid 50% of contributions for health insurance, unemployment insurance, and retirement benefits. Also, the length of the typical work week at 37-39 hours and the annual paid vacation time of 4-6 weeks tended to be generous towards employees, along with regulations for family leave. In addition, Germany's laws regarding codetermination required a higher degree of employee involvement in the running of a business, and letting employees go on short notice became very difficult after a brief period of employment. Furthermore, land and building costs were high, and due to the unstructured layout of many German towns, including many narrow streets, sufficient parking space could become an issue.

---

1 7-Eleven Home Page, "About 7-Eleven, History," www.7-eleven.com/about/history.asp.

2 U.S. Department of Agriculture Foreign Agriculture Service, "Germany: Retail Food Sector 2000," www.fas.usda.gov/gain-files/200003/25647196.pdf.

3 Country Watch, Germany, www.countrywatch.com/cw_country.asp?vCOUNTRY=65.

Competition

Germany's food and beverage retailing sector was highly competitive, existing on slim margins and undergoing considerable concentration. In addition to roughly 25,000 discount stores, supermarkets, and hypermarkets, there were more than 40,000 small and medium-sized grocery stores at the beginning of 2002. Their share of the revenues was only 14%, with about 10 large retailers accounting for 80% of the turnover in foods and beverages, among them Rewe, Aldi, Edeka, Tengelmann, and the German-Swiss enterprise Metro.[4] (See Table 1 for revenue data of the largest grocery retailers in Germany.) Each of these leading retail groups also had a different business structure as well as purchasing and distribution system. Many owned several retail chains, often with various types of retail formats, such as large supermarkets, discounters, and small neighborhood stores. Edeka, for example, operated the Edeka, E-Active, and Condi supermarkets, the discounters Preisgut, Diska, and Treff, the hypermarkets Marktkauf, Dixi, and E-center, as well as several cash-and-carry markets. Since 1997, Wal-Mart had been acquiring and remodeling department stores in Germany, trying to import its philosophy of low prices and friendly service. Losses mounted to above $200 million annually as Wal-Mart underestimated the fierce competition in the German retailing industry, the zoning restrictions, and various limitations on pricing and advertising, prohibiting, for example, resale of products below cost.

TABLE 1 The Largest Retailers in Germany (Sales in Germany in billion Euro)

	Food Sales	Total Sales
Metro	14.4	32.0
Rewe	19.6	28.6
Edeka/AVA	20.9	25.2
Aldi	20.3	25.0
Schwarz	13.8	17.2
Tengelmann	7.8	12.5
Karstadt	0.9	8.5
Lekkerland-Tobaccoland	6.9	8.2
SPAR	7.0	7.5
Schlecker	5.0	5.3
Globus	1.9	3.4
Dohle	2.4	2.9
Wal-Mart	1.4	2.9

Source: Globus Infografik (2003): Die Riesen im Lebensmitteleinzelhandel, Globus publication Ea-8397.

Convenience Stores in Germany
Types of Stores

Convenience stores were among the fastest growing retail formats in Germany, with the expectation that their sales would rise significantly, particularly as their product presentations were updated and enlarged and the variety of products offered was expanded. In addition to nonfood items, the most popular items at convenience stores were beverages, including fruit juice and fruit drinks, soft drinks, beer, and wine, along with pastries, candy, and snacks. Products sold in these stores typically were priced 30% to 70% higher than in more conventional stores. The more-than-80,000 convenience stores could be broken down into four types: gas stations, train stations, kiosks, and bakeries. The latter provided many snack foods and other food and beverage items in addition to bread, pastries, and sandwiches that made Germans the European champions in bread consumption with a per capita consumption of more than 180 pounds annually.[5] Bakeries had such a long tradition in Germany that many Germans would not automatically classify them as convenience stores, but simply as bakeries, typically with average prices.

---

4 Corporate Information—What you need to know, www.corporateinformation.com/desector/Retail.html.

5 "Mischbrot bleibt Nummer eins," (21 March 2003) www.butterbrot.info.

Hours of Operation

Shopping hours in Germany were among the most restricted in Europe since the 1950s. Germany's draconian law governing retailing hours, *das Laden-schlussgesetz*, ensured that stores remained closed after 6 p.m. on weekdays, after 2 p.m. on Saturday, and altogether on Sunday, with the exception of outlets such as gas station and train station shops, which provided necessary items to travelers. Stores were allowed to remain open two hours longer on the first Saturday of every month, on a day called *der lange Samstag*, that is, the long Saturday. In June 1996, the German Parliament gave in to pressure from both business and consumers and eased the *Ladenschlussgesetz*. Shops were allowed to remain open until 8 p.m. on Thursday and eventually on all weekdays, and until 4 p.m. on Saturday. In the weeks leading up to Christmas, shops could remain open until 6 p.m. on Saturday. However, while it made sense for businesses in major cities like Berlin to extend hours, many small shops in towns and villages found that longer opening hours did not necessarily mean more turnover and went back to the old opening hours—Thursday till 8 p.m. but 6:30 p.m. on Monday, Tuesday, Wednesday, and Friday. Some gas stations remained open all night and also on Sunday and were allowed to sell food and other items. In January 2003, the German government entered a new round of discussions, possibly allowing shops to remain open longer, excluding only Sundays and holidays. As of June 2003, the new regulations permitted longer shopping hours on Saturdays. Stores could remain open until 8 p.m. Monday through Saturday.

Consumer Shopping Behavior in Germany

There were a great variety of shops in Germany. For groceries, there were many small and medium-sized stores (rather than two or three large supermarkets) in residential neighborhoods as well as in central shopping streets known for their density of shops. There were many specialty stores for baked goods, for meat

products, cheese and dairy, health food, spirits, candy and chocolate, tobacco and newspapers. In addition, large department stores, particularly in big cities, turned an entire floor of the building into a grocery store with a restaurant and specialty foods. On the outskirts of towns, shopping centers with hypermarkets, furniture, and do-it-yourself stores, and other large markets sprang up and gained popularity due to lower prices, location, parking spaces, and accessibility to many types of products.

In town, many people went to train stations (long-distance stations comparable to Grand Central Station in New York, but also subway and commuter train stations) just in order to frequent the stores, even when they were not traveling anywhere. Since train stations were often located in the center of town, they were accessible by public transportation and on foot, both of which were important means of transportation in Germany. Many Germans used city trains and subways on a daily basis and bought needed items on the way home. Cars and their drivers also frequented train stations, but parking could be difficult, sending drivers routinely to gas stations to make purchases of convenience items. Freestanding kiosks and gas stations became the predominant convenience stores in Germany, offering beer, snacks, sandwiches, and fresh-cut flowers. Some gas stations were open on Sundays and/or during the night. Sales of products other than gas were supposed to be limited to "necessities for the journey," just as in train stations; however, no questions were asked.

Despite the loosening of restrictions, some shops still closed at 6 p.m., with more and more remaining open until 8 p.m. During the week, shopping could still be a hurried affair squeezed into the time between leaving work and stores closing. On Saturdays, shopping became more of an event and a family outing. Families drove to large hypermarkets further away, but offering more parking along with a variety of shops and lunch opportunities. Some stores, and even whole towns, pushed for a loosening of the restrictions on shopping hours. When a regional festival was planned (a frequent event in small German towns), the city might want to allow its merchants to keep the stores open for visitors. Also, supermarkets and department stores were finding that consumers had to be turned away on Saturdays at 4 p.m. as Germans were getting used to the somewhat longer hours and were learning about shopping culture from their many visits to the United States and other countries.

Demographic data showed that there was a large number of single-person households (37% of all households in 2001) and an increasing number of women entering the workforce in Germany. In 2000, nearly 58% of working age women were employed, compared with 51% in West-Germany in 1974.[6] The percentage in the former East Germany had been higher but decreased to the national average. The demographics significantly impacted the food consumption trend and average household income. The growing number of single-person households and more working women resulted in less time available for preparing meals, which increased the frequency of dining out and consumption of convenience foods, easy-to-prepare meals, and snacks.

Germans, like many Europeans, valued quality and freshness. Other aspects shaping the buying decision could include exotic origin, references to a natural lifestyle, and environmental concerns. However, more and more, price became the determining factor. For high-end items, buyers looked at the *Preis-Leistungsverhältnis*, the relationship of price to quality, or performance and value, but price was clearly the decision criterion for routine items. Traditionally, Germans made frequent trips to the store, partially due to small storage spaces and small refrigerators, and also the desire to buy fresh bread products, meat, and produce. Specialty stores were still popular for high-end products because of the value placed on expert advice and the general notion that quality is directly associated with specialization and thorough training in one's field. With increasing frequency, however, Germans bought in bulk at less-expensive outlets, such as discounters (37% of sales) and hypermarkets (42% of sales),[7] often located on the outskirts of towns, and more Germans had a freezer in addition to their refrigerator.

An interesting phenomenon occurred along the borders with central-eastern European countries, including Poland and the Czech Republic. Germans were taking their business to grocery stores, hairdressers, and other retail outlets across the border where prices were lower. On the German side, many businesses had to close shop, as Germans openly and consciously bought their necessities in the cheaper market without regard to national borders. With the entry of these countries to the EU, additional changes were expected to occur.

Culture and Values

German society placed value on the well-being of the whole community. The government, along with churches, unions, and other organizations, has taken an active role in shaping a lifestyle that allows free time, time for family activities and for the pursuit of noncommercial activities, including religion and hobbies, contemplation, and general relaxation, known as *Freizeit und Erholung*. Critics charged that employees in the food service and entertainment industries, in the medical field and the police, fire, or transportation departments routinely worked on weekends and during the night. Nevertheless, some politicians and union representatives held the line as they considered work on Sunday inappropriate for a civilized society.

The values embedded in Germany's social market economy found much support among the people, the government, and the unions, which meant that employee protection, a high quality of life, and a sense of fairness and equality pervaded German thought. In addition, Germans tended to change slowly. They were risk averse and they liked structure and avoided uncertainty. In other words, they liked to plan ahead, make a decision, and stick to it.

More and more Germans spoke English and felt comfortable using the English language. News media routinely introduced foreign language words. This was true especially for English words, at first explaining the meaning, then trying a German translation, and eventually using the original English-language word. Nearly all children began studying the English language in grade school, and many continued to study English all through high school. In business, English had become a *lingua franca*, and television broadcast numerous

---

6 "Frau und Arbeit," 13 March 2000, GLOBUS Infografik GmbH, Ka-6187.

7 U.S. Department of Agriculture, op.cit.

American shows, usually dubbed into German with a generous sprinkling of English words.

U.S. Suppliers and Products in Germany

Business people in Germany at times perceived U.S. suppliers as being unreliable. They considered U.S.-Americans superficial and too focused on the short term. Thus, many U.S. companies were not seen as long-term players in the market and were not viewed as likely to provide adequate after-sales support. A commonly voiced complaint in the German business community was about the "American penchant for being here today and gone tomorrow."[8]

On the other hand, breaking into the competitive German network of retailers and suppliers might be even more difficult. Success in Japan—clearly the most successful international market for 7-Eleven—was the result of achieving integration into the Japanese retailing environment. 7-Eleven Japan established a strong supply chain with domestic suppliers, and not many people realized that the company originated in the U.S. The success of 7-Eleven in Japan was also due to the first-mover advantage back in 1971 and implementation of a POS (Point of Sales) system and alliances with strong local distribution channels. All played important roles. Although some buying habits of Germans were similar to those of the Japanese (more frequent purchases of fresh foods because of smaller kitchens and small refrigerators, patronage of specialty shops), success in the German market was not certain. The restraints of the market and the power of the dominant German competitors create substantial obstacles for 7-Eleven in Germany.

Retailers in Germany usually did not import their own products, but used specialized importers with in-depth knowledge of the market and distribution channels, many with their own nationwide sales network and distribution systems. There were several large wholesalers that supplied food and nonfood products to these convenience stores, among them Lekkerland, Spar Group, and Tengelmann. The leading supplier was Lekkerland–Germany, which more than doubled its sales after acquiring Tobaccoland in 1999. Lekkerland supplied an estimated 70,000 customers, including 14,000 kiosks, 13,000 gas station shops, 9,000 beverage stores, and 8,000 bakeries.[9]

Contrary to the perception towards the U.S. suppliers, German trade and consumer interest in U.S. food and beverage products had been increasingly positive. For many years, the favorable USD/Euro (formerly USD/DM) exchange rate and resultant strong growth in German tourism to the United States appeared to have positively influenced German consumers' attitudes and their propensity to purchase U.S. consumer products. A growing number of restaurants, food service, and retail stores in Germany made USA, California, or other U.S. state/region promotions a standard component of their annual promotional regimen. An increasing number of franchised U.S.-based restaurants, USA-food corners in department stores and supermarkets, and special USA stores and mail-order businesses also inspired German consumers to try new U.S. products or to purchase foods and beverages. The generous and even super-sized portions and drinks so typical at fast-food outlets in the United States were, however, not common in Germany but might be received well if the price were right.

Conclusion

With the introduction of the Euro as the common currency in most member states of the European Union, many prices went up, further curtailing already low consumer spending. In her study of recent news publications, Robin Carter was looking for indications that the retailing environment in Germany might change, presenting new opportunities for the convenience store industry. Competition was fierce, but 7-Eleven already

---

8 "Germany—Food Market Report," 1996, Tradeport, www.tradeport.org/ts/countries/germany/fdmrkt.html.

9 "Daten, Zahlen, Fakten" (22 March 2003), Lekkerland-Tobaccoland GmbH & Co. KG Home Page, http://www.lekkerland.de/lt/de/unternehmen/daten_zahlen_faktenKopie_von_datenzahlen.html.

had a presence in some European countries, and the company had proven its competitiveness in numerous international markets. Also, the Euro had made gains against the dollar, and the recent lengthening of the Saturday shopping hours was a good sign.

APPENDIX 1 International Licensing of 7-Eleven Stores

Territory	First Store Opened	No. of Locations
United States (U.S. Licensees)	1968	432
Canada*	1969	496
Mexico	1971	366
Japan	1971	9,447
Australia	1977	284
Sweden	1978	70
Taiwan	1980	3,187
China (Hong Kong, Shenzhen, and Guangzhou)	1981, 1992, and 1996, respectively	604
Singapore	1983	174
Philippines	1984	168
Malaysia	1984	215
Norway	1986	71
Puerto Rico	1987	13
Guam	1987	8
South Korea	1989	1,401
Thailand	1989	2,042
Turkey	1989	18
Hawaii	1989	55
Denmark	1993	43

*A Wholly Owned Subsidiary of 7-Eleven®, Inc.

Source: 7-Eleven Home Page, International Licensing, http://www.7-Eleven.com/about/globalsites.asp, March 2003.

Brand Kellogg's— Moving Beyond Breakfast?

Lekha Ravi, Shalom Jenifer, and Abdul Samad Syed

"We look forward to carrying forward the legacy our founder began by continuing to provide consumers with the great-tasting, high-quality foods and programs that help promote health and well-being."[1]

–David Mackay, President and CEO, Kellogg's

"All health propositions that disappeared like fads were time consuming and required consumers to reset their existing routine. That's not the disadvantage with Special K."[2]

–Anupam Dutta, Managing Director, Kellogg's India

Kellogg's, one of the world's largest US based multinational food products company, was ranked 7th in *Fortune 500* in 2008.[3] The cereal manufacturer earned revenue of $11,776 million[4] in fiscal year

---

1 "Our History", http://www.Kellogg'scompany.com/company.aspx?id=39
2 Sangameshwaran Prasad "Beyond breakfast", http://www.business-standard.com/common/storypage_c.php?leftnm=10&autono=312528, February 5th 2008
3 "Food Consumer Products", http://money.cnn.com/magazines/fortune/fortune500/2008/industries/198/index.html
4 Ibid.

2007–2008. In February 2008, the breakfast cereal behemoth launched 'Special K', its biggest brand worldwide, across India. Special K's USP is that of being a "shape management" cereal that promises to help one lose up to 6 pounds in two weeks. Special K targets urban women and is positioned as a health management alternative. Kellogg's is promoting Special K as a 'twice daily' meal plan—suggesting that consumers replace it for dinner as well. As consumers in India move towards a health conscious life style, many analysts feel Kellogg's move was well timed. But market critics ask a pertinent question- can this cereal survive in India; in a market where a typical breakfast is a substantial, hot, cooked meal?

Kellogg's: The Breakfast Cereal Giant

Kellogg's is the world's leading producer of cereal and convenience foods, including cookies, crackers, toaster pastries, cereal bars, frozen waffles, and meat alternatives. It was founded by W.K. Kellogg with an entrepreneurial spirit in 1906 with 44 employees in Battle Creek, Michigan. His vision and strong commitment to nutrition, health and quality continued to drive improvement in the products and processes, with the goal of providing great-tasting, nutritious products that met the most rigorous quality standards. W.K. Kellogg began worldwide expansion of the company in 1914. By 1938, Kellogg's had built plants in England and Australia. After W.K. Kellogg's death in 1951, the company continued to expand its operations, by building plants in Latin America and Asia.[5] Kellogg's expanded its operations and innovated by acquiring the vegetarian-based food group Worthington Foods in 1999 and the organic-based food group Kashi Company in 2000.[6]

Kellogg's had begun as a small manufacturer and marketer of breakfast food and has never lost that initial focus. Throughout its history, the company retained many of the values instilled by W.K. Kellogg in its early years. The company carries out its manufacturing activity in over 19 countries and markets its products in more than 180 countries. In 2001, Kellogg's acquired snack leader Keebler Foods Company. The company tried to boost its sales by announcing a deal with the Walt Disney Company. Kellogg's began selling cereal with several popular Disney characters on the boxes, including Winnie the Pooh and Mickey Mouse. In 2002, it formed a multi-year global relationship with Disney to introduce several new cereals and snack food products in the market. In 2004, Kellogg's launched reduced sugar cereals in Europe, to meet 'changing consumer tastes'. The cereals with one third less sugar than the familiar varieties, promised to deliver slightly fewer calories and less impact on blood sugar when consumed.[7]

The products of the company are sold under four brand names such as Kellogg's, Cheez-It, Keebler and Murray (**Annexure I**). The company, over the years, has developed certain mascots like Tony the Tiger™, Snap! Crackle! Pop!™ and Ernie Keebler™ which had become popular characters in Kellogg's advertisements.

The Company has a notable history of operating with values instilled in the Company by Mr. Kellogg. It has a Global Code of Ethics, which instructs workplace health and safety, human rights, environmental and product responsibility, and labor and employment practices. In 2006, the company contributed more than $8 million in cash and $20 million in product to various charitable organisations around the world.[8] The Company focused on three major areas: helping children and youth use their full potential, improving opportunities for minorities and women, and building stronger communities. As part of these efforts, it partnered with groups such as Action for Healthy Kids, the YMCA of the USA, United Way, the NAACP, America's Second Harvest, and the Global Food banking Network.

The company's net earnings had been showing an increasing trend for three consecutive years 2005, 2006, and 2007 (**Exhibit I**). Kellogg's sale of its convenience food products—cookies, crackers, toaster pastries, cereal bars, frozen waffles, piecrusts, ice

---

5 "The history of branding", http://www.historyofbranding.com/Kellogg's'ss.html
6 Ibid.

7 "Kellogg's launches reduced sugar breakfast cereals, but white flour content remains high", http://www.naturalnews.com/001961.html
8 "Social Responsibility", http://Kellogg's'ss.investoreports.com/Kellogg's's_ar_2006/html/Kellogg's's_ar_2006_15.php

Exhibit I   Consolidated Statement of Earnings of Kellogg's

Consolidated results (dollars in millions)	2007	2006	2005
Net sales	11,776	10,907	10,177
Cost of goods sold	6,597	6,082	5,612
Selling, general, and administrative expense	3,311	3,059	2,815
Operating profit	1,868	1,766	1,750
Interest expense	319	307	300
Other income (expense), net	(2)	13	(25)
Earnings before income taxes	1,547	1,472	1,425
Income taxes	444	467	445
Earnings (loss) from joint ventures	—	(1)	—
Net earnings	1,103	1,004	980
Per share amounts:			
Basic	2.79	2.53	2.38
Diluted	2.76	2.51	2.36

Source: "FINANCIAL STATEMENTS AND SUPPLEMENTARY DATA", http://files.shareholder.com/downloads/K/313959660x0x178719/1c05f696-8 6ed-4aa0-99ea-67d26cfc17a2/2007Annual%20Report%20LowRes.pdf

cream cones and meat alternatives—had been high in 2007.

The major competitors of Kellogg's are General Mills, Kraft foods and Quaker Oats. The company faces competition across all its product lines from regional, national and global companies. General Mills, the prime competitor recorded a sale of $12,442 million[9] and Kraft foods $ 24,651 million.[10] Kellogg's had stiff competition with its competitor General Mills in 2007 (**Exhibit II**).

In 2007, Kellogg's announced that it would adopt nutrition standards for all products that it markets to children. It had a policy of not marketing to children younger than six. Its new policy set 'a new standard of responsibility' for the industry. Kellogg's spends nearly 27% of its earnings for marketing its products in US. This includes print, radio, television and internet ads, licensed properties, promotions and web site activities, product placement and in-school marketing.[11] Kellogg's took a major step into a new market when it bought Keebler, the second-largest cookie-and-cracker manufacturer in the United States. Kellogg's ventured into another new area, buying Worthington Foods, the manufacturer of vegetarian 'meat' products. The company founded on cereal meal has moved far beyond breakfast, remaining a major international food corporation.

9   "General Mills Annual Report 2007", http://media.corporate-ir. net/media_files/irol/74/74271/GIS_AR07.pdf

10   "Kraft Foods Annual Report 2007", http://www.kraft.com/ assets/pdf/Kraft_07AR_10-K_only.pdf

11 Gutierrez David, "Kellogg's announces major shift in marketing manufactured food products to children" http://www.naturalnews. com/022058.html, September 24th 2007

Exhibit II   Sales of Kellogg's and its nearest Competitor

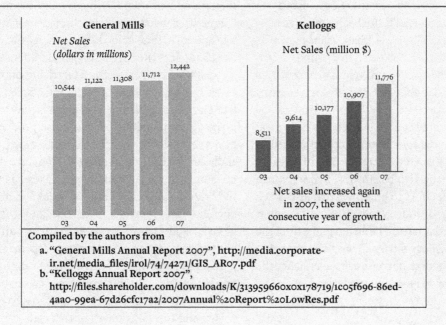

Compiled by the authors from
   a. "General Mills Annual Report 2007", http://media.corporate-
      ir.net/media_files/irol/74/74271/GIS_AR07.pdf
   b. "Kelloggs Annual Report 2007",
      http://files.shareholder.com/downloads/K/313959660x0x178719/1c05f696-86ed-
      4aa0-99ea-67d26cfc17a2/2007Annual%20Report%20LowRes.pdf

Kellogg's Foray into India—Moving with Times

Kellogg's, when it entered India, found the breakfast practice of Indian consumers as the biggest challenge, as most Indian cuisines were based on use of spices and a greater variety of vegetables. Apart from flavors and aromas Indian cuisine is also influenced by religion, geography and climate. Research was conducted to study the Indian consumers mind. Education and intelligence was found to be matters of significance for Indian consumers. Therefore, Kellogg's launched corn flakes brand which enhanced mental performance. It also felt that a change in strategy and a move from core to other segments would increase salience across categories. The cereal market grew steadily at the rate of 20%,[12] and Kellogg's reframed its formats. While Kellogg's corn flakes catered to everyone by improving mental performance, Chocos, one of the products of Kellogg's cereals brought in the taste element favoured by children.

Breakfast cereals, in India, saw an expanded base in 2005. Lifestyle changes led to changing eating patterns, and the importance of breakfast continues to decline as more people either skip breakfast or choose to eat at work. Wheat, corn, rice, oats and barley are the major grains used as breakfast cereals. Although many breakfast cereals contain refined grains and sugars, they are fortified with vitamins and minerals. A new marketing storm was brewing in the Indian breakfast bowl.[13] In 2008, Kellogg's moved from its breakfast cereal to Kellogg's Special K, (**Annexure II**) a diet

12 Goel Surbhi, "Eating habits: Following Indian consumer mind", http://economictimes.indiatimes.com/Interview/Anupam_Dutta_Managing_Director_Kellogg's's_India/articleshow/2817855.cms, February 27th 2008
13 Srinivasan Lalitha, "Cos race to capture fat-free breakfast option", http://www.financialexpress.com/news/Cos-race-to-capture-fatfree-breakfast-option/264451/, January 23rd 2008

cereal to control weight. Special K was launched in Mumbai and Delhi after the test market in Bangalore. It was targeted at urban women in the age group of 25-44 years,[14] positioning Special K as a health management alternative. Special K's USP was 'shape management', a cereal that promises to help lose up to 6 pounds in two weeks.[15] Kellogg's also sells some non-cereal products purely as snacks, like Rice Krispies, Treats, Squares and Nutri-Grain Bars.

Kellogg's promoted Special K as a twice daily meal plan suggesting it as a substitute for dinner as well. It targeted women, instead of children and male executives. The company also began with a nine-month national test in an effort to present cereal as a snack for the nibblers to devour in the evening or at night time. Innovation continues to be an integral part of the company today. Kellogg's tries to meet the changing needs and demands of their consumers to enhance the products and develop new food innovations.[16]

Beyond Breakfast Times—Challenges Ahead

A report by Data monitor[17] stated that the way Indians consumer breakfast is changing. When Kellogg's entered India, it faced several challenges like cultural factors, eating habits (not used to processed foods), easy availability of low-priced traditional breakfast, low awareness about processed foods and calorie requirements and price. But Kelloggs was able to face the competition in few categories through its diet products like Special K. Innovation helped Kellogg's to overcome the challenges. Kellogg's supplemented its launch of Special K with an extensive advertising campaign. In order to adapt to local tastes, it introduced products like Basmati rice flakes and mango-flavored cereal. To attract customers, the company also produced small packs that sold for 10 rupees, or 25 US cents. Kellogg's India continued to make efforts to convince the Indian consumer that a portion of corn flakes has the same nutritional value as traditional breakfast meals. It is currently progressing with its Special K—its biggest global brand—across India. According to an industry analyst, the growth of modern retail format would be a major growth driver for the 'weight management' market in India. Indian consumers were becoming increasingly health-conscious and analysts felt that this would fuel the growth of this category in 2008. According to Anupam Dutta, Managing director of Kellogg's India, "The market's constantly evolving and creating demand for products that you never thought would have had a chance."[18] However many experts feel that change in consumer eating habits as well as rising demand in India for health foods provides growth opportunities for Kellogg's. According to Paul Salyards, Vice President for marketing of established brands at Kellogg's in Battle Creek, Michigan, "The key strategy for us is to drive category volume by expanding eating occasions for cereal well beyond breakfast."[19]

14 Sangameshwaran Prasad, "Beyond breakfast", http://www.business-standard.com/common/storypage_c.php?leftnm=10&autono=312528, February 5th 2008

15 "Beyond Breakfast", op.cit.

16 "Our brands", http://www.kelloggcompany.com/brands.aspx

17 Datamonitor is the leading provider of online data, analytic and forecasting platform.

18 Chandran Rina, "India's processed-food market offers challenges and rewards", http://www.iht.com/articles/2008/03/19/business/cereal.php, March 19th 2008

19 Stuart Elliott "THE MEDIA BUSINESS: ADVERTISING; Kellogg's tries to get cereal lovers to look beyond breakfast", http://query.nytimes.com/gst/fullpage.html?res=9D-04E5D71339F933A25752C0A960958260, January 10th 1996

Annexure I   Kellogg's-Brands

Source: "Our Brands", http://www.Kellogg's'scompany.com/brands.aspx

Annexure II   Kellogg's Special K Diet

With all this variety, see how easy it is to lose 1 inch from your waist in 2 weeks.*

STEP 1
Kick start your day with either a serving of **Special K®** Cereal (any variety) with 2/3 cup skim milk, or a serving of **Special K®** Waffles drizzled with 2 Tbsp of light syrup. Enjoy either option with fruit.

STEP 2
Replace another meal with the delicious new **Special K™** Protein Meal Bar or another serving of your favorite **Special K®** Cereal with 2/3 cup of skim milk and fruit.

* Consume fruits and vegetables for additional snacks
* Drink beverages as you normally do.

STEP 3
Eat your third meal as you normally do.

Snacks!
Enjoy 2 great-tasting snacks everyday:
Special K™ Protein Snack Bars
Special K₂0 ® Protein Water and Mixes
Special K® Cereal Bars
Special K™ Snack Bites

Source: "Kelloggs Special K", http://www.specialk.com/

Negotiating with Chinese Business Partners

What Are You Going to Give Us?

Stephen Grainger

E uropa IT Design and Constructions (EDC) was an international joint venture that took on design contracts and, in some cases, oversaw the installation of computer software and facilities for supermarkets, office blocks, hotels, apartments, villa complexes, and, in general, large buildings in Europe and North America. The directors of EDC were American Bob Michaels, Neil Fortheringham from England, and Pierre Truson from France; they had formed the information technology (IT) architecture, construction, and design company in June 2005, after having worked successfully together on two projects in Saudi Arabia. Since then, they had done all their contracting in Western environments, attracting a steady stream of work, mostly in the design and sometimes in the construction of IT systems for shopping centres and a portfolio of office buildings. After several years of growth, they had noticed an increasing number of their competitors venturing into the growing China market and, as a result, they had decided at a board meeting to direct some of their sales and new contracts staff to keep a watch on requests for tenders in China. Eighteen months later, in 2013, they had found themselves in a stalemate negotiating a contract in China that they thought had been finalized, settled, and ready to put into action. What mistakes had they made to arrive at this impasse? How could they have prepared better, and was there any way they could still generate a successful long-term outcome after coming so close to sealing the deal?

Background

In June 2012, the designated EDC staff watching the market in China had seen a shopping centre project advertised in Hubei Province on a construction tender site on the Internet, and had enquired through the advertised online site to seek more details about the associated IT project, such as size, facilities to be included, materials sourcing, timetable for completion, managing authority, computer specifications, and so on. The Hubei government informed them that the project would be for three shopping centres in their province, with the target date for opening the third and final shopping centre in June 2015.

Five months later, EDC had submitted some introductory drawings and specifications and received a favourable response from Wen Diao, minister for development in the Hubei provincial government. By telephone, in broken English, he had introduced his assistant, English-speaking Zhang Gan, who was to be EDC's official contact from then on. Zhang would source all of the information and specifications required by the tenders, meet all of their requests for more information, and be their contact point over the next six months. The EDC design slowly progressed with regular communication between both parties and several enquiries from the directors seeking confirmation as to when Zhang could confirm that their estimated costs were acceptable and whether they had won the contract. After eight months, they stopped work to await confirmation and were told by Wen three months later that the Hubei government wanted them to do the design, and that they would draw up a contract in the next few weeks.

Michaels, Fortheringham, and Truson were pleased to receive confirmation of their first IT project in China, and they immediately placed two of their best subcontract designers on the project, restarted work, and had their lawyer forward the Hubei government a detailed copy of the standardized international contract they regularly used. This contract included timeline details, an account for a US$100,000[1] deposit to be paid within three weeks, payment specifications detailing the next $450,000 installment to be paid when the IT construction began, the $450,000 to be paid after six months of commencement, and the final $450,000 upon completion. The total project was estimated at $1,450,000.

Zhang replied to the contract after two weeks and said that before the Hubei government paid any part of the contract, they wanted the EDC team to come to China for the signing of the contract, and they wanted the EDC directors to meet the Hubei government consortium behind the project. This was a first-time venture for Truson in China, the second for Fortheringham, and the fifth for Michaels; they were confident that this trip and the associated meeting would merely entail signing the contract, having photographs taken by the media and government officials, and a request that the Hubei government present them with the first payment at the contract-signing ceremony.

The EDC directors knew they would need a translator, and after searching online and through their network of business contacts, they hired Anne Cheung, a Hubei local with international experience, to be their translator. Cheung was an English teacher at one of the local universities and would translate for them during their visit.

Preparing to Sign the Agreement

The final signing of the agreement was to take place at the government office in Wuhan, Hubei, by a small lake in the city. The signing was scheduled for 9:30 a.m. on October 18, 2013, with Jinyu Zhu and Tengan Tung, two officials they had not previously met, representing the Chinese government consortium (CGC) overseeing the project; the EDC directors were told the CGC's role was to ensure all parts and conditions of

---

1 All dollars amounts are in U.S. dollars unless otherwise stated; US$1 = ¥6.1375 on June 30, 2013.

the agreement were undertaken ethically and legally. The EDC team was advised to be there early, so they sent Cheung down at 9 a.m. to meet with the officials and prepare the meeting for them.

Cheung arrived and was surprised to be refused entry to the building by the security staff that were at the gate. She explained that she was representing EDC and that the EDC directors would soon be there; however, the guards told her to move away. It was cold, and there were no restaurants or coffee shops near the government building, so she tightened her sweater and went for a brisk walk around the lake to keep warm.

She arrived back at 9:30 a.m. to meet the EDC team. The guards at the gate were now very apologetic, as they had seen she was a part of the international team. If she had looked like a foreigner she would have been treated much better, but such was the mood in this part of China. She was a local, so her status was not as high or well-respected.

The government representative met the four-person EDC team of Truson, Fortheringham, Michaels, and Cheung; invited them in to sit down; and brought them green tea. Many people were in the nearby vicinity; however, there was no sign of Zhu or Tung. The EDC team was informed they would be arriving shortly. Finally, at 10:25 a.m., Zhu and Tung appeared—two well-dressed gentlemen in suits and ties.

After a number of introductory handshakes, *ni hao*,[2] and acknowledgements, Cheung began to talk about how pleased the EDC team was to be awarded the IT contract and how they looked forward to working together. Tung and Zhu acknowledged the introduction and then asked Cheung whether the EDC team had brought anything to offer, or whether they were prepared to confirm the deal and sign the final contract. Cheung said she understood that everything had been finalized and that this meeting was just to sign the agreement and take some photographs for the local media.

Zhu said a number of issues still needed to be finalized with them (party A) by the foreigners (party B) if the contract was to go ahead. He said that, as a result, they would have to leave the official government building, and they would all need to go to a restaurant for lunch to talk about this further.

Cheung told the EDC team what they would need to do and hinted that she thought Zhu and Tung wanted them (the foreigners) to give them something as a gesture of friendship to confirm the deal. Zhu and Tung stood up, ready to leave, pointed at their driver, made some comments to their assistants, and left. The EDC directors were surprised, but then thought that the signing would take place at the restaurant, and everything would be fine. They asked Cheung about what Zhu had meant by, "What are you going to give us?" She replied that perhaps it meant some kind of gift. Truson was shocked and in disbelief, while Fortheringham and Michaels looked questioningly at each other and wondered what was going on. They thought they were here to finalize the deal worth $1.45 million and to collect the first $100,000 payment; however, they now found themselves being directed into their car and asked to follow the Chinese delegation's car.

Before leaving the car park, they noticed the number plate on the Chinese delegation's black limousine had been covered with a sign reading, "Welcome to Wuhan." They drove across to the other side of the city, following the black limousine, which seemed to cut a clear path through the traffic. The EDC team was unsure of what was happening; however, one of the directors, Michaels, who had some experience working in China, said they should be patient and wait to see what would happen.

They arrived at the restaurant and noticed that the "Restaurant Open" sign had quickly been changed to "Closed," that those enjoying lunch in a small room adjacent to the main dining room were moved to the central part of the restaurant, and that after they had entered this room, all the doors were closed and the window shades lowered. The EDC team was confused and began to worry; however, after another 15 minutes, Tung and Zhu entered the room.

They sat down and called for the menu and a large ashtray, so they could smoke and prepare for lunch. They explained to Cheung in their local dialect that the foreigners were guests in China and needed to give the Chinese officials something in order to have them consider signing this contract. She explained to the EDC team how Tung and Zhu represented a

---

2 *Ni hao* means "hello" in Mandarin Chinese.

large Chinese business conglomerate whose task was to ensure all of the foreign business done in China was done correctly, and how this contract would need their approval to be ratified.

The bottom-line message was, "What were the foreigners going to give us?" After being informed of this message by Cheung, the EDC team spoke among themselves for an extended period to buy more time. They wanted to go back and check through the agreements and dialogue they had made previously and perhaps find an appropriate gift. Before the food arrived, they asked Cheung to convey the message to Tung and Zhu that they needed more time to check the details. They suggested that perhaps a second meeting in a few days would give them time to check everything. After some considerable discussion among the Chinese officials, Cheung reported back to say that unless this situation was decided now, there would not be a second meeting of the two parties.

The EDC team was surprised by these developments, as they thought everything had been finalized. The directors could see their significant deal slipping away; they had thought the officials were present only to sign the contract and hand over the deposit. Nobody had hinted that this might happen; Truson was disgusted and said they should pack up and go home. Fortheringham thought it must be a minor problem. He remembered that he had purchased three bottles of fine Scotch whisky from London's airport duty-free store. He said he would go back to the hotel to get the bottles, and when he returned, he would present them as gifts. Michaels thought it was worth a try. Fortheringham left for the hotel while the room began to fill with smoke, and the Chinese officials waited for lunch to arrive.

Michaels and Truson sat down with Cheung and the CGC delegation and asked Cheung whether she could tell them anything more about what was going on. What was the norm? Whom should they talk to about getting some more information? Cheung said she was not sure, as she had only been asked to do the translation. Did they have someone from their side, perhaps a *Zhongjian Ren* (intermediary) they could call? Michaels and Truson looked even more perplexed and sat back to await Fortheringham's return. Forty minutes later, Fortheringham arrived back with the Scotch whisky as a gift; however, by this time, the banquet was

in full swing with all of the Chinese officials enjoying a wide range of dishes and drinks. It seemed that whether or not the agreement was going to be signed, they were still going to enjoy themselves.

Fortheringham sat down and asked Cheung to find out when would be an appropriate moment to present the whisky. She went to speak to Zhu, who immediately called for silence so that the EDC team could present their gifts. Fortheringham stood up and in English said that as a gift of friendship, they would like to present one bottle of this fine Scotch whisky to Zhu and one bottle to Tung. A nearby official took the third bottle and asked whether they should open it for a toast. At 1 p.m., the EDC team thought it a little early; however, the Chinese officials thought it was a great idea. From then on the Scotch drinking complemented the number of cigarettes smoked after the banquet was complete. The Chinese team was looking quite content, and they let Cheung know that they would call a second meeting the following week to discuss what the EDC team would give them to secure the contract. Fortheringham, Michaels, and Truson were again surprised and realized that the Scotch was not enough. They knew they needed to discuss this situation further before meeting again. The Chinese officials, party A, said they would notify Minister Wen and Officer Zhang (who were in Laos) about what had happened and would call the EDC team the next day to notify them when the next meeting would take place.

The Second Meeting

Two days later, the EDC team received a telephone call at their hotel to say the meeting would take place five days later. The EDC directors asked why it would take so long; they would have to wait in this city where they did not know anybody, and their hotel bill was climbing. They began to wonder whether winning the $1.45 million contract was worth trying to sort out or wait for. Why were the contacts they had worked with from the beginning, Zhang and Minister Wen, nowhere to be seen? What were Zhang and Wen doing in Laos when the directors thought they were going to be here? They tried to contact them several times over the next few days but found it complicated to make contact in Vientiane, Laos. They hoped that the next meeting would be easier. They discussed what additional small gifts they could bring to pre-empt the meeting.

Five days later, the directors and their translator were asked to assemble at another restaurant where they went through the same process of arriving on time and then waiting for more than an hour for Zhu and Tung to arrive.

After presenting Tung and Zhu with some silk scarves from India, a long discussion began between Zhu, Tung, and Cheung. After 20 minutes, Cheung told the EDC team that to gain the Chinese officials' approval, they would require something more. They said that a number of Zhu and Tung's friends had spoken to them about a holiday in the Maldives and that such a trip would be an appropriate gift. The EDC team of directors was stunned and said they needed to discuss this suggestion and think about it. They all thought this trip was excessive, but as a last resort, after coming all this way and waiting all this time, they would consider it. They were quickly doing some calculations and thought they could transport and accommodate Zhu and Tung for a five-star, week-long holiday for approximately $5,000. Cheung told Zhu and Tung that EDC would be prepared to fly the two of them there and provide five-star accommodations for a week if they were prepared to sign the final contract that day.

The Maldives

Another lengthy discussion in Mandarin took place between Zhu, Tung, and Cheung. At the end of the conversation, Cheung took a deep breath and began to translate what Zhu and Tung had said. They wanted the EDC directors to provide flights and accommodations for their entire 18-person CGC team. Cheung later added that she thought that by flying the 18 Chinese officials together, nobody would be left out, which would avoid anyone exposing how the trip had been arranged. It would look as if the trip had been a gift rather than a forced corrupt payment or bribe demanded from EDC, in return for having the contract finalized.

The EDC team was shocked again. The three directors looked at each other. What should they do? They thought of giving the officials the choice of flying to Paris, London, or New York, as those trips would cost much less, and they could use their own social capital in those locations to negotiate significant discounts on the cost. After another lengthy discussion between Cheung, Zhu, and Tung, Cheung said the Chinese officials did not want to go to those destinations, as they could not speak the language. The EDC directors wondered why this same rule did not apply to the Maldives, as surely they could not speak the language there either.

In an act of desperation, the directors asked Cheung if she, as translator, would be prepared to take the Chinese delegation to Europe, the United States, France, or even the Maldives. She said that she did not want to go with this Chinese delegation, as they were too demanding and disrespectful. After coming all this way and wasting all this time, what were the EDC directors to do?

Heritage Manufacturing Company

John Mathis, Darian Narayana,
and Paul G. Keat

Senior Management Issues

George Long, Chief Executive Officer of Heritage Manufacturing Company, had in the past successfully directed his company's export sales to industrial countries. But now, to improve the company's performance, he wanted to turn his attention to emerging markets. Jeffrey Parker, who was recently hired as Vice President of Global Marketing to spearhead this effort, supported this strategy wholeheartedly. However, John Otis, who had been the company's Chief Financial Officer for the last 20 years, was concerned about the ability of these emerging markets to pay their bills.

In June 1998, Jeffrey was notified by the company's representative in the Middle East that the company had received an order for about $25 million pieces of equipment to be sold to an Egyptian government agency.

Brad Lanker was the corporate lending officer for Egypt at International Bank of North America (IBONA). It was his task to arrange financing for Heritage's first major export order from an emerging market—Egypt.

Background Information on Company and Its Business
Heritage Manufacturing Company—History and Products

Heritage was founded in 1950 as a small construction company doing projects for the oil industry. Shortly thereafter, it became a dealer for oil storage buildings and tanks. The most recent additions have been the acquisition of a competing supplier's line of oil storage tanks and buildings and the purchase of a manufacturing facility in England.

Today, Heritage, headquartered in Lehigh, Pennsylvania, is primarily engaged in the fabrication and sale of steel products and cement and steel oil storage facilities and support buildings. The steel fabrication business includes the manufacture and distribution of oil transport and pumping facilities and expandable oil storage tanks. Quality and durability are hallmarks of Heritage products, and the company offers some of the most comprehensive warranties in the industry. These characteristics have contributed to Heritage's becoming one of the world's largest suppliers of oil pumping facilities and storage facilities. The company's tanks are available in a wide range of capacities for commercial transport and storage.

History of International Expansion

The Heritage Manufacturing Company began its activity in international markets in the 1980s and has achieved some successes. To increase its presence in the international marketplace, the company purchased two existing oil tank manufacturing facilities in Europe: Heritage Company-UK, Ltd., located in Fogge, Wales, and Lobb Industries, S.A., located in Baangs, England. Emboldened by their successes in the more-developed markets of Canada and Western Europe, Heritage's CEO began to look for opportunities in emerging markets of Latin America and the Middle East. In general, competition was not quite as stiff in these locations and Heritage might be able to enjoy higher margins on its sales.

The problem with these markets, however, was that there were not many buyers able to pay the prices for the company's oil product storage systems. In order to be able to afford them, potential buyers typically requested financing from Heritage—often for up to five years.

Heritage had very little appetite for extending credit in emerging markets, and certainly not for five years. Within the company, there was a group (which included the CFO) that had always been dubious of the company's push into less-developed countries. Jeffrey Parker, the VP-Global Marketing, saw the potential, but also realized that he would meet heavy resistance internally if the company had to hold long-term receivables from Latin American or Middle Eastern buyers. George Long, the CEO, was supportive of these sales—for now—but had also let Jeffrey know that Heritage was not experienced with international credit and that he had no intention of learning the hard way.

The Transaction

It was within this context that Jeffrey received a fax one morning in 1998 from his representative in Egypt informing him that they had won an order to sell $25 million in equipment to an Egyptian government oil institution. This was a major order and meant that the Marketing Department would meet its sales target for the year several months early. The VP-Global Marketing was elated—until he read the terms of the sale.

The Egyptian institution would open a letter of credit (L/C) through the National Bank of Egypt, a government-owned bank. The L/C called for payment in three tranches:

1. A 15% down payment—Heritage would obtain this down payment by documenting that the oil storage system had been shipped from the U.S.
2. When the system was installed and operating in Egypt, Heritage would be paid 75% in stages

over 18 months as the system met certain performance criteria.

3. The final 10% would be paid three years after initial installation, representing a partial indemnification or warranty on the system.

As it would take one month to ship the equipment and installation would take another four months, the company would receive 90% of its money over 23 months, and the last of its money almost 3-1/2 years after shipment.

Heritage's risk in this transaction would be the National Bank of Egypt (NBE), a government-owned bank. Although this was essentially sovereign Egyptian risk, nobody at Heritage appeared to have the credit skills to take a three-year risk on a sale of this magnitude. It would be necessary for a U.S. bank to take the Egyptian risk for the company to undertake this transaction.

A Letter of Credit (L/C) opened by NBE is usually sent first to a U.S. bank, which in turn passes it on. If requested to do so, the U.S. bank can add its confirmation. By confirming the L/C, the U.S. bank accepts the credit risk of NBE. Heritage definitely wanted a U.S. bank to confirm the L/C. In addition, the company also wanted to receive its cash at the time of shipment. It, therefore, wished to have the U.S. bank discount the proceeds. Subsequently, the U.S. bank would receive the payments from NBE as Heritage made good on installation and the performance criteria. In order to get its funds quickly, the company was willing to accept a lower amount of cash at start-up in exchange for not having to worry about repayment from Egypt over 3-1/2 years.

The National Bank of Egypt's (NBE) principal U.S. correspondent bank was the International Bank of Pennsylvania (IBOP)—New York office. NBE proposed that the L/C be sent through the International Bank of Pennsylvania, and NBE indicated that IBOP was willing to confirm the L/C and discount the payments under the L/C, thus giving Heritage exactly what it wanted. IBOP indicated that it would charge Heritage 1.50% per year to confirm the L/C; the discounts would be priced at LIBOR + 3.50% per year. At the time, this worked out to an all-in rate of about 9.00%.

Economic and Political Environment in Which Decision was Made

Egypt was not an easy country to analyze. Although there were signs in 1997 that it was turning around economically, opening up its markets, beginning to privatize many industries, and promoting capitalism, there were also worries that the economic crisis in Asia (which was just starting at the time) might spread to infect all emerging market economies.

On the political front, there were concerns over a recent spate of fundamentalist Muslim attacks on Western tourists, including a horrific massacre at Luxor, which had occurred only a few months before the order was received by Heritage. This was followed in 1998 by U.S. embassy bombings in Cairo that again focused attention on Egypt's militant exiles. Social and political discontent remained issues of concern as Egypt drew closer to its next presidential election in October 1999 in which Hosni Mubarak was expected to win a fourth six-year term.

Despite some internal political tensions, the external political environment with other Middle Eastern countries continued to improve gradually. The government was working to smooth political relations inside the country and promote greater cooperation with other Middle Eastern countries. Egypt was also working to establish some sort of partnership arrangement with the European Union that could conflict with efforts to form an Arab regional trade area.

The Egyptian economy had recorded favorable economic performance over the period 1992 to 1997. Annual real Gross Domestic Product growth averaged 5% and inflation as measured by consumer prices averaged about 10% until the increase to 20% recorded in 1998. Strict fiscal policies and conservative monetary policies were expected to keep inflation in the range of 6-8% over the next several years.

Increasing investment from both the private and public sectors was driving economic growth. Recent tax increases were expected to boost government revenues and not result in an increase in inflationary

Economic Data for Egypt

EGYPT	1992	1993	1994	1995	1996	1997	1998
Exchange rate (pounds/$) end of period	3.3386	3.3718	3.3910	3.3900	3.3880	3.3880	3.3880
International reserves excluding gold US$ bil.	10.8	12.9	13.5	16.2	17.4	18.7	18.1
Current account US$ mil.	2,812	2,299	31	-254	-192	-711	-2,552
Of which: Trade balance	-5,231	-6,378	-5,953	-7,597	-8,390	-8,632	-10,215
Capital account US$ mil.	548	-2,281	-1,195	-1,573	-1,533	-1,171	1,761
Consumer prices %	13.6	12.1	8.2	15.7	7.2	9.4	20.3
Interest rates %	20.3	18.3	16.5	16.5	15.6	13.8	13.0
Investment %	8.0	14.8	8.4	9.1	17.3	20.6	20.0
Real GDP growth %	2.9	4.0	4.6	5.0	5.5	5.6	5.0
Foreign debt service ratio %	15.3	12.6	12.4	12.9	12.0	12.4	13.5

Source: International Monetary Fund, *International Financial Statistics.*

pressures. The government budget deficit was expected to remain low, but it might have been difficult to reduce it much below its current level of about 1% of GDP over the next couple of years. It was hoped more efficient tax collection and the move to a generalized value added tax would help to offset revenue lost through lower import duties and investment incentive tax rebates on capital goods.

The government had again introduced new investment incentives, and tariffs had been reduced to stimulate the competitiveness of domestic industry and eventually boost export growth. Efforts to privatize various government-owned industries were talked about, but actual progress was slow and could not be counted on to provide a significant contribution to new business investment. In mid-1997, a new reform-minded economy minister was appointed in a cabinet reshuffle, and this may have helped calm rural protests over rent increases. The decline in the number of rural protests reflected the growing consensus behind the economic reform program. Even so, the pace of privatization was likely to remain disappointingly slow relative to the desires of the international investor community.

The strong GDP growth had caused a rapid increase in imports, which resulted in a sharp deterioration in the trade deficit and, to a lesser extent, the current account deficit. Key exports included petroleum and petroleum products, raw cotton and cotton yarn, textiles and garments, engineering and metallurgical goods, and other oil products. Egypt was increasing its imports of oil from Libya and expanding its production of gas and LNG (Liquid Natural Gas), much of which would be exported to Turkey. Exports were increasingly becoming a priority. President Mubarak was convinced that Egypt could only become a major regional economic power through export-led growth. Consequently, the government was removing institutional obstacles that hindered achieving a targeted 10% annual growth in exports. The government also honored its promise to the IMF to reduce the standard maximum tariff rate from 50% to 40% by June 1998.

Despite the trade deficit and much smaller current account deficits, foreign exchange reserves remained at $20 billion. Consequently, the exchange rate was not expected to come under any selling pressure in the near term. Large capital inflows were being successfully sterilized to stabilize the currency and prevent any financial crises. Egypt's first sovereign bond issues have been used to retire domestic debt.

The outlook for the next several years indicated that real growth will continue near the 5% level driven by increasing private investment and foreign capital inflows. This outlook would demand political stability and continued good management of the economy by the government.

Description and Analysis of Possible Decisions

Heritage's CFO, John Otis, had never dealt with IBOP in the past, and had never handled a transaction with Egypt requiring more than 90-day financing. He had no idea whether the terms being quoted by IBOP were reasonable or not. The company had historically done its domestic banking with the International Bank of North America. John did recall that during the last visit by IBONA's Relationship Manager, Carla Peterson, she had mentioned that IBONA had just established a new International Division and was expanding its capabilities. John did not think IBONA had much of a chance to help him. However, he thought that it would not hurt to see with what kind of pricing they could come up, so he put in a call to IBONA's Relationship Manager.

Carla immediately informed the IBONA's International Specialist, who in turn called the officer responsible for Egyptian business. Both Carla and the International Specialist told the Egyptian desk officer how important Heritage's relationship was to IBONA, and how this was a first test which could lead to a lot more international business.

The Egyptian desk officer, Brad Lanker, was one of the most responsive officers in the International Division, and very sensitive to the needs of the bankers in the field. However, he had to deal with some significant problems.

Banks typically establish an overall country exposure limit, which sets the maximum amount and type of financial exposure they are willing to take for any given country. Second, they establish limits for individual borrowers within a country. In order to do the transaction for Heritage, IBONA needed to have a $25 million country limit for Egypt (going out 3-1/2 years) and a $25 million credit line for the National Bank of Egypt (also going out 3-1/2 years). Further, Brad had to

complete all his work in two weeks, because that was when NBE was scheduled to open the L/C.

Brad's problem was that he did not have *any* country limit for Egypt and, consequently, did not have any credit lines for NBE. At the time, IBONA's International Division was less than four months old and other countries had taken priority over Egypt. Furthermore, the International Division Credit Manager was determined that any new country limits of over $10 million should be documented properly—with a complete write-up, marketing strategy, economic and political analysis, etc.

IBONA's International Credit Manager wanted to establish credibility with his boss, the Bank's Chief Credit Officer, and he did not see that requesting a relatively large, medium-term limit for Egypt was a way to make this happen. In no uncertain terms, he told Brad to forget getting a country limit and credit line approved so that IBONA could handle the entire transaction itself. He indicated that he would feel uncomfortable with anything more than $1 million, and nothing more than one year.

Under such circumstances, exporters and U.S. banks frequently turn to the U.S. Export-Import Bank to insure export sales. In this case, however, the ExIm Bank was not an option. They were already at their limits for NBE, and any request for an increase would take at least two months.

Brad was in a quandary—he knew how important this transaction was to IBONA. He knew that NBE was pressing Heritage to deal with the International Bank of Pennsylvania, and he knew that the International Bank of Pennsylvania was pursuing the deal with the company. He also had heard that the International Bank of Pennsylvania was not very complimentary about IBONA's international capabilities. At the same time, he knew that there was no way he would get the Credit Manager to approve more than $1 million, and that only for one year.

Brad took the dilemma to his boss, Gordon Becker, a very experienced international banker. Becker had dealt with similar situations when working in Latin America, where borrowers demanded attractive credit terms but credit managers were reluctant to lend them even cab fare. Becker was used to "getting blood out of a stone."

Becker suggested that Brad arrange to sell the risk of the transaction to one or more other banks, and gave him names of banks to try. One of these was the New York office of IBOP. These banks were usually foreign banks or out-of-state banks operating in New York. There were over 250 foreign banks with offices in New York and maybe as many out-of-state banks represented. They set up shop in New York because it is the financial capital of the world, because they see their competitors setting up shop, and because they believed that they had to have an office in New York to be considered a serious bank.

As a brief digression, it should be mentioned that the reasons given above for these foreign banks' presence in New York are really not very persuasive. Having located their offices in New York, and after digesting the expense of offices and accommodations, they began to look around for ways to pay for "their slice of the Big Apple," only to find that it was not easy. Thus, many of these banks were hungry for opportunities to book a deal—almost any deal. It was not uncommon for U.S. banks to sell participations in credits to these foreign banks. This helped the U.S. banks to manage their overall exposure under country limits and credit lines, and it enabled the foreign banks in New York to cover some of their expenses. In general, foreign banks' operations in New York were not really profitable.

Brad began calling the banks that were most likely to have an appetite for Egyptian risk—the Germans, Japanese, and Canadians. Relatively quickly, and much to his delight, he found takers for the NBE risk. However, no one was willing to take the risk for more than two years. He could stretch this out to cover the 90% of the credit represented by the down payment and the progress payments, but he could not cover the entire exposure. The 10% residual due in three years would still put him over his $1 million country limit and credit line for NBE. Furthermore, the foreign banks purchasing the assets always wanted the selling bank to retain a portion of the risk—they did not want to feel that they were having credits stuffed onto their books.

Brad knew he would have to keep some of the credit and its inherent risk, but he was not sure how to solve the third-year part of the credit. Consulting again with Becker, he was encouraged to learn about the possibility of obtaining insurance for the third-year portion. Brad contacted several insurance companies and finally found a private insurance company that insured export trade receivables. This company was willing to insure 85% of the three-year receivable.

At last Brad had a package he could take to the International Credit Manager: 90% of the transaction was to be sold to foreign banks, and 85% of the 10% residual would be insured. IBONA's exposure would be less than $400,000. Admittedly, it would be a three-year deal, but the total fees retained by IBONA would be almost the same as the exposure. Even the International Credit Manager was happy with this deal.

In the end, IBONA beat IBOP's pricing and won the business with Heritage (and went on to win much more international business). IBONA also established a relationship with the National Bank of Egypt that led to other transactions.

In Summary

To facilitate the consideration of the case, a diagram of the export transaction and a synopsis of the two alternatives open to the Heritage Manufacturing Corporation are presented below.

Transaction Details

Heritage Manufacturing can close a $25 million transaction with an Egyptian government institution. The payments (as shown in diagram [on the next page]) would stretch over 3-1/2 years. Heritage had two alternative methods to transfer the risk.

International Bank of Pennsylvania—New York Office

1. If IBOP confirmed the L/C, risk would be transferred to a U.S. bank.
2. If IBOP discounted the L/C, Heritage would receive funds in six months (immediately following installation).
3. Cost to Heritage: 1-1/2% to confirm L/C, LIBOR + 3-1/2% to discount.

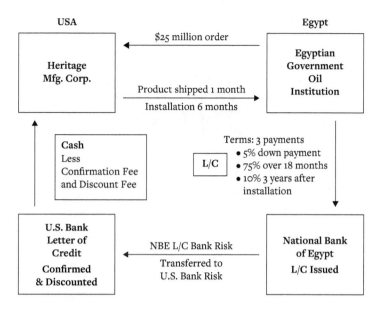

IBONA and Insurance Company

1. IBONA constraint: Country limit for Egypt was $1 million for 1-year maturity.
2. IBONA solution: Sell risk of transaction to another (foreign) bank.
   a. IBONA could sell only 90% and only up to two years.

   b. Remaining third-year portion (10% of total contract) was insured with an insurance company that was willing to cover 85% of amount.
3. IBONA's remaining exposure was now less than $400,000 for three years. But fees from the transaction more than equaled the amount of this exposure and were paid up front.

Ruth's Chris

The High Stakes of International Expansion

Ilan Alon and Allen H. Kupetz

"Well, I was so lucky that I fell into something that I really, really love. And I think that if you ever go into business, you better find something you really love, because you spend so many hours with it ... it almost becomes your life."

Ruth Fertel, 1927–2002
Founder of Ruth's Chris Steak House

In 2006, Ruth's Chris Steak House (Ruth's Chris) was fresh off a sizzling initial public offering (IPO). Dan Hannah, vice-president for business development since June 2004, was responsible for the development of a new business strategy focused on continued growth of franchise and company-operated restaurants. He also oversaw franchisee relations. Now a public company, Ruth's Chris had to meet Wall Street's expectations for revenue growth. Current stores were seeing consistent incremental revenue growth, but new restaurants were critical and Hannah knew that the international opportunities offered a tremendous upside.

With restaurants in just five countries, including the United States, the challenge for Hannah was to decide where to go to next. Ruth's Chris regularly received inquiries from would-be franchisees all over the world, but strict criteria—liquid net worth of at least US$1 million, verifiable experience within the hospitality industry, and an ability and desire to develop multiple locations—eliminated many of the prospects. And the cost of a franchise—a US$100,000 per restaurant franchise fee, a five per cent of gross sales royalty fee, and a two per cent of gross sales fee as a contribution to the national advertising campaign—eliminated some qualified prospects. All this was coupled with a debate within Ruth's Chris senior management team about the need and desire to grow its international business. So where was Hannah to look for new international franchisees and what countries would be best suited for the fine dining that made Ruth's Chris famous?

THE HOUSE THAT RUTH BUILT

Ruth Fertel, the founder of Ruth's Chris, was born in New Orleans in 1927. She skipped several grades in grammar school, and later entered Louisiana State University in Baton Rouge at the age of 15 to pursue degrees in chemistry and physics. After graduation, Fertel landed a job teaching at McNeese State University. The majority of her students were football players who not only towered over her, but were actually older than she was. Fertel taught for two semesters. In 1948, the former Ruth Ann Adstad married Rodney Fertel, who lived in Baton Rouge and shared her love of horses. They had two sons, Jerry and Randy. They opened a racing stable in Baton Rouge. Ruth Fertel earned a thoroughbred trainer's license, making her the first female horse trainer in Louisiana. Ruth and Rodney Fertel divorced in 1958.

In 1965, Ruth Fertel spotted an ad in the *New Orleans Times-Picayune* selling a steak house. She mortgaged her home for US$22,000 to purchase Chris Steak House, a 60-seat restaurant on the corner of Broad and Ursuline in New Orleans, near the fairgrounds racetrack. In September of 1965, the city of New Orleans was ravaged by Hurricane Betsy just a few months after Fertel purchased Chris Steak House. The restaurant was left without power, so she cooked everything she had and brought it to her brother in devastated Plaquemines Parish to aid in the relief effort.

In 1976, the thriving restaurant was destroyed in a kitchen fire. Fertel bought a new property a few blocks away on Broad Street and soon opened under a new name, "Ruth's Chris Steak House," since her original contract with former owner, Chris Matulich, precluded her from using the name Chris Steak House in a different location. After years of failed attempts,

Tom Moran, a regular customer and business owner from Baton Rouge, convinced a hesitant Fertel to let him open the first Ruth's Chris franchise in 1976. It opened on Airline Highway in Baton Rouge. Fertel reluctantly began awarding more and more franchises. In the 1980s, the little corner steak house grew into a global phenomenon with restaurants opening every year in cities around the nation and the world. Fertel became something of an icon herself and was dubbed by her peers *The First Lady of American Restaurants.*

Ruth's Chris grew to become the largest fine dining steak house in the United States (see Exhibit 1) with its focus on an unwavering commitment to customer satisfaction and its broad selection of USDA Prime grade steaks (USDA Prime is a meat grade label that refers to evenly distributed marbling that enhances the flavor of the steak). The menu also included premium quality lamb chops, veal chops, fish, chicken and lobster. Steak and seafood combinations and a vegetable platter were also available at selected restaurants. Dinner entrees were generally priced between US$18 to US$38. Three company-owned restaurants were open for lunch and offered entrees generally ranging in price from US$11 to US$24. The Ruth's Chris core menu was similar at all of its restaurants. The company occasionally introduced new items as specials that allowed the restaurant to offer its guests additional choices, such as items inspired by Ruth's Chris New Orleans heritage.[1]

In 2005, Ruth's Chris enjoyed a significant milestone, completing a successful IPO that raised more than US$154 million in new equity capital. In its 2005 Annual Report, the company said it had plans "to embark on an accelerated development plan and expand our footprint through both company-owned and franchised locations." 2005 restaurant sales grew to a record US$415.8 million from 82 locations in the United States and 10 international locations, including Canada (1995, 2003), Hong Kong (1997, 2001), Mexico (1993, 1996, 2001) and Taiwan (1993, 1996, 2001). As of December 2005, 41 of the 92 Ruth's Chris restaurants were company-owned and 51 were franchisee-owned, including all 10 of the international restaurants (see Exhibit 2).

---

1 *Ruth's Chris Steak House 2005 Annual Report, pg. 7.*

FIGURE 1 Ruth's Chris Restaurant Growth By Decade

Decade	New Restaurants (total)	New Restaurants (company-owned)	New Restaurants (franchises)
1965–1969	1	1	0
1970–1979	4	2	2
1980–1989	19	8	11
1990–1999	44	19	25
2000–2005	25	12	13
	93[2]	42	51

Source: Ruth's Chris Steak House files.

Ruth's Chris's 51 franchisee-owned restaurants were owned by just 17 franchisees, with five new franchisees having the rights to develop a new restaurant, and the three largest franchisees owning eight, six and five restaurants, respectively. Prior to 2004, each franchisee entered into a 10-year franchise agreement with three 10-year renewal options for each restaurant. Each agreement granted the franchisee territorial protection, with the option to develop a certain number of restaurants in their territory. Ruth's Chris's franchisee agreements generally included termination clauses in the event of nonperformance by the franchisee.[3]

A World Of Opportunities

As part of the international market selection process, Hannah considered four standard models (see Figure 2):

1. Product development—new kinds of restaurants in existing markets
2. Diversification—new kinds of restaurants in new markets
3. Penetration—more of the same restaurants in the same market
4. Market development—more of the same restaurants in new markets

FIGURE 2 Restaurant Growth Paths[4]

Restaurant Brands		
	Existing	New
Existing Market	**Penetration** (more restaurants) *Same market, same product*	**Product development** (new brands) *Same market, new product*
New	**Market development** (new markets) *New market, same product*	**Diversification** (new brands for new market) *New product, new market*

The product development model (new kinds of restaurants in existing markets) was never seriously considered by Ruth's Chris. It had built a brand based on fine dining steak houses and, with only 92 stores, the company saw little need and no value in diversifying with new kinds of restaurants.

The diversification model (new kinds of restaurants in new markets) was also never considered by Ruth's Chris. In only four international markets, Hannah knew that the current fine dining steak house model would work in new markets without the risk of brand dilution or brand confusion.

---

2 Due to damage caused by Hurricane Katrina, Ruth's Chris was forced to temporarily close its restaurant in New Orleans, Louisiana.

3 *Ruth's Chris Steak House 2005 Annual Report, pg. 10.*

4 *This diagram is based on Ansoff's Product/Market Matrix, first published in "Strategies for Diversification," Harvard Business Review, 1957.*

The penetration model (more of the same restaurants in the same market) was already underway in a small way with new restaurants opening up in Canada. The limiting factor was simply that fine dining establishments would never be as ubiquitous as quick-service restaurants (i.e. fast food) like McDonald's. Even the largest cities in the world would be unlikely to host more than five to six Ruth's Chris steak houses.

The market development model (more of the same restaurants in new markets) appeared the most obvious path to increased revenue. Franchisees in the four international markets—Canada, Hong Kong, Mexico and Taiwan—were profitable and could offer testimony to would-be franchisees of the value of a Ruth's Chris franchise.

With the management team agreed on a model, the challenge shifted to market selection criteria. The key success factors were well-defined:

- Beef-eaters: Ruth's Chris was a steak house (though there were several fish items on the menu) and, thus, its primary customers were people who enjoy beef. According to the World Resources Institute, in 2002, there were 17 countries above the mean per capita of annual beef consumption for high-income countries (93.5 kilograms—see Exhibit 3).[5]
- Legal to import U.S. beef: The current Ruth's Chris model used only USDA Prime beef, thus it had to be exportable to the target country. In some cases, Australian beef was able to meet the same high U.S. standard.
- Population/high urbanization rates: With the target customer being a well-to-do beef-eater, restaurants needed to be in densely populated areas to have a large enough pool. Most large centers probably met this requirement.
- High disposable income: Ruth's Chris is a fine dining experience and the average cost of a meal for a customer ordering an entrée was over US$70 at a Ruth's Chris in the United States. While this might seem to eliminate

many countries quickly, there are countries (e.g. China) that have such large populations that even a very small percentage of high disposable income people could create an appropriate pool of potential customers.

- Do people go out to eat? This was a critical factor. If well-to-do beef-eaters did not go out to eat, these countries had to be removed from the target list.
- Affinity for U.S. brands: The name "Ruth's Chris" was uniquely American as was the Ruth Fertel story. Countries that were overtly anti-United States would be eliminated from—or at least pushed down—the target list. One measure of affinity could be the presence of existing U.S. restaurants and successful franchises.

What Should Ruth's Chris Do Next?

Hannah had many years of experience in the restaurant franchising business, and thus had both personal preferences and good instincts about where Ruth's Chris should be looking for new markets. "Which markets should we enter first?" he thought to himself. Market entry was critical, but there were other issues too. Should franchising continue to be Ruth's Chris exclusive international mode of entry? Were there opportunities for joint ventures or company-owned stores in certain markets? How could he identify and evaluate new potential franchisees? Was there an opportunity to find a global partner/brand with which to partner?

Hannah gathered information from several reliable U.S. government and related websites and created the table in Exhibit 4. He noted that many of his top prospects currently did not allow the importation of U.S. beef, but he felt that this was a political (rather than a cultural) variable and thus could change quickly under the right circumstances and with what he felt was the trend toward

> If you've ever had a filet this good, welcome back."
>
> Ruth Fertel, 1927–2002
> *Founder of Ruth's*
> *Chris Steak House)*

5 *World Resources Institute, "Meat Consumption: Per Capita (1984-2002)," retrieved on June 7, 2006 from http://earthtrends.wri.org/text/agriculture-food/variable-193.html.*

ever more free trade. He could not find any data on how often people went out to eat or a measure of their affinity toward U.S. brands. Maybe the success of U.S. casual dining restaurants in a country might be a good indicator of how its citizens felt toward U.S. restaurants. With his spreadsheet open, he went to work on the numbers and began contemplating the future global expansion of the company.

Exhibit 1 Fine Dining Steak Houses by Brand in the United States (2005)

Company Name	Number of Restaurants
Ruth's Chris	92
Morton's	66
Fleming's	32
Palm	28
Capital Grille	22
Shula's	16
Sullivan's	15
Smith & Wollensky	11
Del Frisco	6

Source: *Ruth's Chris Steak House files.*

Exhibit 2 Ruth's Chris Locations In The United States (2005)

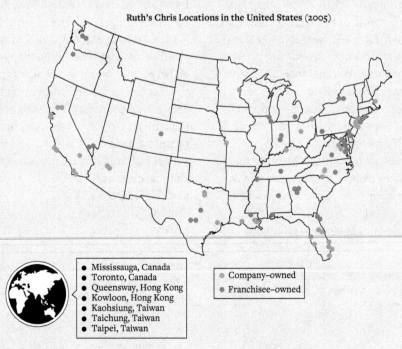

Ruth's Chris Locations in the United States (2005)

- Mississauga, Canada
- Toronto, Canada
- Queensway, Hong Kong
- Kowloon, Hong Kong
- Kaohsiung, Taiwan
- Taichung, Taiwan
- Taipei, Taiwan

- Company-owned
- Franchisee-owned

Source: *Ruth's Chris Steak House files.*

Exhibit 3 Meat Consumption Per Capita[a] (in kilograms)

Region/Classification	2002	2001	2000	1999	1998	Growth Rate 1998-2002
World	39.7	38.8	38.6	38.0	37.7	5.31%
Asia (excluding Middle East)	27.8	26.9	26.6	25.7	25.4	9.45%
Central America/Caribbean	46.9	45.7	44.8	42.9	41.3	13.56%
Europe	74.3	72.5	70.5	70.6	73.1	1.64%
Middle East/North Africa	25.7	25.7	26.0	25.1	24.7	4.05%
North America	123.2	119.1	120.5	122.2	118.3	4.14%
South America	69.7	68.4	69.1	67.6	64.2	8.57%
Sub-Saharan Africa	13.0	12.9	13.1	12.8	12.6	3.17%
Developed Countries	80.0	78.0	77.2	77.3	77.6	3.09%
Developing Countries	28.9	28.1	28.0	27.1	26.6	8.65%
High-Income Countries	93.5	91.9	92.0	92.2	90.9	2.86%
Low-Income Countries	8.8	8.6	8.4	8.3	8.2	7.32%
Middle-Income Countries	46.1	44.6	43.9	42.7	42.3	8.98%

[a]*World Resources Institute, "Meat Consumption: Per Capita (1984-2002)," retrieved on June 7, 2006 from http://earthtrends.wri.org/text/agriculture-food/variable-193.html.*

Exhibit 4   Data Table

Country	Per Capita Beef Consumption (kg)	Population (1,000s)	Urbanization Rate (%)	Per Capita GDP (PPP in US$)
Argentina	97.6	39,921	90%	$13,100
Bahamas	123.6	303	89%	$20,200
Belgium	86.1	10,379	97%	$31,400
Brazil	82.4	188,078	83%	$8,400
Chile	66.4	16,134	87%	$11,300
China	52.4	1,313,973	39%	$6,800
Costa Rica	40.4	4,075	61%	$11,100
Czech Rep	77.3	10,235	74%	$19,500
France	101.1	60,876	76%	$29,900
Germany	82.1	82,422	88%	$30,400
Greece	78.7	10,688	61%	$22,200
Hungary	100.7	9,981	65%	$16,300
Ireland	106.3	4,062	60%	$41,000
Israel	97.1	6,352	92%	$24,600
Italy	90.4	58,133	67%	$29,200
Japan	43.9	127,463	65%	$31,500
Kuwait	60.2	2,418	96%	$19,200
Malaysia	50.9	24,385	64%	$12,100
Netherlands	89.3	16,491	66%	$30,500
Panama	54.5	3,191	57%	$7,200
Poland	78.1	38,536	62%	$13,300
Portugal	91.1	10,605	55%	$19,300
Russia	51	142,893	73%	$11,100
Singapore	71.1	4,492	100%	$28,100
South Africa	39	44,187	57%	$12,000
South Korea	48	48,846	80%	$20,400
Spain	118.6	40,397	77%	$25,500
Switzerland	72.9	7,523	68%	$32,300
Turkey	19.3	70,413	66%	$8,200
UAE/Dubai	74.4	2,602	85%	$43,400
U.K.	79.6	60,609	89%	$30,300
United States	124.8	298,444	80%	$41,800
Vietnam	28.6	84,402	26%	$2,800

Source: World Resources Institute, "Meat Consumption: Per Capita (1984-2002)," retrieved on June 7, 2006 from http://earthtrends.wri.org/text/agriculture-food/variable-193.html and World Bank Key Development Data & Statistics, http://web.worldbank.org/WBSITE/EXTERNAL/DATASTATISTICS/0,,contentMDK:20535285~menuPK:232599~pagePK:641 33150~piPK:64133175~theSitePK:239419,00.html, retrieved on June 7, 2006.